Living in Words

Living in Words

Literature, Autobiographical Language, and the Composition of Selfhood

GARRY L. HAGBERG

Great Clarendon Street, Oxford, OX2 6DP,
United Kingdom

Oxford University Press is a department of the University of Oxford.
It furthers the University's objective of excellence in research, scholarship,
and education by publishing worldwide. Oxford is a registered trade mark of
Oxford University Press in the UK and in certain other countries

© Garry L. Hagberg 2023

The moral rights of the author have been asserted

All rights reserved. No part of this publication may be reproduced, stored in
a retrieval system, or transmitted, in any form or by any means, without the
prior permission in writing of Oxford University Press, or as expressly permitted
by law, by licence or under terms agreed with the appropriate reprographics
rights organization. Enquiries concerning reproduction outside the scope of the
above should be sent to the Rights Department, Oxford University Press, at the
address above

You must not circulate this work in any other form
and you must impose this same condition on any acquirer

Published in the United States of America by Oxford University Press
198 Madison Avenue, New York, NY 10016, United States of America

British Library Cataloguing in Publication Data
Data available

Library of Congress Control Number: 2022948822

ISBN 978–0–19–884121–0

DOI: 10.1093/oso/9780198841210.001.0001

Printed and bound in the UK by
Clays Ltd, Elcograf S.p.A.

Links to third party websites are provided by Oxford in good faith and
for information only. Oxford disclaims any responsibility for the materials
contained in any third party website referenced in this work.

For Eva May Hagberg

with love

Contents

Acknowledgments	ix
Preface: On the Self-Formative Power of Literature	xv

1. Imagined Identities   1
   1.1 Pragmatism and the Relational Conception of Selfhood   3
   1.2 Autobiography at One Remove   12
   1.3 A Person's Words: Literary Characters and
   Autobiographical Understanding   19

2. Boundaries of Selfhood   50
   2.1 Multiple Interpretations and Singular Selves   52
   2.2 Interpretive Rightness, Reconsidered   59
   2.3 Self-Description, Action-Individuation, and Virginia
   Woolf's "A Sketch of the Past"   73

3. Structures of Autobiographical Understanding   86
   3.1 The Thinker and the Draughtsman: Wittgenstein's
   Perspicuous Relations and "Working on Oneself"   86
   3.2 Aristotelian Frameworks   100
   3.3 Narrative Catharsis   107

4. Three Tragedies of the Unexamined Life   118
   4.1 The Self *in Absentia*: Leporello's Question (Mozart's
   Don Giovanni)   118
   4.2 Aware Too Late: Dencombe's Final Moments (Henry
   James's "The Middle Years")   134
   4.3 Lear as a Tragedy of Errors: "He hath ever but slenderly
   known himself" (Shakespeare's *King Lear*)   149

5. Moments of Self-Definition: Forging a Self in Language   162
   5.1 Possible Selves and Webs of Belief   163
   5.2 The Textually Cultivated "I": Making up One's Mind   178
   5.3 Metaphorical Identification and Self-Individuation   196

6. The Sense of Self   206
   6.1 The Self Rewritten: The Case of Self-Forgiveness   206
   6.2 Wittgenstein, Rereading, and Self-Understanding   218
   6.3 Coda: Self-Compositional Reading, Seeing Connections,
   and the Self as a Work-in-Progress   238

Bibliography	243
Index	251

Acknowledgments

Like human selves, this book, happily for its author, was not formed in isolation. I am indebted to what is at this point a rather sizeable assembly of journal and book editors, conference and colloquium organizers, philosophical compatriots, fellow symposium participants, colleagues ranging across a number of fields, and many others for having so generously produced the circumstances that engendered this book.

The first two sections of Chapter 1 began as my response to Ralph Cohen's kind invitation to write for a special issue of *New Literary History* (in connection with a delightful conference at the University of Virginia) on the question "What Is Literature Now?"; I knew at a glance that in extending the invitation Ralph had provided the perfect occasion to set out the foundational ideas of this project. His far-seeing comments on it helped considerably. Because this piece sets out the foundations, I was particularly fortunate to be able to present it at a number of places as it grew and took shape: these included my Inaugural Professorial Lecture at the University of East Anglia (where Jon Cook provided a fully comprehending and insightful commentary), and the Cambridge University Seminar on Criticism and Theory in the English Faculty (where Mary Jacobus and David Hillman provided incisive and constructive comments and questions). The third section of Chapter 1 had its origins in an invitation from Christopher Cowley to write for his collection, *The Philosophy of Autobiography*; earlier versions of it were presented to a stimulating meeting of the American Comparative Literature Association at Harvard University, and to an unforgettable conference devoted to "The Source of Meaning for Literary Works" in Beijing, where conversations with Thomas Pavel in particular were simultaneously enlightening and distinctively heartening.

The problem of interpretive rightness (as it concerns self-interpretation) was an issue I knew this study would need to take up (Chapter 2), so I was particularly pleased to receive an invitation from Andreea Deciu Ritivoi to write a piece for a collection she and G. L. Pandit were editing entitled *Interpretation and Ontology: Studies in the Philosophy of Michael Krausz*. This was presented at a meeting of the American Philosophical Association in Atlanta, and a subsequent piece, the second part of this chapter, was prepared in response to Andreea's and Christine Koggel's invitation to write for their volume *Interpretation, Relativism, and Identity*, which was presented at a conference at Bryn Mawr College. The third part of this chapter was included as part of a symposium in *Philosophy and Literature* on "Davidson and Literary Understanding"; it was presented to Bard's

X ACKNOWLEDGMENTS

Philosophy Research Seminar, where my students displayed the inimitable combination of an exaggerated respect for subjectivism with an overcautious respect for authority for which I owe them so much.

It had been plainly evident from the outset of this undertaking that I would need to include an examination of the life-structuring power of narrative as a source of, or vehicle for, self-understanding. The first part of Chapter 3, on the special kind of work the self-narrator does, began as a paper for a conference on "Wittgenstein, Art, and Architecture" at the Canadian Centre for Architecture in Montreal to which I was invited by Céline Poisson; it was published in her *Wittgenstein et l'architecture* (in French translation by Jean-Pierre Cometti), and also in its original English as "The Thinker and the Draughtsman: Wittgenstein, Perspicuous Relations, and 'Working on Oneself'" in *Philosophy as Therapeia*: Royal Institute of Philosophy Supplementary Volume, edited by Clare Carlisle; it is incorporated here in revised form (in fact all these pieces are revised and extended for inclusion here). I also had the welcome opportunity to present versions of it, as it developed, to a meeting of the Nordic Wittgenstein Research Network in Bergen, where it benefitted from enjoyable and lively exchanges, as well as to a meeting of the Modernist Studies Association in Montreal, where it received further helpful commentary. Then along this book's way John Gibson, Wolfgang Heumer, and Luca Pocci conveniently emerged to ask for a chapter for their collection *A Sense of the World: Essays on Fiction, Narrative, and Knowledge*. My piece for that volume, "Narrative Catharsis," happily took me back to Aristotle's *Poetics* in connection with issues of self-formative narrative, and was presented at a meeting of the Welsh Philosophical Society in Gregynog (where the session's chair, David Cockburn, and Catherine Rowett asked particularly helpful questions); it provided the basis for the second and third sections of this chapter.

I had wanted for some time to return to Wittgenstein's remarks on a special mode of perception or attention that he called "an attitude towards a soul" in connection with this growing project, and when I set out to write on the tellingly soulless Don Giovanni (soulless because he lacks both the reflective self-composing consciousness that I describe in Chapter 5 and the overarching sense of self pursued in Chapter 6) for a symposium in *Philosophy and Literature*, this one on "Music, Politics, and Morality," I saw my chance; it was my good fortune to receive particularly helpful and detailed expert commentary and advice from Lydia Goehr on it in its formative stages. The second section of this chapter (in which I saw a chance to explore the issue of the presence or absence of self-awareness or the kind of self-constitutive mindfulness in connection with an ever-evolving life-narrative that I am exploring throughout this volume) was my response to an invitation from Susan Griffin to write for a special issue of *The Henry James Review* on James and philosophy. A version of this was presented to the Seventh Ghent Conference on Literature and Theory; I am indebted to Sascha Bru and Daniel Steuer for this stimulating and memorable experience. The third section of this chapter's little catalogue of what I take to be among the most interesting kinds of human ruin directly caused by insufficient self-understanding pursues an understanding of King Lear's Big Problem. It is, I suggest, philosophico-linguistic in nature, and the comments and suggestions of Emily Caddick Bourne and Craig Bourne, who invited this piece for their *Routledge Companion to Shakespeare and Philosophy*, were most helpful. I have long believed in the power of instructive examples of a very detailed kind (not "for example, Tolstoy") in philosophy and in conceptual work in literature, and also in the morally explanatory power of cautionary tales; my hope is that the three cases examined in this chapter do both at once.

But in planning this volume I also wanted to consider, really as the conceptual backbone of the book, the role that belief plays in the formation of identity and the way in which, when we make up our mind (often by a process of identification with and comparison to a literary protagonist), we in a sense make up ourselves, and I had the opportunity to do just this in my chapter for *The Blackwell Companion to Philosophy of Literature*, which I had the pleasure of co-editing with Walter Jost; it became the foundation of Chapter 5.

In offering a model of how the materials and processes described throughout this book come together to create a sense of self, or a sensibility strong enough to make us (in significant part) who we are, I wanted to close the book with three things: a consideration of how it can happen that we become misaligned with who we are and what we can do about it; a discussion of the way in which the texts with which we engage for the self-compositional experience that I'm examining in this volume change over time, so that, seemingly paradoxically, a text that obviously has not changed in its written content has, for us and across a span of time, very importantly changed; and a brief concluding mention of what all of this means in terms of the possibility—or impossibility—of a settled or "finished" self.

With the first of these rounding-out topics in mind I was thus particularly attracted to an invitation from Christel Fricke to write for her volume *The Ethics of Forgiveness*. Self-forgiveness is an interestingly doubled form of human action within which the self that forgives is changed both as giver and as recipient of the forgiveness, under circumstances where the self recognizes, suddenly or slowly, that a misalignment between words (of self-description) and deeds (of character-manifesting action) has emerged. What is in play here is, I suggest, illuminatingly akin to rewriting—if of a self-referential kind. I was privileged to have the opportunity to present versions-in-progress to the lively King's College London Philosophy Society and, thanks to Wolfgang Huemer, to a conference on Art, Ethics, and Cognition at the University of Parma. There, Wolfgang provided a characteristically acute and detailed commentary, from which I took away a good deal.

So if rewriting came into play in the preceding section, rereading comes into play in the next one. With that question concerning change in textual meaning across time in mind, the second section of this final chapter came into being at the invitation of Sascha Bru, Wolfgang Huemer, and Daniel Steuer for their volume *Wittgenstein Reading*; it benefitted from their comments and from presentations of various parts and versions of it as it developed at a conference on Literary Fiction and Rationality at the University of Tampere, Finland; at Stanford University's Program in Philosophy and Literature; at the International Wittgenstein Symposium in Kirchberg, Austria; and at the Cohen Center for the Study of Technological Humanism at James Madison University. The lively and attentive audiences at all these places helped me arrive at what I wanted to say about the experience of rereading, its importance, and what it tells us about selfhood, about who we are, and about who we have become. Then the final section of this chapter, interweaving themes from throughout the book, offers a brief retrospective overview along with a few remarks concerning the nature of the life patterns we perceive and why the phrase "a work in progress" locks in so well with the concept of a human being; I had the luxury of presenting and discussing these ideas with new friends at a meeting of the International Comparative Literature Forum in Shenzhen.

Parts of this book-in-progress were also presented to the conference "Acknowledging Cavell: His Multi-Disciplinary Legacy" at Cambridge University at the kind invitation of Rachel Malkin, where Raymond Geuss provided helpful questions that sharpened that piece of the project; to the Fellows' Work-in-Progress Seminar at the Centre for Research in the Arts, Social Sciences, and the Humanities, also at Cambridge, where, among others, Denise Riley offered insightful comments that nicely expanded the frame of what I was trying to do; to the Temple University Colloquium in Philosophy (where especially Philip Alperson and Susan Feagin offered finely focused stimulating questions); to the Bard College Faculty Seminar (where I received what at Bard is the usual special mix combining exacting and demanding questions with intellectually generous and wide-ranging connection-making); to a conference on the work of Stanley Cavell at Harvard University; and to the Department of Philosophy at the University of Bergen and to the Bergen Wittgenstein Archive, where, during an unforgettable week as their guest, Kjell Johannessen and Alois Pichler were particularly philosophically helpful and generous (amongst a most stimulating larger group). And thanks to Roberta Dreon and Daniele Goldoni, I also had the pleasure of presenting some of this material at a conference in Venice on Aesthetics, Ethics, and Communication, where conversations (especially with Daniele over some days) proved helpful on a number of fronts. And a visit to the University of Virginia to deliver a Rushton Lecture, as well as a conference that would have been at Charles University in Prague on Literature and Philosophy (but moved online owing to the pandemic) allowed me to present and discuss the central ideas of this book with savvy and engaged audiences.

I am very aware that it is my extremely good fortune that there are many more family, friends, colleagues near and far, students, and others who have helped this project than I can name here; they have helped in ways ranging from a telling remark made in passing that sticks and then quietly provokes further reflection (Henry James's "air-blown particle") to sustained conversations over extended periods of time. Special thanks to Leon Botstein, president of Bard College, for supporting this project with both understanding and the elusive commodity that usually means the most to academics, i.e., time. I am once again indebted to Peter Momtchiloff for handling this book so very well along its way from initial idea to print, and Tara Werger has also been unfailingly helpful in its production. The sensitive and acute copyediting, for which I am also grateful, is the eagle-eyed work of Kim Richardson. But last and the opposite of least: it is certainly not only this book that would be unimaginable without my wife, the art historian Julia Rosenbaum, and my daughter, the author Eva Hagberg. Without them (for reasons involving the deepest and inestimably valuable aspects of relational selfhood ...), for me—how does one say it briefly?—nothing in this world would or could be lighted in the way that it is.

G. L. H.

Annandale-on-Hudson, New York

Preface: On the Self-Formative Power of Literature

Everyone at bottom really knows (or at least so I imagine) that who we are as persons is in part determined by the literary-aesthetic experience we have and the reflective lives we cultivate as a result of those experiences—our valuing of the narrative arts and aesthetic experience as we do is based on that fact. This book is an attempt to articulate a number of the senses in which this claim concerning self-constitution is true, and the conditions within which it can be true. This task, at least as I undertake it here, involves the interweaving of philosophers as diverse as Wittgenstein, Aristotle, Rousseau, Stanley Cavell, the American pragmatists (C. S. Peirce, William James, Josiah Royce, and George Herbert Mead), Donald Davidson, Richard Rorty, Arthur Danto, Michael Krausz, and Raimond Gaita, among others, co-mingled with a perhaps unpredictable cohort of writers including Virgil, Virginia Woolf, Henry James, Mozart's librettist da Ponte, Goethe, Shakespeare, Dostoevsky, T. S. Eliot, Borges, Iris Murdoch, and Milan Kundera. The figure in this carpet is a conception of reading—a distinctive kind of deeply absorbed and self-examining literary engagement—that is active to the point of self-making; it is, I suggest, a mode of aesthetic experience that, in its way ontologically empowered, brings into existence and stabilizes something—specifically, important elements of the content of our character, to borrow a phrase—that previously did not exist. This is a phenomenon that becomes explicable through the conjoining of a relational conception of selfhood to a narrative conception of self-understanding, and it is a process that is both depicted in literary character development and—more importantly to this discussion—enacted within the reader through a doubled process involving (1) a vicarious identification with those developing characters and (2) a parallel act of definitionally strong self-reflection. But then it is not merely a set, fixed, or invariant process, one prior to and separable from its product, that yields at its conclusion a predictable and fixed result. Rather, it is a progressive or steadily evolving form of (non-pejoratively understood) "bootstrapping" into an ever more exactly defined self-identity.

I will say more about the ground I attempt to cover in this book in a moment, but to briefly enumerate the fundamental aspirations of this undertaking, I hope herein:

(1) To offer a reading of the conception of human selfhood developed in American pragmatism that seems particularly well suited to bring to prominence, and to place in perhaps a new light, the powerful role aesthetic (and particularly literary) experience plays in self-formation.

xvi PREFACE: ON THE SELF-FORMATIVE POWER OF LITERATURE

(2) To bring the preceding into contact with questions and answers concerning the distinctive ways in which human selves are (and against too-facile presuppositions concerning autonomy, are not) bounded, relating this to a discussion of the ways in which human experience is, and instructively (again, against too-facile empiricist presuppositions) is not, bounded.

(3) To look into the deep analogies between the work of a draughtsman who renders all the relations between the parts of a building perspicuously and the autobiographer who does very much the same in achieving self-understanding, then progressing to an intertwined discussion of the literary structuring devices we use (of a broadly Aristotelian kind) as "self-architects" in this process.

(4) To examine some cases, I think powerfully instructive with regard both to all the themes so far in play and in regard to the themes to follow, of the kinds of human tragedy that ensue from insufficient self-knowledge (first, of a kind resulting from a walled-in denial of both self and other acknowledgment—Don Giovanni; second, of a kind resulting from an encompassing mindfulness of the structure and content of one's life too long delayed—Henry James's character Dencombe; and third, of a kind resulting from a presupposition that language is just an instrument for the naming and blunt description of externalities—King Lear). To see how these three cases bring out in high relief what a self-draughtsman (or as I will say later, self-composer on a musical analogy) can sometimes tragically and always regrettably either obscure, minimize, or leave out entirely, shows three foundational elements that are necessary for the sense of selfhood that I discuss in Chapters 5 and 6.

(5) To articulate, in the light of all the preceding, a conception of reading (and rereading), of literary engagement (or by extension, engagement with any psychologically mimetic narrative), that exhibits its own complex architecture, where such reading ("double reading," as I call it here) uncovers (a) the often underappreciated role belief-acquisition plays in identity-construction, (b) the self-constitutive authority exerted within the act of making resolute decisions concerning what we would do if..., and (c) the refining of self-individuation that ensues from an attentive metaphorical (I will explain this in Chapter 5) identification with a self-defining protagonist.

(6) To also reconsider metaphor in light of problems of constitutive self-description, the relation between self-reinvention and self-redescription (and the problem of how to better understand the senses in which self-redescription is, and is not, a creative act), and the imaginative process of parallel reading in connection with a broadly philosophical conception of the examined life.

(7) To offer a nested set of suggestions about the self-constitutive aspects of the reader's inner world (this is dangerously put—and interestingly so, for reasons we will see: in short, it is inner but not autonomous or hermetically sealed) that might augment the extensive discussions of recent decades about the politics of identity with a discussion of what one might then call the aesthetics of identity. Or perhaps

better (because the former way of putting it can suggest that it is external forces on self-creation that are primarily in play), to augment discussions of ethical self-fashioning with what we might now call aesthetic self-fashioning, where this in turn articulates in extended form what we can mean by "sensibility," a word still too little examined in investigations into both the nature and content of selfhood.

(8) To look at how that personal and self-defining sensibility is developed and displayed in autobiographical writing, and to more fully articulate what we mean by "the sense of self" particularly in connection with ever-evolving long-form narrative.

(9) To help diagnose, disentangle, understand the sources of, and ultimately quiet the intellectual impulses that would lead us so quickly and so deeply into the misbegotten picture (itself indeed a self-portrait in a convex philosophy) of autobiographical language as an afterthought or mere reflector rather than as a shaper and maker of who and what we are.

But because—in books as in life—it is better to know how each part fits into a larger whole, a more detailed map viewed in advance may prove helpful. So in finer resolution: Chapter 1 sets the stage for the entire project by considering that, of a rather extended family of ways we engage with literary works, one in particular constitutes an occasion for self-reflection of a very distinctive kind. That distinctive mode of literary engagement is, as I will suggest, supported by the relational conception of selfhood—one that acknowledges connections as much as the things connected—as initially developed in American pragmatic thought. And where that relational conception is viewed against the culturally embedded Cartesian or mind-body dualistic picture of the self (where the self is viewed most fundamentally as an ontologically sealed consciousness only contingently related to what we then call outward things), it allows us to see in higher relief the way in which the detailed and often quite nuanced comparisons we make between ourselves and literary characters yield highly particularized forms of self-knowledge. And more strongly—and this is the fundamental point for all that is to follow here—the relational conception of experience derived from pragmatism allows us also to see with greater clarity how autobiographical or reflexively engaged literary experience itself becomes self-*constitutive*, how it becomes the material out of which we compose, in part, ourselves. Our self-negotiated identities are both sharpened by, and indeed in part constituted by, serious literary engagement. (This, incidentally, is most fitting for the philosophy of a country whose deeper cultural ethos remains centrally concerned, from its founding up to the present, with the possibilities of self-creation, self-renewal, and self-reinvention.) If *we* are in part composed of relations of the kind William James, Josiah Royce, and George Herbert Mead emphasized, then the selves that enter imaginary fictional worlds, insofar as they are relationally reconfigured, do not remain unchanged by those worlds. William James wrote, "No one ever had a simple sensation by itself. Consciousness, from our natal day, is a teeming multiplicity of objects and relations," and if our consciousness, our self-awareness, is in part given content by aesthetic experience, then our relations to artworks and works of literature are, in terms both of self-formation and autobiographical understanding, no small matter. And if such a claim concerning the self-constitutive power of aesthetic experience seems excessive, that I believe is only because our present patterns of attention more generally, and our epistemological hierarchies more specifically, do not give particular aesthetic experiences, and indeed the entire aesthetic dimension of life, their due.

In the last section of Chapter 1, I extend the discussion from a relational conception of a person to a relational conception of language. We will have seen that, according to the traditional Cartesian conception of selfhood, the human self, as a repository of inwardly knowable content, exists prior to and separable from any context, situation, or relation into which it contingently enters. Corresponding to this view is the conception of linguistic meaning as being wholly determined by the inward mental content of the speaker also independent of any external relations. But what are the implications for language if the classical American pragmatists and others since are right about seeing the self as created within, and constituted by, the webs of relations into which it enters and within which it actually acquires its identity and its content? I suggest here that there is a parallel way of looking at words, and that to truly understand a person is in part to genuinely understand the webs of relations, references, allusions, connotations, and cross-circumstance resonances that give a person's words their context-sensitive meaning. This, I suggest, is close to what Wittgenstein referred to as "the field of a word," which for good reason he insisted is decisive in determining a word's meaning. Thus the understanding of a person biographically requires an understanding, with this relation-embedded complexity, of their words; and to understand ourselves autobiographically is to work through an understanding of our own words, our own ways of seeing meaning-determining relations. I examine these ideas in examples drawn from Milan Kundera, Iris Murdoch, and Rousseau, suggesting that what is at issue here in terms of human understanding is true in life just as it is in literature.

But the aesthetically fueled process of becoming who we are brings quickly in its wake the issue of knowing what we are. I return to this more fully in connection with the cautionary tale of Don Giovanni in Chapter 4 and the instructive case of Virgil's Aeneas in Chapter 5. But at this early stage in Chapter 2, I lay the groundwork for that part of the later discussion by looking into what is—and what is not—entailed by our ability to distinguish right from wrong interpretation (as a philosophical model for right or wrong self-interpretation), looking first at the clarifying analysis Michael Krausz brings to this issue. Here we see that the ontological commitments many have perceived in the positions of interpretative singularism and multiplism are not given, not necessary. For example, starting with the option of singularism, we might quickly—too quickly, as Krausz shows—assume that fixed-property realism is necessitated. That is, in order for there to be one uniquely correct interpretation, the object interpreted—in our case a human self—must have a finite set of determinate properties, so that the interpretation is correct in virtue of rightly describing or identifying just and only those properties. This would imply that the self is composed of a finite set of determinate, if not properties, strictly speaking, then bounded experiences or bounded mental events, e.g., intentions, motivations, and so forth. By contrast, multiplism, we might similarly think, implies a variable or non-fixed ontology. But in the first section of this chapter we see that such ontological pictures are not necessitated by either of the two interpretive positions (once we have the American conception of selfhood in focus against the entrenched Cartesian view), and the discussion proceeds to a fuller consideration of the many diverse things covered by the generic term "interpretation." And we also see (here introducing a theme weaving through the entire book, i.e., the deep analogies between artworks and human selves) that many artworks, such as Christo's *Wrapped Reichstag*, exhibit a boundary-indeterminacy that does not endorse a subjectivized or reckless relativism, but it does endorse a pragmatic contextualism. That is, it is within, and only within, particular contexts that we will know how and where to draw boundary lines around artworks. Human selves, it emerges, exhibit similar fluidity or—cautiously speaking—indeterminacy. So the interpretation, the understanding, we have of ourselves will not be a matter of simple correspondence to preverbal fixities. Autobiographical language is not a mere matter of inward reportage.

In the second section of this second chapter we move to a reconsideration of what I take to be Wittgenstein's helpful analysis of understanding, but—advancing the discussion one more step—where we see such understanding manifested in action as well as in speech. Here the characterization of the knowledge displayed, the understanding that is shown and not only said, becomes a fairly delicate matter, precisely because the very idea of a *manifestation* of understanding in action seems to revivify the very dualism to which the pragmatic conception is most fundamentally opposed: it seems to require us to say that we show outwardly what we first know inwardly. And this then links in clear (but perhaps heretofore-too-little examined) ways to self-understanding and to the ways in which we show that understanding in action and say it, or write it, in language. Indeed, Wittgenstein's remarks, read in this light, show that we can be impelled to try to get hold of *the* mental process of understanding, where this process appears at first glance to be metaphysically hidden. It is a short step from there—indeed if it is a step away at all—to an interestingly misleading and also deeply embedded picture of correct autobiographical self-understanding: we would understand ourselves rightly exactly to the extent that we locate and identify the hidden mental process contained within the "inner" and then portrayed in the "outer," i.e., autobiographical writing. But as we see in philosophy and especially in literature, the actual criteria we employ in contexts of self-investigation, while they do allow such a thing as interpretive rightness, instructively do not conform to this entrenched conceptual mold.

In the third section of this chapter we turn to writings of Donald Davidson's that are particularly pertinent to these issues, namely his writings concerning the problem of the boundedness of human experience (where he is developing, extending, and refining some of the pragmatic themes we saw in Chapter 1). Both narrowing and sharpening the issue with Davidson, we see that if the content of experience cannot be accurately captured by any description that fails to acknowledge the interpenetration of one (allegedly determinate) experience by another, if we fail to acknowledge what Nabokov, as we will see here, called the "resonances" between them, then any attempt (1) to atomistically isolate a single human action or experience and then (2) to rightly capture that in an autobiographical description would be to simultaneously mischaracterize both the nature of rightness or correctness in self-description and the content of human experience itself. If mental content is *constituted* holistically (and as William James argued, relationally), then we could not get so far as to grasp which experience it is we are attempting to capture in a correct description—in autobiographical or self-descriptive writing or in speech—without a full grasp of the context, the sensibility, the lived life within which that experience will have its Nabokovian resonances. Then to broaden the discussion back out, these observations, properly understood (an understanding that bringing philosophy and literature together in this way encourages), hold rather deep significance for our understanding not only of what kind of identity-forming process an engaged reader undergoes, but also of what kind of task one who sets out to understand a life, i.e., a biographer or autobiographer, as a describer of selfhood, undertakes. Indeed, we see here in the case of Virginia Woolf writing a memoir of her earliest experiences, the necessity of relational connectedness and context-sensitivity in getting so far as even initially identifying and generically describing that experience. She wants to write of experience, as she says, "as it should be written"—by which she means capturing in language the grainy particularity that makes an experience what it is, and writing of it in a way that does not make what she regards as the cardinal mistake of biographical or autobiographical writing, i.e., "leaving out the person to whom things happened," or failing to capture the sensibility of the individual in question. (I will argue later, in Chapters 5 and 6, that such sensibility can be understood in large part as one's present complex network of relations to one's own past.) The philosophically entrenched idea (which is the most deeply seated part of the distorting legacy of eighteenth-century empiricism) of hermetic or atomistic boundedness of human actions, of experiences, and of selves, is, it emerges here, a picture-driven myth that wants replacing by a far more particularized, individualistic, often messier but invariably far more interesting, sense of real, i.e., context-sensitive and sensibility-sensitive, experience.

(To over-encapsulate: much of the rest of this book tries to describe that more complicated sense of human experience.)

Focusing on the active process of narrative structuring as it provides the architecture of self-understanding, Chapter 3 in the first section looks into the distinctive kind of connection-finding work a self-narrator undertakes. Wittgenstein notes the deep similarity in labor that unites the thinker and the draughtsman; the draughtsman strives to "represent all the interrelations between things," and the thinker—the philosopher—can be seen to pursue strikingly similar ends. (Indeed one important line of philosophical work in the mid-twentieth century was called "connective analysis.") And given what we will have seen by this point concerning the relational embeddedness and the constellation of awakened associations that serve to make remembered and retrospectively described experiences what they are (as examined in Chapters 1 and 2), the task of first clarifying and then structurally situating such relations now emerges as centrally significant to any autobiographical undertaking—precisely because we use such clarified relations to build a structure of self-understanding. (Wittgenstein also noted, as we shall see, that "Working in philosophy—like work in architecture in many respects—is really more a working on oneself. On one's way of seeing things.") Here close and illuminating similarities emerge (a) between the way that following out an interpretation of a work of art or music brings thematic strands out in higher relief and thus, in an important sense, makes that work what it is within that interpretive frame,[1] and (b) the way in which following out an interpretation of a life and its structure does much the same thing, i.e., it determines, in Wittgenstein's sense, our way of seeing things within that evolving life-narrative. It *makes sense* of a life, and it thus constitutes the content of self-understanding—of a kind very unlike model-driven causal explanation in the (so-called) social sciences.[2] And we see here how such retrospective connection-clarification serves to provide what Wittgenstein called a "perspicuous overview"—but here not of a philosophical problem-field but rather of the self's past or one's own intellectual genealogy. But then what tools do we have at our disposal for the structuring of a life's narrative once the connections, as structural elements, are made or identified[3] and clarified? And what is a *structurally* clarified past, and does the structure within which we see a life reveal, or

---

[1] The *locus classicus* in modern aesthetics for this point (concerning our dependency on the interpretive frame) is Kendall Walton, "Categories of Art," *The Philosophical Review*, 79(3), July, 1970: 334–67.

[2] The skepticism intimated here by the words "so-called" derives from Peter Winch, *The Idea of a Social Science* (London: Routledge, 1958), and Rupert Read, Phil Hutchinson, and Wes Sharrock, *There Is No Such Thing as a Social Science: In Defence of Peter Winch* (London: Routledge, 2008).

[3] The distinction between "made" and "identified," or created versus discovered, connections of the self-descriptive kind is not as simple a distinction as it may at first glance seem; I offer a discussion of this in *Describing Ourselves: Wittgenstein and Autobiographical Consciousness* (Oxford: Clarendon Press, 2008), ch. 5, sec. 2: "The Pain and the Piano," pp. 163–75.

impose, sense-making interconnections (or is the "revealed-versus-imposed" dichotomy too stark to capture the intricate truth of the matter)? These questions (although they introduce and point toward issues to be covered in Chapter 5) occasion a close examination, in the second section of this chapter, to Aristotle's exemplary treatment of the narrative elements in drama that yield teleological evolution, thematic interconnectedness, narrative power, and the sense of closure. Here the conception of selfhood and the conception of literary experience being developed in this study will fully come together.

Aristotle makes clear that we do not understand a human action without understanding its teleology, the larger frame of reference within which it has its point, its purpose, and its intentional content within an expanded field. And he famously speaks of the beginning, the middle, and the end of a plot: a beginning sets themes that themselves carry teleological potential and thus establish narrative drive (a drive that becomes inexorable in the strongest cases), the middle is a phase in which those teleologies and developments become manifest or actualized in such a way that they point to subsequent development (and where other possible developments submerge as unactualized), and the end is the narrative thread-tying that yields the sense of closure or the sense, as it has been put by Frank Kermode, of an ending. And in seeing an action within such an expanded frame we see the causal antecedents that made it possible, that made it make sense, and that situated it in a way that gives it its meaning-specifying character, and we see the thematic and causal linkages running to, through, and from it. Aristotle observes that, given these plot-defining elements, "it is right to contrast and compare tragedies largely in terms of plot structure." Tragedy or (as one hopes) not, the same can be said of life-narratives—but then one needs to sort out that life-narrative's literary quality from its truth, because of course a good story is not by virtue of that goodness a true story. And so the third section of this chapter goes into the question of the difference between the clarification and the literary clouding of a life-story, which leads to the distinction between the productive versus the unproductive (and this links back to the pragmatism of Chapter 1) employment of literary architectural devices in the structuring—and importantly restructuring—of a long-form narrative. This in turn leads us to the examination of the complex (and in some cases interestingly unobvious) role that memory plays as a criterion for determining the verisimilitude of one set of narrative connections over another.

All of the Aristotelian elements of plot construction thus can—when employed cautiously and judiciously in ways we will explore—provide ways of articulating the interconnections of a life that constitute its internal resonances, and more deeply, its structure. And such articulations, as they organically emerge within the autobiographical situation, can, as I also suggest in the final section of this chapter, prove in both intellectual and emotional senses cathartic. But here again, the ways in which that happens are not simple, not reducible to a neat formula. This is to

PREFACE: ON THE SELF-FORMATIVE POWER OF LITERATURE   xxiii

say: the Aristotelian themes are not brought in here as a matter of *application*, for that would be to falsify a life-narrative by dramatizing it with structuring devices prior to and separable from that life. Rather, rightly understood—and as we will see in the closing parts of this section—they are in truth housed *within* relationally interwoven experience to begin with (which is not to say that we will initially see them or see them clearly), and as we shall see the language-games we evolve to describe the content and the coherence of such experience reflect that fact.

But one distinctive aspect of self-interpretation, or self-referential narrative composition, has not yet been addressed. Turning to detailed examples, I explore this in the first section of Chapter 4 by considering a text that can be taken as a fine and close study of (a) this distinctive aspect's absence, (b) its presence as the common background against which we can see such absence in stark relief, and (c) its foundational role as a precondition for self-reflection of any kind (and thus its role in inflecting the words we use in our complex networks or language-games of self-description). *Don Giovanni* is an opera that houses deep insight—and an instructive object lesson—about what a number of philosophers have discussed as the precondition of selfhood, of what we call inner human content, that makes the distinctive and irreducible attitude or stance we take toward other persons so much as possible. Wittgenstein called this *Eine Einstellung zur Seele*, an attitude towards a soul. Indeed, the opera serves to frame Giovanni, to comparatively (as in Chapter 1) situate him in relation to the other characters, as a person—or rather as an entity—lacking precisely the interior content that renders humane acknowledgment possible and that constitutes the fundamental difference between our perception of a human being and our perception of anything else, animate or inanimate. Through a close reading of this philosophically significant libretto, we come to see that the statue scene constitutes, at one level, a confrontation with the fallen Commendatore as the possessor of the interior life Giovanni so woefully lacks. But at another level, it becomes a scene of refusal of self-confrontation and that confrontation's consequent self-knowledge; indeed Giovanni's case illustrates, in telling and circumstantially acute detail, an inner vacuity that precludes not only a genuine imaginative vision into the lives of others, but also a capacity to see into himself. And as such, it becomes nothing short of a tragedy of an unexamined, or in his case unexaminable, life—where that examination would have taken place in precisely the kind of autobiographical language under investigation in this book. Giovanni's life is situated against the backdrop of *persons*, not entities, and unlike him, we thus understand them as beings with developing life-narratives and the articulated sense of self that such narratives engender. And we see them as beings whose experience resonates across time (as articulated in Chapter 2) and through their life-narratives, yielding ever more individually defined sensibilities. Giovanni sees entities that constitute little more than matter in motion. We see persons who express themselves verbally; he sees word-generating automata on which he might exert a causal influence. Giovanni (whatever that name actually refers to) teaches us that person-perception is the precondition of self-perception, humane acknowledgment the precondition of self-acknowledgment. At masked balls (like the one in this opera), in the ordinary cases persons are behind the masks. In Giovanni's case, the mask is redundant.

In the second section of this chapter we are witnesses to Henry James's exquisitely acute examination of the inner life of a character who, in an earlier phase of his life, felt himself full of ever-new potentialities, but who now believes that he only fleetingly was once, but will never again be, "better than himself." And he knows, and warily recalls from his earlier life, that some hopes for self-transcendence, or for (in a sense paradoxically) being better than he is, can prove dangerous for their power to wash out, to diminish, to make seem thin, the present—but this turns out to be a self-admonition he (ruinously) cannot heed. He thinks back to his long-seated desire to begin his life as a writer anew (but to do so with all the skill and ability he had to that later point acquired, so like what we call a new beginning in a life's narrative, it can never truly be that, never be truly new—it is always an Aristotelian middle), and now feels alienated from that previous self and its higher aspirations. But he then experiences a "high and magnificent" epiphany of selfhood that such a new start is still possible—where the power of that epiphany is only possible after, or as layered over the top of, the self-alienation. Indeed he now sees, at a very late stage, that "it had taken too much of his life to produce too little of his art," and given this late-stage high-resolution focus and reachieved sense of the self-transcending value of a new start, a second chance at selfhood, he desperately grasps, from a rapidly deteriorating medical condition, at "another go." But the tragedy we see unfold here is not merely the tragedy of a life that comes to outlive its higher aspirations and then to regain them too late, but rather a life that, because of its chronic desire to do something that is "better" in his special sense and thus (in his imagination) truly expressive of who he is, is blinded to the body of work that he has in fact done throughout his productive life—work that is in fact the true expression of himself, and for others admirably so. That blindness places self-alienation in place of self-integration, self-alienation in place of a life-narrative that would have earlier, in time for a sense of genuine narrative closure, meaningfully incorporated, rather than denounced, all he has done. Unlike Giovanni, he has a soul (I employ this term as one denoting the humane depth of personhood and not as one dependent upon any theological picture for its meaning) and he is a person. But all too like Giovanni he has been until his final moments—final moments that, however briefly happy and thus in their way capable of reducing the tragedy we see here, nevertheless sadly show what might have been—incapable of achieving *within* his life (and not only at its last retrospective moment) the edifying state of self-acknowledgment or of, again in Aristotle's sense, narrative closure. He was a person who, in the name of a false and blinding self-image borne by false self-descriptions, tragically did not see who he really was, with the result that he did not really live his life. Genuine words—architectural words building and supporting a structure of self-knowledge and self-understanding—would have saved him.

Last in Chapter 4, we see another moral disaster induced by linguistic limits, but of a different, and in its own way especially instructive, kind. King Lear is a character who, taking language only as a blunt instrument for naming and describing the outside world, both cannot truly hear the words of others (his earnest daughter, most centrally) and cannot understand himself. He is a character deaf to a person's words of the kind considered in the third section of Chapter 1, and deaf to the special way words can accrue meaning or deepen for a user over time (to be discussed in Chapter 6, concerning rereading). From him, utterances and pronouncements erupt without a sense of composure (of the kind we will explore in Chapter 6) or inner reserve or a reflective life behind those utterances. He sometimes utters sentences about others that in a revealing sense have form but no authentic content. Proving himself the opposite of a cultivated moral imagination, and in this way like Giovanni showing something deep through its visible absence, Shakespeare in *King Lear* captures the intrinsic connection between language and character. Indeed, late in the play we see Shakespeare developing this very theme, where personality is discerned in speech, and where a change of language indicates a change of person.

Reading such cases and learning from them is, as I have suggested we all really know, part of what makes us who we are. But given what we will now have behind us from the previous four chapters concerning human identity and identity-manifesting language, human action and its description, the experience of reading, the building of the self's narrative, and instructive failures of self-examination, it will be time to examine more closely the precise experiences that an engaged reader has that yield aesthetically induced self-transformation. If as I have suggested the identity of the self that enters into serious literary engagement is altered by that engagement, more needs to be said about the minute details of the process within which that change to selfhood occurs. And so in Chapter 5 I offer an examination of the distinctive kind of self-compositional reading that resides at the core of the view I have been advancing throughout.

In the first section of this chapter we consider the powerful role belief-acquisition plays in the formation of identity. Our point of departure is the polemical opposition between (1) views of selfhood that argue for, or presume, fixity of identity impervious to and ontologically separate from the vicissitudes of experience, versus (2) those arguing for, or presuming, the indelible and cumulative power of experience to such an extent that such experience becomes part of the person. Both of these models, within particular cases (or selective groupings of particular cases), have their plausibility, although both are too extreme and too overarching to accommodate the more delicate truth of the matter. The important issue, as it will emerge here, is how experience, as it changes belief and webs of belief, changes self-identity. And insofar as the range and scope of a self's thought is circumscribed by that web of beliefs, it becomes important to look into the ways in which, within those webs, certain beliefs make certain thoughts possible and others not. As Donald Davidson puts it (whose views we will consider in connection with the belief-centered issues taken up in this section), "Having a thought requires that there be a background of beliefs." In literature, we can imaginatively identify with (and so learn, in Thomas Nagel's[4] resonant phrase, what it is like to be) characters whose system of interlocking beliefs render a range of cognitive explorations possible; by identifying in that way, we can come to know what it is like to hold that alternative set of beliefs and to be enabled to extend our thought into a cognitive range that otherwise would have remained closed. We also encounter characters in literature who themselves entertain, but do not yet hold, possible beliefs, and so who entertain possible or variant selves, which we then witness from a reflective or spectatorial distance. And we see characters who, in seeing the possibility of changed belief, see the possibility of significant reconnections and thus redescriptions of life-defining experience. We see how in literature—as in life—we get to know characters (or persons) not only by their thought but also by the scope and range of their possible thought. Differing webs of belief become, in this sense, differing possible selves.

We also see in the first section of this chapter the view that Richard Rorty has advanced (albeit both too generally and too generically) called "the contingency of selfhood," but as we will see this overarching polemically situated thesis makes (to put it briefly) too much too contingent. However, this is not to say that there is not a grain of valuable truth here, and in the second section of this chapter we turn to ways in which we can and do make up our minds where they were previously, on a particular belief or set of nested beliefs, un-made-up, not yet resolved, and how we can undergo a self-defining process of irresolution-to-resolution within literary experience. Here we will see Goethe placing what will be within the context of this study deeply significant emphasis on the dialogical character (including inward-dialogical) of the process leading to resolution. And Goethe shows the self-constitutive power of inward-directed identification, comparison, contrast, differentiation to the most subtle degrees, and—in a sense given precision in his writing—self-selection, i.e., where we in a real sense choose to actualize one self from a number of possible ones. A story from Borges then provides a well-tailored allegory for this special kind of active reading, suggesting something that can be important about the perennial openness to reconsideration, to new aspects that we

---

[4] Thomas Nagel, "What Is It Like to Be a Bat?," *The Philosophical Review*, 83(4), 1974: 435–50. See also (lest we become insensitive to the contexts in which "What it is like" is meaningful and thus take it as a generically meaningful phrase that would be invariably or universally applicable), P. M. S. Hacker, "Is There Anything It Is Like to Be a Bat?," *Philosophy* 77, 2002: 157–74.

PREFACE: ON THE SELF-FORMATIVE POWER OF LITERATURE   xxvii

experience in this kind of literary engagement.[5] That openness is the potential for relational reweaving and correlated redescription, even as it presents itself in places where we have attained the narrative fulfillment of teleology discussed as Aristotelian-cathartic closure above. This suggests something that can be rather important about the depth of insight, of humane understanding, that is required to genuinely comprehend some self-constitutive beliefs (as we will see in what is required to comprehend the scene of Odysseus' return, among other instructive examples).

But at this stage of the discussion we will not yet have seen with sufficient clarity the process of *settling* self-constitutive belief (where that belief in turn settles others, opening some avenues of thought while closing others), so we will look to an author who has devoted much labor and many morally intricate pages to the elucidation of the fascinating complexity of this process, Iris Murdoch. Here the settling of belief about guilt and responsibility for profound loss determines both who a character is to himself and what it is then subsequently possible for him to think and feel both about himself and in relation to others. And then in Virgil, in his exacting literary depiction of the inner phenomenology of Aeneas' final act, we see in a lucid microcosm the reader's doubled process of (a) witnessing (and comprehending in the way examined in Chapter 1, Section 1.3) a literary character's act of resolution, yet simultaneously (b) having a self-reflective moment of self-definition that is occasioned in us as readers by reading Virgil's description of the act bifocally, that is, focused on the character and focused on ourselves in a "what we would and would not do if..." mode.

So at the altitude of an overview: The language (1) within which we identify who and what we are, (2) and that in part makes us who and what we are, constitutes the language within which (3) we recognize who and what we are to each other. But how these three linguistic strands of selfhood intertwine now also calls for closer inspection. Thus in the third section of Chapter 5 we trace out, and extend, some helpful observations Arthur Danto has made on this subject. We might expect, far too simply, and as Danto's remarks wisely warn us against, that the language within which autobiographical reflection is captured falls into either of two classes: statements concerning how things are in the world external to my mind (objective descriptions) and those statements concerning how things are within my mind independent of that world (subjective statements). This historically entrenched dichotomy—actually, as we will see and as some literature shows, an appalling oversimplification—opens the space for a false and facile skepticism, and it also falsely dichotomizes elements of self-descriptive life that are

---

[5] I discuss aspect-perception in connection with literary interpretation in *Meaning and Interpretation: Wittgenstein, Henry James, and Literary Knowledge* (Ithaca: Cornell University Press, 1994), ch. 4, "Aspects of Interpretation," pp. 104–48; and in *Describing Ourselves: Wittgenstein and Autobiographical Consciousness* (Oxford: Clarendon, 2008), ch. 6, sec. 3, "Iris Murdoch, the 'Unfrozen Past', and Seeing in a New Light," pp. 202–22.

far more interestingly interconnected—and inextricably interconnected—than this simple picture or conceptual template would suggest.[6] As Danto puts it, we can not only significantly be changed, but moreover we can transfigure ourselves, through literary engagement, and we do this with language that itself forms a metaphorical relation between ourselves as readers and the text (and it is here that we see the fuller explanation of the role of metaphor as promised above). The simplifying picture of the two classes of statements resting beneath this much-oversimplified dichotomy (out of which Danto's remarks show us the way), however, is more difficult to dislodge than anything a superficial or blunt repudiation of it could achieve. This section thus ends with a reconsideration of how self-defining resolution in human life (as opposed to what we might expect from a hermetically mental "class-two" statement) actually *works*, independent of underlying metaphysical pictures that we too easily bring to issues that intimately connect to questions concerning the meaning and power of autobiographical language.

The first section of Chapter 6 looks into some of the nuances of the phenomenology of, and some of the nuances of the meanings of the words involved in performing, a self-directed act that has the power to change the actor both as giver and as receiver simultaneously. Self-forgiveness is an interestingly complex and multilayered phenomenon, and it is one that reaches into the past, is enacted in the present, and projects into the future. Here we see a number of the ways in which this complex act, as it (1) is performed initially as a temporally located yet relationally unbounded episode, as it (2) is reflected upon (and thus temporally extended) by its agent, and as it (3) is maintained and preserved in future forgiveness-based thoughts, words, and actions, not only reflects the present state of the self, but as it more powerfully and actively reconstitutes the self. As and after the self-forgiving agent forgives, that agent reflects not only on what she or he has done, but indeed on what she or he now, as a person, *is*, and this self-constitutive process demonstrates in action a fundamental fact about the relational conception of selfhood—it shows in the microcosm of a single act of self-directed forgiveness how our volitional reconfigurations of our relations to others at the same time reconfigure ourselves. And we also here look into the meaning of phrases such as "This should never have happened"—as though the plot line of a prewritten life-script had been somehow ruptured or violated.

---

[6] In literature, it is perhaps the writings of Proust and James Joyce that most powerfully show the insufficiency of this too simple dichotomy in any attempt to portray human experience. I discuss their contributions in this light in "The Mind in Time: Proust, Involuntary Memory, and the Adventure in Perception," *The Proustian Mind*, Routledge Philosophical Minds, ed. Anna Elsner and Tom Stern (2023), and "A Portrait of Consciousness: Joyce's *Ulysses* as Philosophical Psychology," *James Joyce's Ulysses: Philosophical Perspectives*, ed. Philip Kitcher (Oxford: Oxford University Press, 2020), pp. 63–99.

PREFACE: ON THE SELF-FORMATIVE POWER OF LITERATURE   xxix

This microcosm of volitional self-constitution—self-forgiveness—has been shown and examined in numerous literary examples. But more importantly, such literary cases allow an occasion not only for the close study of mimetic depictions of self-defining actions, but they also allow actual occasions for them on the part of the reader; this section thus extends the notion of the self writing and rewriting its own text or script, and it sets the stage for the interrelated discussion of rereading.

So the second section of this chapter suggests that our reasons for rereading can be philosophically instructive in light of all the foregoing issues, and this is true in a perhaps unobvious way. If we were to see word meaning as fixed or invariant across contexts (as we will see, what Wittgenstein called "the dream of the straight highway"), the purpose of rereading would be uniformly simple: it would be to remind ourselves of what we forgot. But we see that memory comes into rereading in ways far more complex, and ways far more interesting, than that simple "reminder" picture would suggest: both the context of the rereading, and the relevant experience of the rereader, inflect (and as we shall see, give nuanced content to) word meaning—even with a word as seemingly simple as a proper name (which we will consider in the case of Alyosha Karamozov introducing himself in a scene in Dostoevsky's *The Brothers Karamozov*). An examination of these issues will help clarify some of the connections between aspect-perception or "seeing-as" and word meaning, and it brings into sharp focus what Stanley Cavell has called "our relations to our words"—an idea central to our understanding of the nature of autobiographical language. It was Hume who said that at twenty years of age we may prefer Ovid, at forty, perhaps Horace, and at fifty, probably Tacitus. The answer to why this should be the case in our ongoing negotiations between text and self is revealing. And we will ask: Does Wittgenstein's liberated conception of word meaning provide insight into what may be lurking in the conceptual subterrain here, and does it further illuminate the constitutive strength of self-referential words?

In the final section of Chapter 6 we return to the notion of parallel or double reading introduced in Chapter 1, but here, now from the vantage point of the end of the present volume with a perhaps revised or enlarged understanding of self-descriptive language and its powers, and conjoined to a way of articulating the long-form sense of self that is the result of word-borne self-investigation and the mosaic work of self-composition, we are able to see the full reach of this idea. This brief coda does what codas in music do: having seen what we have seen, it looks back over all the ground we have covered. And this coda points to the significance of these reflections for our understanding of the importance—in some quarters underestimated—of aesthetic experience and the role of literature in our lives.

Lastly in this introduction, a word on my subtitle: I have not used "construction," for the reason that it may suggest too arbitrary a process in the creation of selfhood—as though anything goes, all narratives are equally plausible, and anything from any moment is possible. And I have not used "constitution," which may perhaps seem to place too much emphasis on external forces—as though we are the passive recipients of external societal or political forces that alone that make us who we are. (They do, of course, in part.) And so I have used "composition," a musical analogy, which I hope is suggestive of an active and creative undertaking, but within limits that are themselves interesting: Stravinsky said that a blank sheet of music manuscript paper was paralyzing, but once he had an interval, a single pair of notes in place that carried a range of implications and possibilities within themselves, he could fly. But with the foregoing nested themes in mind, we can now, at a point of I hope reasonably prepared departure, ask: How should we answer the question that asks what literature is or can be in connection with the conceptual issues explored in this book, and what was it that the American pragmatists said about selfhood that proves so important in these waters?

1

Imagined Identities

The general question "What is literature?" suggests, at a glance, an essentialist strategy of the kind first and most influentially formulated by Platonic philosophy. In asking a question of the "What is x?" kind, we are, as it is thought on that model, really asking: "What is the definitional essence shared by all members of the class x, where the presence of that essence in each of the members of that class explicitly justifies its membership in it?" If we were able to answer this question in the case of literature, we would then be able to draw sharp boundaries between those works that are, and those works that are not, literature, and—if we were Platonists of an explicit, or the more common implicit, sort—we would be answering that question once and for all. Any new question concerning the identity of a piece of writing and its proper classification that might arise would then of course be settled by reference to that same, invariant, definitional criterion. And for many, if not all, Platonists of this kind, we would have not only a classificatory, but also an evaluative criterion at hand: the greater the amount of the definition-demarcating essential quality, the greater the work of literature as literature.

With this in mind, we can now see that there was more than a small dose of irony present in some of the exaggerated claims of a recently past generation of literary theorists; that is, recoiling in moral horror at the very thought of any variety of essentialism, they proceeded to proclaim that, now free of a pernicious hegemonic presumption of category-determining essence, we can for once see literature for what it (in essence) is: a thinly disguised form of politics. But the full elaboration of that particular phase of literary theory will have to wait for another day. The present concern in bringing up the definitional and category-clarifying aspirations of Platonist question formulation is hardly to criticize the logical consistency of one school of literary theory, or to defend any form of Platonism or essentialism, but rather to provide a frame, or conceptual backdrop, for the more constrained, and perhaps slightly more manageable question "What is literature *now*?" Meaning, which of its aspects or features do we find it important or particularly valuable to focus upon and bring out in higher relief in the present context that is asking about its power vis-à-vis selfhood and sensibility?

This question, with the conceptually reorienting supplemental words "now" or "in this context," subverts the presuppositions of the Platonic formulation, redirecting our attention away from the search for the timeless and invariant criterion and toward the immediate, toward the emergent patterns of the present moment.

Living in Words: Literature, Autobiographical Language, and the Composition of Selfhood. Garry L. Hagberg,
Oxford University Press. © Garry L. Hagberg 2023. DOI: 10.1093/oso/9780198841210.003.0001

2   LIVING IN WORDS

It is a question that asks us to take a freeze-frame snapshot of the present state of play within a larger, continually evolving flux. Among latterday philosophers it was Nietzsche who most lavishly praised Heraclitus, setting aside his name, as he put it, with high reverence, from the rest of what he derisively called "the philosopher crowd," precisely because he (Heraclitus) saw that it was, in the philosophical search for the reality behind the appearance, the *change* that was real. But the project of answering the question "What is literature now?" when seen in polemical opposition to the Platonic question can too quickly (and here too ironically) freeze itself into what is in fact a static picture of constant change— thus what is taken to be definitively and unchangingly true of literature is just that it is in constant flux.

Is there a middle way? Is there a way of approaching the question without the stultifying rigidity of the Platonic question, but also without the extreme conceptual disorder of the all-is-flux thesis? We would do well here to recall two related moments in the history of philosophical thought. The first is the methodological maxim formulated by the Cambridge philosopher Frank Ramsey: he observed that, when a seemingly perennial philosophical problem continues to generate polemically opposed arguments on each side of the debate without genuinely progressing toward resolution, "it is a heuristic maxim that the truth lies not in one of the two disputed views but in some third possibility which has not yet been thought of, which we can only discover by rejecting something assumed as obvious by both the disputants."[1] The second is the suggestion, made by Ramsey's friend and colleague Ludwig Wittgenstein and illustrating Ramsey's point, that in considering the logic of classes we might break free of long-embedded presumptions and consider a family-resemblance metaphor. Rather than being constituted by definitional essence (the essence that both polemical sides take as obviously important), categories might be organized, or made to cohere, by features that overlap in interconnecting ways as do, say, the facial features of a family—the daughter has the father's eyes, her brother has the mother's nose, they both have the maternal grandmother's chin, the daughter's child years later has the grandfather's smile, and so on. These overlapping features make the class recognizable, and they make each member recognizable as a member of it, but no *single* feature is definitionally prerequisite for class (in this case, family) membership.

Keeping the potentially constricting character of the invariance/flux polemic in mind, and keeping the family-resemblance metaphor in mind along with it, we might then ask: What are some of the features of the family of practices and engagements that we call literature or literary experience? Of those features, are there a few that seem to emerge more frequently? And, because in asking

---

[1] Quoted in P. M. S. Hacker, *Wittgenstein's Place in Twentieth-Century Analytic Philosophy* (Oxford: Blackwell, 1996), p. 100.

questions concerning literature we are often asking questions about literary experience in the mind of the reader, what more might we need to know about human experience, and what more might we need to know about the reader in general (if there is such a thing), or a reader in particular (of which there are many), in order to better articulate the character of our literary engagements?

1.1 Pragmatism and the Relational Conception of Selfhood

It was in the American pragmatic tradition that we encountered a relational conception of the self that was developed in opposition to the Cartesian conception. On the Cartesian model of selfhood, the human being is pictured as a hermetically sealed point of consciousness with transparent introspective access to its own contents; on this view the self would predate any of its engagements with what we would then, under the influence of this model, call the "outside world," and it would only contingently associate with that outside world. The relational conception, in stark contrast, sees the self as not merely contingently associated with that world, but rather as constituted by it: the contents of selfhood are not hermetically sealed inside a mental world prior to those external engagements, and they are not necessarily transparently available to introspection. C. S. Peirce mounted the attack on the Cartesian presuppositions in his brief polemic "Some Consequences of Four Incapacities,"[2] where he argued that we do not seek truth through an internally private inspection of mental contents in the way Descartes suggested. That is, it is not, he argued, through the close scrutiny of a hermetically isolated mental content possessing a degree of clarity and distinctness sufficient to call it true, but rather through a (necessarily, and not only contingently) public search within a community of philosophers.

We have, Peirce claims,

(1) no reliable or privileged power of introspection;
(2) truth is guaranteed by no private or internal intuition;
(3) we have no power of thinking, as he says, "without signs" (or, as we might put it now, we have no genuine understanding of what mental content might be that existed prior to its propositional expression, against the foundational Cartesian presupposition that hermetic mental content

---

[2] *Journal of Speculative Philosophy*, Vol. 2, 1868, pp. 140–57, reprinted in *Pragmatism and Classical American Philosophy: Essential Readings and Interpretive Essays*, 2nd ed., ed. John J. Stuhr (New York: Oxford University Press, 2000), pp. 54–67. Because Peirce's original publications are in journals from the second half of the nineteenth century and very hard to find, in the following I will include references to Stuhr's edition. For ease of access I will do the same below with William James, Josiah Royce, and George Herbert Mead.

4 LIVING IN WORDS

would be prelinguistic or only contingently attached to, or expressed in, language); and

(4) we have no distinction between the real and the unreal, between truth and illusion, that is inviolably private or contained within the Cartesian interior, but only as it arises, and indeed is multifariously used, within a community.

Indeed, for Peirce (as he argues in his essay "How to Make Our Ideas Clear"),[3] meaning itself is in fact the reverse of what a thinker under the influence of a Cartesian picture of selfhood would expect; that is, it is external, relational, and in the realm of praxis rather than originating within the solitary privacy of the hermetic mind. "There is," he writes, "no distinction of meaning so fine as to consist in anything but a possible difference of practice."[4] And the concepts of our language function *in situ*; they are not inwardly held mental entities that we can deploy as a purely inwardly contained mental act.

Thus Peirce finds Descartes's starting point for his epistemological project impossible from the first instruction: Descartes begins by asking us to apply universal doubt to all of our mental contents, in effect "trying on" the belief that they are all illusion rather than real. By washing everything away that is not for a distinctive self-confirming logical reason (the *cogito*) immune to the acid bath of doubt, Descartes sought to find an Archimedean platform upon which to build a superstructure of knowledge. Peirce, having said in his "Some Consequences" article, "Let us not pretend to doubt in philosophy what we do not doubt in our hearts,"[5] insists—to encapsulate his complex point—that doubt is not volitional in that sense. *We* are the ones who may or may not doubt, and one comes "laden with an immense mass of cognition already formed, of which you cannot divest yourself if you would."[6] Situating the phenomenon of doubting into the world in which that experience has its life, the stream of life within which the concept of doubt has its meaning, Peirce asks if you call it doubting "to write down on a piece of paper that you doubt?"[7] This solitary exercise, we might see on reflection, is no more in and of itself doubting than writing down on a piece of paper "I intend" is intending. "Do not," he urges, "make believe; if pedantry has not eaten all the reality out of you, recognize, as you must, that there is much that you do not doubt, in the least."[8] For Descartes, the concept of doubt would be one more piece of transparently introspectable mental content, and it would by its internally contained nature be subject to a similarly internally contained volition. For Peirce, that is, indeed, "make-believe": doubting is a complex humanly embodied

---

[3] *Popular Science Monthly*, Vol. 12, 1878, pp. 286–302, reprinted in Stuhr, ed., pp. 77–88.
[4] In Stuhr, ed., p. 81.   [5] In Stuhr, ed., p. 55.   [6] In Stuhr, ed., p. 108.
[7] In Stuhr, ed., p. 108.   [8] In Stuhr, ed., pp. 108–9.

phenomenon that arises in countlessly differentiated ways within the particularized circumstances of lived reality, where the criteria for its application emerge in similarly context-specific ways. It is anything but a single, unitary, and isolable mental act only contingently applied to its external setting. Doubt, as an act that may initially appear (under the distorting influence of the Cartesian picture of selfhood) hermetically sealed within the mind of the doubter, is in fact itself relationally embedded. In his "Issues of Pragmaticism,"[9] Peirce puts it succinctly: "Genuine doubt always has an external origin."[10] This, as we shall see in the final two chapters, shows us something of considerable importance about the nature of the reader. But this, so far, only hints at what is deeper.

The conception of selfhood that is for the most part implicit in these and related writings of Peirce is brought out fully and explicitly by his pragmatist successors. William James saw himself as an empiricist, but of what he called the radical kind; that is, he believed that theoretical philosophy departed disastrously from actual experience in modeling experience as an isolated set of sensations that come in with neatly delineated boundaries. That would be rather more like the philosophical positions of Locke's tradition, and while it would provide a conceptually neat model of human experience, it would in truth severely falsify its genuine character. In "The Stream of Thought,"[11] James wrote, "Most books start with sensations, as the simplest mental facts, and proceed synthetically, constructing each higher stage from those below it. But this is abandoning the empirical method of investigation."[12] That is, those who would pay the requisite attention to the details of genuine experience would see conceptually untidy constellations of relations everywhere, with the possibility of isolating single sensations as the basic or unanalyzable atoms of a combinatorial model receding rapidly into the realm of the theoretically misbegotten. Radical empiricism, for James, takes experience as it actually is and resists any attempt to force it into conformity with a philosophical template or conceptual model. He thus adds, "No one ever had a simple sensation by itself. Consciousness, from our natal day, is of a teeming multiplicity of objects and relations, and what we call simple sensations are results of discriminative attention, pushed often to a very high degree." And in a manner reminiscent (actually, chronologically, anticipatory) of Ramsey's maxim and Wittgenstein's working methods, he adds, "It is astonishing what havoc is wrought in psychology by admitting at the outset apparently innocent suppositions, that nevertheless contain a flaw."[13]

---

[9] In Stuhr, ed., pp. 116–26.   [10] In Stuhr, ed., p. 118.
[11] In *The Works of William James: The Principles of Psychology*, 3 vols., ed. Frederick Burkhardt (Cambridge, MA: Harvard University Press, 1981 [orig. pub. 1890]), pp. 219–40, 262–78; in Stuhr, ed., pp. 161–81.
[12] In Stuhr, ed., p. 161.   [13] In Stuhr, ed., p. 161.

6 LIVING IN WORDS

It is here that James argues against the very possibility of repetition, strictly speaking,[14] and the considerable significance of this particular point for the nature of selfhood has to my knowledge yet to be fully articulated. Thought, for James, is in constant change—that is indeed the one thing that remains constant—and he emphasizes that "no state once gone can recur and be identical with what it was before."[15] Now, if the Cartesian picture of the mind were correct, there would be no reason for repetition of the strictly exacting kind to be impossible: the inner consciousness would bring the same item onto what the generation of Gilbert Ryle discussed as the inner stage and direct its inner gaze at it just as it had before. Similarly, if the Lockean empirical model of perception (which has Cartesian elements) were correct, if the identical isolated sensation were to be presented to the perceptual faculties, the identical experiential episode would ensue. James sees both of these as impossible: we might hear the same note again, or see the same shade of green, or smell the same perfume, or feel the same pain, to use his examples, but insofar as these experiences are presented, they are presented *to a sensibility*, or to a self, that has been altered by the previous experience that it is now (in the looser sense of the term) having again. It is thus not that the self is sitting back within its inner citadel gazing upon its objects of consciousness; it is rather that the self is, here again, in part constituted by that experience—the very idea of the self is given content by the relations into which it enters. And this is just as—as we will be in a position to see with increasing clarity as the pragmatic conception of the self and its experience unfolds—the reader is in part constituted by literary experience.

James puts his position in neurophysiological terms at one point, but it is clear from his larger discussion that he means it in phenomenological terms as well: "For an identical sensation to recur it would have to occur the second time in an unmodified brain. But as this, strictly speaking, is a physiological impossibility, so is an unmodified feeling an impossibility."[16] And he here likens his position to that of none other than Heraclitus: he suggests that just as we never step twice into the same river, so we never step twice into what he calls "the river of life."[17] Consistent with the strong and conceptually reorienting emphasis on relations first made by his sometime colleague Peirce, James writes, "When the identical fact recurs, we

---

[14] It should be noted that there is a tension that surfaces here between the pragmatic and the Wittgensteinian tradition. James is observing that repetition, strictly speaking, is impossible; for any Wittgensteinian, "repetition" is a word that we use in many contexts, and within those contexts we will know, or find out how to know, what counts as what we call an exact repetition, a similar repetition, a "somewhat of a" repetition, and so forth. But the tension is resolvable: James, as he says, is "strictly speaking," that is, he is here observing that the person experiencing the repetition will be changed, however slightly, by the previous experience now repeated. That is the point I want to bring out presently as it relates to the experience of the reader of literature; James's point does not preclude the common or ordinary multiform uses of the term. That is, he is not claiming that, once his point is in focus, we will or should never use the word "repetition" again.

[15] In Stuhr, ed., p. 164.   [16] In Stuhr, ed., p. 165.   [17] In Stuhr, ed., p. 165.

must think of it in a fresh manner, see it under a somewhat different angle, apprehend it in different relations from those in which it last appeared."[18]

The deep significance of these thoughts for aesthetic experience is not lost on James. He writes:

> [I]n the senses, an impression feels very differently according to what has preceded it; as one color preceding another is modified by the contrast, silence sounds delicious after noise, and a note, when the scale is sung up, sounds unlike itself when the scale is sung down; as the presence of certain lines in a figure changes that apparent form of the other lines, and as in music the whole aesthetic effect comes from the manner in which one set of sounds alters our feeling of another; so in thought, we must admit that those portions of the brain that have just been maximally excited retain a kind of soreness which is a condition of our present consciousness, a codeterminant of how and what we shall now feel.[19]

One of the most notable features of literature and the distinctive experience it affords us just is, I want to suggest, aesthetic experience of this relational kind: and insofar as it presents full descriptions of characters who move, think, act, speak, respond, and do a thousand other things within the web of complexities of a depicted stream of life, it provides characters with whom we imaginatively engage. The precise nature of that imaginative engagement I will describe more fully below (after we have seen more of the pragmatic conception of selves and the experience of those selves upon which this discussion is based), but we may already see this at least in outline: If our selves are relationally constituted in anything like the way Peirce and his philosophical compatriot James are suggesting, then literature can be far more than a *description* of human experience. It is, far greater, a tool employed for nothing less than the relational construction of selfhood. But again, first, what more have the pragmatists given us to help articulate this conception of, this emergent pattern of practices of, our literary engagements?

In terms of the history of philosophy, we know that, just as Peirce is fundamentally opposed to the Cartesian conception of the mind, James is fundamentally opposed to the atomistic conception of experience adumbrated in British empiricism. He indeed refers to "the Humean doctrine that our thought is composed of separate independent parts and is not a sensibly continuous stream"[20] as a historically embedded misrepresentation. That model, again, would place the internally contained and fully pre-constituted self at the center of one psychic universe, with isolated or atomistic experiences being sent in through the five sensory modalities to that hermetic self. It would then assemble, or construct, the image of the stable world out of those similarly hermetically

---

[18] In Stuhr, ed., p. 166.   [19] In Stuhr, ed., p. 166.   [20] In Stuhr, ed., p. 167.

isolated atoms of raw data. But "consciousness," he says, "does not appear to itself chopped up in bits."[21] And for him the words "chain" or "train" fail to fit conscious experience: "It is nothing jointed: it flows." Rather, a "river" or a "stream" provides the metaphor of choice; hence, he famously says, "*In talking of it hereafter, let us call it the stream of thought, of consciousness, or of subjective life.*" James's self, as we have begun to see, is a very different kind of relationally constituted entity than that pictured by any empiricism of the non-radical kind (again, his self is, as we shall see in Chapter 5, the kind of entity constituted in part by its literary engagements). But James as philosopher is rarely content to leave his psychological target alone once brought up to the tribunal of actual lived experience: in a manner reminiscent of a Wittgenstein or a Nietzsche, he also wants to unearth, carefully identify, and disarm the forces or conceptual pressures leading us to that misrepresentation. And in this case (also like Wittgenstein and like Nietzsche), he identifies language as the culprit.

Although James does not explicitly name Locke here, it is the Lockean theory of language-as-names-of-individuated-sensory-experiences that he finds dangerously potent as a misleading model ("Here, again, language works against our perception of the truth").[22] He illustrates the conception of language that blinds us to experiential nuance with the example of hearing thunder: thunder is not one experience of an undifferentiated kind that we may have again and again. The uniform word "thunder" in its repeated uses may well make us think that it names a correspondingly uniform experience that is in turn uniformly repeated. But that is to fall prey to the misleading appearance of what Wittgenstein called the grammatical surface of our language. In truth—against what this single and seemingly unitary term suggests—the experience of thunder is *inextricably and in its nature* relational, and not a self-enclosed or bounded event contingently set into a relational web *ex post facto*: "Into the awareness of the thunder itself the awareness of the previous silence creeps and continues; for what we hear when the thunder crashes is not thunder *pure*, but thunder-breaking-upon-silence-and-contrasting-thunder-breaking-upon-silence-and-contrasting-with-it." Hence for James the relationally constituted nature of aesthetic experience mentioned above is in fact a model for, or microcosm of, our experience of no less than the world—and this thus gives us as well a new way of articulating the mimetic function of literature; that is, literature provides a microcosmic replication, not only of the events of life, but of our relational engagement with it.

We often use sonic metaphors to allude to these experiential interconnections—we speak of resonances, of soundings of depth, of being on the same frequency, and so forth—but James's point is here again more radical than that: the very idea of the name of a thing or a thought or an experience is in an important sense a fiction. He

---

[21] In Stuhr, ed., p. 169; this and immediately following quotations.
[22] In Stuhr, ed., p. 169; this and following quotations.

would not, I think, dispute the fact that it is a convenient fiction: life is too short, and indeed pragmatic needs too urgent to fully describe everything in the world with long strings of hyphenated phrases (in truth they would be far longer than the strings he uses here). However, when we can approximate such fuller descriptions, we avoid generating, or shake loose the grip of, a false picture of human experience set in place by that false picture of naming. "We name our thoughts simply, each after its thing, as if each knew its own thing and nothing else. What each really knows is clearly the thing it is named for, with dimly perhaps a thousand other things." If in the rush of life our descriptively truncated language were fuller, we would—as indeed we sometimes do—speak a language of cognitive nuance, a language that would capture the mental life as lived, not as given in practical-world shorthand. The language of literature, of course, is not in that rush of life, nor, usually, is the literary experience of the reader, and it is in the highest achievements of works that capture this enriched conception of experience, for example those of William's brother Henry (who indeed said "relations end nowhere"),[23] that we see a mimetically accurate depiction of the "stream," the "river." Such depictions are composed in an extraordinary language that is mindful, not only of the one thing named, but also of William James's "thousand other things." But again, the fundamental point at present is to identify the elements of Peirce's and James's philosophy that place us in a position from which we can see not only the relational self but also the corresponding self-constitutive power of literary experience.

James next draws an ontological distinction only to subvert it. Like a bird's life, a life of "alternations of flights and perchings,"[24] what James calls the rhythm of language (where we express thought in sentences and then end sentences with periods—our cognitive-linguistic resting places) reflects this as well: we have "substantive" parts of our thought-life, and "transitive" parts. The substantive parts, we are inclined to believe, are thoughts engendered by the sensations given to us by static objects, by (non-Heraclitean) fixed things, and we can hold them in mind for an indeterminate time and, as he says, contemplate them without their changing. The transitive, by contrast, are "filled with thoughts of relations, static or dynamic, that for the most part obtain between the matters contemplated in the periods of comparative rest." And these are elusive when we try to "stabilize" them, when we try to inwardly scrutinize them as we might scrutinize (outwardly, as we would then say in this contrast) a physical object. James uses memorable images to express his point, and they all show that if we stop such transitive moments in their tracks to scrutinize them, we inadvertently annihilate them: if we try to arrest that moment's flow, it "ceases forthwith to be itself," as does a

---

[23] "Really, universally, relations stop nowhere, and the exquisite problem of the artist is eternally but to draw, by a geometry of his own, the circle in which they shall happily appear to do so," in Henry James's preface to *Roderick Hudson*, in *The Novels and Tales of Henry James*, Vol. 1 (New York: Scribner's, 1907), p. vii.

[24] In Stuhr, ed., p. 170; this and following quotations.

10 LIVING IN WORDS

snowflake we want to inspect that becomes a drop when caught in the hand; if we grasp for that fleeting transitive experience we will find only a static substantive thing in our hand, like seizing a spinning top to capture its motion. Or, perhaps his best example, it is all too like attempting quickly to turn up the light to see how the darkness looks.

James progresses to a point of (and here subverting or, better, overcoming his distinction) putting the transitive, interconnecting, relationally interweaving experiences on an equal par with the substantive moments. This is to make radical empiricism even more radical: perhaps the most time-honored tradition in epistemology is that which places the viewer on a perspectival platform out from which we observe the viewed thing, and then asks by what theory or argument we can ascertain beyond any doubt that we know that thing as it is independent of any projection or distortion brought in by the observer. The observation is conducted in the interest of knowing a *thing* (objectivity is thought of in terms of objects), and the relations into which that thing may enter (itself, again, a picture that is insufficiently radical for James) are irrelevant to the brute facts we know about it. As we have seen, James lives in a world of constitutive relations, where the extensionalism presumed by this epistemological tradition is seen as a grand but misbegotten by-product of a false picture of naming. "Now pragmatism, devoted tho she be to facts," he says in his "What Pragmatism Means,"[25] "has no such materialistic bias as ordinary empiricism labors under." Rather like his brother, he said, "relations are numberless," and (rather unlike his brother, both in what Henry said and in the exacting descriptive project to which he devoted his life), "no existing language is capable of doing justice to all their shades."[26] The relations are as real as what we think of as the independent objects into which they enter.

In his "A World of Pure Experience" collected in his *Essays in Radical Empiricism*,[27] James emphasizes the point:

> To be radical, an empiricism must neither admit into its construction any element that is not directly experienced, nor exclude from them any element that is directly experienced. For such a philosophy, *the relations that connect experiences must themselves be experienced relations, and any kind of relation experienced must be accounted as 'real' as anything else in the system.*

For James, that is true in microcosm of our aesthetic perception, it is true in macrocosm of our perception of the world, and—most importantly for our

---

[25] In *The Works of William James: Pragmatism*, ed. Frederick Burkhardt (Cambridge, MA: Harvard University Press, 1975 [orig. pub. 1907]), pp. 27–44; in Stuhr, ed., pp. 193–202, this quotation p. 200.

[26] In Stuhr, ed., p. 171.

[27] In *The Works of William James: Essays in Radical Empiricism*, ed. Frederick Burkhardt (Cambridge, MA: Harvard University Press, 1976 [orig. pub. 1904]), pp. 21–44; in Stuhr, ed., pp. 181–93, this quotation p. 182.

self-understanding—it is true of, indeed, ourselves. Philosophical rationalism, as James observes, may well have made a kind of place for relations, but they were there seen as secondary, as of a less stable ontological kind, as an organizational network in which the more real (because extended as matter in space) things are organized. His view, he insists, will, as he says, do conjunctive relations full justice;[28] they are constitutive of the world, and constitutive of us. And insofar as we are constituted by such relations, and insofar as some of those relations are with other persons, other minds, the radical empiricism espoused by James does not face a *problem* of other minds. We are, he insists, interrelated with each other from the start, and a skepticism that would lock us into our individual and autonomous hermetic shells and then ask how we could even so much as know each other only falsifies that foundational truth of selfhood, that contextually interwoven *bildung* that is depicted in the *roman*.[29] None of these foundational thoughts of Peirce and James were lost on their successors in the tradition of pragmatism, particularly when they turned to the task of articulating not only an ontology that gives full weight to relations, and not only a form of empiricism that was sufficiently radical to describe the nature of relationally constituted psychological experience, but of fully and directly describing the nature of the human self.

Josiah Royce took up that task in one way: like Peirce, he opposed the Cartesian view of the self, and like James, he emphasized relations in psychology. So of the self, he stoutly claimed: "Whatever the self is it is not a thing. It is not, in Aristotle's sense, . . . a substance."[30] For Royce, the contrast between the self and the not-self—indeed the most fundamental contrast for personal identity—is constantly in play, and reflection on the experience of literature suggests that this operates in ever more subtle ways. He wrote, "I affirm that our empirical self-consciousness, from moment to moment depends upon a series of contrast effects, whose psychological origin lies in our literal social life..."[31] Our engagement with literature is in one inescapable sense social, and our imaginative identification with the protagonists and other figures in those literary worlds changes from moment to moment, and our own selves are further attenuated through such self-and-not-self "contrast effects." And a self, for Royce, is more a process than a product: it is not the *kind* of thing that is, once achieved, static, nor is it (as his philosophical forebears suggested) definable in any way independent of the social relations into which it enters and by which it is in significant part constituted.

The community into which, and in a sense from which, the self is woven, is thus, for Royce, one necessary part of any full description we would give of the self we are describing, the person we may be trying to define. Just as Machiavelli famously

---

[28] In Stuhr, ed., p. 182.
[29] See the section "The Coterminousness of Different Minds," in Stuhr, ed., pp. 189–93.
[30] Quoted in Jacquelyn Ann Kegley, "Josiah Royce: Introduction," in Stuhr, ed., p. 249.
[31] In Stuhr, ed., p. 250.

12 LIVING IN WORDS

donned his scholarly garments for his evenings of imaginary scholarly "dialogue" with the ancient authors, the authors of the books that absorbed—and in significant part, made—him, so we become members of a Roycean community of reading. And indeed a literary sensibility is from this vantage point just a preference for, and deep acquaintance with, a particular subset of authorial presences. Yet, while joining such a community and thus in part being relationally constituted by it, we do not sacrifice our individuality to it: we do not, as he says, forget ourselves "in a common trance."[32] For in acts of interpretation (and Royce declares, "Interpretation is, once for all, the main business of philosophy"),[33] we ask, in the continual processes of contrastive comparison-making, not only "Wherein does A resemble B?" but also "Wherein consists their distinction?"[34] or for us, once having recognized a larger similarity or resemblance between the protagonist and ourselves, our enduring character traits, our habits of thought and feeling, our patterns of reactions, and James's "thousand other things," we then ask what more subtle contrasts mark the differences?

If we feel an impulse—for the pragmatists a philosophically recidivistic impulse—to categorize such "self-and-not-self" comparisons in the terms of empiricism and rationalism, Royce is there to point out the conceptually claustrophobic limitations of any such epistemology of self-consciousness:

> But a dual antithesis between perceptual and conceptual knowledge is once for all inadequate to the wealth of the facts of life. When you accomplish an act of comparison, the knowledge which you attain is neither merely conceptual, nor merely perceptual, nor yet merely a practically active synthesis of perception and conception. It is a third type of knowledge. It interprets. It surveys from above. It is an attainment of a larger unity of consciousness. It is a conspectus. As the tragic artist looks down upon the many varying lives of his characters, and sees their various motives not interpenetrating, but cooperating, in the dramatic action which constitutes his creation,—so any one who compares distinct ideas, and discovers the third or mediating idea which interprets the meaning of one in the light of the other, thereby discovers, or invents, a realm of conscious unity which constitutes the very essence of the life of reason.[35]

1.2 Autobiography at One Remove

As will be clear by now, it is my contention that:

(1) One of the centrally discernible and frequently emergent family-resemblance features of literature is that we accomplish precisely such acts of comparison within the imaginative world of literary experience; that

---

[32] In Stuhr, ed., p. 284.   [33] In Stuhr, ed., p. 287.   [34] In Stuhr, ed., p. 288.
[35] In Stuhr, ed., p. 292.

(2) Such comparisons are neither the stuff of empirical verification nor of rational deduction; that

(3) Such comparisons are at once interpretive and—first by a broader imaginative identification and then with the attendant finer distinctions of similarity and difference within that comparative framework—self-interpretive; that

(4) Such experience is productive of the larger unity of consciousness of which Royce and James speak; and, most importantly, that

(5) Such interpretive labors are, in the manner we have seen above and that is only visible having first brought together and expounded the relational conception of experience and the self, self-constitutive or, as I prefer, self-compositional.

But here again the Heraclitean question arises: Does it follow that we are, owing to the emphasis on relations, on shifting comparisons, and on process rather than product, doomed to embrace the thesis that all, with regard to the relationally constituted self, is only flux? Royce is quick here too: If, as he says, "the relative and the transient" take possession of the field, might we then suppose that such acts of comparison would furnish us only "with instances of relative, shifting, and fluent truth?"[36] "As a fact," he writes, "this is not the case," for comparison, while it deals with the "fluent and the personal," also treats of "the exact and . . . the necessary," and indeed—if we stop to reflect on the matter with the preparation of all the foregoing pragmatic thought assembled as what we might, with Wittgenstein, call reminders of what we actually do (thus dismantling the impulse to mischaracterize in the name of philosophical theory)—so it does. Royce goes on (coining a phrase that has since become common currency) to discuss what he called "a Community of Interpretation." The stability of a self—a self that is, for reasons we have begun to see, in one significant part constituted by relational interaction with literary texts—might be explained in much the same way that the emergent patterns of regularities that constitute the enduring unity of vision that makes the community coherent in the first place explain its stability.

But then while not Heraclitean, this position is not Platonic either: truth, he insists in light of these and related reflections, "is nothing static";[37] it "changes with the expediencies of your experience." Truths, not about the world but about the self, would follow in suit. And with this articulation he points out a middle way between the extreme poles of Platonic invariance on the one end and Heraclitean flux on the other. We would take just such a middle way in the process of learning from, and indeed being shaped by, or given humane content by, our experience with literary texts. Some Roycean comparisons confirm what we are (for example,

---

[36] In Stuhr, ed., p. 293; this and following quotations.   [37] In Stuhr, ed., p. 310.

14 LIVING IN WORDS

when we feel a deep affinity, or a "fellow-traveler" feeling in poetry, such as we might sense upon reading Emily Dickinson's line "I dwell in possibility"). Some confirm what we are not—for example, the murdering Meursault in Camus's *The Stranger*. Some show what we can imagine ourselves (if, as we say, in a different life) to have been like but fortunately are not—for example, David Lurie in Coetzee's *Disgrace* or Roquentin in Sartre's *Nausea* or, in a rather different vein, Kingsley Amis's "lucky" Jim or David Lodge's Morris Zapp. Some show what we cannot imagine ourselves to be or have been (for example, Dostoevsky's Underground Man), some (Bellow's Herzog?) show that we need to think harder, which in literary experience often means we need to gain more imaginative range and depth through further reading or reading again (as we will discuss it in Chapter 6) to place ourselves into any of these categories. And some comparisons will confirm that while we may have once been one way, we now are another: consider Hume's example of preferring Ovid at twenty, Horace at forty, and Tacitus at fifty (to which we will also return in Chapter 6). Patterns of regularities or constancies over time and across cases will emerge, but they will change with the expediencies of the self-negotiations brought about by literary experience.

If relations themselves warrant ontological respect, and if the relations we have with literature possess self-constitutive power, what then of those relationally constituted selves' relations to their own pasts? Here we turn, if only briefly, to another of the successors of the Peircean-Jamesian tradition. George Herbert Mead put the point in provocative terms, claiming that the past is as uncertain, and in a distinctive sense as unpredictable, as the future. He did not mean to embrace, of course, any form of extreme pan-temporal skeptical relativism or wholesale revisionism, but he did mean to suggest this: the truth of any claim pertaining to the past will not be judged true by virtue of a verified correspondence between present description and past fact (precisely because we cannot travel into the past to compare the present description to the historical fact), but rather by reference to an emergent set of criteria in the present that lead us to describe or redescribe the past as we do. What he calls the "accepted past," he insists, "lies in a present and is subject, itself, to possible reconstruction."[38]

"We are constantly reconstructing the world from our own standpoint. And that reconstruction holds just as really with the so-called 'irrevocable' past as with reference to a future." And thus he says, indeed memorably: "The past is just as uncertain as the future is." "Every generation re-writes its history," and no such rewriters should go so far as to "contemplate the finality of their findings,"

---

[38] Quoted in James Campbell, "George Herbert Mead: Introduction," in Stuhr, ed., p. 544; this and following Mead quotations. I discuss this issue at some length in *Describing Ourselves: Wittgenstein and Autobiographical Consciousness* (Oxford: Clarendon, 2008), ch. 5, "The Question of True Self-Interpretation," pp. 154–84.

for they "are always subject to conceivable reformulations, on the discovery of later evidence..."

These phrases capture what is in the context of the question concerning the relations of the self to its past most relevant: the evolving self, at various stages along the way of its unfolding process of negotiating its relational self-identity, describes and redescribes itself in accordance not with an overarching and static truth, but in accordance with what William James called its present perspectival "perch," its presently relevant relational associations and connotations, and its "later evidence." This, in terms of the polemics of fixity versus flux as we have seen, sides with neither Scylla nor Charybdis. Mead writes, "The histories that we have transcribed would have been impossible to the pens of our fathers as the world we live in would have been inaccessible to their eyes and to their minds..." And just the same is possible within the span of a single subjectivity, a single self and its history. New aspects can dawn, new ways of seeing emerge, and, more deeply, profound change in self-understanding can occur such that the present state of mind would have been inconceivable prior to the change. This can of course occur independently of literary experience (although here it will, I believe far more often than we might originally think, be inflected by that experience), but we should not forget that such change can and does occur within it or as a result of it (which we will see in Chapter 5, Section 5.2 in detail).

What Mead sees so particularly clearly is the distinctive way in which what he calls "the emergent" (that is, the act, utterance, gesture, deed, thought, object, invention, and so on) seems to display the power to realign acts, utterances, and deeds behind it into a pattern that, taken together, constitutes the conditions of that particular "emergent's" possibility. The emergent, he says, "has no sooner appeared than we set about rationalizing it, that is, we undertake to show that it, or at least the conditions that determine its appearance, can be found in the past that lay behind it." *The past that lay behind it*: indeed this is what works rather like iron filings in a magnetic field, where the "switching on" of the present or recent event repositions other (perhaps initially or heretofore seemingly unrelated) events into a linear progression, a kind of retrospectively discerned teleology. And while those retrospective patterns may well become familiar, Mead warns us that we should not allow that familiarity to blind us to future possible realignments. Precisely this happens with our retrospective identifications of the episodes or emergent patterns in a life that go to make up a character trait, and the occasion of those identifications is often precisely the reflections or speculations given rise by our serious engagement with literature. Yet it is still another notion of Mead's that is of perhaps greatest significance for present purposes.

"Sociality," as James Campbell succinctly presents the idea in his lucid survey of Mead's contribution, is the term Mead uses for, as Mead himself puts it, "the capacity of being several things at once." Campbell gives the example of a stone, which might be an element contained within (or we might now say taking on significance within and exerting pattern-determining power within) "chemical, thermal, gravitational, and perhaps visual and architectural systems." With the question of the nature of literature framed in terms of our present question of its self-forming power in mind, it is but a short step to the claim that a single act or gesture or utterance or deed on the part of a literary character may function within multiple "systems," as Mead uses the word. And then it is short step from there to the point of greatest relevance given the emergent patterns of interest of the present occasion: an act or gesture or utterance or deed, and so forth, can function within the world of the text as part of a pattern or as the emergent element that reveals the pattern behind it, and it may function at the same time in a "system" extending outside the text, as one of the Roycean comparisons or contrasts that give further content and specificity to what we might call our growing and ever-evolving self-profile (to which we will return in the next section and more extensively in Chapter 5). And even there it may function doubly or triply, as an element in three systems that variously, from one vantage point, confirms one aspect of a self-image, from another challenges or threatens to undercut it, and from still another confirms an ambivalence or ambiguity about it.

"Sociality," for Mead, is the ability of any thing, animate or inanimate, to take a meaningful part in varying and multiple "systems" or networks of interests and—indeed—relations. Events and deeds and utterances, along with all the varying kinds of things depicted in literature, exhibit precisely such "sociality." As do the particularized contents of the Roycean comparisons undertaken variously in the back, the middle, or the front of the mind of the absorbed reader of literature.

To stand back, then, what ground have we covered? We began with the question "What is literature?" and its implications, looking then into the presuppositional contrasts to the question "What is literature now?" We saw, in Plato and his followers, a presumption concerning the necessity of invariance for anything deserving the name truth; we saw, in Nietzsche and his distant hero Heraclitus, a Dionysian celebration of flux, of constant change. And we saw Wittgenstein introduce a new metaphor, that of family resemblance. Against that backdrop and the aspiration to identify some members of the family of practices we call literary experience, we then proceeded to some central concepts of pragmatic thought as they help articulate some features of the experience of absorbed reading. And how have they helped us?

Peirce, opposing the Cartesian conception of selfhood as hermetic consciousness, laid the foundations for a relational conception of the self. Doubting, we saw, is a human phenomenon inextricably embedded in its context, and is perhaps in some aspects volitional but in many ways very much not so. As a mental event, doubt is thus not hermetically sealed, not purely of the Cartesian mind: it is relationally situated to circumstances, *just as is the mind that entertains the doubt*. And with that step, we are put into a position to see in a single stroke that the contents of the mind are relationally constituted, and that our self-concept (as one rather expansive item of mental content) is relational as well. And one very complex network of relations into which the mind enters in a deep and sustained way is, indeed, literature (or film or theater or other narrative artforms), and so whatever else literature may be (whatever other family resemblances it may exhibit), it is one significant determinant of the contents of selfhood.

But then that claim needed greater precision: just how does this relational content-determination work in literary experience, and what circumstances—circumstances clearly at variance with the Cartesian picture of mentally hermetic content-determination—make it possible? William James argued that experience *in and of itself* is intrinsically relational, and that the traditional empirical picture of isolated or bounded sensation falsifies far more than it clarifies. There is, he insisted, no such thing as "a simple sensation by itself"; for our present concerns, this serves as a potent double-pronged reminder that, first, human experience itself, if depicted with a degree of verisimilitude, will be situated into the dense weave of a relational matrix in its imaginary literary world, and second (and still more importantly for present concerns), the experience of the reader will not be accurately describable with classical empirical boundary determinacy. The self that has the experience will, in James's distinct sense, be in a state of perpetual change; the literary sensibility engaged with the text will be, however incrementally, altered by that text. And here we moved forward one significant step: the self that is experiencing that literature is a self that is in part given content by it. The river of Heraclitus merges with Wittgenstein's stream of life (within which our words and deeds have meaning, have a point), but it is not only that the river has changed; as the pragmatists have insisted, we have too. Thus, for James, the note in an ascending phrase is importantly different from (what we might call in some contexts) the same note in a descending phrase, the red against azure in a color-field painting is different from that red against violet, and the sound of thunder is not the same to the pre- or post-thunder sensibility. The note, the color, and the sound do not exist as atomistic sensations separate from and prior to the mind of the beholder. The self, for James, is not bounded separately from its experience any more than one experience is bounded from another. The stream of thought is continuous, and consciousness is not, as he rather starkly said, chopped up into bits. There may be markings that represent words on a page in a book stored in isolation away from a literary sensibility, but literary experience itself is not, nor is it anything like, a parading of that isolated content before a static perception device. (That would describe, rather than a humane sensibility, a reading machine.) We may have the simplifying picture that uniform words name uniform experiences, but in truth language is as complexly relationally interconnected as is the self that uses it.

A simple picture of ostensive definition, of names-directly-attached-to-things, we saw to be somewhat less than innocent: the very idea of a name of an experience can suggest that the name is a unitary marker of a hermetically

18   LIVING IN WORDS

contained experience, one that is both in principle and in empirical fact exactly repeatable. Indeed, on such a model, the very name "literary experience" would suggest just such experiential uniformity and hence naming invariance. But James argued that the relations, the "transitive parts" and the "thousand other things," are as constitutive of any experience as are what we take to be the "central" part of the experience, that is, the basic experience without the attached connotations, the resonances, the interconnections, (what we only uncomprehendingly take to be) the supplements. James's radical empiricism rebukes the very idea of central experiences, of basic experiences, and indeed the relegation of the interconnecting sinews to a position of secondary ontological importance. Experience—and absorbed and reflective literary absorption is of course one subspecies of that— is far more intricate; as he said, we annihilate its nuanced content if we try to make it look more stable than it is. And if no existing language, as we saw him say, is sufficient to capture this content, then we can at least see a graded scale from the most blunt to the most intricate that we have. And these gradations are more finely marked in literature than anywhere else—Jane Austen, George Eliot, his brother Henry James, and countless others since show them with a precision well beyond what William James seems to have thought possible.

Royce's self-defining "contrast effects" are as much in play within the imaginative world of literary experience as they are anywhere. This next step forward in pragmatic thought offers a new way of describing the reader's psychology, the reader's identification with the protagonist: it is not only that the reader imagines undergoing the events in the life of the protagonist (or any other character) and thus expands the backlog of imagined experience—to say only that is too simple and it misses more than it captures. Rather, it is, with Peirce, James, and now Royce behind us, a process of relationally and self-comparatively engaging with that protagonist (or other character), so that the self-negotiated profile of our own identity is sharpened by the comparison, by what Royce calls the "not-us." If that relational engagement is, as we have seen, powerful to the (too often underappreciated) point of being constitutive of us, then a slogan such as "we are what we read" is, if far too crude to capture the nuanced facts, at least pointing in the right direction. And if Mead is right about the realignments of the past in memory, if he is right that we are forever engaged in restructuring the past and its sense-making networks of relations, then we are in that distinct sense what we reread as well.

What literature is thus not is diversionary entertainment (and here might be one way of limning the distinction between literature and commercial fiction): it is not merely an escape from our fixed selves into an alternative fictional universe, where the self that enters that other imaginary world remains unchanged. It is, rather, an irreplaceable mode of cognitive engagement wherein the most subtle interactions and interpenetrations of resonant human experiences are both shown and occasioned, and whereby the most specific contents of the self are variously provided, altered, refined, removed, and attenuated. If we ask if this process is itself the unique essence of literature—what literature is in a Platonic sense—then the answer is no: other things in life, other self-constitutive relational interactions, have this power too (indeed literary mimesis depends on that fact). But if we ask whether this process is merely a contingent feature of literature that it might just as well do without, we would probably have to answer that in the negative as well. It is, as a third way that moves between the poles of invariant essence on the one end and a mere fleeting social consensus that would only momentarily and falsely appear to stabilize the contingent flux of literature on the other, a feature that appears often enough to recognize, if with variations, the distinctive profile of a family. It is a feature (or set of related features on a finer level of analysis) that would help account for our valuing humane learning as we do, precisely because it not only expands the reach of imagination, but more profoundly—if the pragmatists are anything like right about the non-hermetic nature of experience and the relational nature of the self—it makes us in significant part who we are.

In imagining self-identities like our own, we better understand, and are better able to articulate, ourselves. In imagining identities unlike ourselves, we sharpen the articulation of the differences. Some of those differences are large and crude, but many more will be small, precise, and particular, and as such will render our self-understanding that much more exact, that much more intricate. In imagining identities in minute ways like, and in minute ways unlike, ourselves, we gain the self-knowledge to see who we are—and as such, literary experience often takes on the character of an autobiographical exercise, if at one remove. But then that itself describes this family of literary experiences too crudely, for it suggests that the self is what it is prior to, and remains unchanged after, those profound, humane, self-constitutive aesthetic engagements. The self is not invariant.

1.3 A Person's Words: Literary Characters and Autobiographical Understanding

So we have seen that what has been widely discussed as the Cartesian conception of selfhood, the notion or conceptual picture of a human being claiming that the most fundamental fact of human existence is autonomy or metaphysical isolation, has been illuminatingly challenged by the American pragmatic tradition. Let's review in brief scope to keep in focus what is most central to what will follow shortly. On the Cartesian view,[39] the self is existent prior to any relation into which it enters; it has consciousness, and it has unmediated introspective access to

---

[39] The *locus classicus* of this view is Descartes's second meditation, in *Meditations*, ed. John Cottingham (Cambridge: Cambridge University Press, 1996). Gilbert Ryle, in *The Concept of Mind* (London: Routledge, 2009 [orig. pub. 1949]), criticized, on linguistic grounds, the picture ("the ghost in the machine") Descartes's theory seemed to paint. For a discussion of the impact I believe this view has

20 LIVING IN WORDS

the contents of that consciousness. Anything external to it is secondary and merely contingent. On the pragmatic-relational view, the self is instead no less than constituted by the relations into which it enters. It is made by, and it is given its content by, the complex, intricate, and layered networks of relations surrounding it. Indeed, for all the foundational pragmatists we considered—William James, Josiah Royce, and George Herbert Mead—the connections between things are as important as the things connected. Thus in truth (and this is another way of putting the fundamental point from the preceding sections), "surrounding it" is not quite the right phrase, in that this way of describing the matter implicitly preserves what the pragmatists regard as the fallacious and widely unexamined preconception of the autonomous entity existing prior to those interconnections. Extending the thoughts of his that we considered above, William James also argued that we have never truly seen any given thing *wholly* by itself, so the model of object autonomy (where we see a given isolated object first, and then, only contingently, situate or relationally interconnect it) mischaracterizes the actual phenomenology of human perception from the start.

And so now we move forward: Some of those interconnections, those relations, are born (as we shall see in detail in Chapter 5) of an imaginatively creative act, or as we revealingly put it, of *making* comparisons, so that to perceive a thing for what it is, is to perceive that thing within an often expansive and always indeterminately bounded network within which the object in question is positioned. And what I will suggest now, as the next step, is that not only do persons exhibit a similar relational ontology, but indeed those persons' words do as well. This means that:

(1) To understand their words in a full and deep sense is to understand who and what they are (and what they are made of, which, to a striking degree—once we are positioned to see it—are complex networks of endorsed words);[40] and

(2) The true understanding of their words requires seeing those words within complex constellations of evolving relations.

This I believe is close to what Wittgenstein called "the field of a word,"[41] which he rightly insisted proves decisive in determining a word's meaning as it is used in a context.

---

had on our pre-reflective intuitions concerning autobiographical writing, see my *Describing Ourselves*, in which I also discuss briefly the possible difference between what Descartes intended and what many philosophers since Ryle have meant by the term "Cartesian."

[40] This particular issue will be taken up more fully in Chapters 5 and 6 below; the fundamental point is that our varying relations to our words—endorsed and with full conviction, or casually tossed off, or half-believed or hypothesized, or countless other stations along these ways—contribute to and inflect the meanings of our words as we use them.

[41] Wittgenstein writes: "A *great deal* can be said about a subtle aesthetic difference—that is important.—The first remark may, of course, be: '*This* word fits, *that* doesn't'—or something of the kind. But then all the widespread ramifications effected by each of the words can still be discussed. That first judgement is *not* the end of the matter, for it is the *field* of a word that is decisive." *Philosophical*

IMAGINED IDENTITIES 21

But after considering how other-understanding works in these relational terms, I also want to suggest that:

(3) Autobiographical labor, the work of self-understanding, functions in precisely these relational-linguistic terms as well. It is work in words.

This, as we will explore below in literature, biography, and autobiography, is in large part a matter of conducting subtle inquiries into the telling comparisons (again, in words) between:

(a) ourselves and others;
(b) competing self-descriptions;
(c) narrative descriptions of the connections between our present and past selves;
(d) what we hoped for and what we actually have (where we express these distinct categories linguistically);
(e) words we used and words we should have used, or things we said and better things we should have said;
(f) one way of connecting past experiences and another in making narrative unity of a life; and numerous further comparisons (some varieties of which we shall shortly see) all the way down to the very finest linguistic detail.

Awareness of the content of these word-borne comparisons, for the relational view of selfhood, becomes a defining part of the content of the consciousness that—as we discover in the act of undertaking this kind of autobiographical reflection—was not and could not have been hermetically sealed in accordance with the Cartesian picture of autonomous interiority. Indeed, we can come to see that it is instructively difficult to so much as imagine a self—not a philosophical caricature, placeholder, or cipher, but an actual human self—prior to, or without the defining content of, those networks of self-defining comparison-generated relations, or without, to adapt Wittgenstein's phrase, the "field" of a self.

We will discuss this in much greater length in the following, but one neatly contained example of the kind of word-borne acuity of perception to be investigated in the following is found in Iris Murdoch's diaries. Writing of John Bayley (later to become her husband), she writes: "JB rang up this morning. His voice was consoling. How can I describe how remarkable he is?... A grace of soul— humility, simplicity, and a way of being very acute & subtle without ever

---

Investigations, revised 4th ed., ed. P. M. S. Hacker and Joachim Schulte, trans. G. E. M. Anscombe, P. M. S. Hacker, and Joachim Schulte (Malden: Wiley-Blackwell, 2009), "Philosophy of Psychology—A Fragment," sec. xi, no. 297, p. 230.

22 LIVING IN WORDS

protecting oneself by placing and despising other people." The tone, the musical aspect of the voice, consoles; this implicitly describes him as a sympathetic person, and this quality itself is discernible in a description she gives of another matter seemingly independent of word meaning, that is, tone or sound. And to discern a grace of soul is perhaps at once an intrinsic and relational description: with a double aspect, it tells us of him—but then this quality only stands out against the background of unnamed others. And then, with the kind of complexity of comparative and relationally embedded description we will look into below, while we see humility and simplicity standing out in the same way as grace of soul, we get "without ever protecting oneself by placing," that is, judging from above and rank-ordering, thus showing that she perceives the defensive purpose of such acts of "placing," and that she sees the special way in which he has transcended any such impulse to invidiously place people in order to attempt to position oneself as superior, an action she rightly sees as in truth lowering the person trying to be superior. So this description of him is undeniably about him, but it is also at the same time a form of comparison to others contained within that description; it is revelatory of what she sees in him; it is about the human folly of "placing and despising"; it is about ulterior motives; it shows what she sees as an embodiment of a moral ideal and her admiring stance toward that ideal (and this carries within it the as yet unconfirmed possibility of implicit self-criticism); it is about the possibility of being acute and subtle without demonstrating these features in the negative judgment of others; and it is about an interesting form of moral backfire. This web of complex relations is indispensable to understanding what she is saying of him, and it is indispensable to our understanding of what she has revealed about herself in this brief diary entry description of him. Thus it becomes rather unclear what the very idea of a hermetic, purely factual and intrinsic, or non-relational, description of a person amounts to or could amount to.

Seeing all of this clearly will involve, as we progress:

(a) Seeing how (that is, in which verbal terms) one literary character comes to understand another, where this proves to be a rather complicated, intricate, layered interrelational undertaking or, equally important in terms of this discussion, misunderstanding them;

(b) Seeing ourselves in the act of reading coming to understand a literary character, where this functions as a model, or a special kind of acuity-enhancing rehearsal, for actually understanding another person, and so within that readerly self-reflection seeing what it takes to achieve such understanding;

(c) Thus seeing how it is that we can come to an ever-fuller understanding of ourselves through a self-reflective process of making ever more nuanced comparisons on the model of understanding a literary character, of grasping their meaning.

And then lastly, reaching just beyond the bounds of these three previous intertwined considerations, we will see in detailed examples how:

(d) It is not only self-knowledge that can result from a distinctive kind of literary absorption, but rather as introduced above, nothing less than an act of self-composition takes place, where, again, in the imagination the reader makes resolutions (resolving, as it were, in a subjunctive mode: getting clear about what one would do if...) concerning self-identity that then become, as a real result that runs parallel to the fictional world, stabilized or solidified in character, that is, in the reader's identity.

Central to this process of self-definitional reading, and connecting directly to considerations (a) and (b) just above, will be a cultivated understanding of what it *actually* is to thoroughly understand a person's words in a highly particularized sense.[42] As my focus case I will look closely at the chapter "Words Misunderstood" in Milan Kundera's *The Unbearable Lightness of Being*,[43] and then, working through the lists of four themes above, consider the significance this holds for autobiographical understanding as we will see it in self-investigative writings of Iris Murdoch and Jean-Jacques Rousseau.

So there is in the remainder of this section some ground still to cover. But given the ground covered so far, we can say (consistent with the step of this section that moves forward from relational selfhood to relational language):

---

[42] One way of expressing this particularity is to specify the aspect, or set of aspects, in which they use or understand the word in question, and how they thereby make it their own, or (I will return to this below) how they make it *of* them. In this connection see Stanley Cavell's emphasis on the distinctive, centrally important, and often missed sense in which we are, in speaking, showing a distinctive attachment to our words. See Stanley Cavell, *The Claim of Reason: Wittgenstein, Skepticism, Morality, and Tragedy* (Oxford: Oxford University Press, 1979), pp. 355ff. See also his discussion in his "The Touch of Words," in William Day and Victor J. Krebs, *Seeing Wittgenstein Anew* (Cambridge: Cambridge University Press, 2010), pp. 81–98, where he writes, "A striking idea among Wittgenstein's remarks about seeing aspects is his saying that the importance of the concept lies in its connection with experiencing the meaning of a word and with our attachment to our words...Some idea of the attachment to our words is indispensable to Wittgenstein's fundamental procedures in the invocation of ordinary language (which, as I often emphasize, highlights the fact of language as *mine*)...(p. 85). Philosophy, it seems, too rarely says this; literature frequently shows it. I offer a discussion of some of the relations between aspect-perception, word meaning, and self-knowledge in "In a New Light: Wittgenstein, Aspect-Perception, and Retrospective Change in Self-Understanding," *Seeing Wittgenstein Anew*, pp. 101–19. I will return to Cavell in Chapter 6 below.

[43] Milan Kundera, *The Unbearable Lightness of Being* (New York: Harper Perennial, 1987), pp. 81–127. Closely related philosophical themes emerge in other novels of Kundera's: in *Slowness* (New York: Harper Perennial, 1997), we see the tale of two seductions, separated by over two hundred years, but where they interweave in such a way that the influence of the past on the present and, more strongly, what we see as the events taking place in the present are informed by that history (and so they are relationally or thematically intertwined with a seemingly separate narrative of a long-past episode). One could well read this as a dramatization of how we, as individuals, experience a non-hermetic, or in William James's sense, relationally intertwined present. And Kundera's *Identity* (New York: Harper Perennial, 1998) concerns person recognition and the character of our knowledge of others close to us, where that knowledge is, after all, made by and carried in words of and about them.

24 LIVING IN WORDS

If the broadly Cartesian conception of selfhood and the self-transparency thesis that is its immediate corollary were true, we would have unmediated access to the meanings of our own words just as we are thought to have unmediated access to our inner contents of consciousness.

If that were the case, autobiographical writing would simply be a matter of reading off internal content and reporting it externally. But indeed, here also in an instructive and perhaps surprising way, we can discover that we have to *work* autobiographically to understand the fuller significance of our own past words just as we may have to work to understand the present and past words of others; *this, it will turn out, is true in life just as it is literature.* And so what this suggests about words is that an atomistic conception of word meaning is as misbegotten as an atomistic, or non-relational, conception of the perception of an object or the perception of a human being: words are in part the makers of the networks of relations in which we live and have lived and in which we perceive and have perceived. So words, as the instruments of the comparative processes under investigation, deserve the closest attention in terms of their contextually distinct nuanced content and—when working in one distinctively reflexive way, their powers of self-constitution or self-composition. But all of the foregoing suggestions will reveal their plausibility, and their more specific content, only in the contexts of detailed examples. So we turn to Milan Kundera's "Words Misunderstood," part 3 of his *The Unbearable Lightness of Being.* Franz is a professor of literature; Sabina is his secret mistress.

In stepping into this text we enter a verbal context that has already described itself as a kind of private reserve: Franz has finished his university lecture in Geneva and is going to see Sabina, with whom he has been in love for a few months. This love, comparatively gauged against the alternative context of his married life, is "so precious to him that he tried to create an independent space for her in his life, a restricted zone of purity" (p. 82). We readers are told that he has been accepting all invitations and speaking engagements around Europe and North America in order to be able to take her with him; he has also started inventing such engagements and is thus further lying to his wife so that he and his mistress can take still more frequent secret trips. With this as immediate background (as we shall see shortly, the full background is much more extensive in a way that shows something important about linguistic meaning), on arriving at her apartment studio (she is a painter) he asks, "How would you like to go to Palermo ten days from now?" (p. 82). Her seemingly simple answer, "I prefer Geneva," is actually a complex, relationally intertwined set of three words with a multiplicity of connections, and Franz is quick to sense this, even if he could not articulate all of them in advance of the following successive exchanges.[44]

---

[44] See in this connection Frank Cioffi, "Wittgenstein and the Fire-Festivals," in his *Wittgenstein on Freud and Frazer* (Cambridge: Cambridge University Press, 1998), pp. 80–106.

He replies, "How can you live without seeing Palermo?"; she replies that she has seen it; and he replies in turn, "You have?" with, as Kundera's narrator tells us, a hint of jealousy. We immediately imagine that, because he travels with her (preserving the integrity of the "zone") to conduct his affair with her, that she may have traveled with someone else to Palermo. Thus the question, "You have?" is hardly reducible to a combination of the dictionary definitions of the words "you" and "have" followed by a question mark; this question's meaning is not contained within a request to confirm what she has just said, nor would any such reconfirmation coherently answer what he has said or follow along its conversational trajectory; instructively vis-à-vis the problem of word meaning, any such answer would be uncomprehending and oddly deaf to inflected content.[45]

But she does follow the conversational trajectory, and it immediately emerges that she was toying with him (by playing within the range of significance that her knowing Palermo, in this context, might entail or carry in its particular and distinctive trail of connotations), and that she has seen Palermo in a photograph on a postcard. But that settled, still "Franz was sad. He had grown so accustomed to linking their love life to foreign travel that his 'Let's go to Palermo!' was an unambiguous erotic message and her 'I prefer Geneva' could have only one meaning: his mistress no longer desired him" (p. 82).

These sentences not only induce his somewhat crestfallen state (where that state is inseparably bound up with their meaning); they also open an avenue of psychological explanation within this exchange: his words functioned to send her "an unambiguous message" in addition to—or actually, within—the words inviting her to Palermo. And her reply, which we see is felt as rejection, establishes implicitly what Kundera's narrator expressly articulates next: as the antithesis to Franz's public life, in which we are told he is powerful and even feared for his arrogant tenacity in putting forward his views, he sees love as a form of longing, where that takes psychological shape as "putting himself at the mercy of his partner" (p. 83). This transforms him, making him "like a prisoner of war" who has given up his weapons, and is "deprived in advance of defense against a possible blow." Thus his longing for antithetical love (that is, secret and transgressive love

---

[45] There is an exact parallel here to an issue in the interpretation of art, where some claim, on formalist grounds, that only formal features strictly contained within the work itself (as though we know what that would describe and where to draw that line) are aesthetically relevant to the appreciation, understanding, or criticism of the work. For an insightful discussion showing what this conception systematically loses, see Richard Wollheim, "Art, Interpretation, and Perception," in his *The Mind and Its Depths* (Cambridge, MA: Harvard University Press, 1993), pp. 132–43. He writes: "However, the question that has to be asked is whether this autonomy is purchased at too heavy a price. How circumscribed will the meaning of a work of art turn out to be if the only properties of the work relevant for its ascription are those which are perceptible without benefit of cognitive stock?" (p. 136). See also his discussion of Panofsky's example of Rogier van der Weyden's Bladelin altarpiece in this connection, where he writes, "it is hard to see where the line is to be drawn" (p. 137). I would add to Wollheim's observation that the cognitive stock of which he rightly speaks is not always, nor in any case fully, immediately available to introspection—we cannot always immediately articulate it; here also, the web of relations and thematic resonances can require self-investigative work within aesthetic experience.

26 LIVING IN WORDS

of a kind antithetical to his public persona) is for him always psychologically present in the form of his "wondering when the blow will fall." All of this prepares us for our comprehension of the meaning of the sentence that is itself giving the meaning of a word in this context: "That is why I can say that for Franz, love meant the constant expectation of a blow."

We saw above how the perception of objects for William James is a relationally intertwined matter, and in this section we are developing that idea in terms of the parallel relationally intertwined understanding of words: "While Franz attended to his anguish, his mistress put down her brush," and returning with a bottle of wine, "she opened it without a word and poured out two glasses." What is the content of this wordless but meaningful presentation of an object? Franz, upon seeing it, is greatly relieved and suddenly feels "slightly ridiculous": the significance of the object, the glass of wine, in this circumscribed context, corrects his earlier utter misapprehension of the significance of her words. "The 'I prefer Geneva' did not mean she refused to make love; quite the contrary, it meant she was tired of limiting their lovemaking to foreign cities" (p. 83).

Now, it is true that one might here insist that the meaning of the words as used is in essence simple, direct, and invariant across context, just as are the objects perceived: "I prefer Geneva" means "I prefer Geneva"; to see a bottle of wine is just to see a bottle of wine. But that would be to exclude, in the name of a superimposed uniformity or an imposed simplifying interpretation, everything in play here that concerns cultivated human sensibility—in short, it would exclude everything that concerns *actual* language as spoken, words as used by us. It would very largely exclude, in the name of a neat theory, the linguistic world in which we live. One could also say, locating a sort of halfway house between the conception of fixity of meaning or invariant semantic content[46] on the one extreme and context or occasion sensitivity[47] on the other, that the meanings are fixed but that they here are speaking in code, where the encoded content is itself in any case fully expressible in direct and non-relational terms. But at a glance one can see that they are decidedly not speaking in code: that would be to agree in advance that one word stood for another, or one phrase stood for another (as, for example, when bank robbers agree in advance that when the leader says to a teller, "Good morning," that means "Pull out your guns"). This exchange, by contrast, is unfolding in the partially improvisational way actual language does, in a way that is aware of prior moves in the linguistic game but that is not preordained by prior explicit agreement.

---

[46] See, as an exceptionally clear and lucid orientation to this issue of fixity of meaning or invariant semantic content, Herman Capellen and Ernie Lapore, *Insensitive Semantics* (Malden: Wiley-Blackwell, 2005).

[47] For a powerful and helpful defense of this position of context or occasion sensitivity in the philosophy of language, see Charles Travis, *Occasion Sensitivity: Selected Essays* (Oxford: Oxford University Press, 2008).

So one could say next (and now locating a position at a sort of three-quarters house), that the meanings of the words in this exchange are fixed by circumstantial detail, so that the words as used are fixed with singular semantic content by these speakers on this occasion. But Kundera's next passage addresses this, showing that the truth of the matter is more interestingly intricate than this "three-quarters house" formulation[48] of meaning content would capture. While being "overjoyed that her refusal to go to Palermo was actually a call to love" (and thus that he now is rightly positioned in relation to her words), Franz is slightly crestfallen, but now for the reason that the action that redirects the trajectory of her words carries with it, in its meaning-contributing undercurrent, twin possibilities. The first is her being for some reason intentionally and comprehendingly determined "to violate the zone of purity" we learned of above, thus shifting by brute force the transcendent union he believes they share into the objectionably quotidian. Or, the second possibility, she has uncomprehendingly "failed to understand his apprehensive attempts to save their love from banality and separate it radically from his conjugal home" (p. 83), thus leaving him feeling the slight chill of the psychic isolation that comes from the incomplete or imperfect understanding of a lover. It is thus not only that the meaning, as corrected, is not mono-dimensional; one could express "non-mono-dimensionality" in a simplifying theory of word meaning in terms of doubled or layered significance. It is rather, more deeply, that the very question of *word* meaning is slowly but steadily losing its intelligibility: to understand the language in play here, we do not begin with linguistic atoms (parallel to the point about the perception of objects that William James and his colleagues made) that we then add together; nor do we (we will see this more clearly in Chapter 4) understand the words and grasp meaning in any way independently of an understanding of the persons using them. Biographical or other-understanding (and as we shall see in the following, autobiographical or self-understanding) is neither prior nor posterior to the understanding of the words of those persons; rather, persons are the vehicles of words while words are simultaneously the vehicles of personhood. Kundera does not say this: more convincingly, he shows this with considerable precision and philosophic exactitude; indeed, he does so with a degree of subtlety that requires close attention to detail to make its force and significance philosophically explicit.

Sabina, painter-mistress-intricate-speaker, next (again silently), while removing garments in a measured tempo, becomes curiously autonomous and acts as if unaware of his presence; she is indeed "behaving like an acting student whose improvisation assignment is to make the class believe she is alone in a room and no one can see her." She then fixes Franz with a long stare, but of a kind that is not

---

[48] This formulation is central to what is often discussed as "contextualism"; for a helpful orientation to the issue and arguments in favor of this position, see Keith DeRose, "Contextualism: An Explanation and Defense," in J. Greco and E. Sosa, eds., *The Blackwell Guide to Epistemology* (Malden: Blackwell, 1999).

28 LIVING IN WORDS

of them, of their relationship, of who *they* are together. Kundera's narrator describes this as her transgressing implicit rules of the game that, he correctly claims, "all lovers unconsciously establish" (p. 84); important for present considerations, this leaves Franz unable to understand this look, and he had "not the slightest notion what it was asking," what it meant. We, as readers, do not yet know that she will shortly reflect, with incredulity, on how many years she has spent "pursuing one lost moment" (p. 86); what we do know is that Franz is disoriented, that what he is witnessing is a fragment of theater not of them and their evolving embodied conversation, and that the trajectory of these gestures is disconnected and seems, dangerously and threateningly, to come from elsewhere. "The stare she had just fixed on him fell outside their rules."[49] This comes, suddenly and intrusively, from another language-game,[50] another relationship, another identity-constitutive interactive style; it treats him as absent—or, far worse, as another person he does not know—and thus painfully not as the self she sees in and with him. It moves beyond the bounds of what he can, within this context, understand. Meaning escapes him. This is a perfect microcosm of other-misunderstanding, where that misunderstanding derives from the superimposition of one expressive/interactive style that one does not know over the top of another that one does know and where that superimposition is motivated by a private or unshared (and, given its wholly separate origin, perhaps unsharable) desire to recapture something lost, something unfinished, something with a teleology or internal trajectory that stopped short of a cathartic or settled conclusion.[51] And it is a perfect miniature of linguistic incomprehension—it is not that one does not know, in dictionary terms, the meanings of the words. It is that one does not recognize the interrelations between the words and the person, and one does not see the complexly intertwining relations that connect what is happening now with what happened before.

Sabina leads them to a mirror, before which she directs her still-alien gaze to herself for some time, and then, in a secondary way and only glancingly, only with a thin and constrained acknowledgment of his (or of at least some) presence, to him; she reaches out to retrieve, and don, an old bowler hat. We get a description

---

[49] There is an entire wholly untouched field connecting the ongoing debate on rule-following and meaning-determination to meaningful gestures and facial looks within a rule-enacting (not exactly rule-governed) relationship; this will have to wait for another time, but the raw material is waiting in literature such as this.

[50] I refer here of course to Wittgenstein's discussion in *Philosophical Investigations* as well as his earlier introduction of language-games in *The Blue Book*, in *The Blue and Brown Books* (Oxford: Basil Blackwell, 1958). I examine the aesthetic relevance of this idea in *Meaning and Interpretation: Wittgenstein, Henry James, and Literary Knowledge* (Ithaca: Cornell University Press, 1994), ch. 1: "Language-Games and Artistic Styles", pp. 9–44; all subsequent mentions of the language-game idea in this book build out from that discussion.

[51] This experience will be the topic of Chapter 3, Section 3.3 below; it is at this point important to see that "settled" does not mean "sealed and frozen" or "immune to any further relational narrative intertwining."

IMAGINED IDENTITIES   29

of what the mirror reports back to him: "instantaneously transformed," we learn that "suddenly it was a woman in her undergarments, a beautiful, distant, indifferent woman with a terribly out-of-place bowler hat on her head, holding the hand of a man in a gray suit and tie" (p. 85). Distant, indifferent, out-of-place, a (not *this*) woman: all the result of words and gestures from elsewhere—so much so that he now describes himself also as an unknown generic. He is not enmeshed in the relations that they have woven together, and he cannot find himself.[52] He knows he understands nothing. And so now he longs for restoration to the context of their convergence from this alien, slightly chilled, disorienting place. Seeing that the disrobing has yielded not "erotic provocation" but rather only "an odd little caper" (p. 85), and beginning to feel that this caper has gone on too long (the time for romantic union, if it was ever there within this estranging mini-drama, is now gone), he gently removes the bowler hat as his attempt at restoration, making within his perception a metaphorical connection to what the strange hat is not in order to better capture what it is, to better describe the content of his gesture of romantic restoration for him and, he hopes, for Sabina. "It was as though he were erasing the mustache a naughty child had drawn on a picture of the Virgin Mary" (p. 85). And with all that has transpired, he now asks what has become a very different question, a considerably more interesting and complex one—if clothed in the same garb of the previous one: "Will you come with me in ten days to Palermo?"[53] Now, "she said yes unquestioningly, and he left." The field of these words has changed; their relational web complicated. To understand them, as readers imaginatively entering their word-borne world, is to see this. And from this conceptually intricate example, we get a glimmer, or more, of what constitutes the real content of understanding another.

Sabina, now by herself, puts the bowler back on and contemplates herself in the mirror. And it is here that she found herself "amazed at the number of years she

---

[52] See Stanley Cavell, "The *Investigations*' Everyday Aesthetics of Itself," in *The Cavell Reader*, ed. Stephen Mulhall (Oxford: Blackwell, 1996), pp. 376–89, esp. p. 380; Cavell is developing Wittgenstein's remark "A philosophical problem has the form: 'I don't know my way about'" (*Philosophical Investigations*, sec. 123), which he retranslates as "A philosophical problem has the form: 'I cannot find myself.'" I discuss the significance of these passages at greater length in *Describing Ourselves: Wittgenstein and Autobiographical Consciousness*, pp. 240–57.

[53] The connection (the relational comparison) between this kind of linguistic phenomenon and music, particularly in a theme and variations, is informative: the theme, reheard at the end, is in one sense the same exact theme, and in another sense now entirely different. This is nicely illustrated by a remark in the diary of David Pinsent, close friend of Wittgenstein's: "At 7:15 I dined at the Union, then visited Wittgenstein and with him went to a concert at the Guildhall. The programme was splendid and included Bach's Chaconne, a Mozart Sonata for 2 pianos, the Kreutzer Sonata of Beethoven and Brahms' Variations on a Theme by Haydn. The latter was amazing—the most wonderful thing I had heard for a long while. The theme itself is indescribable—the variations typical of Brahms at his very greatest, and finally when at the end the theme emerges once more, unadorned, fortissimo and in tremendous harmonies, the effect is to make one gasp and grip one's chair! I simply cannot describe how it excited me." *A Portrait of Wittgenstein as a Young Man, from the Diary of David Hume Pinsent 1912–1914*, ed. G. H. von Wright (Oxford: Basil Blackwell, 1990), p. 53. Words, as Kundera is showing, can work in the same way.

30 LIVING IN WORDS

had spent pursuing one lost moment" (p. 86). Why? Her previous lover, Tomas, with whom she has remained in a kind of sustained private imaginative contact of the mind, once was lifted, very much *with* her and *of* them, from a fleeting comical joke with the hat to a shared moment of transcendence that seared its way into both of their identities. To summarize an extended passage, Kundera here makes clear that the erotic encounter was in a sense the vehicle of, but by no means the whole content of, the experience. Thus the perception of the relationally consti-tuted object, the hat, is gaining in complexity. But he as quickly shows that it is still much more than what we, as readers, presently see in this artifact. As if explicitly clarifying the philosophical significance here, Kundera's narrator makes for us a catalogue. The list includes:

(1) The bowler hat (recall the "what one would look like as a mayor" line above—a phrase that itself is now being more fully situated into a constel-lation of meaning determinations) "was a vague reminder of a forgotten grandfather, the mayor of a small Bohemian town during the nineteenth century" (p. 87).

(2) It "was a memento of her father"—but this too is not the case in any simple way: "After the funeral her brother appropriated all their parents' property, and she, refusing out of sovereign contempt to fight for her rights, announced sarcastically that she was taking the bowler hat as her sole inheritance." She thus sees the symbol of her own act of defiance and assertion, even if (or perhaps especially because it is) self-defeating, in the memento (and for her, not separable from her perception of the object).

(3) "It was a prop for her love games with Tomas." One might understand this as a special kind of externalized "object memory" or objectified emotive-erotic mnemonic.

(4) "It was a sign of her originality, which she consciously cultivated. She could not take much with her when she emigrated, and taking this bulky, imprac-tical thing meant giving up other, more practical ones." That is, to see what the object means for her, and thus to come to know her perception of the object as parallel to her employment of any particular set of words as she means them and as they are meaningful for her, is in this sense to also see what it is not—the hat was not any of those more practical, manageable, and predictable items. And here again, the flouting of that predictability in circumstances of pressing practical necessity is not only a symbol of herself; rather, the act performed with that hat becomes a defining part of who she is and of who she is (this is how the word "consciously" functions here) to herself. When she refers to it, she refers, in a perhaps subtle but meaning-contributing sense, to part of herself and her inner historical genealogy.[54]

---

[54] In this connection see the powerfully illuminating study by Alexander Nehamas, *Nietzsche: Life as Literature* (Cambridge, MA: Harvard University Press, 1985).

The fifth entry in the narrator's catalogue is however the deepest: earlier, when she went to Zurich to see Tomas, she donned it just as he opened the hotel room door. She thought she was jokingly playing, but she underestimated the power of the shared relationally expansive perception of the artifact.

(5) The hat suddenly became "a monument to time past" (p. 87), and rather than only "a continuation" of the established "game," it "was a recapitulation of time, a hymn to their common past, a sentimental summary of an unsentimental story that was disappearing in the distance."

All of their past time together, everything they were to each other, was telescoped into that moment by the unexpected power of this shared relationally enmeshed perception, by this network of increasingly compressed meaning. And the sense of the uniqueness, of the irreplaceable nature of *that* connection, conjoined to the sense that this could not last, lifted this moment above and beyond its time—indeed, in a sense above and beyond time. And thus Sabrina was condemned to try, endlessly and futilely, to recapture it—precisely the driven repetition she is presently enacting with Franz. Thus what is calling to her with the enchanting grip of Sirens in the mirror is a repetition compulsion that is for us as readers brought within the bounds of the comprehensible through the process of coming to a cultivated understanding of her words.

But, with our initial reminders in mind of (a) what William James and his pragmatist colleagues said about relational perception, along with (b) the suggestion about the similarity of this to a properly nuanced account of word meaning, and (c) the significance of this for person understanding, what might we now say of *how those words are actually working*? What, in this still further evolving context, is the meaning of the artifact, and of its name, "bowler hat"? Kundera, philosophical novelist, captures the matter precisely:

The bowler hat was a motif in the musical composition that was Sabina's life. It returned again and again, each time with a different meaning, and all the meanings flowed through the bowler hat like water through a riverbed. I might call it Heraclitus' ("You can't step twice into the same river") riverbed: the bowler hat was a bed through which each time Sabina saw another river flow, another *semantic river*: each time the same object would give rise to new meaning, though all former meanings would resonate (like an echo, like a parade of echoes) together with the new one. Each new experience would resound, each time enriching the harmony.   (p. 88)

Wittgenstein said that words have meaning only in the stream of life. And in this particular stream, in these threatening words, gestures, and facial expressions,[55]

---

[55] The connections between these could be investigated at length; on this matter see the groundbreaking study by Mitchell Green, *Self-Expression* (Oxford: Oxford University Press, 2007).

32 LIVING IN WORDS

Franz will forever be a stand-in: the audience (Sabina) wants to see (and is condemned to forever attempt, hopelessly, to see) the real actor, the original. And so—marking the progress in our slowly earned ability to understand the meanings in play here—Kundera's narrator says:

> Now, perhaps, we are in a better position to understand the abyss separating Sabina and Franz: he listened eagerly to the story of her life and she was equally eager to hear the story of his, but although they had a clear understanding of the logical meaning of the words they exchanged, they failed to hear the semantic susurrus of the river flowing through them. (p. 88)

Language-games, in Wittgenstein's sense, can come together and generate new vocabularies that are, or become, comprehensible: the language of hydrodynamics merged with the language of mental activity produces a Freudian language of pressure, blockage, flow, release mechanisms, and so forth (they may be disguised metaphors that can be mistaken as literal descriptions, but that is another matter). And some language-games, merged, generate uncorrectable incomprehensibility: asking for the color or weight of an abstract number or the committing of a Rylean category mistake.[56] It is the more sophisticated and more human form of incomprehensibility that Kundera is investigating: Franz, in a simple sense, understands every word Sabina is using—again, he does not need a dictionary, nor would one help him now. In a real, that is, a complex, enmeshed, relational, sense—in the sense of a *person's* using language—he understands very little. "And so when she put on the bowler hat in his presence, Franz felt uncomfortable, as if someone had spoken to him in a language he did not know. It was neither obscene nor sentimental, merely an incomprehensible gesture" (p. 88).[57]

What Franz understands from within the context of their relationship he in an unmediated sense grasps (and he does so in an important sense without having to learn it, to work it out) in a way that is internal to who they are to and with each other. What he confusedly sees before him that Sabina brings from outside of their relationship (and that she is inwardly compelled to bring, despite knowing that both its gesture language and spoken language are alien to who she and Franz are) he will not and could not understand without working through the process of gradual, careful, attentive, internally interconnected, and exactingly nuanced

---

[56] See Gilbert Ryle, *The Concept of Mind* (London: Routledge, 2009 [orig. pub. 1949]), ch. 1.

[57] Kundera's phrase here is "as if someone had spoken to him in a language he did not know." This is not "like someone speaking to him in a language he did not know." The difference is important for present considerations: The latter could be explained in terms of atomistic or dictionary word definitions that he does not know; by contrast, the kind of misunderstanding here is not reducible to this nor explicable in its terms. Hence the need to find a way of providing (which, I am suggesting, a philosophical reading of literature can provide) at least an intimation of what Franz is here missing and what would be necessary for full understanding (we will return to this below, where we see this serving as a model for self-understanding in autobiography).

IMAGINED IDENTITIES   33

understanding that Kundera's case study illustrates. And she will not, within their world, give him what he would need to know about Tomas in order to patiently earn a true understanding of what he sees before him in terms of a transcendent moment and her unquenchable and ultimately ruinous compulsion to attempt to recapture it. And so the analogy to musical composition again:

> While people are fairly young and the musical composition of their lives is still in its opening bars, they can go about writing it together and exchange motifs (the way Tomas and Sabina exchanged the motif of the bowler hat), but if they meet when they are older, like Franz and Sabina, their musical compositions are more or less complete, and every motif, every object, every word means something different to each of them.   (p. 89)

Kundera follows this with a section he calls "A Short Dictionary of Misunderstood Words," proceeding through the words "woman," "fidelity and betrayal," "music," "light and darkness," "parades," "the beauty of New York," "Sabina's country," "cemetery," "the old church in Amsterdam," "strength," and "living in truth." Each case shows, with a detail that only an intricate close reading can capture, the way in which the learning of what a word or set of words means to a person constitutes significant, and I want to argue irreplaceable, content of our understanding of that person. And as mentioned above, this shows (here also a point to which we will return in Chapter 3 in terms of autobiographical understanding) that our understanding of a person significantly deepens by coming to understand how that person came to learn the meaning of a word or set of words that are constitutively important for that person.[58] A fully revelatory close reading would proceed microscopically and thus at length, but briefly, it can be said here: "woman," for Sabina, is a given, a fact of one's existence into which one is born. But for Franz, it is an ennobling honorific—not all women, for him, deserve the term. And he makes a distinction between respecting Marie-Claude (his wife) and respecting the woman in Marie-Claude. "But if Marie-Claude is herself a woman,

---

[58] It may seem slightly odd—it is certainly unusual—to quote from an acknowledgments page of a book. But in this case there is a world of philosophy in it. And what I want to suggest is that we know, at some intuitive level (philosophy's task here is to clarify and articulate it), the human importance of what Kundera is showing in his novel (and we thus better recognize it when we see it in life). At the close of his autobiography *Little Did I Know* (in which one finds countless details relevant to this discussion), Stanley Cavell, an author steeped in the philosophy of Wittgenstein and Austin—and an author richly alive to the kaleidoscopic relevance of literature to philosophy—thanks Cathleen Cavell with "and to Cathleen, who continues to know the words." *Little Did I Know: Excerpts from Memory* (Stanford: Stanford University Press, 2010), p. 558. "To know the words" is not a phrase where minimal definitions of these words (actually words about words) will help; a humane appreciation of the great sophistication of actual linguistic usage, along with an appreciation of the importance of words for personal identity, will. The final few books of Aristotle's *Nicomachean Ethics* are on the nature and value of friendship; a modern supplement to that discussion could concern the profound value we can have to each other in (in this more fully articulated sense) "knowing the words."

34 LIVING IN WORDS

then who is that other woman hiding in her, the one he must always respect?" (p. 90). Kundera's narrator asks if the internal woman might be the Platonic ideal of woman in some sense contained within but metaphysically separate from the individual, but he quickly corrects this: it is his mother of whom he would never say that he respected the woman in her. He respected her as identical with the ideal.

This brings into focus the difference between their understandings of the word, but we learn next how, for Franz, this difference is indissolubly connected to his learning of the meaning of another word; our understanding deepens accordingly. "When he was twelve, she [his mother] suddenly found herself alone, abandoned by Franz's father" (p. 90). The boy sensed something very significant had just happened, but his mother "muted the drama with mild, insipid words so as not to upset him." We see here that phraseology can itself be the primary expression of an act of kindness. But the important connection is: when he and his mother went into town that day he saw that her shoes did not match, and although he wanted to point this out, the boy sensed that this might somehow hurt her and so refrained. (We see here that sensitive reticence, not speaking or withholding words, can be the primary expression of kindness or sympathy as well.) But during the two hours they spent walking in the city, he kept his eyes on her shoes. "It was then that he had his first inkling of what it means to suffer" (p. 90).

This case suggests one way of putting the point: knowing what it means to suffer is what is actually involved in knowing the meaning of "suffer." And to understand how he acquired this concept, the circumstances of its emergence in his awareness and the way in which this early experience resonates throughout his sensibility, is to begin to understand him as a person. (It is for this reason, I believe, that Wittgenstein often returned to the question not only of the meaning of a word, but of learning the meaning of a word, or what Stanley Cavell would later call the scene of instruction.[59]) Learning what it means to suffer; the protecting of a boy from the harshest reality of the content of that suffering; the bearing of that suffering with a quiet dignity; the role of his mother at the center of this relational matrix; his having carried with him all of this as a formative memory throughout this life—these are the constituents, the resonances of the word "woman" for him, and it is why, with the exception of that maternal center or hub of associations, he makes the distinction between "the woman" and "the woman in her," a distinction not within the consciousness of Sabina. (I will suggest in Chapters 5 and 6 that this is precisely one central way in which, upon reflection of a particular kind, we come to know ourselves.)

---

[59] See Stanley Cavell, *The Claim of Reason* (Oxford: Oxford University Press, 1979), "Learning a Word," pp. 169–80. For a discussion extending the issue of word learning into aesthetics (and particularly the illuminating comparisons between being taught language and being taught art), see Richard Wollheim, "The Art Lesson," in his *On Art and the Mind* (Cambridge, MA: Harvard University Press, 1974), pp. 130–51.

IMAGINED IDENTITIES   35

Similarly, for fidelity and betrayal: Franz, in speaking about his mother, displays fidelity, and he does so with the ulterior motive of charming her and ultimately winning her over not just for now but permanently. But "what he did not know was that Sabina was charmed more by betrayal than by fidelity" (p. 91). This of course cannot be understood when stated in that reductive way (without making her sound morally alien to a point of incomprehensibility), but the picture starts to change when we learn that Sabina at fourteen was in love with a boy her age, and so her father would not let her leave the house unaccompanied for a year. Her father painted sunsets and vases on Sundays, and once made fun of Picasso in her presence. Not being able to love the boy, she loved cubism, and after completing schooling she went off to Prague where she could—in order to become who she was—betray her home and its conventions. So while she had been told betrayal was the most heinous offense, for her "betrayal meant breaking ranks. Betrayal means breaking ranks and going off into the unknown. Sabina knew of nothing more magnificent than going off into the unknown" (p. 91). But after the death of her mother and the suicide of her father a day later out of grief, she now wanted, as she conceived it, to betray her betrayal—and that recursive act became self-defining in turn. All the while, with each expression of maternal fidelity against this unknown background, Franz makes himself ever less magnificent, ever less adventurous, ever less able or willing to make himself who he is or could be by self-willed action against a background of conventional expectations. Without genuine understanding, they are perennially doomed to work at cross purposes within the same word.

There is a distinct sense in which we can do this within ourselves, working against or blinding ourselves to self-knowledge by using a conventional or simplified meaning of an important word or phrase as a shield behind which we hide precisely the kind of rich content being shown here by Kundera; our false confidence in our grasp of what we take to be perfectly clear significant phrases of our past or present becomes a form of self-deception precisely in cases where what we need is an analogue of close-reading practiced upon our own lives.[60]

And then of the word "music": for her, it is endless noise (going back to summer camp with loudspeakers blaring from 5 a.m. to 9 p.m.); for him, it is the escape from endless words, realizing that "all his life he had done nothing but talk, write, lecture, concoct sentences, search for formulations and amend them."

---

[60] The result of keeping up the barrier of presumed word knowledge to the kind of self-reflection required for true and deep autobiographical knowledge is not easy to describe succinctly, but Martin Amis finds a phrase that serves well in his remarks on an Iris Murdoch novel. Amis writes of the characters Murdoch develops in her *Nuns and Soldiers* that they live within a "suspended and eroticized world, removed from the anxieties of health and money and the half-made feelings on which most of us subsist." Half-made feelings would be those that we have while presuming that our words require no further work. Amis's phrase is "half-*made*," not "half-felt," thus rightly and insightfully emphasizing that there is an active element here. In Peter J. Conradi, *Iris Murdoch: A Life* (New York: W. W. Norton, 2001), p. 559.

36 LIVING IN WORDS

Against this non-stop verbiage, he longs for an "all-encompassing, over-powering, window-rattling din to engulf, once and for all, the pain, the futility, the vanity of words. Music was the negation of sentences, music was the anti-word!" (p. 94). We have the expression: What a given thing—a diamond ring, a diploma, a yacht, a deceased father's pen—*stands for*. This is importantly distinct, and often more revealingly complex, than the expression: What a given word—"diamond ring," "yacht," etc.—refers to. This is one way of marking the contrast between merely understanding a word in a minimal or dehumanized sense on the one hand and the humane understanding of a person through understanding her use of words on the other. For Franz, what music stands for comes from its significance as connected to his identity; this content of the "stands for" kind is thus a subset of the associations sometimes dormant, but always present, within his use of the word "music." So, in this way, to understand that is to understand him. And his knowing this is one part of the content of his autobiographical self-understanding. "He yearned for one long embrace with Sabina, yearned never to say another sentence, another word, to let his orgasm fuse with the orgiastic thunder of music" (p. 94). Kundera does not say so, but a reader expects that the irony contained within this inward antagonism is not lost on the professor, that is, that his "anti-word" thought is only expressible in words, and moreover that its content is only definable against words or polemically, in a way that necessarily implicitly includes what it explicitly attempts to exclude. Words won't go away.

The remaining terms in Kundera's dictionary reveal more subtle differences that weave together as a fabric of biographical understanding in literary form: "darkness" for her means the willful negation of what is seeable, an act of refusal to see, a disagreement with what is seen. For him, it is to descend into a world of unbounded, consuming sensory pleasure. And we see Europe's intentional, designed beauty standing in contrast to New York's "accidental" beauty; Sabina's first mature painting emerged because of an accidental drip of red paint—for her, "beauty by mistake" is much richer, more evocative, and varied than Franz's preferred "composed beauty of human design" (p. 102). In this case, to understand the meaning of a term on a human level within a context of usage is at the same time to uncover an aesthetic predilection (born of meaningfully interlinked past experience) that becomes a constitutive part of a distinct sensibility. To understand a person's aesthetic life is far more important to understanding their personhood than is widely recognized; that aesthetic life, even if centered on visual art or music, is cultivated in words, in a vocabulary of criticism and appreciation. "Sabina's country" is a phrase for her associated with the words (which Franz hears her utter in connection with this phrase) "prison, persecution, enemy tanks, emigration, pamphlets, banned books, and banned exhibitions" (p. 102); for him, it is a phrase relationally entwined with a romanticized conception of "life on a large scale," "a life of risk, daring, and the danger of death," all combining to renew his "faith in the grandeur of human endeavor" (p. 103).

"Cemetery" means a place of green, of flowers, of undisturbed peace even in a world of conflict; it means "an ugly dump of stones and bones" (p. 104); in some cases in this text, we learn that the difference is there (as in the cemetery case); in other cases, we are shown why the difference is there, and in those cases we understand not merely that a word happens as a mere contingency to have different associations. Rather, we understand the person ever more exactingly. Like the distinction between "refers to" and "stands for," the "that" versus "why" contrast can also serve to mark the difference between shallow and deep autobiographical understanding.

But then, as Kundera's philosophical novel also shows, the meaning of the phrase I have used throughout, "understanding a person," does not itself reduce to one simple or unitary thing. As we can see across the range of examples I have discussed to this point, and as we can also see throughout Kundera's book (and indeed throughout Kundera's entire oeuvre), we can utterly fail to understand, superficially understand, partially understand, misunderstand, fully if narrowly understand, fully and deeply understand, and so forth along what we might picture as an Aristotelian continuum.[61] But as quickly as we picture that continuum ranging from nothing on the one pole to everything on the other, we see that Kundera has shown—an important point in these waters—still more: we can fully understand a part of a person, deeply understand one side of a more complex matter, only superficially understand one aspect of an utterance while more deeply, but not entirely, fathoming the significance of another aspect, and so forth through countless epistemic variations of human comprehension.

Kundera is showing us the fascinating and often layered complexity of the process of gaining an understanding of another: we see this, within his fictional text, at a reflective distance inside the verbal world of Sabina and Franz. We are shown what it is or would be for one person to gain a word-borne understanding of another, what it is or would be for the other to reciprocally understand the first, what it is or would be for those literary characters to understand the other's words, what it is for us, as readers, to understand not only each of them but also the limits of their mutual understanding. And, equally important, we gain insight into the nature or character of the exchanges between them, their language-game, and what it is to understand the words that constitute the linguistic grounds of their identities[62] and to understand the words with which, as an active process of self-constitution, they compose themselves.

---

[61] I refer here of course to Aristotle's *Nicomachean Ethics*, trans. Martin Ostwald (Indianapolis: Bobbs-Merrill, 1962).

[62] These conceptual linkages are not new. There is a marvelous passage by Marcus Aurelius in his part-autobiography, part-philosophical-Stoical notebook *Meditations*: "With everyone you meet, begin at once by asking yourself, 'What ideas does this person hold on human goods and ills?' For if he holds particular views on pleasure and pain and the causes of each, and on reputation and disrepute, and life and death, it will not seem extraordinary or strange to me if he acts in some particular way, and I shall remember that he has to act as he does." *Meditations*, trans. Robin Hard (Oxford: Oxford University

38   LIVING IN WORDS

But, with all of this behind us—actually, only with all of this behind us—I want to say explicitly what I have suggested throughout: the forms of understanding shown here—one literary character understanding or not understanding another, a reader understanding literary characters, a reader understanding the relationship between two characters—are all direct models for, and indeed present in, the active processes of autobiographical writing. Or to put it another way: a person, working toward and ultimately gaining an understanding of herself or himself, proceeds in precisely the foregoing terms, that is, just as we have seen them operating within a literary world, and as we have seen them in our reading of and reflecting upon that world. Language, with all the nuances we have seen within Kundera's text, carries the content of the autobiographical process in precisely the same, intricate ways. But to properly make this link between the depicted understanding of one person by another within fiction and self-understanding in real life, we should look, if briefly, at the intermediate case of biographical understanding, that is, the understanding of one person by another in written form. This is a hybrid of literary and real life, and can be revealing as a halfway point between the two.

In Peter J. Conradi's[63] biography of Iris Murdoch, after more than five hundred pages of tellingly informative detail ranging throughout her life, he writes, "As for Iris's dress-sense, after marriage she gave up feminine impersonation. Before then she could disconcert at dances, wearing a velvet dress and full make-up including mascara and lipstick" (p. 512). *Impersonation?* This captures in one compressed word the relation this multidimensional person had to one distinct idiom of her own self-presentation—she was too complex a person to fit into one single projection or self-image. But it is not only that: in the details to follow, Conradi connects a number of dots pertaining to Iris Murdoch's issues about clothing, including ways she was perceived and described by others as well as issues of clothing and appearance she herself brought up with others. What these individual episodes, these now-connected dots, show is that "impersonation" is nowhere near as harsh a word as it initially seems, and that beneath its misleadingly nasty first impression it carries a message. Murdoch could be adroit at dress: "Iris could also be stylish ... she arrived in a splendid antique military coat made of the finest

---

Press, 2011), p. 72. This is a profound remark. Its profundity lies in the clarity and depth with which it captures (a) the fact that the true understanding of words and sentences people find they deeply endorse or to which they hold fast (expressed here as the beliefs they hold—but these are invariably expressed or expressible in words) is the substance of our understanding of them as persons, (b) that what they do will make sense (even if wholly objectionable, which is another matter), and will no longer seem extraordinary or strange, once we see what they do in light of the articulated beliefs they deeply endorse, and (c) that he will, in a sense, be constituted by those word-borne beliefs in such a way that (given that those are deeply engrained) he has to act as he does. (The "has" here neatly connotes the great constitutive power on personhood of endorsed words.) As we will consider more directly in subsequent chapters, we can come to an autobiographical understanding of ourselves through a similar process.

[63] Conradi, *Iris Murdoch: A Life*, pp. 512ff.

black cloth with gilt buttons" (p. 513). But she also went to the other extreme: she asked an acquaintance at a dinner party if her present attire would be suitable for her appearance as a guest of honor at an Oxford college the following week; she was wearing a "black karate-like tunic and trousers lightly marked by what could very possibly have been scrambled egg" (p. 512). And she could cultivate a deliberately "bohemian or eccentric" look, as with "the tangerine-coloured plastic mac with purple outfit she wore in a filmed interview around 1970" (p. 513).

But what this collection of episodes (along with others described in Conradi's biography) shows with a collective force is precisely the fittingness of the word "impersonation"; the logic of the concept of impersonation plainly requires that there be a real person beneath the exterior doing the impersonating. It is that real person beneath, the person who has enduring and truly self-defining traits, that these fleeting sartorial episodes implicitly point out in a sense negatively: to see these episodes together is to see that the matter of real interest is beneath them. Or: to see them rightly is to see what they are not (or not unto themselves), or to see them in a web of relations that point out their deeper meaning beneath their own surface. We are put into a position, by these anecdotes, to better understand the words describing the real person beneath those merely contingent appearances. And the words we next get from Conradi's biographical composition—words describing what is of the essence of the person—are those of Murdoch's friend Frances Partridge; she writes of "her magnificent realism, her Joan-of-Arc-like quality, her way of attending to what everyone said, weighing it (to the accompaniment of a very Oxford 'Yes, yes, yes') and then bringing out her response" (p. 513). This is the kind of incisive, fully present, close attention and cultivated interaction (i.e., the close reading of a person) that one rightly values highly; this is the true person beneath the indirectly truth-telling episodes, one who on the score of human attentiveness never once fails throughout Conradi's biography. And it is the person doing (once the deeper truth of her character and intellectual style is brought into focus) the "impersonating."

Conradi increasingly understands Murdoch, both as novelist and as person, as his book progresses, and he places the reader, by assembling details that together show the fittingness of particular descriptions, in a position to achieve the same. We see within this biography numerous moments that show what it is for two central subjects within it (Murdoch and her husband John Bayley) to be bound together, to live inside a mutual understanding. On this score one philosophically instructive passage may stand for many:

> Some friends, they decided, were 'elephants', others 'angels'. John's brother Michael was Iris and John's premier example of the great category of elephants; later friends—Stephen Spender, George Clive who farmed and entertained in the Welsh Marches—were others. The defining characteristics of an elephant included quietness, secretiveness, impenetrability, small eyes, being kind and

40 LIVING IN WORDS

> easy to be with, someone who might, in the pleasantest of ways, under an always polite exterior, be pursuing their own ends... 'Elephants' cannot be 'angels': angels have the wonderful capacity of never belonging entirely to themselves: there were not many angels. Elephants definitely do belong to themselves. They lead, however, unexamined lives, and don't desire self-knowledge.

One could say one knows perfectly well the meaning of the words "elephant" and "angel," and in some circumstances one would be right to say this. It depends on what the emergent criteria for knowing the meaning of these words are within that conversational circumstance. But there is no generic or universal or case-insensitive super-context in which one would always be right to say it—how would we describe such a super-context? What Murdoch and Bayley meant by these terms, we get a glimpse of here (a glimpse of Wittgenstein's "field" as they, like Sabina and Tomas with the bowler hat, have idiosyncratically expanded it, or like Kundera's "musical theme" that they have developed together), and the truth concerning the cultivated high-focus attentiveness Murdoch exemplified beneath the seemingly trivial details of clothing inflects and informs it: what we see under those connected dots gives further specific content to their humorous yet deeply serious term "angel." Angels, in not entirely belonging to themselves, are always in part constituted by their relations to others, always *truly* attentive to others, and always (in Stanley Cavell's sense of philosophy itself[64]) tirelessly responsive (which this kind of attentiveness, as a moral achievement, requires). "Elephants," overtly or covertly (beneath a covering of politeness or clothing), are always in some sense mindful of pursuing their own ends, and so to that degree imperfectly attuned to the other or imperfectly attentive to the inner life, the nuanced content, of the person with whom they are communicating.

One could work through Conradi's entire biography and patiently show how well what we see herein corresponds to the process of word and phrase under-standing as Kundera presented it, but suffice it to say for the present: cases of characters inside literature coming to understandings (or not, in informatively differentiated ways, or to a degree, within limits) of each other through the very highly nuanced understandings of the words in play are without question different from cases of biographers coming to an understanding of their subjects; this is true for the simple reason that the former is of fictional characters and the latter is of real persons. But this should not blind us to the very striking similarities, and indeed to the possibility of understanding the latter in terms of the former; that is, articulating the process of growing and deepening understanding in literature and

---

[64] See Stanley Cavell, *This New Yet Unapproachable America: Lectures after Emerson after Wittgenstein* (Chicago: University of Chicago Press, 1989): "Philosophy's virtue is responsiveness. What makes it philosophy is not that its response will be total, but that it will be tireless, awake when others have all fallen asleep."

then, having learned the language of that process, shifting that to life. The similarities run deep.

However, as mentioned above, the biographical case is transitional to the case that is our final target here, that is, the content of self-understanding that takes shape in autobiographical writing. It is true that there are a number of reasons that commonly suggest themselves (some of which we saw at the outset of this section) to radically divide autobiographical from biographical understanding: to put it most briefly, the problem of other minds, the problem of knowing the contents of the mind of another, does not (as we imagine the contrast in overly stark terms) arise in the first-person case. As *auto*biographers we are, as it seems to us, always already one with the subject. And this leads us to the belief that all the content is always already there—we need only turn our inward attention to it. This philosophical myth, born of the dualistic picture of immediate or privileged access to first-person mental content,[65] can itself blind us to the striking similarities to biographical understanding, which, as I am suggesting, are—once one is prepared to look in the right way—strikingly similar to the understanding of fictional (or wholly word-borne) characters. But—as is true of so much of philosophical thinking—the steps that are decisive in setting out the lines of the ensuing discussion are the very first ones, taken as given or taken as granted in such an obvious or unproblematic way that to pause to reflect on them would seem to only unnecessarily retard the progress waiting to be made. Such presuppositions are almost always either false, misleading, or both, as they are here. But what are these presuppositions, specifically?

I used the phrase just above, "all the content is always already there—we need only turn our inward attention to it," as though we readily and transparently understand all the elements making up this phrase. Because I used the phrase "philosophical myth" just after it, one might be forgiven for concluding that I would simply put a negation sign in front of the phrase, and argue its contrary, that is, that I would simply argue that the content is not there, ready for attention or, indeed, for transcription[66] into written form (thus seeing autobiographical writing on a model of inner-to-outer correspondence). And having claimed, as the antithesis to the thesis, that the content is not there waiting, I might then argue that the autobiographical narrative is wholly created, wholly contingent on what I happen to say, wholly constructed. This negation assumes that I know what prepackaged autobiographical content is or would be; my claim would then be stated polemically against that picture as presumed intelligible from the outset. But that way of proceeding, that is, accepting the initial presupposition of *the very*

---

[65] For a useful set of articles covering much of the field here, see Quassim Cassam, ed., *Self-Knowledge* (Oxford: Oxford University Press, 1994).

[66] I offer a discussion of the instructive dangers of the transcription (or "reading the self") model of autobiographical writing in "Wittgenstein's Voice: Reading, Self-Understanding, and the Genre of *Philosophical Investigations*," *Poetics Today* 28(3) (Fall 2007): 499–526.

42   LIVING IN WORDS

conception of ready transparency, would block the kind of progress we actually need to make on this issue—progress that takes form as freedom from the grip of this picture—a picture that manifests its foundational influence whether we argue for it or against it. So, if not positioning our argument polemically, where we presume the ready intelligibility of the opposition and then argue to refute it, how do we proceed? We might use a passage from Iris Murdoch on getting ready to write her second novel to begin to loosen the grip of the underlying conceptual picture that both thesis and antithesis would share. (The way of proceeding, briefly stated, is what Wittgenstein called "assembling reminders for a particular purpose.")

Only a few days after completing her first novel, Murdoch registered the fundamental idea of her second. She wrote at that time: "The next thing. Which is already present, only I have not yet turned to look at it. Like a king whose bride has been brought from a far country. But he continues to look out of the window, though he can hear the rustle of her dress" (p. 389). What I am suggesting is that we too easily think of autobiographical content, waiting to be externalized in written form, in precisely this way, as though we need only turn our attention to it to fully and thoroughly know it—an inward gaze at memory images would yield instant self-knowledge. But the more interesting truth is otherwise—indeed to a degree that our confidence in the intelligibility of the phrase "all the content is there" as employed in the context of autobiography is shaken rather badly: her phrase was "Which is already present." Except, as she learned the hard way, it wasn't. We learn shortly that she worked through multiple drafts over the next two years of steady and rigorous labor, working out all kinds of problems (a close study of the notebooks and drafts would show how involved a process this actually was). So what then was present in advance? What she in truth had was: a very general idea (which she registered or in that sense copyrighted), an idea that required an enormous amount of labor to articulate, to exactingly express, to specify in language.[67] This, I want to suggest, is very like the difference between the generic idea of self-knowledge as imagined in the abstract and the reality of actually working through the painstaking process of understanding self-defining

---

[67] We encounter in Stanley Cavell's autobiography a perfect example of using a phrase but in using it knowing that there is content contained within that remains to be investigated and elucidated; or perhaps it is more a sensing on a general level of the aptness of a phrase while at the same time sensing that there is much more to it, and knowing that to find that out will require labor. (It is a form of sensing content that could not be accommodated by the Cartesian picture of introspectively transparent word meaning.) Cavell writes, of a 3 a.m. television search, "On one such memorable pre-dawn excursion I came upon Howard Hawks's *Only Angels Have Wings* as it was beginning, made in 1939 but looking earlier, in I guess the reverse way that Hawks's *Bringing Up Baby*, made in 1938, looks later. (I do not know what the descriptions, or impressions, 'looking later and earlier' are based upon. But I have been at this long enough to want to know, and to be fairly good at waiting for a chance to know)," *Little Did I Know*, p. 541. (Neither waiting, nor the very idea of having a *chance* to know, would make sense on the picture of transparent Cartesian speaker meaning; rather, we would, as imagined of the king and the arriving new queen, just momentarily inwardly look and then instantaneously know.)

and self-composing words as Kundera has captured the matter. Murdoch had to create selves with pasts in language so that they can within the textual world be made to understand each other and so that her readers can understand them.

Murdoch wrote that nothing ever came out right the first time, that she had to write and rewrite; thus recasting was not merely, not only, a matter of polishing something already there, but rather a labored process essential to acquiring and stabilizing the language that carried these characters through their word-dependent lives. Misunderstandings, wrong descriptions, partial or superficial understandings, and prismatic or motivated misperceptions all have to be supplanted by what are often hard-won improvements. Her initial words, recall, were: "Only I have not yet turned to look at it." *Only*?—again, as though this is simply a matter of turning one's gaze in order to fully know the thing in question? In order merely to see the clothes the new queen is wearing, perhaps. But to see the person? And at what does the king presently look? Presumably at a landscape or a garden, from a height and a distance, that is, not *closely*. As though turning quickly, any moment, to the bride with an equally distracted, superficial, and distanced—that is, inattentive—gaze will do. As though that glance will show him who she is. This is the outward source of the misleading model of the inward glance.

But there is still more here: the king hears *evidence* (the rustling fabric) of the presence of the bride. Just as an autobiographer can sense the presence of significant self-knowledge that has not yet been examined with requisite care, the requisite high-focus attention, the very kind of attention Murdoch consistently gave others—but now focused on the first-person case. The bride is a *person*, and so to be understood, indeed seen, for who she is will require very much more than a glance. It will require what William James said of objects, and what Josiah Royce suggested may apply even more strongly with person perception. It will require what Tomas and Sabina had, what haunts Sabina still as a now impossible standard of mutual understanding, and what Franz and Sabina, separated by words—despite all they do have—cannot have, fully, together. Even a quick look into Murdoch's actual practices as they refuted her initial misled words—words that we might have thought lend credence to the picture of ready-to-write internal autobiographical content—immediately shows not only that such content is not there in any full sense, but more strongly (and it is this that begins to undercut the presupposition of the ready intelligibility of the phrase above) that it is not at all clear what we might mean by autobiographical content being already there, awaiting transcription. We acquire and carry autobiographical knowledge in linguistic form, and those words, sentences, paragraphs, texts, do not come already worked out. Nor is the process of self-descriptive writing anything like simple one-to-one matching. So the vague intimation of autobiographical content in the way Murdoch saw her next novel, yes, but fully articulated content, as she indeed experienced over two years, is another matter. It certainly does not conform to the simple conceptual template or philosophical picture that

44   LIVING IN WORDS

presents itself on first reflection. And so with that, we move to autobiographical writing itself.

Rousseau, in his *Reveries of the Solitary Walker*,[68] provides in microcosm the more complex process that I am suggesting is in play here: he provides this microcosm, fittingly, while autobiographically reflecting on his prior autobiographical writing. By the time we see the following passages (passages, like much of his book, in which he is reflecting on the nature of the autobiographical truth he captured—sometimes wholly, sometimes partially, sometimes not at all, and sometimes in ways that do not fit onto the linear continuum that these categories suggest—in his *Confessions*[69]), he has repeatedly emphasized the significance he now sees in what he (a) decided to put into language, (b) what he did not, (c) what he elided, (d) what he overextended or exaggerated, (e) what he reframed from one version to a better or different one, (f) what he recast in more carefully chiseled terms—in short, the very things Murdoch did during those two years and what we see that Franz needs to work out and work through in connection with Sabina's past, with his past, with their past, and with the differences of meaning between them. Rousseau writes, "I have never felt more keenly my natural aversion to lying than when I was writing my *Confessions*, for it is there that I could have been frequently and sorely tempted to lie, if I had been so inclined" (p. 44). We might well think that autobiographical lying here is a simple matter: he either tells it as it was, or he fabricates—another initial-stage unexamined presupposition that is all too consistent with the one examined above. But this simple picture is immediately, and importantly, made more complex:

> But far from having passed over or concealed anything that could be used in evidence against me, by a turn of mind which I struggle to understand and which perhaps derives from my antipathy towards all kinds of imitation, I felt more inclined to lie in the opposite way, by accusing myself too severely rather than by excusing myself too indulgently, and my conscience assures me that one day I shall be judged less severely than I judged myself.   (p. 44)

Lying, like word understanding, is not one thing, and it too falls on a continuum that itself is here again then seen to be too simple, too reductively monodimensional: his impulse is to lie in the self-incriminating way in order to express, within that lie, what he regards as a virtuous dislike of imitation. (We then understand his complex soul within these complex words.) And of course he says here that he "struggles to understand" this impulse, and he is speculating about, and not reaching a settled conclusion about, what drives it—this is hardly

---

[68] Jean-Jacques Rousseau, *Reveries of the Solitary Walker*, trans. Russell Goulbourne (Oxford: Oxford University Press, 2011).

[69] Jean-Jacques Rousseau, *The Confessions*, trans. J. M. Cohen (Harmondsworth: Penguin, 1953).

the look of ready, immediately available inward autobiographical content. (And a reader might now ask—especially having read about self-interested "elephants" above: Is what he says his conscience assures him in fact a polite, thinly disguised invitation to his future readers to enact what he predicts and judge him less severely? If so, the words function in still another way—where manipulation and self-protection converge, and so we understand him, characterologically, correspondingly differently.) He quickly expresses pride in his truthfulness, concluding the passage with "and so I told the whole truth."

But then things become suddenly very much more interesting. He writes, "I never said less than the truth, but sometimes I said more than it, not in the facts themselves, but in the circumstances surrounding them, and this kind of lie was the result of my confused imagination rather than an act of will" (p. 44). What he more fully articulates now in retrospect that he at the initial time of writing only intuitively sensed as a necessity, and that he now sees himself as having taken autobiographical license at that time to provide, is precisely the filling in of what we saw Wittgenstein above call "the field of a word," or what separated the understandings of Sabina and Franz. Rousseau knows that the circumstances surrounding the description of an event, an action, a thought, a person, fill in relational content that determines—in countless, subtle ways—meaning. This, for Rousseau, at this meta-autobiographical point, initially seems one kind of lie. But then he now sees more clearly that precisely such filled-in content is what the imagination demands to make language real, to make it—in exactly the way that ordinary language philosophy investigated imagined and real cases to understand and clarify the meanings of words—intelligible. So reflecting on what a lie actually is (A deliberately gets B to believe P when A knows not-P), and seeing how he was forced by his deeper sense of the demands of intelligibility to fill in what he did, he adds, "I am in fact wrong to call this a lie, since none of these additions was actually a lie." These additions specify meaning; they make significance determinate.

But why is this not an autobiographical lie, precisely? Because his memory "only provided [him] with imperfect recollections," he "filled in the gaps with details which I dreamed up to complete those recollections, but which never contradicted them." The completion of those recollections, to fill in the gaps, was, in this self-descriptive project, to surround the words that were central to his narrative with the rich contexts (of exactly the kind we saw in Kundera and in Conradi on Murdoch) that will indicate the fuller, human, *employed* sense of a word. Without this, Rousseau sensed as writer that his narrative would be schematic—really only a mere skeleton of a narrative at best, and mere detached bones at worst. And the element of truth he claims to have preserved is captured by his words "but which never contradicted them." He extrapolates from the truth he knows to be the case, without allowing his added content that directs the sense of the words to come into conflict with the accuracy of the fundamental elements

46 LIVING IN WORDS

of his narrative. This is thus not lying, but it is not, as he now reflects, wholly, or perhaps better, *strictly* truthful either; it is not exactly nothing but the truth. Yet the added content truthfully directs the senses of the words—but with content extrapolated, not remembered. So again: lying, like truth-telling, is not one thing—the formulaic definition mentioned above is thus only a start. How does Rousseau say this?

> I embellished them with ornaments which my fond regrets provided me with. I talked about the things I had forgotten as I thought they must have been, or as they perhaps really had been, but never contradicting what I remembered them to have been. I sometimes invested the truth with exotic charms, but I never replaced it with lies to cover up my vices or to lay claim to virtue.   (p. 45)

The fact that we sense here an important difference between "exotic charms" and "as I thought they must have been" is itself instructive—the continuum ranging from blunt truth on one pole to blunt falsity on the other does serve in some cases; if we picture truth on the left pole, then "exotic charms" falls farther to the right than does "as I thought they must have been." And our sense that there is an important, if subtle, distinction here reminds us that autobiographical writing is full of fine shades of gray and fine distinctions we make in context on the ground of our actual practices—true or false, bluntly understood as trans-contextual terms, will not suffice. (Rousseau, like Murdoch and like Kundera, knows—or has discovered within the process of writing—that fact.) Invented content can deliberately mislead; another kind of superadded content can unwittingly mislead; and another kind still can rightly and truthfully convey the sense (in, indeed, Kundera's sense of "sense") of the centrally important words in play. And then, of course, one could make the line between remembered and extrapolated content explicit—although that too would be a line that emerges only *in situ*, only in the particular case. And, going back to the relational themes opening this section, we could, as I said, *make* new comparisons, new informative relations, in retrospect, that are new at the stage of autobiographical reminiscence (i.e., they were not comparisons made at the time of the episode being recounted). And yet they may be wholly truthful in conveying the sense of the words used at the time and wholly truthful in describing the past event exactingly (recall Franz's making the comparison between removing the bowler hat and feeling as if he were erasing the drawing of a mustache on a picture of the Virgin Mary by a naughty child in order to describe with some precision what he felt he was doing). As philosophical literature shows, a schematic model or conceptual picture of word-to-world correspondence for autobiographical truth is simply far too crude an instrument to measure these finer distinctions.

Rousseau, it is clear, shows that he recognizes the importance of the distinction between filling in for intelligibility and willfully misdescribing to cover vice or to falsely accentuate virtue. And he appeals to a kind of compensatory justice within the complex autobiographical situation of writing his *Confessions*: when he says he may have "painted himself in profile" in order to "conceal the ugly side," he insists that such omissions were more than made up for by his omissions on the positive side. He offers a number of examples (with the earlier compunctions concerning self-congratulation now apparently no longer exerting moral pressure) that show "the fine qualities with which his heart was endowed" in his early years. The central importance of this for us is that he repeatedly refers here to "the story" and what it requires from him as author to be made comprehensible, what it requires to be fully told, and he repeatedly shows the kind of human detail that is prerequisite to the fuller understanding of the words he is using to tell it. He makes it clear that, without such detail, we will not, and cannot, understand him— it is *he* who uses *his* words, not what a generic person (e.g., a man in a grey suit in front of a mirror) might generically say. Philosophical literature can prepare us to see what an autobiographer of Rousseau's stature means by such a claim, how this claim fits into our larger understanding of what autobiographical writing actually is over and against some too easy initial-stage philosophical presuppositions and conceptual pictures, and what it would indeed mean to map out the field of the word "autobiography" itself.

I briefly reviewed at the outset of this section what we saw the pragmatists assert in the first two sections of this chapter, i.e., that the relations between things are as important as the things related, and that objects, persons, and words can all be seen in this light. Frank Kermode has said of Rousseau's autobiographical project that "Rousseau is in hot pursuit of a closure to be achieved by leaving nothing out, by inserting, and then later supplementing, innumerable bits of truth and leaving the reader to make them whole."[70] This conception of closure is not compatible with the way in which the understanding of a person's meaning emerges as examined here: even a complete assembly of every episode of a life, if not connected in a meaning-revealing way, would be only raw material for understanding, not the content of understanding itself. It is the *connections*, of the various kinds we have now seen, that are essential to understanding. It would be to merely see the dots, but not the pattern(s) presented by their structured relations. A settled interpretation, as the result of reflection, contemplation, and active arranging and rearranging of those interrelated particulars, would be a different, and more fitting, sense of closure. Kermode, reviewing a number of positions on this matter, says next:

> Nabokov's artful autobiography is full of elegantly rendered and various detail, but, as he once remarks, what gives such a work its formal value is thematic

---

[70] Frank Kermode, "Memory," in his *Pieces of My Mind* (New York: Farrar, Straus, Giroux, 2003), pp. 289–306; this passage p. 296.

48 LIVING IN WORDS

repetition. He illustrates the point with an anecdote of a general who amused him as a little boy by playing tricks with matches. Years later this general turns up, dressed like a peasant in a sheepskin coat. He stops the boy's father, now in flight from the Bolsheviks, and asks him for a light. While hoping that the general also escaped Soviet imprisonment, Nabokov adds: "but that was not the point. What pleases me is the evolution of the match theme... The following of such thematic designs through one's life should be, I think, the true purpose of autobiography."[71]

Nabokov's *Speak, Memory*[72] could be closely studied in connection with the foregoing discussion, and it would show us a great deal more about the process of understanding a life on the model of literary understanding, where that understanding is carried within the intricacies of words. But even a first glance at this passage shows us the importance, for understanding Nabokov as a person, for understanding his aesthetic sensibility, for understanding his literary conception of understanding itself (here, like Kundera, also expressed in musical-thematic terms). The true purpose of autobiography, Nabokov says, is the following of such thematic designs through one's life. I want to suggest that we can only do this with an enriched conception of word meaning (or again, really to move beyond a narrow conception of *word* meaning) of precisely the kind Kundera has shown and Conradi has put into biographical practice, with a grasp of what the pragmatists were claiming in terms of the importance of seeing a thing, person, or their speech within an expanding web of relations. Such understanding will never emerge from a condition of hermetic, Cartesian enclosure.

But I also said at the outset that I would make a final, if brief, supplementary suggestion based on all the foregoing: it is not only that we follow such thematic designs and connections. Like comparisons, we also *make* them, and so through these processes of imaginative reading and autobiographical writing we both find and—if we resolve matters one way or another—make ourselves, compose ourselves, within those descriptions.[73] And those descriptions are made of words that we ourselves can have to work to more fully understand. Is this a process we finish in a carved-in-stone fashion? Kermode says of Wordsworth's great autobiographical *Prelude* that, while we may think of it as "aspiring to or even achieving some

---

[71] Kermode, "Memory", pp. 296–7.

[72] Vladimir Nabokov, *Speak, Memory* (New York: Vintage, 1989).

[73] This is of course not to suggest for a moment that anything goes, i.e., that we are free to reflexively describe as we like. Criteria for the acceptability of autobiographical descriptions may arise within particularized contexts, and they may be distinctive to, or indeed unique to, that context. The way in which they function within Iris Murdoch's diaries, within Rousseau, within Wordsworth, and within many other autobiographical works may require the kind of heightened sensitivity to word meaning that we saw in Kundera. But that is not for a moment to say that there are no criteria at all, and so any "constructed" description is as good as any other. We will return to this matter in the final two chapters below.

sort of provisional totality," in fact "it represents the growth of a poet's mind," and that through a decades-long process of revision and expansion, "The pattern changes." It can change by becoming more nuanced, more thematically resonant across one's life, or it can change in a more fundamental way, by restructuring the fundamental connections of a life-narrative. Kermode says, rightly, "It changes because the self knowledge of the autobiographer becomes more complex."[74] The character of that complexity, something that philosophy might help articulate while looking at autobiography, is what I have tried to intimate in this chapter. And so with the three sections of this chapter behind us, we turn in Chapter 2 to a further discussion of selfhood, of our words of self-interpretation, and the descriptions of self-revelatory actions—issues that will take another step forward in bringing together the pragmatic-relational conception of selfhood with a narrative conception of self-understanding.

[74] Kermode, "Memory," pp. 300–1.

2

Boundaries of Selfhood

We have seen in the first chapter that there exists a fairly clear link between a common conception of what it is, what it means, to understand and the broadly Cartesian or dualistic conception of the self, the conception of the self as an inner point or place of consciousness within which mental (and, thus it is thought, private) events occur. We know that Wittgenstein challenged in a multiplicity of ways the (philosophically imagined) ontological neatness of the inner/outer dichotomy, but it is particularly the conception—or more accurately, here again the preconception or underlying philosophical picture or conceptual model—of understanding that one can all too easily hold that lends strong, if often only intuitively felt, support to the inner/outer strictly dichotomized distinction. This metaphysically enclosed preconception of understanding accords very well with (and may indeed be seen as the consequence of) the pictures or schematic conceptions of thinking, of mental experience, and of meaning that we have already seen the pragmatists combat in the previous chapter. And this conception of understanding would lead us to construe self-understanding in a parallel way; its component mosaic pieces are:

(1) Any act of self-understanding would be constituted by a state or a process;
(2) This state or process would be purely mental in the metaphysically significant sense (i.e., it implies that it is a private event only contingently attached, in a way as yet unspecified, to outward behavioral manifestations);
(3) One knows whether one is in possession of it or not, inwardly, by self-inspection or indeed introspection; and
(4) Any expression of understanding in verbal form would thus be in essence a report on the existence and nature of that inner state or process.

As we can even at this early stage of play predict, in what follows we will see that Wittgenstein is deeply and illuminatingly critical of all four of these elements as they together make up what he shows to be a misleading, and sometimes conceptually pernicious, conception—or again, more accurately, half-buried preconception—of understanding. And like the views of selfhood that the pragmatists found so misleading (and blind to the nuances of human experience that make human experience what it is), I want to suggest that this conception's perniciousness lies precisely in its power to make the broadly Cartesian self (with unmediated and privileged access to transparent contents), and thus the

---

Living in Words: Literature, Autobiographical Language, and the Composition of Selfhood. Garry L. Hagberg,
Oxford University Press. © Garry L. Hagberg 2023. DOI: 10.1093/oso/9780198841210.003.0002

ontologically neat inner/outer dichotomy, seem obviously true and, indeed, no less than inevitable with regard to any experience of understanding or, as we shall see, any experience of right or correct interpretation (including self-interpretation). But before turning to a consideration of the details of what Wittgenstein offers (as not so much a counterargument but rather a project joining therapeutic excavation with conceptual undermining), we should spell out more clearly the link between this common preconception of understanding and the corresponding but foundational idea of the self. And we need in this particular context (where we are over the course of this study reconsidering the contribution literary experience and autobiographical or self-descriptive language make to the formation of human identity) to know what, in greater detail, is the conceptual source of the seeming inevitability of the broadly Cartesian picture of selfhood in these regions of the mental landscape.

One essential component of this seeming inevitability emerges, I believe, from the thought—formed in perfect accord with the underlying inner/outer picture—that, as already hinted in (2) above, any *manifestation* (as we are inclined under the influence of the inner/outer picture to characterize it) of the understanding is secondary, and again only contingently attached to the hidden source behind it, the (primary) state of understanding. Indeed, the very term "manifestation" does help to insinuate and subsequently buttress this conception: to make any entity manifest is to imply that that entity has its existence independently from and prior to the (contingently associated) manifestation. It accordingly becomes a precariously simple matter to severely miscast the significant contribution Wittgenstein makes to the clarification of the very concept of understanding, erroneously expounding his view in terms either of:

(1) Eradicating the mental side of this particular variant of the inner/outer dichotomy (i.e., eradicating the inner understanding) and thus reducing the position itself to reductive behaviorism; or

(2) Insisting that the inner state or process of understanding needs to invariably and necessarily be *accompanied* by external manifestations to be rendered publicly intelligible (thus remaining within the clutches of the very dichotomy Wittgenstein is taking great pains to escape).

The line Wittgenstein follows in this matter is considerably more subtle than either of these options. But before turning to that line of thought in the second section of this chapter, we will first consider the work of an author whose writings significantly help clarify the logic of the distinctive interpretations that give the very notion of self-understanding its content; we will then be in a much better position to appreciate the significance of Wittgenstein's work in this area for our larger concerns about the distinctive power of autobiographical or self-defining language.

2.1 Multiple Interpretations and Singular Selves

Michael Krausz's *Limits of Rightness*[1] offers not only the rare combination of humane depth, cultural breadth, and analytical precision, but I bring it in here not for those virtues; it is also a book that holds considerable significance both for questions of self-interpretation and for our understanding of the language, the words, within which those interpretations take place.

Many discussions of interpretive pluralism (the view that many, or at least more than one, interpretation of an object, a work of art, or for us a person and their words) in philosophical aesthetics and still more in literary theory and cultural studies, and certainly the present discussion, can benefit from a fundamental point that Krausz makes clear: we must articulate interpretive pluralism in such a way that the plurality of interpretations address strictly the same cultural entity (for us this includes persons and words). As Krausz shows, we can easily and mistakenly believe that pluralism's plausibility depends on there being differently constituted cultural entities. For example, your *Brothers Karamazov* is different from mine in our varying subjective constitutions of the text, and so pluralism appears a natural theoretical option in that we are interpreting different objects. But with different interpretive objects, even if named similarly (like different people with the same name), interpretive singularism (meaning that only one interpretation is right) would be equally plausible. And with identifiably different interpreted objects unique to our own idiosyncratic readings, multiplism would be called for only if we each had different and competing interpretations of our *Brothers Karamazov*. Krausz clarifies this, and then pursues the more pressing question: *Can* there be multiple and equally admissible interpretations of the exact same interpreted cultural entity? And then once that is answered, to what extent does the self truly fit the mold of "cultural entity" (so that every insight we gain here concerning artistic or cultural-artifact interpretation will apply with equal force to both biographical interpretation and self-interpretation)?

To begin to answer such questions, we might turn to the question of the ontology of the cultural object. In the grip of the intuitively supported notion that:

(1) Any cultural entity subject to interpretation will possess a finite set of determinate properties, and

(2) Those properties will together constitute that object's fixed identity prior to and separate from any interpretive intervention by the observer, we may then, seemingly naturally,

---

[1] Michael Krausz, *Limits of Rightness* (Lanham: Rowman and Littlefield, 2000). I also allude throughout this section to his earlier *Rightness and Reasons: Interpretation in Cultural Practice* (Ithaca: Cornell University Press, 1993).

(3) Believe that such fixed-property realism would quite unproblematically imply interpretive singularism. On this view only that single interpretation formed in direct correspondence to those fixed properties is true; all others, failing the correspondence to fixity, would be false.

But the polemical opposite to this singularist position quickly and naturally suggests itself as well. In the grip of the picture that:

(1a) A cultural entity subject to interpretation will possess an indeterminate collection of properties that are in continual flux, where
(2a) This flux is allowed by the constructivist nature of the object and sustained by the highly variegated and ever-evolving perceptual and interpretive interventions of the observer, we then, also seemingly naturally,
(3a) Believe that such variable-property constructivism would imply multiplism. It is then a short step from this more general ontological polemic between fixity and flux to claiming that this analysis applies with equal force not only to the interpretation of works of art but also to human selves and to their language.

It is, however, the signal achievement (and this is why we need to weave his work into the present discussion) of Krausz's contribution to have demonstrated that the contest between singularism and multiplism is detachable from ontological commitments, and that the intuitive linkages we may too quickly grasp between realism and singularism (and then correspondingly between constructivism and multiplism) are the conceptual equivalent of optical illusions. To fully settle the ontological question concerning the nature of the interpreted cultural entity would thus not be to also settle, by implication from that ontology, the single-right-interpretation question. This is not a small matter in connection with present issues. If the veracity of the single-right-interpretation were insured by the ontological fixity of the object, then we would also have ready to hand a stable criterion for the adjudication of any two competing interpretations. Simply stated, that interpretation which more closely approximates the ideal would be preferable. And then—keeping the deep analogy between the interpretation of works of art and the interpretation of human persons in mind—this interpretive logic would apply with equal force to the question of the interpretation of human selves, and indeed to self-interpretation. But, as we already have reason to believe from the preceding chapter (there seeing the fixity/flux dichotomy from another vantage point), matters are not as simple as this clearly structured ontological polemic might suggest.

And so, both rightly and internally consistently, Krausz himself looks at the issue of singularism versus multiplism from a multiplicity of perspectives. He shows why (in a way that may be surprising to some) in some cases neither the

54   LIVING IN WORDS

interpretive ideals of singularism or multiplism apply, precisely in those cases where we lack the grounds to determine if competing interpretations in fact address one object in common beneath the two interpretations (as we shall see in the following sections of this chapter, particular circumstances of self-interpretation constitute just such a case). Here Krausz demarcates what he has identified as the limits of rightness. And he shows that the very term "interpretation" is not itself univocal and that we do not follow narrow and uniform rules for its singular and correct application. The concept of interpretation is used multifariously, and Krausz will not allow the unifying demands of theory to falsify the diversity of our practices (in a manner deeply congruent with the letter and spirit of Wittgenstein's writings).

That instructive diversity of interpretive practice is explored through an expansive range of cases, including Indian burial rites and attendant concepts of moral purification and transmigration; the paintings of Vincent Van Gogh, Paul Klee, and Anselm Kiefer; Joseph Gingold's Stradivarius; phlogiston and subatomic particles; contrasts between Hindu and Buddhist soteriologies; and Christo's *Wrapped Reichstag* as a problem in artistic boundary indeterminacy. It is in the course of his investigations into these culturally enmeshed cases that his analysis turns to ontological options for the theoretical construal of the interpretive artifacts that lie between the polar extremes of realism and constructivism (again, in a manner newly free of misleading picture-driven presumptions concerning the linkage to the singularism/multiplism debate). And this project is particularly significant for the achievement of a larger understanding of self-interpretation, precisely because the ontology of the self is often too quickly articulated in fixed-property realist or (polemically opposed) variable-property constructivist terms, an either/or proposition.

Taking Wittgenstein's critique of ostensive definition (here emphasizing that ostension alone does not individuate) as his point of departure, Krausz revivifies our appreciation of the importance of the intentional background for the individuation of the object to which we ostensively point, be it a broom (Wittgenstein's famous example) or Christo's *Wrapped Reichstag* (or, as we will see in the next chapter, ourselves). This is a conceptual opening that leads into Krausz's distinctive articulation of constructive realism, which acknowledges that objects are not "given" as such. Instead they are—as shown by our world-interpretive practices quite apart from what a desire for theoretical concision might like to find—"taken" within the intentional frame of the observer, that is, within the symbol system, or representational system (in a manner reminiscent of Nelson Goodman's philosophical project[2]), of the observer. Challenging the insistent view that we can begin any such inquiry with a basic description of an

---

[2] See Nelson Goodman, *Ways of Worldmaking* (Indianapolis: Hackett, 1978).

uninterpreted reality, above which the interpretations "float," Krausz acutely uncovers some of the deep linkages between problems in metaphysics and the philosophy of language. For example, the description of an uninterpreted realist world of pre-represented objects will invariably proceed within and not prior to a language, within an interpretive matrix. Thus it is best to relinquish the desire or overcome the temptation to speak of that pre-interpreted world. (This is reminiscent of the German Idealists' critique of Kant's noumenal world, but here in linguistic form.) But one needs to be clear that the process of conceptual therapy Krausz takes us through does not deliver us into an ever-new world of chaotic flux and rampant subjectivism. It is a constructive *realism* he is after, and the contingency (a matter to which we will return in Chapter 5 in connection with Richard Rorty) must thus in some sense be constrained—we as interpreters cannot make the world into just anything we want, nor can we interpret ourselves into just anything.

But then on Krausz's view, could these interpretations be constrained by the conditions of the preverbal world unto itself, or by what we (as ontologically empowered linguistic interventions—to which, in connection with self-description, we will also return in Chapters 5 and 6) say about that world? It is the presumed dichotomy undergirding the formulation of this question that Krausz rightly wants to unearth and remove: that undergirding, as we will increasingly see throughout this discussion, is a deeply embedded formative influence on our thinking and our corresponding subsequent expectations as to how an answer, to be satisfying, must proceed. The constructivist point concerns the necessity of any description of the interpreted object proceeding inside of language, thus never to be free of constructivist interventions no matter how scientific our descriptive language sounds. The realist replies that this point concerns not what is, but rather only what we say about what is—a debate of course absolutely fundamental to the question of autobiographical or self-descriptive truth. But what Krausz sees here with bracing clarity is that it does not follow from the impossibility of elucidating realism *cleanly*, i.e., in a manner free of the human hand's rather smudgy intervention in the proceedings, that thus we might as well abandon the notion of constraints on interpretation. In truth we do not have to choose sides in a doctrinaire and polemically inflexible all-or-nothing fashion; for Krausz, the dialectical p or not-p structure is only the surface manifestation of an undergirding conceptual picture that we should therapeutically excavate and eradicate or at least earn our conceptual freedom from it.

I am perhaps casting Krausz's project in terms that are more Wittgensteinian than he actually uses, but be that as it may it is clear that Krausz both sees and says that the impulsion to ask the question—the answer to which would identify the constraints on interpretive chaos in (1) words, constructively, or in (2) the world, realistically—originates in an underlying picture of a bifurcated separability. That separability, having first severed our myriad and highly variegated connections

56 LIVING IN WORDS

and relations between what we in a metaphysical and highly generalized voice call on the one side words, and the other the world, then leads us seemingly inevitably to search out the one fundamental and ontologically significant relation that obtains between the two metaphysical categories. Thus in relation particularly to the problem of selfhood and the special nature of the autobiographical project— that is, the self taking itself as its object of investigation, we would bifurcate the self as an entity that is (a) in ontological fact hermetically sealed unto itself (analogous to the world as originally sealed from the word) and then only (b) contingently spoken about in the ontologically separate words we use to describe it. This is evidently a complex matter, but most directly stated: the self is pictured as a fixed given, like the world on this ontologically bifurcated world-word conceptual template, and so the language of the self, autobiographical writing, is pictured as *ex post facto* descriptions that, like the words that describe but do not in part constitute the world on the realist model, are irremediably secondary to the prior facts that obtain in the prelinguistic world. And so here again, this schematic model or philosophical picture engenders its polemical opposite: speaking of the world, the linguistic constructivist (here in a manner reminiscent of medieval nominalism) will argue that words make the world and exercise the constitutive power they are unfairly denied on the opposing realist view. The corresponding constructivist view of the self is that autobiographical speaking and writing makes, or is linguistically constitutive of, the self. So the grand bifurcated categories of world and word are anything but innocent when we turn to the question of selfhood and autobiographical knowledge and the self-constitutive role of language—on the contrary, they lay down grooves of thought of which it becomes very difficult to steer clear.

The vital point here emerging from Krausz's reflections (as reconstructed in this chapter within a Wittgensteinian/conceptually therapeutic idiom) is that we will feel impelled to espouse a radical constructivism only so long as we retain the dichotomy that the realist and constructivist share (recall Ramsey's maxim as it appeared in the previous chapter). Because the fixed referents with real properties are not accessible via language or perception, the constructivist position is in an important sense defined negatively. That is to say, constructivism is defined in terms of how we must identify and describe the interpreted object, because we obviously could not intelligibly do it by capturing the prelinguistic in language. This vital point will emerge as indeed all the more vital as our investigation into the self-constitutive power of the autobiographical language we appropriate from literature unfolds in subsequent chapters.

But for the present, moving with Krausz beyond this dialectic of polarized opposites that share a common foundational dichotomized picture makes possible the development and more thorough grasp of what a constructive realism means—and particularly what it means for us. In this articulation of realism the role of our interpretive practices is acknowledged without embracing a reckless interpret-what-you-will, or saying-so-makes-it-so, constructivism. And so elements of realism, such as questions:

(1) of the "fit" of a description of a cultural object or entity;
(2) of whether a given property is in the interpreted object, either the artwork or the self; and
(3) of the abiding qualities of a work or object or self that have gone unseen by that work's or object's (or again, person's) contemporary audience;

all can and do arise in particular contexts of inquiry. But then elements tipping toward constructivism also arise as well. We find questions about:

(1) the "historied" nature of the perceiving eye or ear;
(2) the potentially prismatic nature of an aesthetic property we think we are seeing clearly (where the perceptual error is discerned in retrospect, thus calling into question our other perceptions of the object); and
(3) the power of the particular background, interests, and sensibility of the interpreter where these powers become constitutive of that object's relational properties (of the kinds examined in the previous chapter).

All these context-specific issues that intelligibly arise only within particular contexts of interpretive inquiry are compatible with Krausz's synthesis-ontology of constructive realism. But the leading idea to keep in mind for us is that his ontological position does not internally or necessarily entail singularism, multiplism, or—here again moving beyond a dichotomy and what it enforces with regard to our expectations of an answer—either one, in those cases that extend beyond what he terms the limits of rightness.

A number of such particular interpretive issues arise in the case of Christo's *Wrapped Reichstag*; of Krausz's cases listed above, I focus on this one because of its strong and immediate relevance to questions of person interpretation (both of other and of self).

Krausz uses this particular case to good effect to show that the issues it presents, taken together, reveal an aesthetically significant boundary indeterminacy that will help us later. Does this work include only, and precisely only, the German parliament building, over 60 tons of billowing silvery fabric, and over 10 miles of blue rope, all put in place around the building? Or, as Christo asserts, does it include both the prehistory of the work, its conception, its long and arduous process of obtaining permissions and the files of correspondence and drawings leading to the permissions, and also what we might then call the work's post-history, i.e., the revelers around the building, the art students sketching it, the storefronts displaying silver-in-blue wrapped objects, and so forth through a long causal chain of influence? Here, as Krausz shows, precisely where one draws the

58   LIVING IN WORDS

line between work and non-work is indeed constitutive of the work. But that line could be drawn at a number of different places, and from those demarcations a number of implications follow.

Krausz shows how such cases quickly unsettle any presumption we may have concerning the "fixed-object with a finite list of properties" model, but on reflection it appears—and I think Krausz would accept this extension of his point—that such cases also quickly unsettle the opposite presumption concerning the power of the interpreter of the object *as envisioned by the constructivist*. Again, we can draw the lines in many plausible places. But, importantly, we cannot draw them just anywhere. For example, we cannot possibly include the fabric and exclude the blue rope in the way we can include the fabric and the blue rope and not the documentation preceding the act of wrapping. Similar non-arbitrary constraints naturally emerge in the interpretation of selves, biographically or autobiographically (to which we will return in connection with the significance of Aristotle's *Poetics* for self-understanding in Chapter 3).

I thus see here Krausz's fundamental point concerning artistic boundary indeterminacy, but also a further point concerning the context-occasioned nature of particularized questions that sometimes lean toward the realist view, sometimes toward the constructivist. The power of the judgments we make is indeed in some respects constrained by the properties of the object. And in some different respects they exert work-determinative control over it. But it is just at this juncture that a fundamental difference of epistemic priority may emerge in our thinking about such cases. Should the facts of our interpretive practices be construed as surface-level manifestations of a deeper truth to the matter yet to be analyzed, in such a way that our praxis should be organized around the principle of interpretive constraint imposed by the fixed properties of the object for the realist, or around the principle of work-constitutive interpretive power for the constructivist? Or, should those practices, for all their diversity and noncommittal stature vis-à-vis the realism/constructivism polemic, *themselves* be given priority as instructive sources of what knowledge we can have on this issue? Should not the messiness and diversity of the particularities be regarded as a more accurate, if far more unwieldy, report on, as we will say in some cases, the way things are, and in other cases, the way we take them? Perhaps they should not even be organized into a pattern of cases supporting the synthesis ontology of constructive realism of the nuanced variety Krausz favors? I endorse these less constrained views. (In that case, if an "ism" were to apply at all, this would be to endorse a radical particularism—radical for reasons similar to those William James relied upon in calling his position radical empiricism in Chapter 1).

Krausz uses some passages of Wittgenstein's to good effect in the course of his analysis, and a quick look at them will help clarify what we will take with us from Krausz into the subsequent discussion. Investigating the issue of boundary indeterminacy in relation to identity, he quotes Wittgenstein's question:

Has the name "Moses" got a fixed and unequivocal use for me in all possible cases?—Is it not the case that I have, so to speak, a whole series of props in readiness, and am ready to lean on one if another should be taken from under me and vice versa? (quoted in Krausz, p. 107)

Wittgenstein is directing our attention to our practices and contexts of linguistic uses, in order to glean what we can about the meaning of a word. He does so quite apart from any preconceptions we may bring to the inquiry as shaped by an underlying model of meaning as a template to organize and systematically arrange those otherwise unwieldy practices. Throughout *Limits of Rightness* Krausz sees all this clearly. Yet (and this point too we will take with us), we might still ask whether Krausz goes as far as the powerful collection of cases and the fundamental insight of the book concerning the limits of theoretical concision warrants. I mean something like the following (the point itself allows multiple yet accurate expression):

"Interpretation" is itself a word. Given the complex and intricate interpretive practices Krausz so adroitly assembles, good reasons exist to acknowledge interpretation's diversity in practice, its wide range of possible employments, uses, and applications. Might a reasonably close look at some further passages of Wittgenstein that pertain directly to questions of interpretation prove helpful? And might these passages redirect our attention to differences and nuances that unsettle a common presumption concerning an underlying unity in the concept of interpretation, belief in which is sustainable only by insufficiently attending to the finer particularities? With regard to the question of autobiographical knowledge and the language within which we capture and form and sculpt that knowledge, this question would prove indisputably central, since the precise way in which we understand "interpretation" will determine the way we picture or understand the concept "self-interpretation." With this in mind, we might reconsider the following case.

2.2 Interpretive Rightness, Reconsidered

In investigating the case of a pupil assigned the task of writing down a sequence of numbers according to a particular rule (initially simply natural numbers in decimal notation from zero to nine), Wittgenstein (*Philosophical Investigations* §143)[3] observes that if the pupil copies the series 0, 1, 2, 3, 4, 5, . . . in this way, 1, 0, 3, 2, 5, 4, . . . , we will be inclined to say that he has "understood *wrong[ly]*," or

---

[3] Ludwig Wittgenstein, *Philosophical Investigations*, revised 4th ed., ed. P. M. S. Hacker and Joachim Schulte, trans. G. E. M. Anscombe, P. M. S. Hacker, and Joachim Schulte (Malden: Wiley-Blackwell, 2009).

60 LIVING IN WORDS

misinterpreted our meaning. We will do so because we can easily discern a pattern to the mistake, because it is indeed a "*systematic* mistake." But to forestall the quickly advancing (picture-buttressing) notion that in such cases we are (inferentially) identifying the presence of a mental state as that meaning, although the wrong one for the assigned task, Wittgenstein adds that there is "no sharp distinction between a random mistake and a systematic one," or that cases we are inclined to call "random" and cases we are inclined to call "systematic" are not sharply, categorically distinguished. (In some cases the details will tell us which is right, and in others the decision as to its random or systematic nature will be constitutive; this distinction, especially where as Wittgenstein observes it can be non-sharp and yet still there, holds considerable significance for the process of self-formation discussed in Chapter 5 below.) But so far, the philosophical significance is only implicit: *if* we determined such cases strictly according to the presence or absence of a mental state, then categorical sharpness would exist. No such clarity exists. So this, at the least, calls into question the idea that it is a mental state that serves as the criterion of understanding. This too, as we shall see, is directly important for the very concept of self-understanding.

The force of Wittgenstein's question is strengthened next: if the pupil now writes zero to nine in a way we find satisfactory, we will be satisfied in a larger sense only if the pupil does this correctly most of the time, "not if he does it right once in a hundred attempts" (§145). This strengthens the question because the *practice* of the pupil, not an inferred mental state, serves as the criterion of understanding, of the interpretation. We then want to know with some precision what serves as the criterion of correctness, of rightness for the practice. Are we not, at least initially, implicitly positing that the grasping of our own mental state, or successfully communicating it to the pupil, is the criterion of correctness? In the case of self-interpretation, on this model, the correct present grasp of our own prior mental state would serve as the criterion of correctness.

It was Aristotle who delivered an admonition that we not impose upon a given subject matter more categorical neatness or exactitude than that subject itself naturally possesses, and Wittgenstein is following in that tradition here.[4] But still, we find an answer to the question concerning the criterion for correctness—or at least a strong suggestion of an answer—in the following remark: "Now, however, let us suppose that after some effort on the teacher's part he continues the series correctly, that is, as we do it." The words "correctly, that is, *as we do it*" de-psychologize the issue, resituating the emphasis back on practice, eroding the presumption that it must be a mental state hidden beneath these remarks

---

[4] Renford Bambrough insightfully explored these methodological connections in "Aristotle on Justice: A Paradigm of Philosophy," in *New Essays on Plato and Aristotle*, ed. Renford Bambrough (London: Routledge & Kegan Paul, 1965), pp. 159–74, and "How to Read Wittgenstein," in *Understanding Wittgenstein*, ed. Godfrey Vesey (Ithaca: Cornell University Press, 1974), pp. 117–32.

concerning practice that serves as the criterion of correctness or rightness. Reinforcing the earlier point concerning the lack of sharp distinctions between understanding, misunderstanding, and non-understanding, Wittgenstein adds that there will not exist a precise point at which we can say that the pupil has "mastered the system," that he has interpreted our intention rightly.

Wittgenstein's dialogue with his interlocutor advances rapidly, and it shows Wittgenstein's position breaking off in complete independence from the presumption of interior understanding as the criterion for interpretive correctness. This example with the pupil is, after all, what Wittgenstein calls a "primitive language-game": it provides a microcosm within which we can see more clearly. And suppose we say with the interlocutor that, even though the pupil has shown his mastery of the system in carrying the series up to a relatively high number, still "to have got the system (or, again, to understand it) can't consist in continuing the series up to *this* or *that* number: *that* is only applying one's understanding." Encapsulating the insistence we may feel that the having of the understanding is one thing and the showing of it another, Wittgenstein adds in the interlocutor's insistent voice, "The understanding itself is a state which is the *source* of the correct use" (§146).

Asking what one is "really thinking of here," Wittgenstein suggests that the idea behind the interlocutor's insistence is that of the derivation of a series from its algebraic formula or something analogous. This corresponds directly to the distinction between the having and the showing of understanding introduced above. But this ability to *apply* the formula repeatedly need not be characterized in this (fundamentally dualistic) way. Wittgenstein's argument proceeds, observing that even though we can think of more than one application of a formula, and even though the converse point also holds (that "every type of application can in turn be formulated algebraically"), still, the application, and not a mental state existing behind it, constitutes a "criterion of understanding."

At this stage, to agree with the interlocutor, Wittgenstein's imagined opponent, is not difficult. The opponent is shortly given voice again (§147): he insists, quite reasonably, that he has not "'*found out* that up to now'" he has applied the formula in a certain way. He adds, again fairly reasonably if in a more metaphysically loaded way, that in his "'own case at all events I surely know that I mean such-and-such a series; it doesn't matter how far I have actually developed it'." Wittgenstein replies that the fundamental idea motivating this remark is that the knowing of the rule is "quite apart" from "remembering actual applications to particular numbers." And the reply quickly comes in turn, "Of course!" But now Wittgenstein is positioned to advance to the next stage of his argument, and here we can see the direct significance this may have for Krausz's analysis of rightness in interpretation, and thus for our present considerations in turn.

Wittgenstein asks these questions: (1) What does the pupil's knowledge, separate from its applications, consist in? (2) When is the application known: always,

62   LIVING IN WORDS

day and night, or only when the student is thinking of the rule? (3) Is the application known as one knows the alphabet and multiplication table? More generally, (4) Could what is here called knowledge be understood as a state of consciousness or a mental process (§148)? He goes on to point out that if we say that knowing the alphabet is a state of mind, then we must be thinking in terms of a "mental apparatus" by means of which we explain (here again employing the conceptually treacherous word from the preceding discussion) "the *manifestations* of that knowledge" (§149). And the objection to this way of thinking, this way of characterizing our knowing, for example, the alphabet, is that (he says somewhat confusingly) "there ought to be two different criteria for such a state."

Wittgenstein means, as the heart of this step of the argument against the larger misconception of interpretive understanding at issue, that if this is true then we should be able to gain knowledge of the "apparatus" *apart* from its manifestations. And upon investigation, we find, against the expectations formed by the underlying philosophical dualistic picture of understanding, that we cannot separate the manifestations from the alleged "apparatus." It is given content by—and indeed *only* by—a consideration of its manifestations or applications. Although Wittgenstein does not say so explicitly, this calls into question the aptness of the concept of "manifestation" in these cases.[5] And to call into question the word is to call into question the underlying philosophical picture that prompts that word's (mis)use. Against common presuppositions or philosophical preconceptions, self-solidifying self-interpretations may not be an "apparatus" prior to and separate from what we then call its manifestations. Rather, as we shall see, these may be *in* practice, *in* action.

I bring this example of the pupil with the numerical series, along with Wittgenstein's discussion of its particularities, into the discussion because such cases can give us pause of exactly the kind Krausz's analysis gives to those who believe the singularist versus multiplist debate will be solved by realist or constructivist ontology. Krausz wants to dig beneath the oppositional dialectic of that debate and bring to us the value of that philosophical archeology. Should we not, in a broadly parallel way, ask whether the very conception of *interpretation*, of rightly or wrongly interpreting or understanding an intended meaning at work within and perhaps also beneath Krausz's analysis, needs similar re-examination? (In Wittgenstein's case the issue lies in language, but there is good reason to believe that the linguistic case holds direct significance for the interpretation and understanding of the meaning of cultural artifacts as well as the self's past actions.) Is the concept of interpretive understanding in play here excessively or

---

[5] Note that (as Wittgenstein adds) it would only further obscure matters to introduce the distinction between the conscious and the unconscious, presumably in such a way that the formula is known unconsciously and applied consciously. That pair of terms only covers over, he suggests, what is of grammatical (in his philosophically enriched sense of the word "grammar") interest.

exaggeratedly cognitive, or cast too strongly in intellectualist terms? Can an interpretation be non-dualistically embedded within our practices in a way that repudiates an underlying picture much like that between an understanding, construed as a mental state, and its manifestations, construed as an application? Might the practices, which Krausz masterfully puts to work, perhaps prove even more significant than his account to this point acknowledges?

Wittgenstein amplifies the preceding points by contrasting what we *call* mental states (once again returning words to the ordinary voice) with what we have in his foregoing discussion of understanding. Depression, excitement, and pain are called mental states. Is "understanding a word" a natural item on such a list? True, we can say, "since yesterday I have understood this word." But this observation in itself by no means answers the four questions he put forward at the last stage of the argument. Has the word been understood continuously? We do not know quite what to say in response to that (and the point is that, if the criterion of right understanding were a state, we would immediately know how to answer). He also suggests we consider the disanalogy between the questions "When did your pain get less?" and the marginally sensible question "When did you stop understanding that word?" The more we look into such cases, the more it becomes evident that interpretive understanding, if classified as a mental state, behaves *very* differently from the unproblematic or natural entries under that classification. Detailed questions beyond the simple language-game of the pupil and numerical sequence further reinforce the point.

For example, consider the question asking when we know how to play chess, when we have rightly interpreted the complexly interlocking rule-governed organization of the particular pieces before us on the chessboard. Meaning, or the right interpretation, understood as a mental state, is not something we find readily intelligible once we stop to scrutinize the details. As a result of such investigations, Wittgenstein speaks of the proximity of the grammar of the word "knows" to that of "can" and "is able to." This proximity highlights matters of practice over picture-driven characterizations of knowledge generally, and, more especially for our present purposes, of a rightly grasped or understood intention.[6] He suggests that the grammar of this practice-emphasized conception of "knows" is similarly proximate to that of "understands," and he adds parenthetically, for reasons we can now fathom, the phrase "'Mastery' of a technique" (§150). Might it be valuable to consider the possibility of resituating interpretation—of works of art, of human selves—*into* our practices? In general, we too quickly picture it as a determinate mental act that assembles a number of particular perceptual experiences into a composite whole. In this hasty picture, the resulting cognitive

---

[6] I offer a discussion of such picture-driven conceptions of knowledge, versus what (philosophical) literature can teach us, in *Meaning and Interpretation* (Ithaca: Cornell University Press, 1994), ch. 5, "Interpretation and Philosophical Method," pp. 149–78.

structure of the interpretation mimetically mirrors the perceived artifact's structure in the world according to realism; or, the resulting cognitive structure is imposed upon the perceived elements according to constructivism.

In practice, each of these competing descriptions of an interpretation can, within cases, capture the perceptual event. In suddenly seeing that a painting we mistakenly took to be abstract is in fact representational, the representational figure seems to leap out and suddenly "lock" the various elements together into an interpretation corresponding to what it in fact is.

Conversely, we can see the ambiguous line drawing, such as the perceptually reversible Necker Cube, as now having this side forward and that one in back, and then voluntarily switch the perception reversing forward and back, finding in it a case where the cognitive structure of the perceived element is constitutive of what we see. (We will pursue this contrast between two kinds of cases in connection with the too often underappreciated power of self-constitutive language later in this study.) And these are, after all, only two cases: should either case be elevated to a paradigm of all perception? No more, I would say, than the picture of interpretation underlying them should be elevated to a paradigm of all acts and cases of interpretation. The truth of the matter—or matters—of our interpretation—or interpretations—is *in* our interpretive practices, not cognitively prior to them in such a way that those interpretive practices are merely contingently attached external manifestations. But we can say this and yet still retain an underlying, unifying picture or conceptual model of interpretation, where the practices are assembled as illustrations, according to that model. Has Krausz stopped here, or does he want to move to the stronger claim for the practices—indeed the claim that I for one would endorse, that would entail the exacting scrutiny of the kind Wittgenstein gives his case: the model can be found more or less applicable in some cases (like the painting or Necker Cube example) and utterly beside the point in others. The answer is that Krausz has not stopped here, for the salutary reason that he invariably keeps the door open for the practices to outrun the conceptual template at hand, the door open for the practices to teach us that there is more subtlety than the model at hand can accommodate.

And Wittgenstein shows in his case that the model or picture, not the practice, is dispensable. He weaves the different strands of his position together, identifying: (1) the motivations for the initial search for the mental process or state that allegedly constitutes an interpreted understanding; (2) the instructive problems endemic to the characterization of that state as hidden somewhere other than in the practices where they lie open to view; (3) the problem of an essentialistic or unitary definition of correct interpretive understanding and the resultant subordination of all cases and their nuances to that overriding definition; and (4) the illusory nature of the picture-driven attempt to locate the mental process or state. And then (5), Wittgenstein sets a distinct tone of self-diagnostic analytical distance (§153):

We are trying to get hold of the mental process of understanding, which seems to be hidden behind those coarser and therefore more readily visible accompaniments. But we do not succeed; or, rather, it does not get as far as a real attempt. For even supposing I had found something that happened in all those cases of understanding,—why should *it* be the understanding? And how can the process of understanding have been hidden, when I said "Now I understand" *because* I understood?! And if I say it is hidden—then how do I know what I have to look for? I am in a muddle.

The specially problematic nature of the idea of the hidden process or state is most devastating for the interlocutor's intuitions here. If we say "Now I understand" *because* we understand, how could it even make sense to say that at the moment of that utterance—an utterance made *because* of the internal recognition of the understanding—the state of understanding was hidden? This does not and could not describe the moment of understanding, of interpretive rightness. The very concept of hiddenness, as construed in this particular way, is thus bound to severely mislead any attempt to shed light on the moment at which a work of art or a human being or their utterance is understood, the interpreter's moment of felt rightness.

Yet there remains the sense that the interlocutor's insistence has not been exhaustively diagnosed and treated. Is there not something else "behind," or if that is thought too metaphysically freighted a formulation, something else in addition to, the practices? Are we not in pursuit of *something*—a determinate and unitary process, act, or event—apart from them, like the understanding apart from its manifestations? The next step of Wittgenstein's discussion acknowledges and to a degree assuages this sense, and it clarifies what Wittgenstein was referring to as the "muddle."

If, Wittgenstein writes, the phrase "Now I understand the principle" is not equivalent to, or is not exhaustively captured by, "The formula ... occurred to me" or "I say the formula," and so on, we should then ask: Does it follow—and here he is addressing precisely the sense that there *must* be something in addition to the practices—that we thus use the sentences "Now I understand" or "Now I can go on" as a description of, or as a report on, the inward existence of a process or state that occurs either "behind or side by side with that of saying the formula?" (§154). His implied answer is clearly negative. And it is at this final step of the argument that Wittgenstein is able to say that if there is anything behind, beside, or in addition to the formula, then it is "*particular circumstances*, which justify me in saying I can go on—when the formula occurs to me." Here is what legitimately gives rise to a good part of the interlocutor's insistence that more than (brute) practice must enter into the accounting of the phenomena of understanding. This final step in de-psychologizing our conception of the understanding that is interpretive rightness leads us to ask not about the presence, absence, or the

66 LIVING IN WORDS

nature of a hidden inner state or process, but to inquire instead into the *circumstances* of our acting on, and speaking about, understanding. "Try," Wittgenstein adds, "not to think of understanding as a 'mental process' at all.—For *that* is the expression which confuses you," suggesting that we ask ourselves instead in what sort of circumstances we could say that now famous phrase "Now I know how to go on." We shall see in the following chapter how and when we find ourselves in the circumstances to say now we know how to go on in rightly connecting the dots of a life-narrative, now we know how to interconnect the relations of which the pragmatists spoke, now we know how to replace self-deception with self-knowledge. And now we know how to speak, to endorse, to take within the words that both make and describe who and what we are. A singular, isolated mental process is not the material of this kind of autobiographical or self-constitutive work.

But, with these remarks of Wittgenstein's on the phenomenology of interpretation behind us, let us look back to where this section started with Krausz's work: his lucid analysis gives pause to those who would think too quickly about singularist or multiplist interpretation in relation to realist and constructivist construals of cultural artifacts of any kind. It casts much light and clears much ground, and in the final part of Krausz's discussion he turns explicitly to a discussion of life paths and projects, and whether such paths and projects need to be understood in relation to a self that possesses a singularist essence, a realist artifact displaying definitionally invariant properties. Or—as we have seen the question approached in a number of ways in connection with the interpretation of cultural artifacts in the foregoing—is the self, by contrast, a construction whose organizing cognitive structure is imposed by the interpreter? Krausz, articulating and then transcending that often (but not always—the particular case will tell) misleading dichotomy, showed both its value and its limits.

That insistent dichotomy is often (again, not always) misleading in self-interpretation and self-description as well, and what I have described as Krausz's conceptually therapeutic project frees us from it with the following progression of thought. In understanding, in rightly interpreting a life, the orthodox essentialist would insist that essences—of character, of life paths, of potential in a continual process of realization—are there in the person to be found. But, as Krausz says, "rather than actualizing antecedent innate potentialities, antecedent potentialities are posited in light of who the person has become. It is a posit in light of the foreknowledge of actuality. One retroactively infers the past potential in light of the present actual" (143). We will then want to know: Did the past potential preexist its realization as a kind of determining essence of the self, conceived in a fashion resonantly similar to understanding or right interpretation existing metaphysically and temporally apart from its alleged mental content? No, Krausz answers, "such retrospective positing does not establish a preexistent essence of who one was to become" (143). Instead, "when telling the story of one's own actualization, one posits a prior narrative self, but that does not entail a

BOUNDARIES OF SELFHOOD 67

substantive essentialized self. That self as the subject of the story is a posit from the vantage point of the present actualized self" (143–4). Much like the reversing Necker Cube, this way of putting it suggests that the cognitive structure within which we organize all we know of a life—either our own or that of another—is imposed from without: the self as construction. Indeed, sounding like a late-in-the-game endorsement of a radical constructivism concerning selfhood, Krausz continues, "so understood, the subject of the story is no inherent being but is a construction of the presently told story."

So, with regard to selfhood, we come to the bedrock-level question: Does saying so make it so? If one follows Krausz, one might believe that the answer is affirmative from what he says next: "One postdictively postulates the self, the grammatical subject, that makes the narrative intelligible" (144). But, now pulling back from that theoretical polar extreme, Krausz adds in a style reminiscent of pragmatism's relational conception of selfhood, "at the same time, this does not mean that just any story will do. The natures of selves are postdictive constructs of plausibly entertained present narratives." And he goes on to describe constraints that, within particular contexts of self-inquiry, are loose enough to allow a self that is emergent from its practices and its discourse and yet tight enough to make distinctions between what is and is not true of a self.

But one might here ask: Is Krausz, at the culmination of his account, having his cake and eating it too? The self is in one sense an individual corresponding to a realist model and in another constituted and reconstituted through and within its practices, discursive and otherwise. The answer—highly significant for what is to follow in the present study—is, No. And it is important to see that the answer *can* be No. This would appear cake-eating-and-having only to one indissolubly wedded to the polarized conceptual bifurcation from which Krausz's work is designed to free us. Or perhaps I should say: Given the particularities of my own intentional background and the web of meaning-constitutive relations into which I situate this work, that—in a manner at once reasonably free and yet (I hope) rationally constrained—is my interpretation of Krausz's position and its relation to Wittgenstein's contribution to our understanding of the "logic" (or one could say in Wittgenstein's sense the grammar) of interpretation and understanding. And both, taken together, significantly advance the cause of reconsidering—in a manner that has gained freedom from misleading schematic conceptual pictures—the nature of interpretive rightness.

So, taken all together, combined, and encapsulated, what significance do these reflections hold for the interpretation of persons, of selves? If persons are cultural entities, then we can return to the polemical theses considered at the outset, but now with persons or human selves as the focal point. In that case, we would have on the first pole:

(1) Any self-as-cultural-entity subject to interpretation will possess a finite set of determinate properties, and

68 LIVING IN WORDS

(2) Those properties will together constitute that self's fixed identity prior to and separate from any interpretive intervention by an observer-interpreter, we may then, seemingly naturally,

(3) Believe that such fixed-property realism would quite unproblematically imply interpretive singularism with regard to both the content and the interpretation of that person. On this view only that single interpretation formed in direct correspondence to those fixed properties of that given self is true; all others, failing the correspondence to fixity, would be misinterpretations or, as misunderstandings of a person, false.

But as above, the polemical opposite to this singularist position quickly and naturally suggests itself when we think of the interpretation of persons. So in the grip of the picture or conceptual model holding that:

(1a) A self that is subject to interpretation will exhibit an indeterminate collection of emerging and receding properties that are in continual flux, where

(2a) This flux of self-content is consistent with the constructivist nature of the self as a highly variegated and ever-evolving entity inviting and supporting similarly ever-changing perceptual and interpretive content on the part of the observer, we then, also seemingly naturally,

(3a) Believe that this variable-property constructivism of selfhood would imply interpretive multiplism. And again, but now from this side, this more general ontological polemic between fixity and flux demonstrates the parallel between the interpretation of works of art and the interpretation of human selves.

But what I described as Krausz's signal achievement above was that he showed the initially counterintuitive separability of this ontological debate from the interpretive contest between singularism and multiplism. Fixed-property realism does not in and of itself imply interpretive singularism, any more than variable-property constructivism implies in and of itself interpretive multiplism. By considering a number of cases throughout the arts and culture, Krausz showed that there are cases where neither singular nor multiple ideas of interpretation apply in a way that leaves nothing out. That is, we can *stipulate* that a person is fixed in accordance with thesis (1), and then stipulate that the correct interpretation of that person will be singularist, but this will in the case of a real person seem drastically oversimplified and inappropriately reductive. (Indeed the recognition and acknowledgment of the complexity of a person versus the oversimplifying reduction of that person can be a moral matter; we will return to this matter in Chapter 4.) Or we can stipulate as the polemically opposite methodological presupposition that a person, a self, is of a generic kind that is thoroughgoingly constructivist, so that the free-for-all multiplism discussed above is endorsed. But with the connections between the ontological claims and interpretive methods severed (and accordingly clarified), we will see these as what they are: stipulations. And that itself exposes these methodological and categorical simplifications on either side as *themselves* too free-for-all, themselves too unaware of the circumstantial details of context within which criteria for interpretive plausibility emerge. So *both* models of selfhood are too undisciplined (with fixed-property ontology conjoined to singularism falsely promising clarity and rigorous discipline). Interpretation, again, itself is not univocal, and its variations will manifest across different cases: this is true in life as it is in art.

So human beings can be well described, in the terms discussed here, as cultural entities, and the logic of their interpretation can be very much like the *Wrapped Reichstag* case. We can make decisions about what we regard as foundational to the identity of the person, and if we establish and cement in place a commitment to truth, then a perceived moment of dissimulation will be seen against that background and taken for what it is—an exception to the rule rather than itself being an isolated person-defining foundation (although the exception, as an exception, will carry its significance for the interpretation of the person). And with that commitment, and that exception, in place, some further descriptions will then make sense within that person-interpreting language-game, and others not. This will be like including the fabric and the rope, but not the paperwork concerning the permissions. But then Krausz's summarizing phrase was "constructive realism." And this takes us, finally, inside the issue not of other-interpretation, but of self-interpretation. It is true, through the relational engagements of the kind that the classical American pragmatists emphasized, that we make significant contributions to the "making" or the composition of others through the encouragement and solidification of person descriptions. But we would miss a lot of the significance of the present discussion for more intricately understanding self-interpretation if we stopped at that point.

Because we persons are not invariably transparent unto ourselves, and because we can reinterpret, or newly interpret, past action, we can find ourselves in a position of self-interpretation that incorporates everything already discussed concerning other-interpretation (including the deep analogy to the interpretation of a work of art, an analogy from which it seems we can always learn more). But in these cases the decisions we make concerning what is in and what is out as in the *Wrapped Reichstag* case, and the ways in which we make sense of new additions to the unfolding interpretive language-game and consider and evaluate the contextually emergent inflections of our words, become not only in a weak sense self-defining (where the words we use are thought of as coming after the fact and then only contingently so, so that the truth of ourselves was in place prior to language or as Krausz says pre-dictively), but rather in a strong sense self-defining (where we are changed, solidified, or resolutely exemplifying one trait and not another) so

70   LIVING IN WORDS

that language (now post-dictively) not only describes the case but significantly helps makes the case. It is as if the *Wrapped Reichstag* were making its own decisions as it proceeds, making itself what it is and determining its own identity and its own boundaries through a process of unfolding self-constitution. It is, to use a familiar image non-pejoratively, a kind of bootstrapping of selfhood. Any purely descriptive account of the language of self-identity would systematically miss this; if the ontology were fixed in advance of any language, there would be no room for words to exert power. And on the other polar extreme of radical constructivism, there would be no recognition of the stability of the self-descriptions that demand acknowledgment and with which any ongoing constitutively empowered self-description must negotiate.

The kind of truth that emerges in such cases is often like metaphorical truth:[7] like Wittgenstein on the seeing of aspects,[8] we see the truth of a self-defining remark or observation, and assess its interpretive power, by seeing initially unobvious similarities or likenesses, by seeing connections, by seeing subtly emergent patterns. This is not one-to-one matching of language to the world, not simple or direct verified correspondence. But nor is it entirely creative, entirely unconstrained or free-floating, entirely without gradations of plausibility or acceptability. That no man is an island, profoundly true, is not a truth one can verify by matching intrinsic and invariant properties to its subsequent flatly descriptive language. (Instructively, one can verify the very odd *literal* claim that no man is an island in this way, but that would have to be only humorously and deliberately mock-uncomprehending; Donne's truth is not verified in anything like that way.) And Donne's words do not constitute merely a claim that is no better than any other random description of a person or the nature of persons; the truth in it is not a matter of whimsy or shallow subjectivist preference.

It is at this point that one can feel tempted to revert to a simple foundationalist model of self-description and self-interpretation, where we take simple stated correspondences to be the base upon which the more poetic descriptions rest. But on closer inspection (precisely of the kind Krausz encourages), we find that such a model can apply, for example, to parts of bodies, but not to *persons*. That is, a medical doctor may begin with a diagnostic hypothesis concerning a lung, proceed through investigation and testing to a probable explanation of symptoms, finally settling on a confirmed diagnosis. And this can depend on a confirmed physical fact of the case, where the diagnostic language directly follows, and describes, that physical fact. Such cases can falsely revivify our sense of the applicability of the fixed-ontology model of person interpretation, but that

---

[7] For an acute discussion and demonstration of how it is that we see the truth in a metaphor, see Ted Cohen, *Thinking of Others: On the Talent for Metaphor* (Princeton: Princeton University Press, 2008).

[8] For a set of informative articles on this category of perception, here again see *Seeing Wittgenstein Anew*, ed. W. Day and V. Krebs (Cambridge: Cambridge University Press, 2010).

approach will not capture either the complexity or the phenomenology of the self. Indeed, perhaps the best refutation of descriptive reductionism, or physicalistic behaviorism of a humanely anemic kind, is to look at how we actually interpret and understand a person and then ask how much of this we can actually capture on the models of language that such reductionisms insinuate or presuppose.[9] As I mentioned above, there will be cases, and considerations that arise within cases, that tip now toward realism, now toward constructivism. But they *tip*, they do not (unlike some medical diagnoses) wholly fall to one side or the other. It would be the rare exception, and not the rule, that would give us a case in which everything relevant to a moment or self-reflection or self-interpretation would be captured on one polemical model or the other without very significant remainder. The words, the instruments of such reflections, neither dig down to direct foundational correspondence nor fly up to airborne fancy. Like good metaphors.

I identified above what I called the conceptual opening that leads into Krausz's distinctive articulation of constructive realism, a sophisticated articulation of realism that acknowledges that interpreted objects are not in a simple empirical sense "given" as such. Rather, such objects are—as is shown in the real contexts of our interpretive practices—"taken" within the intentional frame of the observer, within the intellectual atmosphere of what Richard Wollheim called cognitive stock. The self, in Krausz's special sense, is an interpreted object, but interpreted by itself inside the mental world of its own cognitive stock, its own web of "seeing-as" relations and aspect perceptions, and its own interacting weave of metaphorical descriptions. So is there a general overarching or organizational rule to follow in putting together an overarching collection of self-interpretations, so that we end with a singular and unified sense of self that singly corresponds to one overarching self-description? Or put it this way: Is there a singular foundational self-description as the reduced essentialized result of a collection of self-interpretations to which every subsequent self-interpretation must be first reconciled before being considered acceptable?

With these questions in mind, let us newly consider the passage quoted above, but in this case where "objects of interpretation" means not only "human selves" but (to encapsulate the project of self-knowledge and its active side as self-composition) "human selves interpreting themselves": Krausz wrote, "The strategies of aggregating and pluralizing objects of interpretation or aggregating and pluralizing interpretations themselves are mandated by no general rules for correct application. Rather, their appropriate deployment is a matter of piecemeal deliberation within the context of pertinent practices." And so in self-investigation,

---

[9] As a correction to the impulse to simplify and to mistakenly take conceptual presupposition in such cases as simple empirical fact, see Krausz on reference frames, in his *Interpretation and Transformation: Explorations in Art and the Self* (Leiden: Brill, 2007), ch. 8: "Changing Reference Frames, Changing Emotions," pp. 85–95.

72 LIVING IN WORDS

the criteria relevant to the adjudication and further reflection on any self-interpretation will emerge, with its language intricately inflected in the way mentioned above and indeed in a fashion reminiscent of Franz and Sabina, and with relevant pragmatic relations intertwining, only within the circumscribed contexts of pertinent practices.

It would take a separate volume to fully show how such case-sensitive criteria emerge within such interpretive practices and indeed exactly what those practices are case by case and how they proceed, but we will return to some illustrative cases in Chapters 5 and 6. For now, however, with this question concerning the possibility of a single "backbone" or foundational fixed-property self-description to the fore, one might recall that we say that we are individuals—that is, non-dividable singular selves hermetically internally contained. But there are cases (as in cases of collective action or joint intention of a kind irreducible to the sum total of individual intentions[10]) in which philosophers and anthropologists are now speaking with considerable plausibility of "dividuals" and "porous subjects" in contexts of distributed creativity. If Krausz is right (and I think he is), as we have just seen the sense of any such word alterations or neologisms will be specified, given content, and inflected within particular contexts of human interpretation and understanding. Of course, whether we would ever want to *replace* the concept of an individual with that of the "dividual" is an open question (and I doubt it). But to augment our conception of selfhood in a way that extends beyond the boundaries of established preconceptions and that would capture more of the nuances of our complex practices would in any case prove beneficial, and it would correspondingly expand our grasp of the range and character of self-description and self-interpretation.

In any case, with an enhanced and, thanks to Krausz, much more acute understanding of the conceptual models within which we can and are inclined to think about the interpretation of artworks and the interpretation (and self-interpretation) of persons (including, as we have seen, fixed-property grounded realism; variable-property unconstrained constructivism; interpretive singularism; interpretive multiplism; and constructive realism), he has shown us how and why it is that sometimes the right thing to say, if I may borrow a phrase, is: we are large, we contain multitudes.

Standing back, Krausz's writings, read in close conjunction with Wittgenstein's, have shown that the question of boundedness and boundary indeterminacy of

---

[10] I offer discussions of this matter in "The Ensemble as Plural Subject: Jazz Improvisation, Collective Intention, and Group Agency," in *Creativity, Improvisation, and Collaboration: Perspectives on the Performance of Contemporary Music*, ed. Eric Clarke and Mark Doffman (Oxford: Oxford University Press, 2017), and in "Playing as One: Ensemble Improvisation, Collective Intention, and Group Attention," in *Oxford Handbook of Critical Improvisation Studies*, ed. George Lewis and Ben Piekut (New York: Oxford University Press, 2016), pp. 481–99.

BOUNDARIES OF SELFHOOD   73

both works of art and selves, is a far more intricate, and indeed interesting, matter than our pre-reflective intuitions and the simplified pictures that nourish those intuitions may have predicted. With that overarching desideratum in mind, we now turn to another contemporary philosopher whose writings show that the question of the boundedness of a human action, and thus any life-narrative that involves a recounting of these actions, is similarly intricate. And this intricacy will, here again, prove instructive.

2.3 Self-Description, Action-Individuation, and Virginia Woolf's "A Sketch of the Past"

Let us begin this section by standing back for a moment: Among the numerous things that make any autobiographical undertaking so interesting is the fact that there exists no one-to-one correlation between a person's belief, intention, preference, desire, hope, fear, expectation, and so forth (through a list including many of the diverse things philosophers now tend to group together as propositional attitudes) and that person's behavior. Were there such a relation, our knowledge of others would be far more transparent than it is, and autobiographical writing would prove straightforwardly simple: for each remembered action there would be a determinate mental event that stood behind it (directly parallel to the manifestation-of-understanding picture examined above), and a recording of the past action by the autobiographer would entail the parallel reporting of the mental predecessor, or indeed cause[11] articulated in terms of the content of a single propositional attitude, of that action.

Of course, this simple dualistic schema, or conceptual picture, has been subjected to various forms of scrutiny: Nietzsche decried what he generically termed the "antecendentia of action,"[12] referring to the explanatory dreamland many philosophers and other theorists have happily but confusedly occupied, wherein the explanations of "outward" human actions proceed in what we will then call prior inward, and ontologically hidden, mental determinants. Focusing on the alleged temporal separation of antecedent and consequent action, Nietzsche with characteristic rhetorical force ridicules the misled many who attempt to explain something in some cases so complex, and in other cases so immediate, as human intentional action. Gilbert Ryle, focusing on the dualistic separation of inner and outer in any such explanatory schema, famously argued against the very

---

[11] See, for example, the analysis offered in Davidson's "Actions, Reasons, and Causes," in *Essays on Actions and Events* (Oxford: Clarendon Press, 1980), pp. 3–19.

[12] See the forceful discussion in Nietzsche's *Twilight of the Idols*, trans. R. J. Hollingdale (Harmondsworth: Penguin, 1968), esp. pp. 48–51.

74 LIVING IN WORDS

conceptual substructure of the "ghost in the machine";[13] the ensuing behaviorism argued against the inner world of mental machinations, yielding a picture of selfhood that was in retrospect fairly close to and anticipatory of one variety of reductive monism, or "animalism," now argued in some quarters.[14] On any such behavioristic-reductionistic view, the project of the autobiographer would be merely to recount past actions, show their relations to other actions both before and after, and give an overarching narrative that displays the shape of a life over time—all without explanatory recourse to ghostly prior causes standing behind, and invariably dualistically linked to, the actions being recounted.

As the philosophical world has seen, Wittgenstein's conceptually reorienting remarks avoid the Scylla of dualism and the Charybdis of behaviorism. And although any summary statement of his position (expressed as an "...ism") is instructively impossible, it can be said that throughout his writings he showed that the language-games of intentional action are intricately, and with an irreducible complexity, interrelated with the language-games of human behavior and—to speak too generally—action description.[15] Equipped with the view, or rather overview (Wittgenstein's *übersicht*), that we might gain of those myriad interrelations between language-games as a result of a consideration of cases (of precisely the kinds psychologically mimetic literature—such as Dostoevsky's[16]—affords), we might outlive our desire to thematically encapsulate the (mythical) unitary nature of the relation between intention and action, and correspondingly free ourselves of a misbegotten picture of autobiographical writing, i.e., the very picture of one-to-one action-causation, and hence of autobiographical truth, as examined above. But deliverance out of the grip of any such picture (to reemploy Wittgenstein's resonant phrase) is not easily won; it is most assuredly not a simple matter of deciding not to think that way anymore, or of being permanently relieved of any such dualistic misconception as a result of reading a few memorable remarks. The impulses to posit Nietzsche's antecedentia, to believe in Ryle's despised ghosts, to cling to a partially submerged belief that autobiographical writing will, with whatever local variations, fit the generic dualistic mold Wittgenstein labors to undercut; these are no more the kind of thing one simply

---

[13] The attack on dualism in various manifestations occurs throughout Ryle's *The Concept of Mind* (New York: Barnes and Noble, 1949), but see esp. chs. 1 and 6, "Descartes' Myth" and "Self-Knowledge," pp. 11–24 and 154–98 respectively.

[14] See, for an exemplary discussion of the issue, Eric T. Olson, *The Human Animal: Personal Identity without Psychology* (New York: Oxford University Press, 1997).

[15] I offer an account of why I find this a dangerously over-generalized way of putting the matter in *Describing Ourselves: Wittgenstein and Autobiographical Consciousness* (Oxford: Clarendon, 2008), ch. 5, "The Question of True Self-Interpretation," pp. 154–84.

[16] I offer a discussion of the philosophical import of this text in *Describing Ourselves: Wittgenstein and Autobiographical Consciousness*, ch. 4, sec. 3, "Wittgenstein Underground (and Dostoevsky's Notes)," pp. 140–53.

leaves behind than one simply drops, upon recognition that it is such, what a Freudian calls a repetition compulsion.

Thus Donald Davidson writes—and (leaving aside what "truer" means) truer words are rarely spoken—that "there is a picture of the mind which has become so ingrained in our philosophical tradition that it is almost impossible to escape its influence even when its worst faults are recognized and repudiated. In one crude, but familiar, version, it goes like this: the mind is a theatre in which the conscious self watches a passing show (the shadows on the wall)."[17] It would be both unfair and untrue to suggest that work on autobiographical, or more broadly first-person, epistemology has not in sum and substance advanced beyond the shadowy knowledge claims of Platonic troglodytes; it has. But the influence of the under-lying dualistic picture of selfhood is nevertheless, as Davidson rightly observes, still very much in evidence. It manifests itself, to take only one kind of example, very often when one inquires into, or puzzles over, the hidden and, as we say, real reason someone did something that we find piques our moral interest in such a way that we are led to search for a concealed mental intention that prefigures the action (so that understanding the action is thought to be wholly and exclusively a matter of matching it to its intentional cause). One might indeed think that the simple one-to-one explanatory schema has been appropriately cast out by the very fact that we are here seeking the real reason lying behind the false appearances of disingenuous antecedentia, and thus have overcome the one-to-one model. But the evident truth, corroborating Davidson's observation, is that the model is still intact, still playing out its repetitions in our thinking, at one remove: the "real" stands as the singular one behind the untruthful many, and while open specula-tion on motives assembles the explanatory candidates, conclusive, and thus closed, description (truthful in the first-person case, accurate in the third-person) of the action's motivating propositional-attitude content still provides that one real reason. The picture Davison refers to is thinly disguised in such cases, but by no means genuinely overcome and supplanted by a more capacious, comprehensive view. Much to his credit, it is just such a view toward which Davidson works in his writings on self-knowledge—and naturally these hold significance not only for understanding just what kind of thing (or, perhaps better, instrument) autobio-graphical language actually is, but also the key to the way out of the grip of the picture of selfhood Davidson identified.

The provenance, as is widely known, of Davidson's repudiation of what we might, given the ground covered in the previous two sections of this chapter, call explanatory singularism with regard to belief and the other propositional attitudes

---

[17] In "Knowing One's Own Mind," *Proceedings and Addresses of the American Philosophical Association*, 60 (1987): 441–58, reprinted in *Self-Knowledge*, ed. Quassim Cassam (Oxford: Oxford University Press, 1994), pp. 43–64; this passage p. 61.

76 LIVING IN WORDS

is found in Quine's influential argument against two dogmas of empiricism:[18] the second dogma concerned the very idea that there exists a one-to-one correlation between isolated sentences and an experience, or neatly circumscribed small set of experiences, that provides their confirmation or disconfirmation.[19] Rather than singular linkages between sentences and their exactly corresponding experiential verifications, "statements," Quine wrote, "about the external word face the tribunal of sense experience not individually but only as a corporate body."[20] Davidson, picking up the same ball and running with it into a different game, argued that the very idea of assigning a belief to a person, in isolation and one by one, on the basis of that person's verbal behavior, choices, "or other local signs no matter how plain and evident" is an extreme and hopelessly reductive mischaracterization of what we humans do: we do not assign single beliefs to persons on the basis of single bits of behavior or neatly circumscribed small sets of behaviors, nor do we—turning the point around, which Davidson does in his later writings on self-knowledge, thus showing the more pressing relevance of this for an understanding of autobiographical language—explain an isolated or single bit of behavior, what we generically (and thus dangerously) call an action,[21] by reference to a single and isolated belief or propositional attitude. On the contrary, as Davidson writes, "we make sense of particular beliefs only as they cohere with other beliefs, with preferences, with intentions, hopes, fears, expectations, and the rest. It is not merely, as with the measurement of length, that each case tests a theory and depends upon it, but that the content of a propositional attitude derives from its place in the pattern."[22]

This anti-reductive view, as stated, holds great significance for both biographical and autobiographical understanding and the central role words play in achieving that understanding; this holism acknowledges, and preserves a place for, the necessity of context in the understanding of human belief and action. And the often more intriguing cases of desire, intention, hope, fear, expectation, "and the rest," all must similarly be articulated in a wider context, or against the backdrop of related cases of the kind that Wittgenstein utilized. That, as stated, would lead us to reconfirm (as seen in the pragmatists in Chapter 1) but now in this context the rather significant conclusion that any atomistic, or conventionally empirical,[23] conception of experience would to that extent falsify the very experience it is attempting to recount. All of which is of direct relevance to the project of

[18] W. V. O. Quine, "Two Dogmas of Empiricism," reprinted in his *From a Logical Point of View* (Cambridge: Harvard University Press, 1953), pp. 20–46.

[19] For a full discussion of these issues, see Simon Evnine, *Donald Davidson* (Stanford: Stanford University Press, 1991); see esp. the lucid examination of the anomalism of the mental, and events and causal explanation, pp. 7–38, to which I am indebted here.

[20] Quine, "Two Dogmas of Empiricism," p. 41.

[21] See Frank B. Ebersole, *Things We Know: Fourteen Essays on Problems of Knowledge* (Eugene: University of Oregon Books, 1967), ch. 14, "Where the Action Is," pp. 282–304.

[22] This and the preceding quotation in Davidson's "Mental Events," in *Essays on Actions and Events*, pp. 207–27; this passage p. 221.

[23] As in the atomistic conception of experience articulated in Locke's foundational empiricist conception of perception, to take only one example.

understanding with some acuity both the nature and the power of autobiographical language.

But Davidson's point goes further: it is not merely an anti-separability thesis being advanced, contra classical empiricism and (that view in a more modern form) the notion of the verification of isolated observation sentences in Viennese positivism. It is rather, and far more interestingly, that the *content* of the experience cannot be accurately captured by any description that fails to acknowledge the interpenetration of lived experiences, the contextually specific seepage of one experience into another.

A sonic analogy is instructive: in recording studios, engineers speak of the sometimes unavoidable "bleeding" of one instrument's sound into the microphone recording another instrument, for example, the saxophone is audible, despite the engineer's best efforts at signal isolation, on the guitar track. And thus one cannot, even when "soloing" the track in the mixing booth after the recording, i.e., leaving that single recorded track on and turning off all of the others, hear the guitar in isolation without the perhaps faint but ineliminable presence of the saxophone. Human experience, rightly understood, is similar— sometimes for better and sometimes for worse—and thus any attempt to atomistically isolate an action, and then to similarly isolate its putatively corresponding ontologically hidden mental antecedent (an intention, desire, hope, fear, expectation, etc.) is to metaphysically mischaracterize the object under investigation, i.e., the lived life of a person. But the sonic analogy—like most analogies—is at the same time misleading in another sense. The sounds of the saxophone and guitar are, at the point of their origin, separate and distinct.

Davidson's memorable point on this particular score—and to repeat, extraordinarily significant for a clear-eyed and capacious recognition of autobiographical language for what it is—is that the interpenetration of experience, as defended as one part of his larger, expansively developed holism, is constitutive of the experiential state in question. The content of the propositional attitude is not discernible apart from the background, the context, and the nuances of the mind (again, Franz and Sabina, and William James perceiving an evolving constellation of relevant relations) undergoing the experience or performing the action in question. Mental content is *constituted*, Davidson argued, holistically. In determining what other people think, feel, intend, mean, and so forth, i.e., in—broadly speaking—biographical undertakings, we cannot get so far as to understand what the experience is without both the broader context within which the experienced action occurs and some grasp of the psychological nuances, among them the reverberations between the present action or experience and past similar or related ones as they, in countless distinctive ways, inflect the present case.[24] And

---

[24] There are clear parallels to this observation concerning the mutual inflections of related experiences throughout the writings of William James (ranging well beyond what we saw in Chapter 1), but especially in his magisterial *Principles of Psychology*; see, particularly in connection with the present

78   LIVING IN WORDS

similarly, any form of self-investigation that inquires into what we thought, felt, intended, or meant must display precisely the same contextual breadth and acknowledge the same constitutive power of relations and associations. In the absence of such full acknowledgment, the intervention of the self-observer would alter the subject—the observed self—beyond recognition. The mind would distort its image of itself through oversimplification.

The holistic character of the mental also lends strong support to Davidson's argument against the very idea of a psychophysical law, and this too is immediately relevant to our gaining of a fuller understanding of how autobiographical language really, i.e., apart from the prismatic distortions of simplifying theoretical templates, works. Any such law would require that an invariant relation obtain between a person's neatly individuated belief, desire, etc., and that person's neatly individuated action. Were such analyses not rendered impossible by the nature of the experience being recounted and narratively situated within the context of an encompassing life interpretation, this here again would make the task of the biographer or autobiographer vastly easier than it is—as well as far less interesting, because such projects in life-writing would thus not require the imaginative understanding and humane depth that they in fact do. They would proceed with the reductive barbarisms of a pseudo-science, claiming that person P in context C at time T with motivation M as a causal necessity performed action A according to psychophysical law L. And predictions of action, were the laws to actually hold invariably, would be as easy as after-the-fact explanations on the bare-boned model Davidson is opposing. Davidson's argument against this picture is not, it should be noted, based upon skepticism: the point is assuredly not, as some have argued, that at our present stage of knowledge, we are unable to perform the prerequisite parallel tasks of belief (etc.) and action-isolation like the music-studio engineer; his point rather is the much stronger claim that any such program in its fundamentals is hopeless. Indeed, he writes that if we are to pursue such a program, "What is needed in the case of action, if we are to predict on the basis of desires and beliefs, is a quantitative calculus that brings all the relevant beliefs and desires into the picture." And assessing the force of the irreducible and context-specific complexity of these beliefs and desires, adds "There is no hope of refining the simple pattern of explanation of reasons into such a calculus."[25]

And if one recognizes, as a result of Davidson's labors, that any such simplified explanatory program would be doomed to failure because the content of the relevant beliefs, desires, etc., as motivations for the actions to be explained

considerations, the section "The Stream of Thought," in *The Works of William James: The Principles of Psychology*, 2 vols., ed. Frederick Burkhardt (Cambridge, MA: Harvard University Press, 1981 [1890]), pp. 219–40 and 262–78.

[25] In "Psychology as Philosophy," in *Essays on Actions and Events*, pp. 229–44; this passage p. 233. This is helpfully discussed in Evnine, *Donald Davidson*, pp. 21–4.

would be schematic, anemic, and decontextualized, then if not to the image of science and that image's progeny in the form of (hopeless) psychophysical laws, where then do we look for a model of full-blooded and richly contextualized descriptions of belief, intention, desire, etc., of a kind that convey humane depth? The answer, of course, is literature, and from this perspective, having followed Davidson through only a few relevant reflections, we can discern one of the ways in which literary work is of irreplaceable philosophical value.

The philosophical psychology resident in, say, Henry James, George Eliot, and Dostoevsky can, within a context of philosophical interpretation, deliver what Davidson is calling for, and in doing so provide models—appropriate measures of psychological particularity—for our understanding of others and of ourselves. Davidson's holism (of a kind, given what we have seen in Chapter 1, that can and should be regarded as a latterday extension of pragmatism), and what he elucidates as the normative background, the broad and unencapsulable knowledge of how we can contextualize human action, how we understand people acting on belief, desire, and so forth, and how we go about determining what people think, is thoroughgoing, i.e., it is not a weak holism arguing only that isolated beliefs and action need to be understood in context, but rather the far stronger claim that there is no fundamental (and ontologically hidden) mental reality that exists prior to and apart from the human processes of contextualization, the normative background, constitutively powerful interactions between experiences, beliefs, and actions, and the ongoing and evolving other- and self-interpretive practices that in part constitute that normative background and the contexts of our action. Literature, of the kind to which I am referring in this context, when read with these philosophical issues in mind shows what Davidson refers to as the anomalism of the mental, and in doing so, it provides precisely the kind of conceptual therapy of which Wittgenstein spoke, allowing us to escape the grip of the picture Davidson articulated and to quell the self-blinding desire to formulaically express *the* relation between an intention and an action.

If, however, the atomistic boundedness of the human action, and the boundedness of the belief, desire, or other propositional attitude are illusory, what must we say about the description of the action, or series of actions, about which the autobiographer is writing? There is, we want to insist, a distinction, of the greatest importance to the autobiographer or biographer, to be made between a true and false description of an action or event. Yet we now have a reasonable foundation to say that this description cannot derive its truth in any simple way, i.e., where the true description of the narrowly circumscribed action corresponds to the similarly circumscribed mental state (belief, desire, etc.) that caused it, and to which it in a sense answers. That, as we have some reason to believe, is a philosophical myth.[26]

---

[26] The fuller reasons supporting this conclusion would take the form of detailed philosophical interpretations of Henry James, Eliot, Dostoevsky, and of course many others. I attempt to show

80   LIVING IN WORDS

How then does one proceed here, in pursuit of understanding how it is that one narrative of a life can be true (or truer—we will come to that) by contrast with another, or some words of self-description more accurate than others? One important step forward is to do here what Wittgenstein very often does in his later philosophical writings, to make progress by explicating what *not* to think, how not to conceptually structure the inquiry. And Davidson, in another part of his work, provides just the tools for this task.

As is well known, Davidson rejects the traditional dichotomy between scheme and content.[27] The ancestry of this distinction is, of course, extraordinarily distinguished, with Locke, Hume, and most powerfully Kant all developing one version or another of this dichotomy—in brief, that the senses provide us with uncategorized or raw experience, and that the mind constructs an order, organization, or structure for them. This dichotomy has generated the belief, severely criticized by Davidson, in the "given" in experience; that raw content then requires a corresponding mental power—a conceptual scheme or set of organizational categories—that refines the given into recognizable and nameable experiential content. Scheme-content dualism, applied to our present concern to seek out a better or fuller understanding of autobiographical speaking and writing, would import into the discussion at the very outset, or, more accurately, pre-position deep in the substructural foundations of the inquiry, a chronic doubt concerning whether or not we have, either as autobiographers looking at our own lives, or biographers looking at another's life, the correct scheme for the content. And this doubt quickly gives rise to both skepticism and a pernicious form of relativism: skepticism in that we would not know to which criteria to appeal in justifying the narrative assembly of a life according to this schema and not that one, and so we might never know the truth; and relativism in that we might to a degree ameliorate the chronic skepticism by embracing a relativism of schema impositions, saying (trying to turn a perceived necessity into a virtue) that it is a superior position to hold out the possibility of a number of diverging and even incompatible schema-generated life-narratives. Taken to its extreme, this would consign the autobiographer to a rather gloomily ineradicable self-doubt concerning not only the veracity of the self-narrative, but indeed whether there might have been some highly preferably alternative schema for the organization (we will look more fully into the issue of the architectural structuring of a life-narrative in the next chapter) of his or her entire life, thus feeling that, as there might well have been a sort of parallel universe in which one's life was markedly better than it seemed to its

---

something of the circumstantial complexity of the sentences that authors use to describe human actions in *Meaning and Interpretation: Wittgenstein, Henry James, and Literary Knowledge* (Ithaca: Cornell University Press, 1994), ch. 3, "Circumstances of Significance," pp. 84–102.

[27] See Davidson's "On the Very Idea of a Conceptual Scheme," in *Inquiries into Truth and Interpretation* (Oxford: Clarendon Press, 1984), pp. 183–98.

BOUNDARIES OF SELFHOOD   81

owner, one missed the real structural large-scale sense of one's own life while busily constructing a far lesser schema-driven narrative out of the raw givens.

The extreme constructionist-relativists among us will accept that—or something all too like it—as part and parcel of the human condition. Davidson's quite radical critique of this entire dichotomy in this respect performs the service Wittgenstein recommends: rather than claiming that there is only one schema for the given content of experience, and thus that the threats of autobiographical relativism are quieted but with the conceptual substructure still intact, Davidson goes beneath the one-versus-many schema debate, uprooting the pre-positioned element of the given itself (here again, Davidson is working in a manner deeply reminiscent of the pragmatists in Chapter 1) and thus preventing a false problem from generating false doubt.

This is not the place to conduct a full review of Davidson's argument on this score, but taking into account what we have already seen to this point about the nature of experience, one can fairly well predict the lines along which his position develops. Seeing that language-in-toto has often been conceived by philosophers and linguists[28] as either the schema itself, or as the intermediary metaphysical instrument that provides the connecting links between schema and content, Davidson provocatively writes, "There is no such thing as a language, not if a language is anything like what many philosophers and linguists have supposed."[29] And seeing that the mind has been construed in the terms he described above, where we see and interact not with the things and persons in the world but rather only with inner mental representations of them, Davidson argues that—in *this* sense—the mind doesn't exist either. Wittgenstein, who with exquisite care extricated himself from the Cartesian dualisms of twin ontological substances, mind and body, inner and outer, still said that there are indeed two differing categories, or types of language-games, the mental and the physical (and that if we try to reduce their interrelations to a formula we will invariably obscure far more than we illuminate). Davidson, within a larger context that seems mindful of this, succinctly says, "in my view the mental is not an ontological but a conceptual category."[30] Neither experience nor description is atomistic, psychophysical laws are a dream (or dehumanized nightmare), language is not the intermediary between scheme and content, and our interactions are with people and things, not with mental representations of them that place us at one remove. And the precontextual, precategorical, given in experience is an illusion, generated by a consort of conceptual pictures of the kind Wittgenstein labored against and the

---

[28] Most notably presented, and most widely discussed, as the "Whorf/Sapir hypothesis."

[29] In "A Nice Derangement of Epitaphs," in *Truth and Interpretation: Perspectives on the Philosophy of Donald Davidson*, ed. E. Lepore (Oxford: Basil Blackwell, 1986), pp. 433–46; this passage p. 446.

[30] In "Problems in the Explanation of Action," in *Metaphysics and Morality: Essays in Honour of J. J. C. Smart*, ed. P. Petit, R. Sylvan, and J. Norman (Oxford: Basil Blackwell, 1987), pp. 35–49; this passage p. 46.

82 LIVING IN WORDS

kind we saw Davidson rightly identify as persisting in their influence on our thinking far beyond the recognition of their worst faults. Working through (on a therapeutic analogy) the etiology of the skepticism and relativism engendered by the scheme-content distinction, and the very idea of the given before that, shows us, in the sense mentioned above, how not to construe the position of the autobiographer and our words of self-description. And this constitutes positive progress, for it clears the way for us to see, in a manner free of the prismatic distortions of simplifying conceptual templates, if not something quite as grand as the universal nature of autobiographical truth, at least what we call descriptive accuracy as we find it in contexts of first-person recollection and the recounting of experience.[31] Fittingly, a number of the foregoing points are readily discernible in autobiographical practice.

Exhausted by the prospect of returning to work on her biography of Roger Fry, Virginia Woolf turned to the sketching of a memoir. Calling it "A Sketch of the Past," she began by noting how many different ways there are of writing memoirs, i.e., that autobiographical writing resists any narrowly circumscribed definition—the extensive practices and the subtleties of the emergent issues invariably outrun any unifying (and thus for her reductive) theory. She then turns to the recounting of her first memory—the close-range perception of red and purple flowers on a black ground (which turned out to be the fabric of her mother's dress), but in recounting this Woolf just as quickly turns to what seems to be her other first memory, which she described in this way:

> If life has a base that it stands upon, if it is a bowl that one fills and fills and fills— then my bowl without a doubt stands upon this memory. It is of lying half asleep, half awake, in bed in the nursery at St Ives. It is of hearing the waves breaking, one, two, one, two, and sending a splash of water over the beach; and then breaking, one, two, one, two, behind a yellow blind. It is of hearing the blind draw its little acorn across the floor as the wind blew the blind out. It is of lying and hearing this splash and seeing this light, and feeling, it is almost impossible that I should be here; of feeling the purest ecstasy I can conceive.[32]

This passage offers a richly evocative description of the experience, but what is central to the experience—the sound of the repeatedly counted wave—itself offers testimony in favor of the interpenetration of related-but-distinguishable experience. The second repetition of the waves, "one, two, one, two," is clearly and

---

[31] This also builds on the discussion of this issue offered in *Describing Ourselves: Wittgenstein and Autobiographical Consciousness*, esp ch. 7, "Rethinking Self-Interpretation," pp. 223–57.

[32] Virginia Woolf, "A Sketch of the Past," in her posthumous *Moments of Being*, 2nd ed., ed. Jeanne Schulkind (San Diego: Harcourt, 1985), pp. 61–160; this passage pp. 64–5.

BOUNDARIES OF SELFHOOD   83

undeniably different from the first immediately preceding experience of them.[33] The boundary is not atomistically drawable, which is further reinforced by the significant linguistic fact that we would in other contexts call them "the same experience," whereas here—given the circumstances of this context—we call them different experiences. (One might say that "The same" is not, as this case shows, always the same.[34]) What does and does not constitute part of the experience, like the *Wrapped Reichstag* case, is context-sensitive,[35] and tellingly not determinable in classical empirical terms. Indeed, Woolf immediately comments that she could spend hours "trying to write that as it should be written, in order to give the feeling which is," she says, "even at this moment very strong in me."

Part of the problem she is identifying, and part of what makes autobiographical writing a fascinating human endeavor, is that the experience cannot, in a neat and bounded way, be successfully described apart from a description of the experiencer. She thus adds (as we saw in an epigraph to this volume), "Here I come to one of the memoir-writer's difficulties—one of the reasons why, though I read so many, so many are failures. They leave out the person to whom things happened." The misleading model of autobiographical truth that is semi-wittingly insinuated along with the picture of experience discussed above, i.e., that of accurately describing, one by one, events as they happened along with the fixed and bounded content of the propositional attitudes that caused, and thus explained them, is—to reemploy Davidson's word in this context, hopeless. Woolf adds to the preceding remark, resonant with everything we have considered, "The reason is that it is so difficult to describe any human being." And this, as we see in her case, includes

[33] Here again we see the close similarity to the conception of experience articulated in early pragmatism (especially in William James on repetition); the repetition of experience is often misleadingly construed as the exact reduplication of experience. James's discussion of the experience of rehearing thunder (where the second and subsequent hearings are all heard relationally against their predecessors) makes the point forcefully; on hearing the second clap, that as we can say is exactly like the first, in experience is not for the straightforward reason that we hear it as following the first and so the phenomenological difference is unavoidable.

[34] See George Pitcher, "About the Same," in *Ludwig Wittgenstein: Philosophy and Language*, ed. Alice Ambrose and Morris Lazarowitz (London: Allen and Unwin, 1972), pp. 120–39.

[35] Of course I am here concentrating on only one aspect of Davidson's philosophical writings for our understanding of autobiography. He does, at one point, offer identity conditions for events that are (in the sense that their conditions for sameness are specified invariantly) bounded—by having identical causes and effects. (He does later abandon this definition in favor of the definition put forward by Quine; for a helpful discussion of this see Evnine, *Donald Davidson*, p. 28.) This is, evidently, quite different both in spirit and letter from the broadly Wittgensteinian line of thought I am pursuing presently. If, indeed, one recognizes both (1) the impossibility of psychophysical laws (owing to the unspecifiability of the boundary around what philosophers call the propositional attitude (the motivating desire or belief, etc.)), and (2) the corresponding unspecifiability of the action boundaries (apart from a highly particularized context of inquiry about, or concerning, that action), one might reasonably ask why one would then turn to the pursuit of acontextual, definitionally invariant identity conditions for events. These—from a Wittgensteinian point of view—seem incompatible, but this is only the tip of another iceberg, that of fundamental differences and incompatibilities that separate Davidsonian and Wittgensteinian perspectives; again, my project here is to draw into service, and only for the present purpose of seeking some clarification of the philosophical problems of autobiographical language, one thread of Davidson's much more expansive intellectual project.

84 LIVING IN WORDS

herself. The autobiographical challenge is not accounted for exclusively in terms of complexity (although that accounts for a good deal of it); it is also that she herself does not know how or where to draw the lines around the experience, or set of interrelated experiences, that together convey and render intelligible and comprehensible to another the intricate and contextually nested phenomenological nuances that make that experience *that* experience. She adds, after attempting a brief account of who she was as a child, her family, a view of their habits and their expressive style, a clear statement of an epistemic limit on the part of this autobiographer attempting to convey that first memory: "But I do not know how much of this, or what part of this, made me feel what I felt in the nursery at St Ives."[36] And later in the same piece, Woolf observes that—despite the difficulty she has just reported in accurately conveying the content of her first memories—the autobiographical events that are at least comparatively easy to describe are from childhood, but only, she says, "because they are complete,"[37] meaning that it is only those relatively few early experiences that are not experientially interconnected across time and place, not inter-constitutively resonant, not in and of themselves irreducibly unbounded.

It is precisely this, I believe, that Nabokov has in mind when, in his autobiography *Speak, Memory*,[38] he writes "the supreme achievement of memory ... is the masterly use it makes of innate harmonies when gathering to its fold the suspended and wandering tonalities of the past." Such resonances, giving such irreducible and holistic experience an ineliminable part of its content—and any description of which would require an inclusion of these tonalities in order to be descriptively accurate, autobiographically true—are hardly unknown to literature. Of Chekhov's story entitled "Gusev," written while on a long sea journey home during which a typhoon nearly capsized the ship and two passengers died and were given over to the sea, James McConkey writes, "I think of this story—in which certain of his homeward experiences are transformed by the larger experience of the whole journey—as a record of what he has learned."[39] The story itself, a microcosm within which the constitutively powerful larger story inflects the particular episodes of the return—thus making them the experiences they are—is an argument for holism on both experiential and linguistic grounds. We understand the particular return episodes in the ineliminable context of the larger tale, and we grasp the particularized meanings of the words and sentences in those descriptions in a way ineliminably resonant with the larger context of the whole story—within, indeed, something strikingly like a richly expanded Wittgensteinian language-game. Without this, neither human understanding, of a kind worthy of the word "understanding," nor a grasp of the meanings of Chekhov's words, would be available. There is, of course, a great deal in Davidson's philosophical essays

---

[36] Woolf, "A Sketch of the Past," p. 65.   [37] Woolf, "A Sketch of the Past," p. 80.
[38] Vladimir Nabokov, *Speak, Memory* (New York: Vintage, 1989), pp. 255–6.
[39] James McConkey, *The Anatomy of Memory* (New York: Oxford University Press, 1996), p. 479.

relevant in one way or another to autobiography not so much as hinted at here, and much of that, if brought to bear here, would in fact be in tension with the broadly Wittgensteinian direction I have pursued; I have here emphasized the conceptually therapeutic nature of the few of Davidson's ideas I have tried to extrapolate to serve the interest of casting some light on the nature of autobiographical language. But the fact remains that his statement concerning the persistence of a philosophical picture—and I would add that this is too often undetected, shaping our pre-reflective intuitions about the nature of the self, of experience, and of that experi-ence's description in writing—is demonstrably true, and it is of the first importance to our removing, with the help of conceptually therapeutic literary antidotes, the motivated misconceptions that would block or severely distort our ultimately self-defining conception of that special circumstance in which the subject takes itself as its own object of inquiry.

Woolf knew that the difficulty of describing a human being was central among the problems faced by any biographer or autobiographer, and we have now seen that special difficulty, experienced by her in a literary context, given its philo-sophical articulation by Krausz and Davidson. Krausz helped us see that the boundedness of a human being (like a work of art) is not the simple matter we may have initially taken it to be, and Davidson helped us to see, again anti-reductively, that the boundedness of a human action is not as straightforward a matter as we may initially have thought. The interconnecting resonances, as Nabokov articulated the matter, are constitutive of an experience, so any accurate description of them would—against the atomistic picture of experience individuation—necessarily include them. Grasping the distinctive nature of this difficulty, as Woolf termed it, is itself to make positive progress in understanding self-description and what we might more broadly call the language of selfhood.

And so now, with the reflections of these two chapters behind us, we are ready to turn directly to the self-investigative project of clarifying the designs for, and then building, the structures that make our self-narratives coherent and that make them structurally stable enough to build further (in some cases retrospectively repositioning the past, in some cases prospectively appropriating the future) upon them. And—to ask a question that captures a central part of what it is to live a life[40]—how do we engage in what architects call "fast-track" architecture, where the foundations are laid down and the lower floors built before the upper stories are even designed? And how is the growth and development of a human self over and across time, where that process is described (for, as we shall see, good reasons) within an architectural vocabulary, interwoven throughout our more expansive autobiographical language?

---

[40] See Richard Wollheim, *The Thread of Life* (Cambridge, MA: Harvard University Press, 1984), pp. 162–96, where, in a chapter entitled "The Examined Life," he helpfully discusses the relation between the questions (a) what it is to live a life as a person and (b) what it is to understand that life as that person.

3

Structures of Autobiographical Understanding

So our questions at this point are: How might we then think of an architecture of selfhood? How might we think of the structuring elements of a life-narrative within which we understand that self? What is it to clarify the relations between parts as in an architectural plan? And is there a cathartic aspect to the achievement of a settled self-narrative?

3.1 The Thinker and the Draughtsman: Wittgenstein's Perspicuous Relations and "Working on Oneself"

In 1931, in the remarks collected as *Culture and Value*, Wittgenstein writes: "A thinker is very much like a draughtsman whose aim it is to represent all the interrelations between things."[1] At a glance it is clear that this analogy might contribute significantly to a full description of the autobiographical thinker as well. And this conjunction of relations between things and the work of the draughtsman immediately and strongly suggests that the grasping of relations is in a sense visual, or that networks or constellations of relations are the kinds of things (to continue the ocular metaphor) brought into focus by seeing the subjects—events, experiences, words about those events and experiences—in the right way.

This should not come as a surprise: emphasis on the visual constitutes a leitmotif running throughout Wittgenstein's writings from the earliest to the latest, and we have already seen that for him one way of making progress in philosophy is to loosen, and then—when philosophical problems have been dissolved—finally escape from the grip of simplifying "pictures" or conceptual templates that attempt to generalize beyond their contextually specific sphere of applicability. And that escape constitutes, and is the measure of, philosophical-therapeutic progress. Indeed, also in 1931 he wrote, in response to people saying that philosophy does not generally progress and that we are still working with, and on, the problems bequeathed to us from the Greeks, that those who level this

---

[1] Ludwig Wittgenstein, *Culture and Value*, ed. G. H. von Wright and Heikki Nyman, trans. Peter Winch (Oxford: Basil Blackwell, 1980), p. 12.

Living in Words: Literature, Autobiographical Language, and the Composition of Selfhood. Garry L. Hagberg, Oxford University Press. © Garry L. Hagberg 2023. DOI: 10.1093/oso/9780198841210.003.0003

complaint do not grasp why "this has to be so."[2] "It is," he writes, "because our language has remained the same and keeps seducing us into asking the same questions." And by seduction, he means the ensnaring grammatical "look" of language: "the verb 'to be'...looks as if it functions in the same way as 'to eat' and 'to drink.'" And we speak of "a river of time" and "an expanse of space," and we have the adjectives "identical," "true," "false," "possible," and so forth (as though we are attributing generic or Platonic properties to the particulars before us, thus giving rise to metaphysical questions concerning the nature not of the particular but of the Platonic quality it allegedly exemplifies or in which it participates). The achievement of conceptual clarity—of, in a word, perspicuity—is also a result of the kinds of philosophical therapy Wittgenstein has shown us throughout his extensive investigations. Indeed, that achieved perspicuity is very often described by Wittgenstein as a perspicuous *overview* ("übersicht"). Without such a clarification (itself of course initially an ocular term), "people will keep stumbling over the same puzzling difficulties and find themselves staring at something which no explanation seems capable of clearing up."[3]

The distinct kind of Wittgensteinian therapy being discussed here has, since the writings of John Wisdom, been likened to psychoanalysis, and this analogy has proven enlightening in a number of ways. But in characterizing Wittgenstein's work one should bear in mind that this is after all an *analogy*, and so it has its limits, can be taken too far, and can insinuate misleading expectations. This distinctive kind of therapeutic work, for example, can be taken as excessively personal (to the point that it loses force or value beyond the individual psychology within which this work takes place) and so be only of correspondingly limited value to the discipline of philosophy. This removal of Wittgenstein's contribution to a distant place far outside the field of contemporary relevance, to put it bluntly, is utterly false and equally utterly uncomprehending. Rush Rhees writes:

Philosophy as therapy: as though the philosopher's interest were in the personal disabilities of the perplexed: and as though he were not perplexed himself—as though philosophy were not discussion. Some remarks which Wittgenstein himself made are partly responsible for this. But he was suggesting an analogy with therapy; and he was doing this in an attempt to bring out certain features in the method of philosophy: to show the difference between what you have to do here and what you would do in solving a problem in mathematics or in science. It was not a suggestion about what it is that philosophy is interested in. If Wittgenstein spoke of 'treatment', it is the problem, or the question, that is treated—not the person raising it. It is not the personal malaise of the 'patient' which makes the perplexity or question important. What has led me to this

---

[2] *Culture and Value*, p. 15.   [3] *Culture and Value*, p. 15.

88   LIVING IN WORDS

perplexity is not my personal stupidity. Rather it is a tendency in the language which could lead *anyone* there, and keeps leading people there.[4]

At the same time, one wants to bear in mind that it is a philosophical or conceptual problem expressed in words, where those are the words of a particular person with a particular sensibility and experiential background as spoken or written in a particular context—all in such a way that the meaning of the words is inflected by those occasion-specific particularities. One can thus go too far in the direction Rhees is pointing out here as well and render the matter in what would then be insufficiently personal terms. The balance—fitting to a nuanced awareness of the multiform determinants of linguistic meaning—is and should be a delicate and in a sense bifocal one. We can learn something larger from following closely in the tracks of an individual or personal philosophical undertaking just as we can learn (to which we will return in Chapters 4 and 5—what we learn is not a matter of a list of ethical declarative propositions) from following in the tracks of a literary character.

So this affords, as we say, a glimpse of some of the content of Wittgenstein's remark about the similarity between the thinker and the draughtsman, but one needs to say more to show why and how the recognition of this similarity can prove helpful. As one part of the task of clarifying relations, the thinker assembles cases in which terms such as "identical," "true," "false," "possible"—and many other philosophically seductive words such as "intentional," "willed," "caused," "planned," "preconceived," "remembered," "recollected," "inner," "content," and "reflected upon"—actually function, and these uses, seen in particularized contexts, often show one of two things. They show either (1) that the uses of such terms in context are very remote from the philosophical or metaphysical use of the term in which the general or Platonic question concerning the nature of the thing (willing, causing, preconceiving, remembering, etc.) is asked, to such an extent that we come to doubt our grasp of the very meaning of the term in the metaphysical sense; or (2) that a wide range of intermediate cases *connects* the seductively puzzling case before us to related unproblematic cases, cases in which the criteria for the use, for the meaning, for the intelligible comprehension of the term or concept in question are given. This kind of "connective analysis," as it was called in the middle decades of the twentieth century, reveals the "interrelations between things," to return to Wittgenstein's words concerning the similarities between the thinker and the draughtsman. And both (1) the sense of disorientation to the language in which the general philosophical question is expressed, and

---

[4] In "Assessments of the Man and the Philosopher," in *Ludwig Wittgenstein: The Man and His Philosophy*, ed. K. T. Fann (New York: Dell, 1967), pp. 77–8. This passage is helpfully discussed in Ronald Suter, *Interpreting Wittgenstein: A Cloud of Philosophy, a Drop of Grammar* (Philadelphia: Temple University Press, 1989), p. 48.

(2) the gradually dawning awareness that the criteria that emerge for particularized usages of these philosophically troublesome words do not (legitimately) carry over to the generalized philosophical case, are themselves also measures of therapeutic progress.

A good draughtsman will clarify the relations between all the various parts in such a way that the drawing itself constitutes a perspicuous overview of the building—and incidentally here we see one philosophical motivation for architectural modernism (of precisely the kind practiced by Wittgenstein in his house for his sister in Vienna), in that the relations will be clearer in a design that is not obscured by ornamentation. But note that, for Wittgenstein as for the draughtsman, not everything visual, or visually "plotted," is by virtue of that fact good, i.e., conducive to perspicuity, be it philosophical or architectural. We have seen above that the "look" of words, the misleading parallelisms on their grammatical surfaces, can deeply mislead. Phraseology that for the user unwittingly insinuates metaphysical pictures in Wittgenstein's sense is a bewitchment of our intelligence by language that is itself pictorial, as in the phrase "the river of time." The visual, or our way of seeing, can be clarified, and it can also be profoundly clouded or confused. A good thinker articulates, in Wittgenstein's phrase, "all the interrelations between things," just as the good draughtsman shows them. If a bad one, then, obscures them, we might think, as an extreme example, of a draughtsman who generates drawings like those of M. C. Escher in depicting impossible or internally contradictory states of affairs and yet who does not realize he is doing so. (Imagine a construction company working from Escher's drawings—"slab," "pillar," "beam," and perhaps "what?!")[5] The "painting" of a false self-portrait in autobiographical writing, or creating what becomes a verbally encrusted, deceptive self-definition (where, to put it one way, the "dots" of a life-narrative are falsely or misleadingly connected), would constitute the parallel unrecognized anti-therapeutic failing in self-understanding.

Of the interrelations that the draughtsman perspicuously represents, some would be the formal elements within the design (say of an architectural façade). The strength, and the significance, of a vertical line is determined not only by its intrinsic height and width, but also by its interaction with the other verticals in the composition, its role in relation to horizontals, its placement within the illusory third dimension or the receding space of the image, and so forth. This makes the rendering deeply analogous to a language-game, to a circumscribed context or

---

[5] I am referring here, of course, to Wittgenstein's imagined microcosm of linguistic usage, the "builders' language"; see Ludwig Wittgenstein, *Philosophical Investigations*, revised 4th ed., ed. P. M. S. Hacker and Joachim Schulte, trans. G. E. M. Anscombe, P. M. S. Hacker, and Joachim Schulte (Malden: Wiley-Blackwell, 2009), §§1–38. See also Rush Rhees, "Wittgenstein's Builders," in *Discussions of Wittgenstein* (London: Routledge and Kegan Paul, 1970), pp. 71–84; Warren Goldfarb, "I Want You to Bring Me a Slab: Remarks on the Opening Sections of the 'Philosophical Investigations,'" *Synthese* 56 (1983): 265–82; and Norman Malcolm, "Language Game (2)," in his *Wittgensteinian Themes: Essays 1978–1989* (Ithaca: Cornell University Press, 1995), pp. 172–81.

90 LIVING IN WORDS

conversational microcosm within which certain verbal "moves" get their inter-relations to other moves, to previously said things, to things left unsaid, to what was implied, and so forth. Here the analogy is indeed deep, and it is perhaps no accident that Wittgenstein begins his discussion of language-games in *Philosophical Investigations* with, after all, the builder's language. And recall that he said there that "[i]t disperses the fog to study the phenomena of language in primitive kinds of application in which one can command a clear view of the aim and functioning of the words..." (*Philosophical Investigations*, §5). Simplicity here functions (as the removal of decoration does in an exactly parallel way in modernist architecture) as that which allows the important elements—elements that, like language, get their *point* within the context of their "utterance"—to be seen. Thus to grasp the larger context of the line, the vertical beam, the horizontal slab, is not an *addition* to the fundamental perception of that particular element—no, the context rather is an ineliminable prerequisite for seeing the beam or slab for what it is in the most elemental sense. The context, within which the archi-tectural element, or "gesture," makes sense or takes its point—or has its "inter-connections"—is just like the language-game within which the word, the phrase, the utterance, gets its point and, indeed, shows its meaning-determining "inter-connections." And to understand that word, or more likely the group of words used collectively, to see it within its meaning-determining web of interconnec-tions, is precisely to make the therapeutic progress described just above, i.e., to see both (1) the remoteness of this actual usage from the linguistically disoriented generalized question and (2) the illicit or linguistically deceptive borrowing of criterial legitimacy that can give those clouded expressions their appearance of sense, their Escher-like false plausibility. But there is more here as well: in the builder's language, we have the words "block," "pillar," "slab," and "beam" and that miniscule set is indeed stripped of the linguistic analogue of architectural decoration. But we also have the range of implication, the setting, the context, in which we already have to know what a word is, what reference is, what a name is, what an object is, what a command is, what a response is, and many other pieces of conceptual preparation that allow the reduction to (seeming) simplicity in the first place. And so again: those names of things function within a network of pragmatic relations, and they function—if they are spoken by human beings, not robots—within fields of irrepressible association and connotation like Franz and Sabina. The reduction to clarified simplicity is made possible by the much more expansive if presently unspoken network or field of pragmatic relations within which that reduction takes place. Precisely the same is true of life-narrative simplification: we may use a few words, or sentences, or paragraphs, to describe the narrative arc of a life. But those reductions, those encapsulations, live, and only live, within a much more expansive conceptual and relational network.

The relation between the work that the thinker does clarifying language and dispelling confusions and the work of the draughtsman or architect who clarifies

STRUCTURES OF AUTOBIOGRAPHICAL UNDERSTANDING 91

the design and its network of interrelations surfaces time and again throughout Wittgenstein's writings. We see it in the 1930 draft of the foreword to *Philosophical Remarks*, where—of his work there in the philosophy of language—he writes: "I am not interested in constructing a building, so much as in having a perspicuous view of the foundations of possible buildings."[6] Judith Genova[7] offers a helpful elucidation of what is meant by the important phrase "a perspicuous view." She begins[8] with Wittgenstein's remark from *Philosophical Investigations*, §5: "It disperses the fog to study the phenomena of language in primitive kinds of applications in which one can command a clear view of the aim and functioning of the words."[9] Genova writes: "Clarity's main virtue is that it reveals the connections between things and thus provides a view of the whole..." (p. 28). Here there emerges a link (also helpfully explained by Genova) between the later Wittgensteinian notion of perspicuity and the early work of the *Tractatus*: in *Tractatus* 6.45 Wittgenstein wrote, "To view the world *sub specie aeterni* is to view it as a whole—a limited whole. Feeling the world as a limited whole—it is this that is mystical."[10] The modernist gaze, as one might call it, could also be succinctly described in just these terms. To see all of the connections between elements perspicuously would be to see that architectural microcosm as a limited whole. And if god is, indeed, in the details, we need to scrutinize these in sharp focus. In *Philosophical Investigations*, §51, Wittgenstein wrote, "In order to see more clearly, here as in countless similar cases, we must focus on the details of what goes on; must look at them *from close to*." This passage is also discussed in Genova (p. 41), in which the need for a "double perspective," one that both moves in for fine detail and moves back for an overview, is well articulated. It is worth recalling in this connection that in 1938 Wittgenstein wrote the entry quoting Longfellow: "In the elder days of art,/Builders wrought with greatest care/Each minute and unseen part,/For the gods are everywhere," adding to it the parenthetical note to himself "(This could serve me as a motto)."[11] Also in the early 1930s he writes: "Remember the impression one gets from good architecture, that

---

[6] *Culture and Value*, p. 7.   [7] In *Wittgenstein: A Way of Seeing* (London: Routledge, 1995).
[8] In Genova, *Wittgenstein*, ch. 1, "Commanding a Clear View," pp. 27–54.
[9] This itself, I would suggest, is deeply analogous to the methodological imperatives of modernism in architecture: to strip away ornamentation, where this is understood as a form of concealment, in order to reveal the aim and functioning of the elements of the structure. It is instructive (as a parallel to subtle differences in distinctive styles of autobiographical reflection that then themselves become part of the subject of the autobiography) to consider varying manifestations of this aesthetic in, e.g., Mies van der Rohe in Chicago, Richard Meier's Getty Center in Los Angeles (where the phrase "an Italian hilltop town seen through the lens of Modernism" itself relationally situates, and thus brings out the properties of, the work), I. M. Pei's East Wing of the National Gallery in Washington, D.C., or Denys Lasdun's Institute of Education, University of London or his University of East Anglia campus. Seeing these works in light of each other better reveals the internal coherence of each (where the interrelated perception of a single element can suddenly lock together the whole composition), and looking closely at any example earlier on this list puts one in a better position to see the stylistic integration of examples later on this list. There are, of course, countless such comparatively enriching examples—just as there are in person comparisons or, in literature, character comparisons (to which we will return in Chapters 4 through 6).
[10] Discussed in Genova, *Wittgenstein*, p. 29.   [11] *Culture and Value*, p. 34.

92   LIVING IN WORDS

it expresses a thought. It makes one want to respond with a gesture."[12] And in 1942 he writes, further cementing the analogy between a purposive and meaningful human gesture made within a context that is in ineliminable part constitutive of its meaning and a "move" or gesture made within architecture: "Architecture is a *gesture*. Not every purposive movement of the human body is a gesture. And no more is every building designed for a functional purpose architecture."[13] Not every life-narrative is a vessel of self-knowledge and self-solidification. If too simplified, if too crude, if too careless, and if too inattentive, it may be a functional building but not architecture.

For Wittgenstein, when philosophers are misled by the tricks (although this word should not for a moment suggest that they are simple or superficial)[14] of language, they use (or misuse) words in ways severed from the particularized context that insures their intelligibility and gives them a point. And as suggested above, the criteria that make this intelligibility-ensuring point-making so much as possible reside within those contexts; they are not brought in with the individual words, item by item. If aestheticians ask of the nature of beauty itself, as at once an abstraction and a substantive, in such a way that no particular case is really relevant to the question, they sever the word from its conversationally embedded criteria in precisely this way. In such circumstances of conceptual vertigo, no answer will seem satisfying. And the real problem, as we can be quick or slow to see, lies with just what this therapeutic approach addresses, i.e., the question and

---

[12] *Culture and Value*, p. 22.   [13] *Culture and Value*, p. 42.

[14] On this point see Wittgenstein's observation in *Philosophical Remarks*, trans. Raymond Hargreaves and Roger White (New York: Harper and Row, 1975), pt. 1, sec. 2: "Why is philosophy so complicated? It ought, after all, to be *completely* simple.—Philosophy unties the knots in our thinking, which we have tangled up in an absurd way; but to do that, it must make movements which are just as complicated as the knots. Although the *result* of philosophy is simple its methods for arriving there cannot be so. The complexity of philosophy is not in its matter, but in our tangled understanding." Applied to the issue of self-understanding (of the kind that is the result of the autobiographical or self-directed therapeutic conceptual work being examined presently), this rightly suggests that the tracing of the etiology of conceptual confusion standing in the way of self-knowledge may well be no less complex and intricate than the life of a human being, but the end result may be a state of clarity that, in contrast to the complexity of the autobiographical labor that led to it, seems liberatingly simple. A deeply absorbing example of this process as it traces layered complexity and multiple resonances across and through a life, but then emerging in moments of perspicuous clarity, is shown in Bela Szabados, *In Light of Chaos* (Saskatoon: Thistledown Press, 1990). In the final passages of this autobiographical novel Szabados articulates the nature of the labor he has actually undertaken from the first page. In referring back to his reading of Popper and Marx with a group of young students and the impulse to not only understand the world but to change it, he writes: "Yes, change it, but for the better, and this can not be done in terms of rigid schemes and systems, where the voice is privileged, univocal, and the source of violence. Perhaps the real revolutionary is he who revolutionizes himself. I incline toward clarification, the dispelling of myth and confusion in the personal life and in the world—my conception is that of a cognitive therapist where the therapist is himself always the therapee, as well" (p. 124). This book also shows the considerable value, the meaning-determining significance, of the most fine-grained particularities in experience as they uniquely allow the kind of "tracing" mentioned just above; Szabados closes the book with the line "I resolve always to stay close enough to see the terrain clearly, never to lose sight of the terrain" (p. 125). (His epigraph is Wittgenstein's remark: "The lover of wisdom has to descend into primeval chaos and feel at home there.")

STRUCTURES OF AUTOBIOGRAPHICAL UNDERSTANDING   93

what it presupposes, and not the answer. Language, like architecture, imposes a certain discipline (of a kind that was brought into particularly sharp focus in the generation of J. L. Austin): not just *any* utterances constitute language, and not just any drawings constitute architecture. Wittgenstein wrote, in 1931:

> Philosophers often behave like little children who scribble some marks on a piece of paper at random and then ask the grown-up "What's that?"—
>
> It happened like this: the grown-up had drawn pictures for the child several times and said: "this is a man," "this is a house," etc. And then the child makes some marks too and asks: what's *this* then?

The "then" here, for present purposes, is especially interesting: the presumption on the part of the child is that *anything* can follow the intelligible drawings and be a drawing. Just as one might believe that, if we have a string of four or five sentences, then *any* combination of words following that would be a sentence, would be coherent, as well. But of course, the discipline intrinsic to language-games, be they linguistic or stylistic,[15] demands much more. The "interconnections" that both the thinker and the draughtsman make lucid need to be present, and they may be in the foreground or in the background. If in the foreground, they can be the formally evident relations between horizontals and verticals, within the plane of the façade, or the connecting thematic sinews between the episodes of an evolving conversation or narrative of any kind. But if in the background, they become in a sense even more interesting. (And this will cast light on the meaning-determining background of autobiographical language.)

Wittgenstein had long been interested in the inexpressible, the unsayable, and in his early philosophical work in the *Tractatus* this concept played a central role. In another remark, also published in *Culture and Value*, we see that by 1931, although he is clearly still interested in the concept of the inexpressible, he is now thinking of it in a different way, with a different inflection, or with a different web of meaning-determining interrelations. He writes: "Perhaps what is inexpressible (what I find mysterious and am not able to express) is the background against which whatever I could express has its meaning."[16] It is thus not now a distinctive kind of content that evades propositional encapsulation or expression, but rather the background against which what is expressed functions—and we can take this in linguistic or in artistic and architectural form. The word "mysterious" here

---

[15] I offer a discussion of the relations between linguistic and stylistic language-games (looking into stylistic limits, the range of possible moves within a style, what it is easy and what it is difficult to say within a context, and the perennially puzzling problem of the coherence of a larger style or individual work) in *Meaning and Interpretation: Wittgenstein, Henry James and Literary Knowledge* (Ithaca: Cornell University Press, 1994); I discuss the matter further in "Wittgenstein, Verbal Creativity, and the Expansion of Artistic Style," in *Wittgenstein and the Creativity of Language*, ed. S. Greve and J. Macha (London: Palgrave, 2015), pp. 141–76.

[16] *Culture and Value*, p. 16.

94 LIVING IN WORDS

plays an interesting role: we sense the presence of, or sense our reliance upon, that unspoken background—the evolved context of the expressive speech, gesture, or work of art or architecture—but it would prove exceptionally difficult to capture in any particular case everything, or even an approximation of everything, in the background that is, again, in good measure constitutive of the meaning of the expression. And what is "mysterious" is thus in a sense a kind of ghostly presence; without it our expressions would not possess the significance they do. It is as though both the thinker and the draughtsman are able to bring to mind some parts of that background, making some strands of a very complex weave explicit, perhaps particularly the elements of the background that resonate importantly with the expression at hand. Thus the literary critic shows how Dante would not have been possible without Virgil, who in turn would not have been possible without Homer. The architectural historian shows how Le Corbusier's villa would not have been possible without Palladio. The musical analyst shows how the possibilities realized in Mozart's *Six Quartets Dedicated to Haydn* would not have been possible without Haydn and yet not foreseeable by him either. The art historian shows how early analytical cubism would not have developed without late Cézanne. But each of these quick examples, as will be evident, are far too brief to really capture the point—and that *is* the point. To genuinely grasp the deeper significance of the great steps taken by Dante, Corbusier, Mozart, and Braque and Picasso, we need to *articulate* a great deal more. And of that vast background content—content that is expressible, but *not presently wholly recollectable*—what is and what is not necessary to articulate will be context-dependent. One particular line of inquiry will make one strand emerge in higher relief; another inquiry will bring out another, and there will not be a point at which this process is complete (which, incidentally, would explain one way in which works of art are inexhaustible). The presence of the past within the present works in precisely this way, and it gives a sense of what Wittgenstein meant by the word "spirits" in his remark of 1930: "The early culture will become a heap of rubble and finally a heap of ashes, but spirits will hover over the ashes."[17] (That for him extremely briefly describes the emergence of modernist culture.) A *sense*, perhaps an intimation, of that surrounding constellation of interrelations that led to, that made possible, what is now rubble and ashes, will persist. That we perceive a work of art or architecture within such a network of relations is implicit in another of Wittgenstein's remarks from 1930, and it reminds us of how important it is, in aesthetic contexts, to be aware of artistic or expressive acts of restraint, to be aware of what was possible, but not done—where what was possible but not done constitutes in a seemingly paradoxical way (only seeming, because acts of omission are nevertheless acts) part of the content of the work. We of course

---

[17] *Culture and Value*, p. 3.

understand persons, including ourselves, with similar layered combinations of commission and omission. "Today," he writes, "the difference between a good and a poor architect is that the poor architect succumbs to every temptation and the good one resists it."[18]

A language-game, be it linguistic or stylistic, opens many avenues of development, opens many possibilities. Understanding that game, in large part, is a matter of grasping those possibilities, seeing the artist within that expanding network, and seeing what he or she did do within that surrounding dense weave of what was left out, what was not done or, for the speaker, what was left *un*said. This too is not uniform: in some cases we will consider what an artist chose not to do (i.e., did not commit a crime of ornamentation within a context where a value on the perspicuous clarification of designed interrelations is paramount); in other cases, critically, we will see a possibility opened that the artist missed, one of which he or she was unaware in an aesthetically blameworthy sense, i.e., it will be something that should have been seen, or was seen by another artist with—as we metaphorically say—greater vision. This stands directly analogous to the fact that we may criticize a person, a speaker of language, for having failed to say what should have been said. Indeed Wittgenstein, in 1940, criticizes himself in just these terms, saying that in his modernist house for his sister he was working with quite a full awareness of the kinds of interrelations and possibilities within the stylistic game I have been discussing, but that a more romantic power is lacking in the building. He wrote: "the house I built for Gretl is the product of a decidedly sensitive ear and *good* manners, an expression of great *understanding* (of a culture, etc.). But *primordial* life, wild life striving to erupt into the open—that is lacking."[19] And if we have some difficulty imagining how the architectural expression of primordial striving might have been incorporated into that cool temple[20] of modernist internally generated consistency, then that itself gives a sense of the way in which possibilities are circumscribed as well as opened within a stylistic language-game.

Be that as it may, everything I have said so far in this excursus into the interrelations between philosophy and architecture is, in the sense of Wittgenstein's use of "background," its own background for what is I think of fundamental importance here in terms of elucidating a notion of therapeutic philosophical work and the kind of progress it affords, and then the relation of this to autobiographical writing and the articulate content of self-understanding

---

[18] *Culture and Value*, p. 3. Good architecture is thus, in a sense, a moral matter (in that there is a prescriptive sense of what ought, and particularly ought *not*, to be done). Conversely, Wittgenstein describes (some) moral issues in architectural terms: in 1937, he writes, "The *edifice of your pride* has to be dismantled. And that is terribly hard work." *Culture and Value*, p. 26.

[19] *Culture and Value*, p. 38. Also in 1934 Wittgenstein had written, "In my artistic activities I really have nothing but *good manners*" (p. 25).

[20] Wittgenstein described his philosophical work in these terms, further underscoring the commonalities between architectural and philosophical work. See *Culture and Value*, p. 2: "My ideal is a certain coolness. A temple providing a setting for the passions without meddling with them."

96   LIVING IN WORDS

and self-composition. He wrote, in 1931, this remark: "Working in philosophy—like work in architecture in many respects—is really more a working on oneself. On one's way of seeing things. (And what one expects of them.)"[21] The phrase "really more a working on oneself" itself invites a changed way of seeing work in philosophy. Working on oneself can mean any kind of autobiographical—in the broadest sense—inquiry, where one works toward a more capacious grasp not only of what one has done, and why one has done it, but also how one has come to hold the views one does, how pressures on one's thoughts have manifested themselves in various beliefs and actions, how what one said was opened—as a possibility—by earlier things one said, and how one has understood the trajectories of one's own life projects. And of course such autobiographical subjects can easily take a more explicitly philosophical turn: they can turn to how one pictures the act of introspection, how one pictures meaning in language (and often, by extension, how one pictures meaning in the arts),[22] and indeed how one conceives of, pictures, a human being. All three of these of course directly interact with any developed conception of autobiographical language.

But more precisely with regard to seeing all of the foregoing remarks as background for a point to be made presently, an autobiographical project can—and very often does—take the form of "representing all the interrelations between things," like the work of the thinker and of the draughtsman. Or at least, as we have seen, representing some of those relations: the interrelations in the web of one's background will stretch beyond any particular autobiographical iteration. And various strands of that life, various collections of past experiences, will be brought into self-interpretative play with, will be enlivened by, a present or recent event whose meaning is in significant part constituted by those past resonances or whose content is in significant part determined by those sinews of association. (Here, incidentally, a deep similarity between autobiographical work of this kind and curatorial work comes to the surface: creative juxtaposition in the display of artworks just is the act of looking for, thinking through, and then making visible resonant relations between particular objects—where the very constitution of the objects is in part determined by those emergent relational interconnections.)

Similarly, like the progress-measuring escape from simplifying "pictures" that would govern our thought and preclude the patient achievement of conceptual clarity, any simple or truncated narrative of a life, or of an episode in a life, will in a

---

[21] *Culture and Value*, p. 16.

[22] I offer a study of various ways in which preconceptions concerning linguistic meaning powerfully shape conceptions of artistic meaning in *Art as Language: Wittgenstein, Meaning and Aesthetic Theory* (Ithaca: Cornell University Press, 1995); I pursue this further in "Word and Object: Museums and the Matter of Meaning," *Philosophy*, Supplementary Volume: *Philosophy and Museums* (Cambridge: Cambridge University Press, 2016), pp. 261–93. Of such connections Wittgenstein notes: "Phenomena akin to language in music or architecture. Significant irregularity—in Gothic for instance (I am thinking too of the towers of St. Basil's Cathedral). Bach's music is more like language than Mozart's or Hayden's ..." (*Culture and Value*, p. 34).

parallel way blind us to the contextually specific particularities that not merely add to the experience, but again, as we have seen in the foregoing, make it what it is. The draughtsman elucidates the complex interconnections; viewing the self's past for its significance in the present, for our present self-understanding, is much like experiencing art in three dimensions, for example viewing architecture or sculpture, precisely because, in moving around and through it, we constantly change our vantage point, which in turn changes what does and does not come into focus, what does and does not take a foreground or background position. Of doing philosophy, Wittgenstein wrote in 1937: "I find it important in philosophizing to keep changing my posture, not to stand for too long on one leg, so as not to get stiff,"[23] which is a nice way of embodying the point concerning the conceptual need for shifting vantage points and assembling a larger mosaic of initially separate perspectival positions; "stiffness" in our present case would thus constitute the hardening of one set of presently perceived relations into what we mistakenly take as the final, singular, definitive, and complete life-narrative.

Also similarly, Wittgenstein claims that what we need in philosophy is a perspicuous overview, where this, as we have seen, is not meant in the sense of a generalized, Platonic concept to which no particular case is genuinely relevant, but rather where that overview is the result of patiently considering cases under that concept, seeing how it functions *in situ*. If we desire a fuller understanding of our own courage or cowardice, or pride or prejudice, we need an overview of the self's words and deeds *in that sense*. This constitutes a kind of connective analysis of the self's past, of one's intellectual genealogy. One may liken this kind of conversation with oneself to creative curatorial work, as I have just done above, but instructive parallels may also be seen in creative artwork itself: in the original Mozart scores, for example, one sees insertions and emendations written in later, over the top of what was first written, in such a way that the revision renders more perspicuously a relation, or thematic or harmonic linkage, that was initially less visible than the revision made it. And it is striking here that one can tell just where Mozart had the thought concerning the relation—in some cases seeing it and in some cases making it, with a rather hazy line between creation and discovery—by the sharpness of the quill; this allows a close reader of the score to see precisely where the thematic material in front of him in a sense realigned, or brought out in higher relief, the earlier material now better, or more clearly, interrelated to it. This is precisely the process one sees in Iris Murdoch's diaries, where the pen or pencil used shows when a passage or entry was revised in light of subsequent reflection or realization. Those changes were by no means wholesale revisionism. Much more interesting than that, she subtly reshaped her description of past experience in the light of later descriptions, themselves shaped by orderings and

---

[23] *Culture and Value*, p. 27.

98 LIVING IN WORDS

interrelations in her autobiographical memory. (Some of these, one can see, are efforts to reconcile her past self with her own descriptions of her present self; this is thus a project particularly like that of reassessing Picasso's early work in the light newly cast by what we now know of Braque, etc.)

We can also be misled by the surface appearance of a person's actions—or in the case of self-knowledge, our own actions—just as we can be misled, as Wittgenstein has shown, by the surface appearance of words. Both the thinker and the draughtsman (if good) clear up these confusions, and the author of a *Bildungsroman* takes both of these roles as she or he contemplates the design, the building, the construction of a life and the thinking, the pressures on thought, that shaped the construction. And again, like a good architect, the good *Bildungsroman* author makes these interrelations clear.[24] Some retrospective constructions of a life's story, its purpose, its developmental trajectory, will, like Escher's drawings, seem initially plausible and yet in the end fail to genuinely cohere, however good they may look on the level of surface design. If ultimately acceptable, we will—as a project that is at once philosophical therapy and autobiographical "work on oneself"—see the connections between the parallels in our personal experience to a series of verticals, a strong horizontal, a set of receding planes, a reiterated angle, a niche, a stylobate, and so forth. And coming to understand what we did do, what we did not, what was possible that we did see, and what was possible that we did not, are all ways of earning self-understanding of a kind that, as narrative girders, stabilize identity. So in a distinctly architectural sense, these are language-games of the self, and we come to comprehend the range of possible moves within a person's character in a way strikingly parallel to language, to language-games. And here as well, grasping the larger context, the relevant sections of a person's experiential background, is not an *addition* to understanding the action in question, for it is within—and here again only within—that relational matrix that the interconnections that make the action what it is become visible. (This way of seeing autobiographical labor is also a corrective to the atomistic or classically empirical conception of experience: as we saw in Chapter 1 with William James and his colleagues, relations are not after the fact; rather, they *are*, in equal part, the fact.) When we speculate about how we ourselves, or another, might have been different, we imagine a different set of experiences, or "interconnections," grafted by contingency onto what we think of as the foundations of that person's character. This, I think, is more than merely incidentally reminiscent of Wittgenstein's metaphorical remark concerning his philosophical work that he is interested, not in constructing a building, but in gaining a perspicuous view of

---

[24] Such progressive interrelational clarifications are precisely what a reader sees while closely following the development of the eponymous protagonist in Goethe's great (and arguably first and most influential of the genre) *Bildungsroman, Wilhelm Meister's Apprenticeship*, ed. and trans. Eric A. Blackall in cooperation with Victor Lange (Princeton: Princeton University Press, 1995).

STRUCTURES OF AUTOBIOGRAPHICAL UNDERSTANDING   99

the foundations of possible buildings. And like the child's doodle after the grown-up's drawings, not just any string of words makes sense, nor does any construction constitute architecture. For deeply parallel reasons, not every undisciplined interpretative suggestion about a person, or about, reflexively, the self, constitutes insight or self-therapeutic progress.[25] The radical relativist's undisciplined speculations, or the extreme postmodernist's "any description goes as well as any other" ethos, turned loose on questions of self-interpretation, are in the realm of human understanding all too like the child's scribbles.

As has emerged already, much of our language of self-understanding and self-description is ocular, and this, as we have now glimpsed, is in differing ways, in differing contexts, either conceptually incarcerating or therapeutically liberating. But it does in any event seem helpful to find a way to speak of what Wittgenstein called—in his later sense of the term—the "mysterious," the background against which our gestures, verbal or artistic, literary or autobiographical, make sense. That expansive and unbounded network of relations gives our person-defining experience the character, the resonance, and indeed even the identity, it has. And yet it lies beyond the reach of the fully sayable at any one time, in any single context of inquiry. Our way of seeing, with regard to our interpretation of ourselves and of others, can change according to which parts of that relational network we focus upon, which parts we make—like the work of the thinker and the draughtsman—particularly clear, which parts we render perspicuously. And what we expect, hope for, or demand of others and of ourselves is just a function of such relationally interweaving inquiry. Skeptics, aware of the limitless nature of this background, might leap to embrace a blanket doubt concerning the very possibility of our knowledge of the self as well as of another. But while a full and final comprehensive articulation of the content of that background may not fall within the bounds of possibility, we need not for that reason embrace skepticism. Through the conjunction considered here of the work of therapeutically inflected

---

[25] Richard Wollheim offers a helpful discussion of some of the constraints under which such an interpretation may proceed in *The Thread of Life* (Cambridge, MA: Harvard University Press, 1984), pp. 171–7. He writes: "That interpretation, properly understood, has something to tell us about the structure of the mind derives from the constraints under which it operates. In all domains interpretation is possible only under constraints—constraints imposed upon the interpreter, and specifying conditions that interpretation of one and the same text, or one and the same legal system, or one and the same person, must satisfy" (p. 171). But lest this be misunderstood, a special virtue of Wollheim's discussion is that he does not import a false (because radically oversimplified) model of belief-consistent rationality as the primary governing constraint in the interpretation of persons; rather, he rightly (and realistically) suggests, "Instead of trying to devise in the abstract constraints upon interpretation intended to capture rationality, what we should do is to examine the actual processes by which persons do regulate, or try to regulate, their beliefs and desires, and then argue back to the constraints. It is to such processes, which are in turn part of leading the life of a person, and not to some idealized rationality, that the constraints upon interpretation must ultimately answer" (p. 173). Wollheim does not say so here, but this suggests why the close and exacting philosophical study of literature, i.e., particularized and highly detailed descriptions of the nuanced moral psychology of characters that show at a reflective distance what it actually is to lead the life of a person, is of irreplaceable value.

100 LIVING IN WORDS

philosophy and the conceptual model of architecture, we can at least begin to see that the projects of self-knowledge and of other-knowledge, are—although they may not have fixed endpoints—possible within our language-games of human understanding. Like works of art—and for parallel reasons—the project may be inexhaustible (and that is itself a wondrous thing). But then Wittgenstein also wrote, in 1938, "In philosophy the winner of the race is the one... who gets there last."[26]

Wittgenstein's work on the house in Vienna for his sister was unquestionably architectural work, just as it was philosophical work. And where these converged, where the labors of thinker and of the draughtsman came together, it became a distinctive kind of autobiographical work, or "work on oneself," as well. Such work is driven by the desire for hard-won therapeutically liberating interrelational clarification. But with those thoughts in place, we should now ask: what resources might an autobiographical thinker, by analogy to the draughtsman who strives to make all the relations between the elements of the construction clear, draw upon in rendering the structural interrelations of a life perspicuously? To pursue this question we will turn back to the classical philosopher who did the most to cast light on the structuring of a life's narrative in drama—where that narrative serves as both a mimetic reflection of, and in a special sense structural model for, lives of our own.

3.2 Aristotelian Frameworks

It is in Aristotle's *Poetics*[27] that we find an account of narrative rich enough to account for the deep and abiding interest we take in the stories of lives past and present, literary and real. With this interest we tend to bring strong intuitions concerning the distinction mentioned above between the truth or falsity of any given life-narrative: veracity is a function of, as the phrase goes, "telling it like it was." And false narrative content is, conversely, made false by virtue of deviation from this verisimilitude. But we also sense a unique difficulty with maintaining this somewhat simplistic criterion when the subject turns from biographical to autobiographical narratives. The problem we sense here was encapsulated by Wittgenstein in 1937: "You cannot write anything about yourself that is more truthful than you yourself are. That is the difference between writing about yourself and writing about external objects. You write about yourself from your own height. You don't stand on stilts or on a ladder but on your bare feet."[28]

---

[26] *Culture and Value*, p. 34.
[27] Aristotle, *Poetics*, trans. Stephen Halliwell (London: Duckworth, 1987).
[28] *Culture and Value*, p. 33.

STRUCTURES OF AUTOBIOGRAPHICAL UNDERSTANDING   101

Of course, as we already know at this point in this discussion, "telling it like it was" is nowhere near as simple a matter as that formula makes it sound (the Russian saying "He lies like an eyewitness" serves as an initial corrective). But these are not the problems, or at least problems to be treated directly, for the moment. The problems that we will presently approach directly emerge in the bringing together of (a) parts of the profound analysis Aristotle provides of the power of narrative form and the structure of a gripping—or indeed satisfying, in a distinct sense to be considered—narrative representation of past events with (b) the problematic self-descriptive circumstance Wittgenstein articulates. So first, what are the relevant elements of Aristotle's account?

In his first sentence, Aristotle brings into play the notion of the unity of plot that is prerequisite to a successful composition (and that, fundamental among his tasks, is explaining such unity).[29] And the mimetic depiction—for us the representation of the self within the narrative—will be, he says with an importance reaching far beyond what he briefly says, of people *in action*.[30] This, as we shall see more fully below, is of vital importance precisely because the representational content of the self-narrative not only is not, but could not be, static: no human action of any significance can be described, or more importantly understood for what it is in the first place, without seeing its teleology, without seeing it within a larger temporal frame of reference (as we saw in some detail in Chapter 2 above). A frozen moment, abstracted from its context, would capture the person with an arm up. A representation of a person in action would depict a person waving a greeting, or warning, or giving the number of persons present (by the number of fingers held up), or indicating that he is unarmed, or "conducting" the music he hears in his earphones, or humorously emulating Plato in Raphael's *School of Athens*, or countless other things depending on the relational threads that weave that representation into a narrative. The description "a person with his arm up" does not describe a person in action, but rather a bodily disposition. Any of these latter, even slightly fuller, descriptions do describe a person doing something. Moreover, we will not in ordinary contexts speak here of a difference between the factual matter of his arm being up and the interpretative (and thus less epistemically firm) matter of the contextualized description. There are cases in which we would speak of interpretations of his actions in far more specific ways stemming from far more specific contextualized prompts. But—particularly important for what is to follow—the fact-versus-interpretation template is not generalizable to anything like this level. The perception or recognition of what the person is doing within a narrative structure does not by virtue of that narrative positioning reduce the factual content of the narrative: indeed here, from this angle of approach also,

---

[29] Aristotle, *Poetics*, p. 31.   [30] Aristotle, *Poetics*, p. 32.

102 LIVING IN WORDS

we see our now-familiar point that we would not so much as know what the action in question was without it.

Aristotle offers a naturalistic account of the pleasure we humans take in mimesis, emphasizing the "great pleasure"[31] derived from the exercise of the understanding occasioned by the contemplation of each element in a mimetic representation. The reasoning faculty, applied to the elements of the mimetic object, works out the interrelations between them, taking an intrinsic pleasure in the solving of the "puzzle," or the assembly of the "mosaic," that in part reveal the unity of plot or the coherence of the object. It is, one can see fairly readily, as if in these remarks Aristotle were actually describing the distinctive character of autobiographical writing itself. And his remark concerning the pleasure we take in mimetic objects, even where we are unfamiliar with the original that is therein depicted (where we take pleasure, for example, in that representation's craftsmanship or color), has its direct analogue in life-narratives as well. For we may know a given narrative to be inaccurate, yet still be very much amused by the cleverness of the reasoning that put the elements of the narrative together in a manner resulting in the false narrative portrait.

But it is, of course, tragedy of which Aristotle is writing, and he famously says of that distinct genre: "Tragedy, then, is a representation of an action which is serious, complete, and of a certain magnitude ... and through the arousal of pity and fear effecting the *catharsis* of such emotions."[32] He has already said that the comic is one species of the shameful, and that while the comic mask is ugly and misshapen, it does not express pain. Epic, by contrast, addresses ethically serious subjects. It is telling, I believe, that no purely or exclusively comedic, or comically diverting, life-story—a biography—would meet with our genuine or wholehearted approval. We would see it, indeed, as a comic *mask*.[33] (And if the biography were both wholly comedic and wholly accurate as a depiction of the life, we would then not wholeheartedly approve of the life.) So the representation of the action (itself, as we have briefly seen, woven into its context with narrative threads), if compelling, if convincing, needs to be serious or, like epic, inclusive of ethically serious considerations. And, he next says, it needs to be "complete," or, as he adds a bit latter, "whole,"[34] in that it has a beginning, middle, and end.

As if giving the necessary and sufficient conditions of narrative (there is, by extension from tragedy, a sense in which he is here doing precisely that), he shows that this matter—like everything in Aristotle's more accessible writings—is not as simple, and far more interesting, than it initially appears. A beginning is characterized as that which "does not have a necessary connection with a preceding

---

[31] Aristotle, *Poetics*, p. 34.   [32] Aristotle, *Poetics*, p. 37.

[33] For example, imagine the monodimensional character of a biographical account of the life of Peter Sellers that included a full description of his phenomenal comedic talent but that omitted any mention of his tortured sense of personal failure, or a life of Charlie Chaplin that was nothing but, as we say, fun and games, or sweetness and light.

[34] Aristotle, *Poetics*, p. 39.

event," but that in and of itself has the potential to give rise in an organic or naturally evolving manner to a further circumstance, situation, or occurrence. Of course the beginning will have a connection with prior events, but not a *necessary* one, that is, it is a point at which we can begin a narrative without requiring the answers to unavoidable questions concerning the causal linkages that led to it in order to understand the actions depicted for what they are. But the linkages that draw our attention will point forward, and not back, in time. A musical theme, from which variations are drawn, is seen for the possibilities it houses, for the developmental trajectories we can see moving out from it. To write, "I sing of warfare and a man at war" is to open twin trajectory lines along which the *Aeneid*[35] can unfold, both of the universal theme of warring conflict and of the exemplification of that universal within the particular story of Aeneas. By a middle, Aristotle means events that exhibit causal connections in both temporal directions; in such cases, in order to understand the depicted action for what it is, we need to see it, in a sense, bifocally, i.e., we need to grasp both the causal antecedents that made it possible or necessary (a separate chapter could be written on that distinction) and the causal linkages running both from it and through it. By "from" it, I mean something like the effects, in *Oedipus Tyrannus*, of Jocasta saying to Oedipus, midway through, "May you never know who you are." This opens a space, it initiates a teleological or developmental line, where we now watch for the incremental steps of Oedipus' progress in self-knowledge to follow those of Jocasta's, or to gradually fill the epistemic space opened by her remark. (The tragic end of the play occurs when that space is filled.)[36] But also, as a middle, "through," since we could not get so far as to comprehend any part of the significance of Jocasta's words were it not for what came before, including actions—like the killing of the old man at the crossroads—performed by Oedipus that he himself does not see within a larger frame of reference as actions with causal antecedents leading back to the prophecy he did so much—or thought he did so much—to avoid. An end, for Aristotle, is an event or circumstance which occurs naturally as a consequence of, or within what we might call the "possibility field" opened by, preceding events and their developmental trajectories. And—even if Aristotle does not quite explicitly say this—it seems reasonable to believe that the degree to which all of the developmental lines are brought to closure in this way, the extent to which all the strands are woven together with none left dangling, will be positively correlated to the depth of cathartic satisfaction we take in the drama, giving us the special sense of completion, of, indeed, narrative wholeness.[37]

---

[35] Virgil, *The Aeneid*, trans. Robert Fitzgerald (New York: Vintage, 1984), p. 3 (line 1).

[36] I discuss this matter of the gradual filling of epistemic space in "In the Ruins of Self-Knowledge: Oedipus Unmade," in *The Oedipus Plays of Sophocles: Philosophical Perspectives*, ed. Paul Woodruff (Oxford: Oxford University Press, 2018), pp. 65–98.

[37] One extensive study of this sense of completion may be found in Frank Kermode, *The Sense of an Ending* (Oxford: Oxford University Press, 1967).

104 LIVING IN WORDS

We have then, thus far, in Aristotle's famous definitional passage the ideas of: (1) the representation of an action; (2) the seriousness of it; and (3) the completeness of it. He next mentions (4) "of a certain magnitude." Scale emerges as relevant to aesthetic evaluation in a number of places in Aristotle's text, and he emphasizes the need for the contemplated object to fall within the thresholds of human perception and attention. That which is too small to be perceived in anything but an instantaneous way, and that which is too large to allow contemplation as a whole, are both found objectionable. Plot structures, he says, "should be of a length which can be easily held in the memory."[38] A life-narrative the length of a haiku may indeed prove interesting as a literary miniature, but it could not—for reasons of the lack of mimetic fit between its scale and the scale of what it purports to represent—command serious respect *as a life-narrative.* (It is for this reason that extremely truncated and grossly simplified narratives of significant life events can prove so demoralizing, insufficient in attentiveness, and indeed in certain contexts morally offensive.) And on the other threshold, we can (whatever our ultimate judgment) imagine problems in seeing the shape of a life as narrated in, say, Pepys or Proust. But Aristotle's fundamental point here concerns our inability, owing to scale, to derive from the very small or very large work the sense of completeness or wholeness, so this fourth criterion in fact serves the third. However, his last criterion, (5) the arousal of pity and fear thus effecting a catharsis, have proven by far the most contentious.[39] It is not my intention to enter that debate here, but rather to suggest, for the particular purpose of explaining the nature of the gratification and satisfaction we derive from successful narrative orderings or structurings, an extension of the concept. This criterion perhaps runs beyond what Aristotle intended (although that itself is by no means a clear matter), but it can at least be said that this extension is built from the explanatory materials Aristotle provides.

In Aristotle's definition above of tragedy that includes the reference to catharsis, there are two further important qualifications. The first is that the tragedy will proceed "in language which is garnished in various forms in its different parts" (his ensuing discussion of metaphor is one important part of what "garnished" means, along with the more obvious matters of rhythm and melody); the second draws a contrast between acted drama versus narrative, and he specifies that the representation of the action will be "in the mode of dramatic enactment, not narrative."[40] This last qualification would seem to draw a rather stark contrast between enactment and narrative, where only the former is suited to achieve the end of catharsis. But Aristotle was speaking here *particularly* of the emotions of

---

[38] Aristotle, *Poetics*, p. 39.

[39] For a particularly helpful study of this much-disputed concept, see Jonathan Lear, "Katharsis," *Phronesis* 33:3 (1988); reprinted (as "Catharsis") in *A Companion to the Philosophy of Literature*, ed. Garry L. Hagberg and Walter Jost (Oxford and Malden, MA: Wiley-Blackwell, 2010), pp. 193–217.

[40] Aristotle, *Poetics*, p. 37.

pity and fear. Now, it may well be the case that, because of the unmediated presence in the enacted drama of both the object of the fear and the object of sympathetic pity (again, where those objects are physically portrayed and not only narratively described), the gripping power of enactment is greater.[41] But if we expand the reach of the cathartic experience beyond the narrowly defined emotions of pity and fear, however, the picture changes.

The representation of an action, for Aristotle, is performed by agents, who, as he says, "must be characterized in both their character and their thought."[42] It is through this combination of thought and character that we are then enabled to "judge the qualities" of their actions. The mimesis of the action is a product of—importantly—plot structure. This observation is only initially counterintuitive: it may seem at first that it is the determinate and isolated action itself that should be re-presented as the mimetic content. But if, as we saw above, the action can only truly be understood for what it is within an enlarged frame of reference or within the context that gives it its significance, tracing back through the threads of its antecedents and tracing forward through its consequences or to what it makes possible, then indeed, as Aristotle says, it is the plot structure that constitutes the mimetic object (he here defines the plot structure as "the organization of the events"). And within that narrative flow, the characterization works with the plot structure, showing us the thought of the agents and thus allowing us, as spectators, both vicarious imaginative entry into their lives and a moral understanding of who they are and why they do what they do. Here again, all of this could function equally well as an analysis of the elements of writing, or thinking through, a life-narrative, biographically or autobiographically. And the emotionally engaging power of that plot, that narrative, will—Aristotle says himself[43]—be determined by the essential components of the plot structure. (He cites here reversals and recognitions, such as the washing scene in the *Odyssey*). Thus, on second look, the emotional power of the drama is hardly limited to the embodied enactment of the objects or provocations of fear and pity, but is, to an equal or in fact greater extent (he says that plot structure is the soul of tragedy), a result of plot structure. It is thus the power of *form*, of what he called the ordering of events (where this means all that we discussed concerning the beginning, the middle, and the end, and the sinews of their interconnections, along with the teleologically embedded character of a represented action), that is felt in our imaginative engagement with a life-story, with plot. And such experiences, I want to suggest, are to greater and lesser

---

[41] And even this is not incontrovertible; consider Tolstoy's case of the boy and the wolf (in which the boy tells, in an unfolding narrative sequence, the story of his sudden and frightening encounter with a wolf, thus engendering in his hearers the feeling of fear he experienced). Leo Tolstoy, *What Is Art?*, trans. Aylmer Maude (Oxford: Oxford University Press, 1898); relevant excerpt reprinted in *Aesthetics: A Critical Anthology*, 2nd ed., ed. G. Dickie, R. Sclafani, and R. Roblin (New York: St. Martin's, 1989), pp. 57–63.

[42] Aristotle, *Poetics*, p. 37.   [43] Aristotle, *Poetics*, p. 38.

106 LIVING IN WORDS

extents cathartic. Reading a work of biography can give us this experience to a considerable extent (we use the word "powerful" to name this)—primarily the extent to which we vicariously identify with the protagonist and find the plot engaging for some of the reasons we have already seen Aristotle elucidate. But the case of autobiographical writing is even of greater interest, precisely for the reason that no such vicarious imaginative entry or identification is necessary—the author *is* the protagonist. And of course the working out of the plot structure—the life-narrative—is in such cases (obviously unlike the cases of the work of the biographer or the playwright) self-description. And it is at this point that we arrive back at Wittgenstein's problem about our not being able to write anything about ourselves that is more truthful than we ourselves, independent of that writing, are.

Aristotle also articulates what is for many a rather deep intuition concerning life-narratives: "A plot structure does not possess unity (as some believe) by virtue of centering on an individual."[44] So a full and exacting recitation of every event in a life (assuming there were an extra lifetime of years to tell and hear it) would not constitute what we desire (to be cathartically satisfied) as a life's *story*.[45] By including everything, such an account would in fact leave out the story. Aristotle, enunciating (as one would expect) an aesthetic classicism, writes of the need for the superior author to construct the plot so that the displacement or the deletion of any single episode within the whole would disturb the equilibrium of wholeness, of completeness. Indeed, nothing that is not contributing to this sense of wholeness can "be counted an integral part of the whole." And he writes of staying within the bounds of probability in depicting events, of focusing on the particular event that nevertheless speaks also of the universal, and of the intrinsic weakness of the purely episodic plot structure that merely strings events together along a temporal continuum without the interconnecting sinews of causal link-ages. "It makes a great difference," he says, "whether things happen because of one another, or only *after* one another."[46] Nothing, one would think, would make a greater difference to the sense-making, or sense-discovering, coherence of a life-narrative, a biographical or autobiographical structure.

Aristotle also writes of the value of the fully explained description of suffering as well as of recognition and reversal to the power of the plot, and of the considerable difference in value between emotions given rise by mere theatrical spectacle and those given rise by "the intrinsic structure of events."[47] And he emphasizes the dramatic importance of showing precisely the differences in the degree of know-ledge and understanding with which actions are performed, noting that a

---

[44] Aristotle, *Poetics*, p. 40.

[45] Just as a video and audio recording device, attached to a person's head for life (thus recording everything seen and heard by that individual), would produce a historical document, but not a narrative, not a story. Some over-inclusive autobiographies have been criticized, and sometimes parodied, on just such grounds.

[46] Aristotle, *Poetics*, p. 42.   [47] Aristotle, *Poetics*, p. 45.

recognition occurring just in time to prevent what would have been an irreversible deed performed in ignorance is particularly powerful (powerful because we as spectators are made clearly to see forward into a disastrous possible future that, narrowly, did not occur). Then in a larger frame of reference, he notes the dramatic value of having seemingly disparate events fall into place so that they ultimately contribute to a common end. All of these, adding to the preceding considerations, yield for Aristotle a sweeping aesthetic generalization: "It is right to contrast and compare tragedies largely in terms of plot structure."[48]

Much, as we have seen along the way, of Aristotle's analysis of the nature of, and evaluative criteria for, tragedies could function as a description of life-narratives too. But here we face a pressing question: Is it right to contrast and compare—to evaluate, in these terms—life-narratives largely in terms of plot structure? Is the cathartic and edifying experience we derive from a deeply engaging narrative—deeply engaging for precisely the reasons Aristotle has adumbrated—itself an indication of that narrative's value, indeed itself a measure of the veracity of that life-narrative? Or is it merely a measure of the *literary* value of that life-narrative wholly separate from any question of its truth? Does what makes it a good story make it—in some or any sense—a true one? Are those literary values *exclusively* literary, and might they, taken together, constitute a collection of temptations to falsify, to provide just the needed materials for autobiographically encoded self-deception? Wittgenstein also wrote, a year after the passage above, "Nothing is so difficult as not deceiving oneself."[49] Why make it even harder? Let us pursue this.

3.3 Narrative Catharsis

If the bathwater is the set of rightly deception-fearing, skeptical questions concerning the potential damage to self-understanding these literary considerations might inflict, the baby is the set of insights into the structures of our lives that those considerations might make possible.

First, it is surely a misstep to characterize the problem here as an all-or-nothing affair: the skeptical questions, as stated above, are framed in the most general terms. Given the vagaries of autobiographical inquiry and the language within which we conduct it, why should we for a moment presume that all self-reflection will be hampered by any consideration of the value and power of the plot structure as discussed above? There is not here, or not yet, a clearly individuated case in which the relevance of plot-structural considerations is at issue (even that way of putting it is too general—the real question would be "In which exact detail or set of

---

[48] Aristotle, *Poetics*, p. 52.   [49] Wittgenstein, *Culture and Value*, p. 34.

108　LIVING IN WORDS

details of a specific life is one or a few of these considerations relevant?"). To make the point obvious: the question "Will every member of the class of autobiographical reflections throughout all human life be distorted by Aristotelian structural considerations?" is disorientingly overgeneral; for good reason, no one could begin to answer that (very likely because no one would accept the question in that form). And so it is not merely that these questions are too general to suit the case, but rather the *cases*.

Second, there is the fact that tragedy, or dramatic forms more generally, are indeed mimetic arts, and what they mime, what they represent, is (if in variations, abstractions, and extremes) *us*. With this fact appropriately recalled, our surprise should thus be reserved for those cases where such considerations as Aristotle investigated in his *Poetics* do not apply, rather than to where they do. We see ourselves in the depictions and descriptions of mimesis; it should seem odd if we did not, in turn, see the organizing structures (made visible by being cast in dramatic high relief) of those mimetic narratives—with innumerable variations and nuances—in our own lives.

Third, given the facility with the rhetorical redecoration of event descriptions that language naturally affords, why should we assume that the language we use that may not be under the influence of these Aristotelian issues is any less epistemologically polluted than language that is under this Aristotelian influence? Indeed, narrative structures assembled under that influence might well help clarify, rather than cloud, a life-story. It is thus not transparently evident that all such considerations, when brought from literature to life, will yield only distortion, falsification, or self-deception. But there is more to say than these first three preliminary points.

Wittgenstein, while remaining in many ways deeply critical of Freud, at the same time, and at the same depth, remarked on some similarities between their methods (declaring himself to be, at one point "a disciple of Freud"); we briefly encountered this point in connection with John Wisdom's work above.[50] Writing on method in psychoanalysis, Adam Phillips observes that the psychoanalytical experience will not invariably lead one to a singular, definitive, and finally settled truth, but it "can be useful in the way it adds to our repertoire of ways of thinking

---

[50] I offer a discussion of some of these issues of philosophical method in *Describing Ourselves: Wittgenstein and Autobiographical Consciousness* (Oxford: Clarendon, 2008), ch. 7, sec. 3: "On Philosophy as Therapy: Wittgenstein, Cavell, and Autobiographical Writing," pp. 240–57. For a discussion of the Wittgenstein-Freud connection, see John Wisdom, *Philosophy and Psycho-Analysis* (Oxford: Basil Blackwell, 1953); Frank Cioffi, "Wittgenstein's Freud," in *Studies in the Philosophy of Wittgenstein*, ed. Peter Winch (London: Routledge and Kegan Paul, 1969), pp. 184–210; Brian McGuinness, "Freud and Wittgenstein," in *Wittgenstein and His Times*, ed. Brian McGuinness (Oxford: Basil Blackwell, 1982), pp. 27–43; and Jacques Bouveresse, *Wittgenstein Reads Freud: The Myth of the Unconscious*, trans. Carol Cosman (Princeton: Princeton University Press, 1995). See also, of course, Wittgenstein, *Lectures and Conversations on Aesthetics, Psychology, and Religious Belief*, ed. Cyril Barrett (Oxford: Basil Blackwell, 1966), pp. 41–52.

STRUCTURES OF AUTOBIOGRAPHICAL UNDERSTANDING   109

about the past."[51] This, I want to suggest, is precisely the way in which the Aristotelian issues can—in a highly productive way—come into play. Phillips discusses a number of forms the self-descriptive projects of analysis (and one of the numerous virtues of his discussion is that he makes clear that "analysis" does not name one thing) can take: these include (1) the removal of obstacles to, and defenses against, memory; (2) the fragmenting, or dismantling, of a too-settled life-story; (3) the making of both new links[52] and new gaps in a narrative; (4) the changing of patterns of exclusion in a narrative by retelling; (5) the "unfreezing"[53] of repetitions in a life-narrative (where repetition, as he reports, functions for Freud as "forgetting in its most spellbinding form"[54]); and (6) the creating of the internal conditions that, through the recovery of a past otherwise frozen in repetition, make autobiographical endeavors possible. This, of course, is not an exhaustive catalogue. But it does illustrate the kinds of things an engagement with the plot structure considerations can also achieve. Phillips emphasizes that the psychoanalytical circumstance is fundamentally dialogical ("it takes two to make a life story"),[55] and the considerations articulated by Aristotle that arise in the process of generating a narrative—in fiction or in life—can give articulate voice to the inward interlocutor with whom one engages in projects of self-investigation. (Wittgenstein's later work—or much of it—was inwardly dialogical in just this respect.)

Psychoanalysis can also—in particular cases, not generically—make us ask ourselves what the narrative we are telling ourselves covers over, what it occludes, what events it turns our self-directed view away from. And it can awaken a sense of "versions" of self-narrative (Phillips notes that the French psychoanalyst J.-B. Pontalis wrote that a person should not write one autobiography but rather ten of them, owing to the "innumerable ways of recounting [our] life to ourselves.")[56] A strikingly similar achievement can be won through the sensitive and judicious "replotting" of a life's story using Aristotle's reflective tools.[57] Of course, the psychoanalytical dialogue, as Phillips makes clear, is hardly identical to

[51] Adam Phillips, "The Telling of Selves: Notes on Psychoanalysis and Autobiography," in his *On Flirtation: Psychoanalytical Essays on the Uncommitted Life* (Cambridge, MA: Harvard University Press, 1994), pp. 65–75 (this passage p. 67).

[52] I discuss some of the considerations relevant to the question of the ontological status of links within a narrative (i.e., are they created or discovered? Do they exist prior to their being perceived in self-reflection?) in *Describing Ourselves*, ch. 5: "The Question of True Self-Interpretation," pp. 154–84; as in earlier and the following references to this book, I am relying on and extending out from those discussions here.

[53] I explore this matter of the "unfrozen past" in Iris Murdoch's sense of the phrase also in *Describing Ourselves*, in ch. 5, sec. 3: "Iris Murdoch, the 'Unfrozen Past', and Seeing in a New Light," pp. 202–22.

[54] Phillips, "The Telling of Selves," p. 69.   [55] Phillips, "The Telling of Selves," p. 68.

[56] Phillips, "The Telling of Selves," p. 73.

[57] Also, Phillips makes clear that psychoanalysis should not assert itself as a "master-narrative" *against* which any life-story should be judged or measured. The same cautionary note should be sounded regarding the Aristotelian tools for the structuring of self-understanding.

110 LIVING IN WORDS

autobiographical labor, to seriously working with self-descriptive words. But the sense of self-interpretive freedom gained through the provision of an articulate vocabulary of plot elements—be they Aristotelian or Freudian—is common to both. And while neither guarantees the truth, neither systematically or generically works against it either. But those thoughts are a second stage of the answer; there is still more to say along these lines about the potential value of adopting life-narrative structuring tools from literature to life.

Jonathan Lear writes: "Wittgenstein made an analogy between philosophy and therapy: each is used to free us from the grip of various illusions about who we are, how we go on, what we mean."[58] That, indeed, goes to the heart of the matter, and my suggestion here is that considerations of the plot-structuring kind in the *Poetics* (and beyond) can be one further way of giving content to the notion of philosophical therapy as discussed in the first section of this chapter. But Lear sees more than that which is captured in the previous passage. Lear adds, "I believe this analogy can be extended. In psychotherapy, a person may (in the presence of another) create a representation of herself: of her belief, desires, wishes, anxieties, and character, all set in a social context of parents, friends, and loved ones' personalities, the environment of childhood, the institutions in which she now operates." This rightly emphasizes the *creative* dimension of any such life-describing project. With that in focus, we might then naturally look to studies of the structural elements of literary creations. This does not, in and of itself, or by virtue of the emphasis on creativity, suggest that the result will be fictional, any more than a portrait of a person will itself be fictional (or depictively false) by virtue of the fact that portrait painting is a creative art. And this passage also rightly emphasizes that the result of that analytical process is after all a *representation*, which clearly links us back to the concept of the representation of action at the center of Aristotle's study of plot structure. But Lear sees still more: "The ultimate value of the therapeutic process, though, is not the creation of this artifact [the self-representation]. Although the agent will become a better 'observer' of herself, the point of therapy is not the observation of an accurately represented person, but nonobservational insight into the person creating the representation. It is insight into the forms of active creativity." It is a commonplace that one gains insight into the grammar and structural features of one's native language by learning a second one; travel is widely valued for performing a parallel service with regard to our own local presumptions, mores, and customs. The careful consideration and reconsiderations of life-structurings that go against the grain of our settled presumptions can function in the same way (to which we will return in detail in Chapter 5), and we of course need a vocabulary and structuring instruments with which to undertake that task.

---

[58] Jonathan Lear, "Transcendental Anthropology," in his *Open Minded: Working out the Logic of the Soul* (Cambridge, MA: Harvard University Press, 1998), pp. 247–81, this passage p. 272.

STRUCTURES OF AUTOBIOGRAPHICAL UNDERSTANDING   111

But of course the gaining of insight need not follow only on the project of contemplating life-structurings *other* than we think them to be. The project Lear is discussing is one in which the subject is pursuing accurate self-description, and that is still a creative undertaking, one productive of the distinctive kind of non-observational insight Lear is identifying. What more, then, can be said about that insight into "the forms of active creativity"? Lear continues this way: "As the forms of mental activity too become conscious, they too can be represented—and thus thought about and modified. In this way, insight into activity—not into any particular mental representations, memories, facts, and so on—can lead to a change in the form of living." And that, I want to suggest, would, in the extended sense of the term suggested above, be a cathartic change. And if we return from the Freudian to the Wittgensteinian emphasis in elucidating the concept of therapy—that is, to philosophical therapy based on a methodological analogy leading us to something like conceptual archeology—we might adapt Lear's phrase to this: In this way, insight into activity—not into any particular mental representations, memories, facts, and so on—can lead to a change in the form of thinking. And thus, I also want to suggest, that would constitute cathartic change in our thought, or, as Wittgenstein often called it, our "way of seeing."[59] And all of this is conducted inside (and not in any sense prior to) the use of autobiographical language. Lear concludes his thought: "In this way, the creation of the artifact can be partially constitutive of a change in the creator." Of his philosophical work, Wittgenstein (at the close of his third lecture on aesthetics) said, "Much of what we are doing is a question of changing the style of thinking,"[60] where that change is an effect of the reorienting power of our words.

With these thoughts in mind, let us look in another direction for a moment: Ensconced within one conventional style of epistemological thinking, one that quietly houses residual influences from verificationism and from the reduction of all forms of human knowledge to correspondence between fact and description, it would be all too

> easy to have a false picture of the processes called 'recognizing'; as if recognizing always consisted in comparing two impressions with one another. It is as if I carried a picture of an object with me and used it to perform an identification of an object as the one represented by the picture. Our memory seems to us to be the agent of such a comparison, by preserving a picture of what has been seen before, or by allowing us to look into the past (as if down a spy-glass).

This remark, *Philosophical Investigations*, §604, articulates a picture of memory verification that: (1) reduces memory to memory images, and (2) reduces the

---

[59] For a full discussion of this aspect of Wittgenstein's conception of philosophical progress, see Judith Genova, *Wittgenstein: A Way of Seeing* (London: Routledge, 1995).
[60] Wittgenstein, *Lectures and Conversations*, p. 28.

112 LIVING IN WORDS

veracity of any such memory image to a matter of correspondence between the memory image and the initial sensation of which it is the memory. Thus, on this picture, when we correctly recognize an object, we see that the memory image "fits" perfectly over the present sensation image. This simplifying template underwrites, in turn, an application to the case of the verification of self-narrative: all and only those narratives are true that "fit" in just this way, i.e., where the memory image, and the memory the image is *of*, are brought into perfect correspondence (as in an optometrist's examination room, where we look into the optical machine and report when two images come into perfect overlay, when they merge into one). This drastically oversimplified model of self-narrative would make all of the Aristotelian considerations seem obviously irrelevant to finding narrative self-descriptive truth: that would, again, be a wholly uncreative act in which the correspondences are verified. Forms of plot organization that we learn from literature, and the tracing of interconnecting threads, would be as irrelevant to fact-finding as the gripping power of plot inexorability would be to the matching of a paint chip to the color of a wall. But this entire line of thinking emanating from that simplifying picture of memory recognition is deeply, if instructively, misled.

First, recognition, here implicitly employed as the essence of memory, is itself grossly oversimplified. Wittgenstein asks if, when we say "Of course!" to the question "Did you recognize your desk when you entered your room this morning?" we should thereby be committed to saying that an act of recognition took place (*Philosophical Investigations*, §602). Indeed, "No one will say that every time I enter my room, my long-familiar surroundings, there is enacted a recognition of all that I see and have seen hundreds of times before" (*Philosophical Investigations*, §603). The concept of recognition is not invariably or clearly in play within all contexts in which memory, or a question of memory, arises. Recognition—like every other concept—will come into play within a language-game in a context-specific way.

Second, it would be consistent with an entrenched style of thinking in epistemology, but not consistent with the facts of our practices, to accept the presumption that memory is either entirely, or even in primary or central cases (are there *central* cases?), visual: olfactory, auditory, tactile, and gustatory experiences are certainly remembered—Schopenhauer called the olfactory sense the "sense of memory"[61]—and there is certainly no *prima facie* reason to assume that these are "translated" into visual form before they are remembered. Of course, one could say that they are not translated, but that the image-recognition matching model nevertheless applies, but there is no reason to assume that recognition functions in

---

[61] On this matter, see Joachim Schulte, *Experience and Expression: Wittgenstein's Philosophy of Psychology* (Oxford: Oxford University Press, 1993), pp. 98–102.

STRUCTURES OF AUTOBIOGRAPHICAL UNDERSTANDING   113

a more consistent and universally applicable way with the four senses other than sight than it does with sight.

Third, the image-recognition template also seriously misleads—and this is the most important point for present considerations—by obscuring a double-pronged fact. The first prong is that many memories are *verbal*—they involve what one said or wrote, or what one heard, and these, like the four non-visual sensory modalities, are not in need of "translation" into the visual in order to be remembered. The second prong is that verbal memories themselves do not behave in a single, consistent way—sometimes we recall what we meant to say without remembering verbatim what we would have said. Nor, of course, is what we meant to say in the remembered moment always or usually inwardly "pre-recorded" verbatim— although it can be.[62] Of course the remembering of certain words—in distinct contexts—may well bring to mind visual memories of the setting in which the words were uttered or heard, but the essential point in such cases is that the verbal memory is prior to, and not dependent upon, the visual memory; the verbal does not follow upon the visual, but rather triggers it. With that in mind, and to return to the first prong, we start to see in this context the significance of Wittgenstein's remark in *Philosophical Investigations*, §649: "And memories etc., in language, are not mere threadbare representations of the *real* experiences; for is what is linguistic not an experience?"

Fourth, there is what we might in too-compact form call emotional memory, and this need not depend for its content on prerequisite visual or verbal memories (although naturally memories of the visual setting of the emotion, as well as— more tellingly in dismantling a unitary image or picture of memory— retrospective thoughts concerning what we might or might not, could or could not have said at the time but did not, may fill out the context of the remembered emotion). In *Philosophical Investigations*, §651, we thus find:

'I remember that I should have been glad then to stay still longer.'—What picture of this wish came before my mind? None at all. What I see in my memory allows no conclusion as to my feelings. And yet I remember quite clearly that they were there.

What these observations do, individually each in their own way but also collectively, is to free us from the grip of the oversimplifying picture of memory as recognition, where that is an inward process of image-matching. Free of that blinding conceptual model, we can come to appreciate the myriad or polymorphous nature of memory, which allows us to see that variegated concept in play

---

[62] I focus on this issue in *Art as Language: Wittgenstein, Meaning, and Aesthetic Theory* (Ithaca: Cornell University Press, 1995), ch. 5, "Against Creation as Translation," esp. part 3, "On Finding the Right Expression," pp. 109–17.

114 LIVING IN WORDS

across a vast range of cases throughout life-writing from Augustine to the present. And it preserves space for what has been called the creative[63] dimension of memory and particularly memory-dependent forms of writing (which accords well with Lear's observations above). Working against the picture of intention as a determinate inner mental act (and that, for present considerations, would give an exhaustive autobiographical account of what one did or did not intend on a given occasion), Wittgenstein writes that, instead of remembering a specific, isolated, inwardly sealed intentional act, what one remembers—what actually comes to mind in remembering an intention—are "thoughts, feelings, movements, and also connexions with earlier situations" (*Philosophical Investigations*, §645).

And also connections with earlier situations. Such connections may be visual—a threatening door may resemble one we saw at an impressionable age in a Hitchcock film; they may be auditory—one person's voice may sound like another's from our past; they may be olfactory, sensory, and so forth. But they will in large measure be verbal, or linguistic, and that in and of itself powerfully links an autobiographical inquiry into one's intentions to the issue of the relations between sentences, between words, in the ways Aristotle discussed in his writings on plot structure. It is important to see here that the significance of the Aristotelian considerations is not one of *application*, i.e., they are not initially isolated from, prior to, and then applied to the connections of which Wittgenstein writes. They are intrinsic to them; they are housed *within* the language we use to describe life experience, or within, and not attached to, the language-games of self-description. We have seen enough in this chapter (and we have seen enough in life, if we are not looking through a conceptually unifying, reductive prism) to expect that those self-descriptive sentences, with regard to statements of our intentions, and our giving of reasons for our actions or inactions, will not be a unitary or simple affair. In the course of his lectures on aesthetics, Wittgenstein also said:

> Giving a reason sometimes means 'I actually went this way', sometimes 'I could have gone this way', i.e. sometimes what we say acts as a justification, not as a report of what was done, e.g. I *remember* the answer to a question; when asked why I give this answer, I gave a process leading to it, though I didn't go through this process.[64]

In solving a problem in musical composition where we want to modulate from one key to another, we may use a diminished seventh chord, using for the old key

---

[63] See Joachim Schulte, *Experience and Expression*, ch. 7, "Memory," pp. 95–119. To make space for what we can call a creative discussion of memory is not to embrace an "anything-goes" subjectivism; Schulte's admirable discussion makes this clear.

[64] Wittgenstein, *Lectures and Conversations*, p. 22.

the top of the four voices of the chord as a leading tone to the tonic; to modulate we repeat that chord but now use the second voice from the top as the leading tone. (Later, we may use the third voice in this way, and later still the root.) When asked why we did it this way—when asked for our reason—we may well say: "Because in a diminished seventh structure, each of the four voices can function equally well as a leading tone to four resolutions, because the structure of the stacked minor thirds yields an internal dominant tritone, with the other two pitches serving as alterations to that implied dominant chord." But of course that is *a* way to get there, or what Wittgenstein calls a process that leads to the conclusion if we follow it now. Or it led to it before in our earlier, more mechanical or student-level musical thinking. Or we may, in analytical retrospect, see that this answer would both justify our harmonic decision now and mark out the path to follow in analyzing it. To then ask which of these is autobiographically true is an intricate—and tellingly irreducible—matter; cases like these do not boil down to one singular, true answer. Perhaps that sequence of thought is one we took as composition students, before such thinking became second nature. Perhaps, differently, we were (as Debussy said he did) working purely from sound alone. The parenthetical doubt expressed in the previous sentence concerning the veracity of Debussy's intentional statement is a layer of questioning concerning whether one could, as a kind of harmonic savant, get there by *pure* sound. Perhaps it was a product of a flash of harmonic insight into dominant-tonic relations in connection with the intervallic structure of diminished seventh chords that comes of long hours working through and beyond the diatonic system in a way that yields a "Work at it as I have for a long time and then you too shall see" kind of answer (frustrating as such answers can be). And we have countless other possibilities that emerge within particular circumstances. Parallel cases can of course be worked out in all the other arts, in mathematics, and—here is the point—in our self-descriptions of ethical reasons and motivations.

Wittgenstein, in those lectures, observes that in answer to "Why did you do it?" questions, we often state as the motive "just what we give on being asked."[65] This is not, or not necessarily, falsification, and nor is it invariably what we call rationalization. It *may* be either of these, *depending on the circumstances of the case.* It may not. And it may be some more complex admixture of both. And, similarly, "Why did you do it?" questions are not themselves unitary in motive: in some cases, it will be a question concerning which "road" one took to reach the conclusion. In others, it will be a question concerning the consequences you envisioned. In others still, it will be a question indirectly asking if the agent feels regret, or a question meant to indirectly evoke an apology. And a thousand other things. As a student in Wittgenstein's lectures on aesthetics noted: "Thus 'reason'

---

[65] Wittgenstein, *Lectures and Conversations*, p. 22.

116 LIVING IN WORDS

does not always mean the same thing."[66] And the variability of these situations can in turn elicit from us a false sense of mystery and of metaphysical privacy[67] with regard to motives, expressed by Wittgenstein in the phrase "Only he knows the process which led to it."[68]

Any autobiographical undertaking moves, not along a simple route of image-matching verified correspondence, but rather through this thicket. To capture anything less intricate is indeed to falsify from the outset the experience we are trying to self-analytically describe. We saw Wittgenstein say at the beginning of this section, "You cannot write anything about yourself that is more truthful than you yourself are." Part of that truthfulness itself takes the form of an acceptance of, and a desire to preserve, complexity. A disciplined philosophical patience will itself show the truth in Wittgenstein's warning concerning the "power language has to make everything look the same";[69] that power works against our grasp of particularity, but a finer and more nuanced use of language (and a perspicuous overview of our uses) is the weapon with which we battle it. Wittgenstein, as we also saw, said, "Nothing is so difficult as not deceiving oneself."[70] And we might now begin to see some way into a new articulation of self-deception, i.e., a losing of one's bearings within the "thicket," where one retrospectively invents pathways that not only one did not take but that this person could not have taken. "When you bump against the limits of your own honesty it is as though your thoughts get into a whirlpool...."[71]

It is at this juncture that some will embrace a generalized motive-skepticism. There will be some cases in which the autobiographical inquiry, in a given case, will not yield definitive results, no settled conclusion. But it is obvious folly to suggest that because some cases are like this, they all are. And some will embrace a larger skepticism about ever arriving at a fully settled, "finished" autobiographical picture of the self. That, because of the truth Henry James captured in his succinct phrase "relations end nowhere,"[72] is in a sense true (as we shall see more fully in Chapter 6), but it is cause for wonderment, not despair. The interrelations between experiences of the kind we saw in the pragmatist's conception of experience in Chapter 1, the complex "weave" of those strands as we saw in Chapter 2, the *active* nature[73] of the project of self-understanding, the clarifications of our concepts of memory and of reason-giving, are all open-ended endeavors. And in

---

[66] Wittgenstein, *Lectures and Conversations*, p. 22.

[67] What is meant here by the phrase "a false sense of mystery and of metaphysical privacy" was the central project of *Describing Ourselves*, ch. 1, "Autobiographical Consciousness," pp. 15–43.

[68] Wittgenstein, *Lectures and Conversations*, p. 22.   [69] Wittgenstein, *Culture and Value*, p. 22.

[70] Wittgenstein, *Culture and Value*, p. 34.   [71] Wittgenstein, *Culture and Value*, p. 8.

[72] In the preface to *Roderick Hudson*; the full passage, highly significant for the understanding of one way of characterizing biographical or autobiographical closure, is "Really, universally, relations stop nowhere, and the exquisite problem of the artist is eternally but to draw, by a geometry of his own, the circle in which they shall happily appear to do so." In *The Art of the Novel*, ed. R. P. Blackmur (New York: Charles Scribner's Sons, 1962), p. 6.

[73] See Jonathan Lear, "Transcendental Anthropology," in *Open Minded*, pp. 274–5.

STRUCTURES OF AUTOBIOGRAPHICAL UNDERSTANDING   117

those endeavors we can employ, in a manner intrinsic to, or woven within, life's plot structures, the profoundly mimetic structuring and sense-making elements Aristotle identified. It is, again, open-ended, but that does not mean we do not make progress. Quite the contrary. And that progress—of a kind produced through the combination of the judicious employment of the life-structuring tools we see articulated in Aristotle's *Poetics* and the meticulous processes of conceptual clarification that we see modeled in the later writings of Wittgenstein—can prove deeply cathartic. Aristotle did also famously say, in the *Nicomachean Ethics*, that we cannot judge a life happy until it is over.[74] Actually, that may have been a conservative estimate of the time required for the task: although autobiographical weaving and ever fuller reweaving will for all of us one day stop, at least biographical reweaving need not. A finally settled life-narrative would be rather like a fully interpreted work of art: we can say the words, but cannot genuinely imagine what that might be. We saw at the close of the first section of this chapter Wittgenstein's remark that in philosophy the one who wins is the one who gets there last;[75] we are now in a position to see with greater depth the conditions within which this remark can be resonantly true.

And so we turn to three cases, really three cautionary tales, in which the kind of self-knowledge, the kind of autobiographical vision and inward understanding, and the kind of long-form narrative stability the foregoing considerations might produce are either wholly absent (Don Giovanni), achieved too late (Henry James's character Dencombe), or present but far too crudely with far too blunt a conception of what language does (King Lear). As I mentioned in the introduction, these cases bring out in high relief what consciousness can look like when either inner vacuity (Giovanni), or self-deception (Dencombe), or a willful and blunt and blinding arrogance (Lear) occupy the psychic space that a reflective psyche might have occupied. Such a psyche might have been: (a) attentive to networks of meaning-determining relations, (b) aware of and attuned to the subtle contents of words, (c) perceptive of the sensitivities of idiosyncratic individuals to whom events happen, (d) free of reductive and dehumanized conceptions of human beings, (e) mindful of the fact that their interpretation of others near them, or their interpretations or understandings of themselves may not be singular, uniquely true, and settled in their one-and-only verbal formulation, and (f) thoughtful concerning the structure and narrative understanding of a human life. Just as silence can be deafening, so absence can, if in a sense paradoxically, make qualities more visible.

---

[74] Aristotle, *Nicomachean Ethics*, trans. M. Ostwald (Indianapolis: Bobbs-Merrill, 1962), pp. 23–7.
[75] Wittgenstein, *Culture and Value*, p. 34: "In philosophy the winner of the race is the one who can run most slowly. Or: the one who gets there last."

4

Three Tragedies of the Unexamined Life

It would be surprising if there were a simple or general and overarching way to describe the relations between language, identity, and self-understanding. Such relations are probably better seen within the detailed contexts of particular cases—from which we gain what is really more a matter of a clarified vision of the phenomena in question rather than a reductive encapsulation of alleged essence. So in this chapter we consider three instructive particular cases: the soulless Giovanni, the self-stunting idealizer Dencombe, and the deaf-to-nuance Lear. They do have some things more or less in common, but they live in linguistic particularities and networks of relations that make their problems all their own.

4.1 The Self *in Absentia*: Leporello's Question (Mozart's *Don Giovanni*)

I mentioned above that one finds in the later philosophical writings of Wittgenstein an elucidation of the distinctive attitude we bring to the perception of human beings. Again, this attitude, called by Wittgenstein "Eine Einstellung zur Seele," an attitude towards a soul, is irreducible—it cannot be analyzed into any more basic constituent parts—and it is the precondition for our sympathetic and imaginative understanding of others. It serves at the same time as the precondition for human selfhood. Stated succinctly, this unique attitude, marking the contrast (of the pragmatic, self-definitional kind we saw in Chapter 1) between our perception of a human being and our perception of anything else animate or inanimate, is constitutive of who and what we are. And while this irreducible facet of the human situation is expressly articulated in philosophy—that is, it is therein said—it is shown in myriad places and ways. Viewed through the lens of Wittgenstein's fundamental concern with this ineliminable human attitude, Mozart and da Ponte's *Don Giovanni* possesses considerable insight into the content of humane acknowledgment, the very concept of selfhood upon which that acknowledgment is based, and how words convey either its presence or its absence.

It is just after voicing his aspirations to become a gentleman himself that Leporello, outside the palace of the Commendatore, provides the interpretive clue to the philosophical significance of the entire opera. Thinking that he hears someone coming, he puts into play within the opening line of *Don Giovanni* the

---

Living in Words: Literature, Autobiographical Language, and the Composition of Selfhood. Garry L. Hagberg, Oxford University Press. © Garry L. Hagberg 2023. DOI: 10.1093/oso/9780198841210.003.0004

intertwined themes of concealment, of person-perception, and of the underlying desire for human avoidance that motivates the particular act of concealment in question: "I don't want to be seen, ah, I don't want to be seen, I don't want to be seen, no, no, no, no, no, I don't want to be seen" (p. 86).[1] However, the deepest clue to the philosophical significance—and the one that resonates most clearly throughout the opera—is given by Don Giovanni himself and comes in his very first line: "You shall not know who I am" (p. 86). He repeats this morally significant epistemic limit a moment later to secure this limitation on person-perception with an emphatic denial (to Donna Anna): "You scream in vain, you shall not know who I am, no" (p. 86).

So if we are to see *Don Giovanni* as an opera that houses considerable insight—and an instructive object lesson—about what Wittgenstein and others have discussed as the preconditions of selfhood, of inner human content, that make the distinctive attitude or stance we take towards other persons so much as possible, we must first investigate how the opera serves to frame Giovanni. That is, we must comparatively situate him in relation to the other characters, as a person lacking precisely that human content, that interiority, which makes the distinctive and remarkable attitude, the essence of person-perception, possible. But before I proceed with the attempt to sketch the philosophical content (concerning the relational constituents of selfhood and the language we use to create, cultivate, and preserve it) to which both Leporello's and Giovanni's first words provide clues, let us consider some preliminary details in the libretto that point out the interpretive direction we will take and how we will draw a philosophical lesson concerning selfhood and autobiographical language from it.

As early as the fatal wounding of the Commendatore, a telling contrast emerges. With the Commendatore dying, Leporello exclaims, "What a tragedy! What a crime!" and then, having made these morally engaged judgments, he describes his inner state with "I feel my heart pounding with fear in my breast." Then, in humanly engaged reaction to the scene, he exclaims with increasing urgency (owing to his moral perception of the magnitude of the profound human loss presently occurring at Giovanni's hand) that he does not know what to say or to do. Showing in his words, his actions, and his felt urgency, his attitude towards the person of the Commendatore, Leporello stands in striking contrast to the humanly disengaged language and posture of Giovanni—a posture or stance that displays only a refusal to acknowledge the humane loss he is presently

---

[1] *Don Giovanni*, trans. Ellen H. Bleiler (New York: Dover, 1964). In addition to the libretto itself, I have found a number of writings particularly helpful. These include Joseph Kerman, *Opera as Drama* (New York: Vintage, 1952); see especially his remarks on Giovanni's "amorous dissimulation" (p. 115), Giovanni's never having taken "the trouble to think" about the Commendatore's death (p. 119), and Mozart's having "dwelt more profoundly than anyone else on men in relation to other men and women" (p. 123); Edward J. Dent, *Mozart's Operas*, 2nd ed. (Oxford: Oxford University Press, 1947), chs. 8–10, pp. 116–87; and *Don Giovanni: Myths of Seduction and Betrayal*, ed. Jonathan Miller (New York: Shocken, 1990).

120   LIVING IN WORDS

causing. Giovanni provides the cold description of a detached eyewitness—one without a trace of imaginative sympathy for the victim—that approximates the outwardly descriptive language of a dehumanized behaviorist: "already the villain is fallen, gasping and breathing his last." This cold vision of the death scene before him, given as a factual report on his ocular experience in strange isolation from any indication of human sensibility, contrasts strikingly not only with Leporello's reaction but also with the Commendatore's himself. Like Leporello, the Commendatore's words express his interior experience, and although he uses phrases similar to Giovanni's, there is an essential difference (here recall Wittgenstein's remark "a whole cloud of philosophy condensed into a drop of grammar"): "the assassin has run me through and I feel my soul parting from my heaving breast" (p. 89). The contrast between human content ("I feel my soul parting") and emptiness (Giovanni's detachment and indifference) is underscored a moment later, when Leporello comically emerges from hiding, asking Giovanni: "Who's dead, you or the old man?" (p. 90). It does not take a Freudian to detect the serious undercurrents that joking remarks can carry, particularly where the origin of the joke lies in the perception of human frailties. Wholly deaf to the critical reverberations issuing from such undercurrents (Franz tried, if failingly, to listen for these in Sabina's words and deeds with the bowler hat; Giovanni, vastly worse, does not know there is such a thing as listening for them), Giovanni replies with only, "What a stupid question! The old man" (p. 90). But one might see the source of the question not in witless stupidity, but rather in Leporello's inability to discern the humanity in Giovanni, to mark the contrast between one whose "soul," whose animating sympathetically imaginative humane attitude, has departed his heaving breast, and one in whom such a morally engaged sensibility has yet to show signs of itself. This contrast is shown by, or in a sense living within, words.

The framing of Giovanni against the setting of the others is advanced on this score by Donna Anna's response to the spectacle of her deceased father. As with both Leporello and the Commendatore, she reports not mechanistic ocular experience, but rather the emotional impact of what she sees as the person she is ("But ah Gods, what distressing sight presents itself to my eyes!" [p. 91]). And a moment later, her words heighten the very contrast that Leporello's half-joke draws. Looking at her fallen father, she is appalled to see that the full humanity she has always effortlessly discerned in him is now cloaked. To her horror, she sees "that face—stained and covered with the hue of death" (p. 91). Don Ottavio adds in the exchange a description befitting a statue (a theme to which we will return): "He breathes no more! His limbs are icy!" (p. 91). Ottavio's moral shock, as registered in these remarks, is tellingly humane: his description of the fallen Commendatore is so alarming to himself and to the others (except Giovanni) precisely because it is the description of a person. The attitude undergirding this moral shock is, as evidenced by his profoundly different attitude, utterly alien to

Giovanni. Act I, Scene I closes with Anna and Ottavio reiterating their humanity, that is, singing repeatedly of the emotional significance, the human power, of what they have witnessed. The last words, sometime back, we have heard from Giovanni (to Leporello) are, vacuously, "Be quiet!" (p. 90). The themes are in play, and the contrasts are drawn. What we now need—and precisely what da Ponte gives—is a clearer enunciation of Giovanni's condition.

The injunction to know thyself is linked to the judgment that the unexamined life is not worth living. One way—and we shall see, a way fundamental to explaining the dramatic power of this opera's deepest moment—to describe the tragedy of Giovanni's life is that, in being wholly given over to one episode of sensory indulgence after another, it is a spectacular failure of Socratic self-examination. In fact, this is true of any life of the kind that Giovanni's life exemplifies; like Greek tragedy, the moral interest of the opera is hardly restricted internally and exclusively to the imagined fictional world of the libretto (we will return to this matter also at some length in Chapter 5). It was Aristotle who wrote compellingly of the moral significance of habituation: the inculcation of habit—including on the positive side the habit of self-reflection and the mindfulness engendered by it—made, for Aristotle, a very great difference. Indeed, as that exactingly precise author at one point said, it makes "all the difference."[2] Giovanni's long and deeply ingrained habit of episodic, unreflective diversion, evidenced by Leporello's catalogue (to which we will return shortly), renders him constitutionally incapable of reflection upon his own life. And this character-based limitation, one that functions within this context, within Giovanni's personality, simultaneously as an epistemological limit, condemns him to self-ignorance—or worse, as we shall see at the moment of his inexorable descent into the flames.

If Socrates and Aristotle introduced descriptions of our moral life into ethics that show what is profoundly true of a good life and profoundly vacant in Giovanni's type of life, it was Locke who introduced into epistemology the distinction between Sensation and Reflection. Without articulating the point of moral-epistemological convergence that defines the solitary tragedy of this mis-begotten life, Locke wrote, first, of the five senses that collect data and, second, of the intellectual power of reflection upon this data (it was Locke who articulated the classical version of empiricism to which, as we saw in Chapter 1, William James was opposed with his "radical empiricism"). Giovanni, as we have already seen, describes his reactions (or internally vacuous non-reactions) not only to things, but to persons, and even to persons *in extremis*, in flatly ocular terms. This particular variety of debasement is reflected in Leporello's catalogue aria, in which Giovanni's enumerated conquests are described in every external way ("there are

---

[2] Aristotle, *Nicomachean Ethics*, trans. Martin Ostwald (Indianapolis: Bobbs Merrill, 1962), Book II, sec. 1, "Moral Virtue as the Result of Habits," p. 35.

122 LIVING IN WORDS

women of every rank, of every shape, of every age!" [p. 101]). Here Leporello describes the objects of desire seasonally ("in winter he wants plumpness, in summer he wants leanness" [p. 101]) and dimensionally ("the tall woman is stately; the little tiny girl is always charming") but never morally. I suggested above that this might be characterized as the language of an unrefined form of behaviorism; it might also, equally aptly, be characterized as the language of sensation-sans-reflection.

Near the beginning of Scene II, Leporello (once again saying more than he knows he is saying) tells Giovanni that he is leading a "rogue's life" (p. 95).[3] This again means—whether or not he could describe it—a life of unreflective, unexamined, episodic sensory diversion. This is to say that, for Giovanni, the next episode of sensory "data" invariably takes the place of any reflection that might have been undertaken in a non-sensation-filled moment of reflective quiescence. Of course Giovanni replies with a stern, characteristically un-self-reflective dismissal to this, but it is his descriptive language that follows that truly reveals his condition.

Giovanni bluntly tells Leporello that he is in love, but as quickly and without giving a single word's worth of either outward expression or interior self-acknowledgment of his emotional state, he speaks exclusively in the language of sensation. In the same sentence (and he returns quickly to ocular terminology in avoidance of any genuine human expressivity) he says, "I saw her, I spoke to her," disallowing—dramatically unlike all of the other characters we have heretofore encountered—any glimpse of a humane reaction to either visage or locution. He then shifts his emphasis to another animal sensory modality, announcing, "Hush! I seem to smell femininity" (p. 95). Underscoring his self-entrapment in the Platonic cave of superficial appearances, he sings: "At first glance, she seems pretty"—and of course Giovanni never really gets beyond the severe epistemic limit of a first glance. He never genuinely knows anyone. Then, in a further act of dehumanization (replacing the *Einstellung* with language befitting not a person but rather the natural environment, and thus obscuring the essential distinction between the discernment of humanity and the brute perception of the inanimate), he says: "Let's withdraw here a little and look over the terrain" (p. 96).

In the remainder of Scene II, da Ponte extends and deepens his description of Giovanni's state. He gives a line to Giovanni in reply to the abandoned and furious Donna Elvira (who has not yet recognized Giovanni), with exaggerated, thinly disguised mock-pity: "Poor little thing! Poor little thing!" It is not so much that this expression also plays on the perception of the inanimate with the word "thing," nor that the explicitly belittling and thus morally distant "little" gives

---

[3] This illustrates, in saying more than he realizes he is saying, precisely the kind of meaning-externalism much discussed in recent decades in the philosophy of language; see for example Hilary Putnam, "Meaning and Reference," in *Analytic Philosophy*, ed. A. P. Martinich and David Sosa (Oxford: Blackwell, 2001), pp. 90–6, esp. p. 92.

offense. It is rather that the sympathy with its exaggerated delivery is wholly false, and, given the vacancy of inner resources, could not be anything but false. Leporello stresses this with another humorous yet double-sided phrase, "that's how he's consoled eighteen hundred of them" (reminding us of the character-shaping force of negative Aristotelian habit). And immediately after a diminutive version of an Aristotelian recognition scene, Elvira describes Giovanni as (among other "refined titles," as Leporello ironically puts it) a "bundle of deceit."[4] Indeed, she finishes the line with a term that our language has developed to most powerfully connote the inability to discern the humanity in a person: "monster!" (p. 98).

Our steadily deepening appreciation of the moral significance of the kind of case Giovanni represents constitutes, in Wittgenstein's sense, a gradually dawning set of aspects as the opera progresses. And for this reason, the opera possesses a good deal more Aristotelian teleological necessity, a good deal more structural cohesion, than those who have complained about the opera's episodic design have heretofore realized (to which we will return). We next see the most fundamental deficit of Giovanni's condition, the absence of a humanely responsive sensibility, being confirmed by Elvira. Accusing Giovanni of making fun of her sorrow (the very capacity for this heartless act serving as litmus test for inner vacuity, which further strengthens the moral point of this scene), she realizes, just after she has sung her line, that indeed Giovanni has already gone, and she is, quite literally, speaking to no one. Leporello, again speaking with meaning that extends well beyond what he himself fathoms, adds only "let him go; he isn't worth thinking about" (p. 100).

One way we have of describing a person without what Wittgenstein refers to as the "soul" toward which we hold the very distinctive attitude he investigates, or without the humanity he discusses that we regularly do (and only in very special, exceptional circumstance do not) discern in a person would be to say that she or he is soulless, is an automaton, or is a person without a heart. (Such a person lives without what I will call in Chapter 6 the sense of self, where that sense is inwardly grown and cultivated through autobiographical reflection and word-born self-composition.) Old-fashioned behaviorism, one of the twin pictures of selfhood to which Wittgenstein strenuously objected, went to one extreme of eliminative reductionism, asserting that the body with its patterned responses to stimuli is, in cold fact, just what we are. With such a reductive picture of a human being, we would see physical bodies in motion, responding to physical stimuli and inter-vening causally in the world in physical ways (we will consider Avashai Margalit's distinction between a scientific and literary conception of a human being in Chapter 6 to further pursue this matter). Fueled by his sensual ambitions, Giovanni wants to manipulate the throng around Zerlina and Masetto, the

---

[4] *The Poetics of Aristotle*, trans. and commentary Stephen Halliwell (London: Duckworth, 1987), pp. 48–50.

124 LIVING IN WORDS

happily engaged peasants, and offers them the stimuli of the senses. He instructs Leporello to divert them with chocolate, coffee, wines, and hams, and to give them the distracting sights of the palatial gardens and galleries. This carrot-dangling physicalism is further reinforced both by a stage direction, where Giovanni gives Leporello an insinuating dig in the side as he orders him to keep Masetto happily occupied, and where Giovanni shortly thereafter cleverly separates Zerlina from Masetto by positioning himself physically between them. He shapes behavior with stimuli, and he communicates, and intervenes causally in the physical world, using only the brute fact of embodiment. The right relation to words would have changed all this.

Da Ponte thus further advances the "argument" of the opera when he shows, as I have said, how behavior looks to a behaviorist, that is, showing bodies, responding to physical stimuli, in motion within a reductively physical world. Tellingly, one cannot, consistent with the larger moral point of Scene III, intelligibly say that he has shown how behavior looks to a behaviorist from the inside. And da Ponte then reinforces his depiction of behaviorism's conceptual impoverishment by linking it to the physical language the likes of which we now know well: Giovanni says to Zerlina, once he gets her alone, that a noble gentleman such as himself cannot suffer seeing "that precious face, that sweet face" insulted by the presence of a "low boor" (p. 108). And making it clear that descriptions of persons on this model (or picture, in Wittgenstein's sense) of selfhood will proceed in terms of facial externalities, adds "you are not destined to be a peasant" because of "those roguish little eyes...those lovely little lips, those white and fragrant fingers." Da Ponte underscores the point by then giving Giovanni lines that congratulate human beauty by employing descriptions of nature-without-consciousness: "it's like touching reeds and smelling roses" (p. 108). A few lines later da Ponte gives Giovanni an unforgettable phrase that perfectly epitomizes this behavioristic picture: using the terminology not of the genuine but of the simulacrum, not of the original but of its Platonically false appearance, Giovanni declaims to Zerlina, "the aristocracy has honesty painted in its eyes" (p. 109).

As the plot advances, the strands are woven together: just as da Ponte has wedded the physical descriptions of the previous scenes with the correlated behavioristic person-perception in the third scene, so he now picks up the thread of framing Giovanni, or positioning him in contradistinction to the others, in contexts that occasion, in Wittgenstein's terms, the further dawning of aspects. In reply to Giovanni's inducements to "join hands," Zerlina evinces a moral ambivalence that betokens an inner life fully capable of reflecting upon itself. Having said, in simultaneous apprehension and excitement, that soon she will likely no longer resist, she gives voice to a bifurcated state only available to a conscience possessing a capacity to reflect upon its sensation: "I would, and I would not" (p. 109). Giovanni neither perceives nor even instinctively responds to her ambivalence. To Elvira's outraged intervention in the proceedings (in which she issues

THREE TRAGEDIES OF THE UNEXAMINED LIFE   125

Cassandra-like warnings to Zerlina), Giovanni speaks to Zerlina here again in the fashion of his earlier mock-sympathy, claiming with the inward emptiness of a parrot (a condition to which we will also return in Chapter 6) that, as Elvira is hopelessly in love with him, he must out of pity pretend to love her. And he immediately adds, with a hollow resonance that can only come from cavernous empty places within, "it's my undoing that I'm a kind-hearted man" (p. 111). Just as Leporello's words have carried greater weight than he realized, so now Elvira— corroborating the picture of Giovanni that da Ponte has to this point drawn—says not that he is lying and deceitful, but rather, significantly, "his lips are lying, his brow is deceitful!" (p. 111). And at this moment, the contrast that separates Giovanni from the others, a contrast that shows us a good deal about the rich human significance of the *Einstellung* in both its presence and its absence, is suddenly sharpened.

As if she were bringing her moral microscope into sudden focus, Elvira refers in a single, philosophically compact line to the language of inward emotive expressivity and to the sympathetic imagination that transcends Giovanni's morally claustrophobic limits. It is precisely the combination of this inward-directed emotive expressivity and outward-directed moral imagination that allows moral-epistemic gain through the acknowledgment of the inward suffering of another. Elvira thus says to Zerlina: "Learn my suffering to believe my heart; and may my danger give birth to your fear" (p. 111). Thus with the theme of the human heart once again explicitly in play within this incrementally expanding language-game, Anna asks Giovanni in a manner that renders her inquiry a more pointed variant of Leporello's "Who's dead?" question: "Have you a heart?" In more explicitly philosophical terms, the question would become: Have you a humanity we can discern? Similarly, the next line, "have you a noble spirit?," now becomes: Have you a soul toward which we can take our distinctive attitude? A little later, Elvira, even with words as damning as these, gives Giovanni perhaps too much of an interior life by inferring the presence of the inward from the physiognomy of the outward. (This inferential model of other-knowledge is itself a conceptual warping of genuine, unmediated, non-dualistic or non-inferential person-perception). She sings: "One ought to recognize your black soul by your ugly face" (p. 115).

The ensemble passage that leads to this remark also shows more than it says. Anna and Ottavio, along with Giovanni, sing of inward feelings, some not yet named: "I feel an impulse of unknown anguish" (p. 114). And, by adding Elvira to the ensemble, they describe the inward mental experience accompanying it, describing the unclear emotional state as a jumble of thoughts and feelings "turning within [their] minds" (p. 114). They then all sing of intuition, which, like the foregoing reports of emotional turbulence, are all clear indicators of the presence of an inner life, a "soul," a sense of self, a fuller humanity. Anna sings of "something that tells me a hundred things in favor of that unhappy girl, which it

126 LIVING IN WORDS

cannot speak" (p. 114). Elvira develops a variation on the theme of mental-emotive content not yet verbally formulated (again clear evidence of an inner life upon which one is shortly to reflect and capture in the form of linguistic expression) with "something that tells me a hundred things about the betrayer, which it cannot speak, no" (p. 114). And Ottavio adds his variation of the line as well. But it is Giovanni who immediately follows Elvira. And Giovanni indeed appears fully to participate in this ensemble that itself constitutes a kind of celebration of interiority—the group senses together unknown or not yet named feelings, intuitions, and the experience we begin to describe with the words "something tells me...," and they share mental turbulence and a felt sense of the limits of language, that is, that what they possess as inward content is not sufficiently expressible in the linguistic forms presently available. They all express the same point: they recognize they need to think more, in words, about the words they need. Why then does this not itself refute the unfolding picture of the vacuous entity that is Giovanni? If we look closely at this ensemble, we see that, unlike Anna, Ottavio, and Elvira—and thus here again but with greater subtlety Giovanni is given further definition not intrinsically or in terms of what he is individually and autonomously, but relationally, in comparison to the others, and negatively, in terms of what he is not—Giovanni does not contribute a single new phrase or even a word of his own. Rather like Anna's more sophisticated variant of Leporello's question, here da Ponte returns to the parroting theme, but he now uses it to show that a parroted "expression" of interiority in fact indicates, within this musical-ensemble-turned-moral-comparison, not the presence of an inner life, but rather its absence.

Indeed, were there such humane interiority, the exacting reduplication of the others' phraseology would be unnecessary; with such reduplication, one sees Giovanni as morally hollow, as merely a speaking automaton. The point for us is that the words are in a thin sense identical, and yet the words are a world apart: in the other cases these words are autobiographically expressive utterances; in Giovanni's case they are empty playback. It is thus exquisitely fitting that, only a few passages later, Anna and Ottavio, given the stage direction to look at Giovanni curiously, do precisely that, and they do so not with the language of humane sympathetic understanding, but with the very dehumanized behavioristic external-feature analysis encountered earlier as Giovanni's vocabulary: they sing of "Those very subdued tones, that change of coloring," and they call such indicators "signs." Moreover, when Giovanni finally manages to pull Elvira away, he does so again with the physical force of the body, and not with any appeal sent, as it were, from his inner compassionate self-composition to her inner volition.[5] Near the close of Scene III, Anna and Ottavio exchange words that

---

[5] One could make a study of the stage directions for Giovanni's comportment and its significance for the description of his condition. See, for other examples, Giovanni dragging Zerlina into the shrubbery

THREE TRAGEDIES OF THE UNEXAMINED LIFE   127

strongly and unambiguously state both what the heart demands (Anna) and the power of the sympathetically imaginative understanding of another's emotional state, toward which we display, precisely, Wittgenstein's *Einstellung*. Ottavio himself expresses the same with "my peace depends on hers"; "If she sighs, I sigh also"; "her wrath is mine, her tears are mine." The very intelligibility of the special human closeness measurable by a mutually interdependent peace of heart rests upon the foundational practice of first having mutually discerned the humanity of which Wittgenstein writes. The contrast to Giovanni's condition thus becomes ever starker: Leporello, upon shortly thereafter seeing a person—well, an entity—who has caused death, loss, pain, grief, and suffering all around him, is offended by what would for a genuine person be the most callous disregard as displayed in Giovanni's happy and untroubled gait, posture, and stance. Taken together, all this shows an attitude towards anything but a soul. Leporello sings: "I ought to leave this madman forever, on any condition! There he is; look how nonchalantly he comes along!" (p. 121).

Don Giovanni is an opera thick with images and themes resonant with the interrelated philosophical issues of self-knowledge or its absence, substantial humane self-content or its absence as displayed in language and in our relation to our words, the nature of our knowledge of others, and the fundamental issues of person-perception upon which the previous issues stand. In addition to the themes we have now followed that dramatically lead inexorably into the second and final act, we also see (1) reiterations of the misidentification of cloaked presences (Anna in Act I, Scene III, p. 118); (2) their use again, along with masks, in the masquerade (in Act I, Scene IV); (3) episodes of dissimulation and ironic truth-claims (Giovanni and Leporello, and then, with sarcastic repetition (and so the same words, but not meaninglessly so) by Masetto, later in Act I, Scene IV, p. 137); and (4) references, not to directly perceived moral qualities or character traits, but to signs of them (e.g., Anna, Elvira, and Ottavio expressing gratitude for signs of generosity, p. 136) where the very concept of a sign introduces skepticism concerning our knowledge (with talk of signs, now indirect knowledge) of that personal quality or trait (to perceive a sign of a thing is not to

---

in Act I, Scene IV (p. 130), and his maneuvering-while-dancing with Zerlina (followed immediately by his trying to pull her through the door) in Act I, Scene V (p. 138). Wittgenstein wrote at one point that "the body is the best picture of the human soul." Stage directions, as embodied depictions, rest upon this fact of our natural history. To put the matter in a related but different way, one might say that Giovanni's behavior in this respect displays the phenomenon of "soul-blindness" as discussed by Wittgenstein and in turn by Stanley Cavell in *The Claim of Reason: Wittgenstein, Skepticism, Morality, and Tragedy* (Oxford: Oxford University Press, 1979). Giovanni's soul-blindness might also usefully be discussed as the instructive polar opposite to the distinctive variety of human attentiveness of which authors as diverse as Iris Murdoch (articulated in philosophy and shown in fiction), Martha Nussbaum, Toril Moi, Cora Diamond, Simone Weil, and again Cavell, on acknowledgment, write.

128 LIVING IN WORDS

perceive that thing). And now Giovanni's words, at the close of the first act, connote more than what at first glance appears.

Confronted by his enemies, he declares that even if the world should fall apart, nothing would ever make him afraid (p. 146). This could be a sign of courage or inner strength. But then it could also be a telling remark about a specific moral impossibility: nothing could ever make him afraid, precisely because there is no present self to satisfy the logical precondition for so much as having an emotion such as fear in the first place. The ambiguity arises because the sense of self behind, or really within, the words is missing.

The extended deception that opens Act II underscores both instability of character (we will examine how autobiographical words can stabilize character in Chapters 5 and 6) and the debased identification of personhood through externalities. With Giovanni and Leporello in each other's cloak and hat, they are mistaken for each other in a number of encounters. Yet, importantly, it is not Giovanni but Leporello who is discovered; a characterless entity would of course be able to sustain the deception in a way no person could. All of this unfolds from the opening exchange of the act, in which Giovanni, asking his servant why he wants to be done with his master, says—with humorous irony on the surface but conceptually linking the trivial with the ultimately inhumane act, where such a linkage is generally conceivable only in the case of the most extreme sociopath or an entity of utter inward vacuity: "Oh, nothing at all, you almost murdered me" (p. 149). Surface-level humor, but offered just above forceful—and in terms of plot development, unstoppable—undercurrents, continues throughout the opera. In response to Leporello's "And you have the heart then to deceive them all?" Giovanni replies with a line that, in many performances, brings forth a burst of readily audible laughter from the audience. But like many remarks evoking sudden outbursts of laughter, it floats atop a deeper, hidden wave of moral significance. Giovanni replies: "It's all love; whoever is faithful only to one is cruel to the others" (p. 151). It was Aristotle, again in *Nicomachean Ethics*, who commented on the impossibility of the truth of any such utterance: love, he said, is an extreme and extreme cases are by definition limited. They are the exceptions, and not, *contra* Giovanni's line, the rule. (Aristotle also said that love takes time, and so, time being for better and worse a finite commodity, love cannot run to large numbers.) Giovanni continues: "I, who feels such ample sentiment in myself, love them all," and with this adds self-deceptive misdescription to the Aristotelian impossibility. It is not only that, given what we know of him, he does not feel this, but rather, and more interestingly, given what we know of the nature of love, he could not feel it. Because of what we know of life, we can judge some autobiographical words to be false or impossible in advance of further inquiry. Concluding the passage by adding insult to self-blinding rhetoric and emotive impossibility, Giovanni sings: "and since women don't comprehend these things, they call my natural goodness deceit." And still deeper beneath this remark, with

THREE TRAGEDIES OF THE UNEXAMINED LIFE   129

latent content reminiscent of the subtextual significance of the "signs" considered above (where a skeptical gap is introduced between a moral character trait and its perception), the very notion of calling the self-proclaimed goodness "deceit" introduces a skepticism, or descriptive relativism, concerning moral attributes. This skepticism implicitly suggests that moral descriptions are, or at least can be, arbitrary linguistic constructions and thus that, for Giovanni-as-radical-subjectivist, any description, however capriciously put forward, is as good as any other. This may perhaps be going too far, but then Leporello's quick response, brimming with irony ("Never have I seen a nature more ample and more kind!"), immediately reestablishes our sense of shared descriptive practices, of the scaffolding or stage setting of which Wittgenstein spoke as the expanded conceptual backdrop against which any action or utterance is made intelligible (which we saw, in microcosm, in the case of the builders' language and all the conceptual stage setting that needs to be in place before we can get so far as minimally understanding it). The power of Leporello's irony here is dependent upon the preexistence, and our shared implicit acknowledgment of, these background practices of moral description. His words will only work against that background. That the characterization of, indeed, character is not linguistically arbitrary is what at once makes Giovanni's claim funny and Leporello's reply pointed.

Throughout the remainder of Act II a good number of the themes already in play are further interwoven: (1) Elvira, reinforcing the contrast between substantive inner content and its absence, reports a "strange sensation awakening in my breast" (p. 153); (2) Leporello refers again to Giovanni's "lying lips," thus reinforcing the growing conception we have of him of vacuous animalism (p. 155); (3) Giovanni instructs Leporello, unreflectively and oblivious to the identity-determining human individualism of the expressive voice, to imitate his own voice (p. 155); (4) the conceptual linking of triviality and death is reinforced by Giovanni's own words "hah, hah, you're dead!" (p. 157); (5) the vacuous rhetoric of the artificially "heartfelt," designed to deceive and manipulate, is robotically articulated by Giovanni—"to the depths of my heart," etc. (p. 158)—thus suggesting the wholesale absence of such depth, so his autobiographical language reveals the reverse of what that language explicitly asserts; (6) the increasingly stark, and increasingly Giovanni-defining contrast of this with genuine heartfelt utterances, e.g., "only death can end my weeping," thus showing in the human cases that emotions are self-defining forces and strong influences on thought and action that involuntarily shape how and even who (to which we will return at length in Chapter 6) one is (p. 165); (7) thoughts, also beyond the grip of volition, churn in the head of everyone but Giovanni, thus indicating both serious moral engagement and humane presence (pp.168–9); and (8) Elvira resumes the Cassandra-like predictions and premonitions (of thunderbolts that will strike, and chasms that will engulf, Giovanni) that point to the developmental trajectory of an increasingly sensed inexorable moral necessity (p. 179). But it is an exchange between the Don

130 LIVING IN WORDS

and his servant, early in the graveyard scene, that encapsulates Giovanni's condition with the greatest density. Leporello reports that, because he was mistaken for Giovanni, he was nearly beaten to death (p. 181). As a perfectly turned depiction of a grotesque failure of moral imagination and an utter, solipsistic incapacity to imagine the reality of the life of another, Giovanni replies—suggesting that to be mistaken for Giovanni is, even if lethal, preferable to being anyone else—"Well, wasn't that an honor for you?" (p. 181). It is with Giovanni in this profoundly vacuous condition, his words here revealing so powerfully what he is not, that the statue of the Commendatore begins to speak.

Having been instructed to read the inscription on the statue, Leporello, while on the humorous surface telling Giovanni that he has not learned to read by moonlight, in the morally serious subtext plants the seed of a theme: the notion of the inscription, the message, the content, that cannot be read, or interpreted, because of its concealment in the dark. Emphasizing corporeality (shortly to be re-emphasized in Giovanni's and Leporello's singing together about his gigantic mouthfuls [p. 190]), Giovanni forces Leporello to issue forth the invitation to the statue to dine. The statue accepts, and the closing lines of Act II, Scene IV also weave into the textual fabric here one strand of an earlier theme: Leporello is terrified and can think only of getting away; Giovanni, commenting impassively on the weirdness of the scene, is—with, in a sense, the world collapsing around him—frightened by nothing.

In Act II, Scene VI Giovanni physically pulls Elvira, who is delivering an entreaty in the comparatively revealing terms of her "oppressed soul" (p. 192), to her feet, and he promptly mocks her most sincere expressive utterances. Leporello, now near the close of the opera but just as in its beginning, offers another essential interpretive clue as to what one should read as philosophically significant in the scene: "If her sorrow doesn't move him, he has a heart of stone, or he hasn't got a heart!" (p. 193). His words tell us what he is, and who he isn't. Leporello emphatically repeats the point in response to Elvira's increasingly hostile (and informatively increasingly dehumanized) invective: "filthy stench! A dreadful example of evil!" (p. 194). Giovanni's disengaged query as to the meaning of Elvira's screams (having just glimpsed the approaching statue) further tells us what we already know about the Wittgensteinian *Einstellung* that is conspicuous for its absence, the inward vacancy wherein we should instead find lodged the precondition of an irreducible humanity.

It is of the greatest significance to the philosophical interpretation of this opera that neither Elvira (who runs screaming) nor Leporello (who after no fewer than four clear orders from Giovanni to answer the basso profundo knock at the door goes to hide under the table) confront the statue. Against his repeated protestations, Giovanni is forced to do this himself. Why this is centrally significant, however, is layered in its complexity. The tragic element of the opera—one might say the opera seria that flows beneath the opera buffa—lies within this display of

THREE TRAGEDIES OF THE UNEXAMINED LIFE   131

character: Giovanni has become, or rather statically remains, through ever more deeply ingrained habit (of precisely the kind Aristotle described as making "all the difference" in the development of a human being), constitutionally incapable of reflection upon his own life. He feeds, as we have seen, wholly upon Lockean sensation at the inestimably high cost of reflection. That is one layer of the moral content of this opera, and as such it contributes to the power of the opera's greatest moment, where the statue of the Commendatore calls Giovanni's name in the most forceful, gripping, stentorian tones. (The statue sings in the strongest harmonic terms available to music, i.e., fifth to tonic, both above and below, which stand in striking morally mimetic contrast to the far less stable melodic lines of Giovanni). That characterological incapacity, as one layer of the opera's tragic content, shows a kind of "self" (or, as we have seen, more accurately an instructive absence of the foundational human content of selfhood) that, despite the Commendatore's injunctions, is incapable of even the slightest hint of gravitas. And the closing line of the opera, where the ensemble sings that Giovanni's death was just like his life, encapsulates this tragedy of character: his death was the same as his life, in that Giovanni—enduring his descent into the flames of the under-world with only redoubled resistance in the place of self-reflective repentance—experiences his own demise, including his interaction with the statue, as simply one more episode in the unbroken string of episodes in his life.

It is at this layer of interpretation that one can see the error of criticizing the narrative structure of the opera as merely episodic: the word "episodic" does describe the opera's structural type, but this is the structure that mimetically reflects the structure of Giovanni's life, the structure of his moral blindness to both others and to himself. And even though Giovanni's life unto himself is a mere series of episodes (most memorably emblematized in the catalogue aria) uncon-nected by any deeper thread of seriousness, of underlying deeply purposeful continuity, we, as moral spectators upon his condition, can clearly see the minimal structure of his life, a structure that fails to satisfy the preconditions of a genuinely humane life. Aristotle identified the episodic as the weakest structure aesthetically:[6] so too, as this opera shows, is the episodic the weakest structure ethically. And we, as moral spectators, also see (in recognizing the moral significance of the very vacuity of his selfhood and its episodic structure) a larger-scale structure of the opera that is, indeed, serious, teleologically interwoven over the long form, and one which generates the inexorability of Giovanni's descent. Giovanni, to the bitter end, remains blind to all this, and a tragedy of moral vacuity thus engenders a tragedy of self-ignorance; the words he would need to become humanized forever unavailable. To put it most succinctly, Giovanni's own life is interwoven

---

[6] *The Poetics of Aristotle*, ch. 9, pp. 40–2.

132   LIVING IN WORDS

into the opera's form in such a way that the opera itself assumes the form of a personal tragedy of nearly wordless self-ignorance.

But again, his world is not ours, and our experience of the opera is—for its content concerning substantive selfhood and the *Einstellung* that defines person-perception (again, including the perception of both self and others)—irreducible to the merely episodic. Indeed, the opera, taken *in toto*, is itself an analogue for the very nature of selfhood that it studies: the opera and the self display a parallel irreducibility, and they show the dangers of externalized behavioristic reductionism. Giovanni cannot see the inexorability (of precisely the kind Aristotle articulated and that we considered in Chapter 3) that we do, and self-blindness, habitual throughout and then defiantly willful at the very end, prevents Giovanni from comprehending the significance of his own demise. And this leads us to the next layer of philosophical significance.

It is true that the opera exhibits, in its most large-scale form, a rounded structure: the Commendatore's death at the beginning is counterbalanced by Giovanni's descent into the flames at the end. And the moral contrast between persons of substance and (in Wittgenstein's special sense) attitude on the one side and an entity of vacuous identity missing precisely these qualities on the other that is drawn in the numerous particularities we have seen along the opera's narrative way is also drawn on the grander scale: it is writ large in the two contrasting losses of life—the loss of conscious, reflective experience, indeed the loss of an inner life—at the death of the Commendatore, and the cessation of episodic sensory existence at the death of Giovanni. And we see the speaking statue as a sculptural reincarnation of that first lost life: the Commendatore, although transfigured into stone, still possesses the capacity for moral self-reflection of which Giovanni remains incapable. The presence of humane gravitas in the opening scene with the Commendatore's death inversely mirrors the Don's end. As viewers with a range extending well beyond Giovanni's claustrophobic intentional world, we witness the tragic triumph of frivolity and a lack of reflective self-examination over autobiographical gravitas, and again, it is precisely this absence that renders Giovanni singularly unequipped to fathom his own, let alone anyone else's, mortality.[7] But the statue, at the deeper interpretive layer, is not the Commendatore, and thus there is greater content to the tragic element of this opera than any interpretation focused exclusively on the first layer could explain.

Aristotle, in yet another famous passage in the *Poetics* where he is describing the powerful grip of some dramatic forms, observes that the case of the bad man falling from a great height is odious, but not tragic, and thus of minimal gripping

---

[7] And so, not unlike Wittgenstein on the problem of a private language where the first-person use of a word is inconceivable without the social fabric within which that word has a life, Giovanni is not able to see, to reflect upon, to autobiographically investigate himself precisely because he cannot truly see another first. His profound self-blindness is a function of what is, for him, the unimaginability of other minds.

power (in contrast to the good man falling from a great height owing to some character flaw or misstep in thought or action making the tragic fall inevitable and the plot leading to it inexorable). Yet the "Don Giovanni moment," where the statue calls his name, is the most spine-tingling and powerful passage of this entire opera. Something deeper than what Aristotle described as the odiousness of a bad man falling must, in order to explain the dramatic power, be at work. And it is clear that we cannot describe Giovanni's case as that of a good man falling due to some character flaw or misstep in word or deed that makes the tragic fall inevitable and the plot sequence leading to it inexorable.

Not all mirroring in the opera is inverted: it is not as simple as the Commendatore-versus-Giovanni of the first layer. The stone Commendatore, one must recall, tells Leporello to disregard Giovanni's instruction to bring another plate, and that (as a soul) he draws nourishment from heavenly, not earthly, things. He is a soul, but one that is now in the graveyard and at dinner manifesting himself in a form that itself mimetically reflects Giovanni: stone as an utter absence of interiority. Unwittingly saying once again more than he understands, Leporello gives voice to the identification of the statue with Giovanni when he describes him as either having a heart of stone or no heart at all. Then, against his will, Giovanni is forced to answer the door himself, and that moment, in portraying so clearly his desire to avoid the direct confrontation with the statue, stands as outward symbol for his own long-avoided self-confrontation. The Commendatore's chilling basso profundo "Don Giovanni" strikes so deeply because it calls for a self-confrontation, the sort of call, philosophically speaking, that demands self-investigation as a first step away from inward vacuity and towards substantive selfhood. It is a call that threatens, indeed demands, self-knowledge, and in doing so it thus demands—with the powerful, authoritative grip of the doubly significant handshake, from which Giovanni struggles to free himself—a regarding of the self by the self, with the *Einstellung* that is the fundamental content of humane acknowledgment. Fleeing, one last time, this demand, Giovanni desires only to remain unreadable unto himself in his darkness.

That most powerful line in the opera, musically with fifth and tonic, verbally with the only name the self could call to itself, speaks not only of the lighter "tragedy" of a libertine brought to account. It speaks far more deeply—and far more resonantly for every human being going back to Oedipus who has fought battles of self-knowledge—of a self perennially *in absentia* unto itself, soaking in sensation and denying reflection. Giovanni's final refusal to repent is not merely that: the power of the call demands that it not be only that. It is a denial of an awakening self, one that calls out to satisfy the first, elemental precondition of humanity. As such, the moment conveys, again in a manner following Aristotle, not merely a particularized historical truth, but a far more gripping universal, poetic truth about what we are and should be both in relation to each other and in relation to ourselves. And that relation, to others and to ourselves, is a relation of words.

134 LIVING IN WORDS

In seeing persons as mere instruments for a shallow diversionary and episodic gratification (or merely what a behaviorist reduction of personhood would leave in view), Giovanni lives in a world populated not by the people, but by the masks, at his party.[8] But we know, here following Wittgenstein, that a masked self is the exception, intelligible only against what Wittgenstein called the "scaffolding of thought" that brings with it the very possibility of identity concealment. Masking is only possible within a much broader context of identity revelation and disclosure; the mask can only make sense *against* this backdrop. Giovanni himself (if the word "himself" is not in this case an oxymoron) is nothing but mask: he is pure appearance. And the reduced entities he perceives on the level of pure sensation around him are similarly, tragically for him and for those with whom he interacts, nothing but masks, nothing but appearances. So Giovanni does indeed open the opera with what we can now deem the most philosophically meaningful line: "You shall not know who I am!" Absent the responsive attitudinal preconditions for humanity (and thus for morality) in the form of both other- and self-acknowledgment and the language that carries those forms of recognition, indeed we never will, and never could, know who he is: the Wittgensteinian *Einstellung* is at once as we have said irreducible, but also, with regard to human understanding and as this opera shows, ineliminable. Leporello's question "Who's dead—you or the old man?" is an interrogatory that does indeed make more than joking sense in reference to what is, to put it one way, a prototypical man without qualities, a man whose accurate mimetic depiction is stone. Bernard Williams began a brilliant essay on *Don Giovanni* with the observation that Giovanni is not us.[9] I think Williams too is right beyond what he perhaps intended: Giovanni is not us because Giovanni is not, instructively, anyone.

4.2 Aware Too Late: Dencombe's Final Moments (Henry James's "The Middle Years")

In *Philosophical Investigations* §426 Wittgenstein presents a dream of fixing a sense unambiguously, of clearing away what is muddied down here on the ground of our usage. He writes:

---

[8] I have discussed problems of the behavioristic reduction of personhood in "The Self, Speaking: Wittgenstein, Introspective Utterances, and the Arts of Self-Representation," *Revue Internationale de Philosophie*, 219, 2002: 9–47, and related issues of person-perception in "The Mind Shown: Wittgenstein, Goethe, and the Question of Person-Perception," in *Goethe and Wittgenstein: Seeing the World's Unity in its Variety* (Wittgenstein-Studien, Band 5), ed. Fritz Breithaupt, Richard Raatzsch, and Bettina Kremberg (Frankfurt am Main: Peter Lang, 2003), pp. 111–26.

[9] Bernard Williams, "Don Juan as an Idea," in *Don Giovanni*, ed. Julian Rushton (Cambridge: Cambridge University Press, 1981), pp. 81–91.

THREE TRAGEDIES OF THE UNEXAMINED LIFE   135

A picture is conjured up which seems to fix the sense *unambiguously*. The actual use, compared with that suggested by the picture, seems like something muddied. Here again we get the same thing as in set theory: the form of expression we use seems to have been designed for a god, who knows what we cannot know; he sees the whole of each of those infinite series and he sees into human consciousness. For us, of course, these forms of expression are like pontificals which we may put on, but cannot do much with, since we lack the effective power that would give these vestments meaning and purpose.

In the actual use of expressions we make detours, we go by side-roads. We see the straight highway before us, but of course we cannot use it, because it is permanently closed.

So this is the dream of (what was called in philosophy's history) an ideal language, and it is, or at least it can be, literature that awakens us from this captivating dream—this illusion of perfection. Or to put it another way, through seeing language as it is actually *used* with point, power, and purpose, we realize that, in seeking the invariant word meaning that would prove insensitive to the vicissitudes of context, of communicative occasion, we are donning vestments without power, meaning, or purpose—without the circumstantially seated particularities that make the wearing of those vestments real. Literature, I want to suggest, shows us where we *actually* travel verbally—the endlessly interweaving side roads we take with our words—and in doing so it shows us not only how much we would have missed by staying to the straight highway, but indeed that, were we to insist on trying to take the straight highway, we would quickly enough realize (with literary detail as our instructor in communicative complexity) that we did not have a genuine means of conveyance that could get any traction. Autobiographical words, in life and as used by persons in the avenues of self-reflection, have this traction, solidifying what we mean and who we are.

And in *Philosophical Investigations*, Part II, sec. iv, Wittgenstein wrote:

And how about such an expression as: 'In my heart I understood when you said that', pointing to one's heart? Does one, perhaps, not *mean* this gesture? Of course one means it. Or is one conscious of using a *mere* figure? Indeed not.—It is not a figure that we choose, not a simile, yet it is a figurative expression.

This suggests that human understanding of some depth (of the kind that, in human tragedies, can come not at all, or too little, or too late) may not be the kind of thing best captured by theories of denotation or by a dictionary's word definitions. In this section, then, I want to pursue, within the larger context of a cautionary tale concerning an insufficiently examined life, (1) what it takes to genuinely understand what we might call a "heartfelt" utterance (in this case, something as seemingly—but only seemingly—simple as an emphatic "It's true!");

136   LIVING IN WORDS

(2) how the complexity of such understanding seriously undermines (or awakens us from the dream of) an ideal language, and (3) suggest how one kind of Wittgensteinian reading of a literary text might unfold, where that reading begins to call into question the categorical separation of literary interpretation from philosophical investigation as it shows us something instructive about our words as we travel with them. And to do these things, I will look back once again to a writer whose work I believe holds deep significance for the philosophy of language, Henry James, in this case in his tale entitled "The Middle Years."

The opening words of this story are "The April day was soft and bright, and poor Dencombe, happy in the conceit of reasserted strength, stood in the garden of the hotel..." (p. 235). As we learned from Eliot, April is the cruelest month. Its cruelty lies in its double aspect, being both a month of a continuing winter in which one comes to long for the spring, but then also—sometimes—that very spring. It is one thing and looks forward to another; it continues the past of the winter, delivering it, wearily, into the present, just as it severs its ties to the past and inaugurates a new season. One might say it is a month of bifocal displacement, looking in two directions at once, displaying a fluctuating identity. Or: It seems to aspire to a condition of being better than it is. April, however, is hardly the only exemplar of bifocal displacement, of double-aspect identity in this story. We meet Dencombe, James's protagonist, in a condition of recovery, and with it the faint promise of renewal. Yet he stands in the garden, James tells us, contemplating "the attraction of easy strolls" with, significantly, "a deliberation in which however there was still something of languour." Languor hangs over from the past, delivering itself into the present, despite Dencombe's explicit forward-looking intention of recovery and his inner psychological displacement—about which James, as moral philosopher in literary clothing, will show us a great deal in very small scope[10]—is mirrored now not meteorologically but geographically: "He liked the feeling of the south so far as you could have it in the north...."

---

[10] Given James's often-stated and always-displayed concern with the literary quality of "compression," it is not surprising that he is able to convey philosophical significance in small scope. See, for example, his remark in the Prefaces to the New York Edition, included in the Kermode edition of "The Middle Years," in Frank Kermode, ed., *The Figure in the Carpet and Other Stories* (London: Penguin: 1986, pp. 235–58) and to which all page references in this section refer, on p. 46: "To get it right was to squeeze my subject into the five or six thousand words I had been invited to make it consist of... and I scarce perhaps recall another case... in which my struggle to keep compression rich, if not, better still, to keep accretions compressed..." He goes on to contrast the form of the *nouvelle* with that of "the concise anecdote," suggesting that "The Middle Years" is of the latter form. And as very often happens in James (particularly in his tales concerning the literary life), his art mirrors his life: Dencombe seeks a "rare compression." James's frequently unstated but always-displayed suspicion of conceptual generality and its articulation in generalization is interestingly expressed in terms of visual perception. "It was indeed general views that were terrible; short ones, contrary to an opinion sometimes expressed, were the refuge, were the remedy" (p. 242). As I have argued elsewhere (in *Meaning and Interpretation*, passim), there is a striking similarity stretching across conventional disciplinary boundaries to the later philosophical methods of Wittgenstein: misleading generalities and their underlying metaphysical "pictures," i.e., thought-governing conceptual models perhaps held unwittingly, are treated, on a

Dencombe in short likes the *idea* of one place while in truth occupying another place of a very different kind. The north delivers the hint, or the faint promise, of the south when it changes its aspect. Dencombe's inward self is one that likes (and as we shall see, longs for) the *idea* of a better self. James first leads us to think that this better self refers to a better *physical* self; this is explicitly shown in Dencombe's reaction to his own quickness to tire. "He was tired enough when he reached it [the bench], and for a moment was disappointed." This flicker of disappointment at the clinging illness he hopes to leave in the past is accompanied by a preliminary reflection concerning the relative or the need for a relationally situated meaning of "better": "he was better, of course, but better, after all, than what?" This thought of relative terms (words that demand a context to be so much as minimally understood) is immediately followed by a far darker absolute assertion: "He should never again, as at one or two great moments of the past, be better than himself." The plausibility of ever-new potentialities and actualities is something Dencombe is rapidly exhausting; as James puts it, the "infinite of life was gone," and of the actual dose of life only a "small glass scored like a thermometer by the apothecary" remains. But again, this is only the physical mirroring of what is of primary interest in this story, that is, the psychological meaning of Dencombe's aspiration to be "better than himself" and our grasp of the true meanings of Dencombe's autobiographical words.

James effects the transition from the concerns of the body to the preoccupations of the mind with characteristic ease. Resting on the bench, with a parcel he has been handed by the postman a little while earlier, Dencombe looks out at the sea. What he sees is "all surface and twinkle," and what he thinks is that this is "far shallower than the spirit of man." With the polarity of surface and depth now directing his subsequent thought, he reflects, seemingly paradoxically, that the human abyss is indeed real, but that the reality of this very abyss is constituted of human illusion. To himself, he says, "It was the abyss of human illusion that was the real, the tideless deep."

Dencombe knows fully well what the parcel contains: an advance copy of his latest book, *The Middle Years*. Something keeps him from opening it, and it is more than another felt incapacity for full revivification: he took "for granted there could be no complete renewal of the pleasure, dear to young experience, of seeing one's self 'just out'" (p. 236); indeed James tells us not just that Dencombe knew this, but that he knew *too* well, he knew "too well in advance" the state that would come over him. This state, given what we know so far of him, not surprisingly is bifurcated: it simultaneously looks at what he has done *and* at the imagined future, the achievement to which he aspires. He knows the hope of what he calls

---

rough analogy to psychoanalysis, as disorders of the understanding, where the treatment, the remedy, consists of closely studied (or closely read) particularity, as we saw in connection with some architectural models of self-constitution in the preceding chapter.

"betterness" will wash out, will diminish the present. Dencombe continues to postpone this half-anticipated state and finds, after the fact, something of a rationalization for it: "His postponement associated itself vaguely, after a little, with a group of three persons" (p. 236) he sees below him on the beach, one of whom, a young gentleman, is reading a book in a state of undistractable absorption. So absorbed is this reader that "while the romance of life stood neglected at his side he lost himself" in the novel, with one companion wandering off with a "martyred droop of the head" while the other imitated a crash-landing on the beach (p. 237). No such histrionics are sufficient to divert the observed reader. Dencombe's attention to the reader is equally rapt until the little "drama began to fail," and Dencombe finally unwraps his latest and—setting the tone for the final reckoning of this delicately unfolding word-borne moral philosophy—what he now describes as "perhaps his last" work.

At this moment the severity of Dencombe's condition—in both physical and psychological terms—becomes apparent. He opens the parcel and sees the newly printed book, but, sensing "a strange alienation," realizes that he does not remember what the book is about. A fortnight in bed, during his illness, "passed the sponge over colour," i.e., washed out any details of his memory of the work and he "couldn't have chanted to himself a single sentence." Physically, he is obviously moving away from recovery, and psychologically, he is momentarily wholly displaced from himself, the possessor of a mind that does not recognize or recall its own literary progeny. Yet in this state he does recall, and vividly, his higher aspirations, his desire to begin again his life as a writer, beginning again in possession of all the skill heretofore achieved but with a freshness unconstrained by force of habit, by the past. "Alienation" is precisely the right word: he is an alien to himself, made so by a momentary lapse wholly into the other, competing aspect of his mental life, the aspect that looks only forward, never backward, and that would disown all he has done, demoting it to the merely preparatory. In this state he "uttered a low moan as he breathed the chill of this dark void, so desperately it seemed to represent the completion of a sinister process." So once again in James we are presented with ambiguity: the sinister process is in fact conceptual but presented as physical; his long-nourished dream—indeed perhaps itself an abysmal illusion of a better future—is robbing him of his present. He has come to the extreme point of psychic division. But "[s]omething precious," he now thinks, has "passed away" (pp. 237–8). The dream of transcending himself and beginning anew with past redefined as prologue, he sees, is impossible. This is the psychological environment from which his words of self-description come, as it is the environment in which the narrator biographically describes him.

Characterized as the "pang" that proved itself the sharpest he had felt in recent years, Dencombe's "sense of ebbing time, of shrinking opportunity" now has seemingly reached its culmination: "he felt not so much that his last chance was going as that it was gone indeed." The narrator caps this condition with another

THREE TRAGEDIES OF THE UNEXAMINED LIFE   139

assertion displaying a chilling, absolute finality: "He had done all he should ever do, and yet he hadn't done what he wanted." Now the prey of dread, he finally opens the book (a single volume, because in this work he aimed—with art within art imitating James's art within life—at a "rare compression") and quickly "everything came back to him." By "everything" James means not just the forgotten (or perhaps really disavowed) contents of the book, but rather the plausibility of the dream of a new start. Dencombe regains this inward vision as something like a miniature epiphany, with a "high and magnificent beauty" accompanied by a sense of wonder—all possible only from the vantage point of extreme self-alienation—without that, its sudden magnificent return to his psychology would not be wondrous. In short, he now fitfully regains his sense of the extended better possible future. "[H]e had a glimpse of a possible reprieve. Surely its [his art] force wasn't spent—there was life and service in it yet." What he had forgotten in his illness, within this part of his identity (or, as we shall see in Chapter 5 below, within this web of articulated belief), was the high quality of the work ("it was extraordinarily good") of the previous year. His talent and his perception had never been so fine, and this he suddenly and newly recognizes—he sees his own work and possibilities under a new aspect.

But what is of particular interest about James's depiction of Dencombe's mind is that, immediately upon recognizing the quality of his new book, he again uses that recognition to fuel the dreamworld of the future in which he will greatly surpass it. He both sees and does not see his own accomplishment. In seeing the quality—now a revelation to him in what one might call his psychologically post-lapsarian condition—he sees the implicit possibility of the new start, and this in effect pulls down a veil between himself and his real work, his genuine achievement. James describes this psychology acutely:

> What he saw so intensely today, what he felt as a nail driven in, was that only now, at the very last, had he come into possession. His development had been abnormally slow, almost grotesquely gradual. He had been hindered and retarded by experience, he had for long periods only grasped his way. It had taken too much of his life to produce too little of his art. The art had come, but it had come after everything else. At such a rate a first existence was too short—long enough only to collect material; so that to fructify, to use the material, one should have a second age, an extension. This extension was what poor Dencombe sighed for. As he turned the last leaves of his volume, he murmured "Ah for another go, ah for a better chance!"   (p. 239)

Thus in what may appear a reintegration of Dencombe's self—in that the acknowledgment of the actual work is restored along with hope looking toward the future—we see in truth a return to a pernicious bifurcation that, again, deprives Dencombe of a full-blooded sense of his present and of his actual achievement. To

140 LIVING IN WORDS

express the matter in fully paradoxical form, the extent to which Dencombe sees and acknowledges his achievement is precisely the extent to which he does not see and acknowledge it, because the degree of plausibility of the dream of a better future just is the degree to which he recognizes what he has before him. To put it less paradoxically, he cannot see the actuality for the potentiality that is implicit in that actuality. And this may, again, constitute a very human reality—the abysmal reality of the illusory, that "tideless deep" from earlier in the story, the real imaginative force that possesses the power to bifurcate, to displace, to alienate. Without the details of his mind and state as described to this point, we cannot understand the meaning, his personally expressive and self-reflective meaning both telling us who he is and speaking and contemplating those words, as they function autobiographically for him as he says them, of the words "Ah for another go!" (In such cases we often say things such as "There was more in those words than it initially seemed"; at the end of this study I will suggest that there is almost always more in our words in this sense.)

As the story progresses, Dencombe meets the rapt reader on the beach: Doctor Hugh, who does not learn for some time that the man before him is Dencombe the author, proclaims enthusiastically "it's the best thing he has done yet!" (p. 242). Tellingly, Dencombe focuses on the pair of words "done yet," which, he observes, "made such a grand avenue of the future"; his focusing on the phrase perfectly encapsulates in verbal microcosm his paradoxical position. The particular way in which James has Dencombe reflect on, and articulate to himself, the unexplored possibilities along that "grand avenue" tells us something about James's own vision of literary creativity: Dencombe puts the matter in terms of *mimesis* (implicitly) and *combination* (explicitly). Dencombe realizes that Doctor Hugh may well be of assistance to him in his convalescence, particularly as a source of new treatments. Yet he reflects that "it would shake his faith a little perhaps to have to take a doctor seriously who could take *him* so seriously" (p. 243). This reflection in turn leads him to the future-directed thought that there would still be a great deal of work to do "in a world in which such odd combinations were presented."

Mimetically capturing this world, not for its grand views but for its nuanced particularities, would indeed create interest, indeed create art, and—in infusing life itself with interest through the mimetic scrutiny and accumulated, reflective comprehension that art allows (to which we return in the second and third sections of Chapter 5)—to that extent create life. With mimesis at the foundation, creativity could unfold in terms of ever-new combinations,[11] or to model the

---

[11] James also sees personalities in combinatorial terms. See for example his description of Doctor Hugh: "Who would work the miracle for him but the young man who could combine such lucidity with such passion?" (p. 251). Personalities, and the process of character formation, can also usefully be seen in terms of belief-combinations; we shall return to this in Chapter 5, Section 5.1.

THREE TRAGEDIES OF THE UNEXAMINED LIFE   141

matter here also as new moves within the circumscribed contexts of the literary versions of incrementally expanding Wittgensteinian language-games. And in so far as life itself is made, or at the very least revivified, intensified, and conceptually clarified, the fictional fiction (i.e., fiction within James's story) that Dencombe wants to create (and has already—if in unacknowledged or semi-acknowledged form—created) and that James has actually created, we might illuminatingly characterize as just what Wittgenstein called a "form of life." James actually and Dencombe fictionally perceive the inexhaustibility of this larger form of life and these language-games as they unfold within it: James's narrator says, "It wasn't true, what he had tried for renunciation's sake to believe, that all the combinations were exhausted. They weren't by any means—they were infinite: the exhaustion was in the miserable artist." The combinations were not—and could not be— exhausted. And the relations—of both Henry and William—end nowhere.

But the fundamental point here concerns the incapacity of Dencombe to acknowledge what he has done as an expression of himself, and thus to achieve self-integration of a kind born of autobiographical veracity. His work, I want to suggest, is itself (not unlike James's entire body of work, finally integrated, polished, detailed, and "framed" with the Prefaces in the New York Edition) a kind of self-portrait, but one in which he cannot yet clearly see himself due to his projection of a different idealized self to be recognized and acknowledged in the unspecified future. James dramatizes this in a passage concerning perennial revision, where Doctor Hugh has caught his newfound literary compatriot (still unknown to him as Dencombe, author of *The Middle Years*) altering the text, penciling in emendations to the published pages. As indeed a kind of emblem of the refusal, or incapacity, to see the self in the portrait (rather like the "aspect-blind" in Wittgenstein's discussion), "Dencombe was," we are told, "a passionate corrector, a fingerer of style; the last thing he ever arrived at was a form final for himself" (p. 246). Moreover—here verifying the existence of the psychic division that Dencombe inflicts upon himself in the form of an idealized future and its correlative dis- or semi-avowed past—we learn that "His ideal would have been to publish secretly." And then, after "sacrificing always a first edition"—at a kind of imaginary altar to a future more real than the past as it for him frustratingly persists into Dencombe's present—and then, not completing, not achieving a sense of integrated closure (or not consolidating the sets of relations, as discussed in Chapters 1 and 2, that in significant part make him who he is), but rather "beginning," *beginning* a slow movement in the real toward the distant ideal with a second edition that will only then anticipate a third.

Dencombe's protracted postponement of divulging his identity can be viewed as an outward reflection of his very protracted postponement of self-acknowledgment of his real authorial identity, and the second major change in Dencombe's consciousness I think takes on layered significance in this connec-tion. Dencombe loses consciousness at the very point at which he is reproached by

142   LIVING IN WORDS

Doctor Hugh for the penciled-in alterations and expected to explain himself. On regaining his senses, Dencombe discovers that Doctor Hugh has now learned of his identity (and a link between recovery and epistemic gain is here rendered explicit: "You'll be alright again—I know about you now" [p. 247]). But a layer above that narrative development we have seen Dencombe, as the perfect expression of his self-alienation, eradicating his consciousness at the precise moment that it would merge with itself by stepping down into his real authorial self, at the precise moment that Doctor Hugh's gained knowledge of his identity reflects his own inner acknowledgment and resulting integration of his identity. He keeps his consciousness out of, or sealed off from, that identity; only on the other side of that hermetic seal, i.e., while Dencombe is *unconscious*, does Doctor Hugh learn the truth about who the person before him, Dencombe, really is.

On waking, Dencombe's divided psychology worsens, reaching a state of existential crisis. Divided yet recognizing the very real limitations of the physical self that serves as the necessary mortal vessel for the idealizing self that directs its gaze only to futurity, Dencombe sees, in a moment of rare lucidity, that he may well be lost:

> The idea of the help he needed was very present to him that night, which he spent in a lucid stillness, an intensity of thought that constituted a reaction from his hours of stupor. He was lost, he was lost—he was lost if he couldn't be saved. He wasn't afraid of suffering, of death, wasn't even in love with life; but he had a deep demonstration of desire. It came over him in the long quiet hours that only with "The Middle Years" had he taken his flight; only on that day, visited by soundless processions, had he recognized his kingdom. He had had a revelation of his range. What he dreaded was the idea that his reputation should stand on the unfinished. It wasn't with his past but with his future that it should properly be concerned. Illness and age rose before him like spectres with pitiless eyes: how was he to bribe such fates to give him the second chance?   (pp. 247–8)

A night of lucid stillness, of intensified thought, the despair of feeling lost, the theme of suffering, of death, of desire, a revelation of possibility that comes perhaps too late, the experience of dread, the pain of being misunderstood, the pitiless fixed gaze of age and illness, the machinations of fate, and—lastly—the subject of chance: this indeed reads like a compendium of existentialist themes and preoccupations. James has contextualized these into an imagined life (recall Chapter 1), an imagined identity, within which these terms and phrases possess an indisputable meaning, display an unassailable sense. And all of these, taken together, show what Dencombe's thoughts about himself mean, how those particular autobiographical reflections have, in Wittgenstein's sense above, traction.

Indeed *showing* meaning is one part of the work of the philosophy of language; again it was Wittgenstein who taught us the value of returning such

THREE TRAGEDIES OF THE UNEXAMINED LIFE   143

terms from their abstract philosophical employments to their ordinary—or fully contextualized—uses, and in one sense James's fiction can be seen as achieving exactly this end.[12] But the present purpose of examining this remarkable passage of James's just above is more specific: particularly, it is, as another step in creating a full and subtle depiction of Dencombe's mental life, a further characterization of the context that will make Dencombe's final utterances below meaningful and, as a contribution to both moral philosophy and the philosophy of language in literary form, well worth remembering.[13] But to move to this conclusion presently would be to cut short the mimetic depiction of that context, thus cutting short our grasp of the significance of those final words.[14]

At the close of the preceding passage the narrator once again delivers a solemn, universal claim: "He had had the one chance that all men have—he had had the chance of life" (p. 248). Although this assertion serves as a kind of moral beacon towards which Dencombe will progress in his exchanges with Doctor Hugh, as stated it is too stark to show its real, or deeper significance; it sounds unforgiving, unsympathetic, and largely uncomprehending of Dencombe's true state. It sounds like the judgment of a person who does not fathom the words in which Dencombe lives. But not surprisingly, given the significance of context for meaning, this remark is deceiving when bluntly asserted; it in truth—if not initially visible— holds the revelation, the very help, that Dencombe now urgently needs. This urgency is underscored in further exchanges, in which Dencombe reveals to Doctor Hugh that only "today at last had he begun to *see*," that he had "ripened too late," that he had to "teach himself by mistakes," and that—fundamentally— he more than anything desires an extension: "I want another go" (p. 250); "I want an extension." At one point Doctor Hugh replies that he prefers Dencombe's mistakes to other people's successes and that he admires Dencombe for what, with an amusing logic, he erroneously calls his mistakes. Dencombe, here resisting movement toward that moral beacon, toward the final revelation, replies with just,

---

[12] For a fine brief exposition of the distinction between saying and showing in Wittgenstein's early philosophy, see Hans-Johann Glock, *A Wittgenstein Dictionary* (Oxford: Blackwell, 1996), pp. 330–6. In the *Tractatus* Wittgenstein engages the idea that some forms of meaning can only be shown, not said. In his later philosophy (and directly in line with the suggestion I am making here) Wittgenstein speaks of showing meaning by returning words from their metaphysical to their ordinary contextualized usages: for expansions and developments in his later philosophy, see Stanley Cavell, *In Quest of the Ordinary: Lines of Skepticism and Romanticism* (Chicago: University of Chicago Press, 1988); see also Glock, *A Wittgenstein Dictionary*, pp. 376–81. The *locus classicus* of this method, and of what I am here suggesting that Wittgenstein taught us, is of course *Philosophical Investigations*.

[13] For helpful discussions of a number of the ways in which we might come to see moral philosophy in literary form, see the essays by Martha C. Nussbaum, Cora Diamond, Eileen John, and Daniel Brudney in the section "Literature and the Moral Life," in Garry L. Hagberg and Walter Jost, eds., *The Blackwell Companion to the Philosophy of Literature* (Malden: Wiley-Blackwell, 2010), pp. 239–327.

[14] In this connection Wittgenstein said, as we saw above, that the one who wins in philosophy is the one who finishes last; I read James's "The Figure in the Carpet" as a kind of allegory on the virtues of interpretive-philosophical patience in *Meaning and Interpretation*, pp. 139–48.

144   LIVING IN WORDS

"You're happy—you don't know"[15] (p. 249). Dencombe spends the next days and nights wondering if the talented young doctor may be able to produce the extension, during which time it becomes clear that Doctor Hugh, retained by a countess fanatically jealous for his medical attention, is alienating his patron with his close attention being paid to Dencombe and his condition. An inheritance from the countess has evaporated despite Dencombe's scheme to keep the doctor away and drive him back to attending her. The significance that "a penniless young man of fine parts" (p. 254) has suddenly lost this imagined future, is that he has chosen not only art over life (which is hardly unfamiliar as a Jamesian theme), but chosen indeed the full engagement in the present over a concern for the future. Doctor Hugh is thus no candidate for Dencombe's mental condition; indeed he provides a polar opposition to Dencombe in this respect, with Dencombe lost to the future while Doctor Hugh is wholly consumed in the present. But Doctor Hugh is also much more than this: he brings home to Dencombe the profound truth contained within the narrator's seemingly stern, universal claims, and leads him, at the last possible moment, to appreciate the human significance of these claims. Up to the last minutes Dencombe is still dreaming of a rescue of his physical self that will permit him the second chance, in which he will display a "splendid 'last manner'," construct the "citadel...of his reputation" and even "the stronghold into which his real treasure would be gathered" (p. 252). But while dreaming of a better future self, Doctor Hugh assures him that "the very pages he had just published were already encrusted with gems" (pp. 252–3). Still later, Doctor Hugh returns to Dencombe's side with a copy of a glowing review, reading passages of high praise: Dencombe's reply is equally predictable. Of the passages, he says, "Ah no—but they would have been true of what I *could* have done!" (p. 256). With this remark the final exchange begins, initiating the most momentous change of consciousness in Dencombe—and here we are moving toward a grasp of the circumstances that constitute the conditions for understanding a heartfelt utterance, a few words of humane depth that convey a world of thought, experience, and perception.

Doctor Hugh replies, "What people 'could have done' is mainly what they've in fact done." This is a clear call to acknowledge one's own life *as* one's own life, to bring the two sides of the oppositional divide between the actual and the ideal together, to merge the greater sense of possibility with the facts of one's past into an expanded sense of the reality of one's life. And this is a process undertaken

---

[15] In stressing the epistemological limits ("you don't know") that separate the happy from the unhappy person, James again puts forward a view also important to Wittgenstein; see *Tractatus* 6.43, "The world of the happy man is a different one from that of the unhappy man." Wittgenstein makes this early claim, because the transcendent self of the *Tractatus* and the world are in truth a unity, they are one—thus the unhappy self, in occupying a world other than that of the happy self, does not and, more interestingly, could not, have epistemic access to the world of the happy person. On this early view, it is more than metaphor to say that the happy and the unhappy speak different languages—because they refer to (or perhaps more accurately, speak within) different worlds.

THREE TRAGEDIES OF THE UNEXAMINED LIFE   145

within (and not, according to a dualistic myth, prior to) our ever-expanding family of self-descriptive words, where those words are used in the course of, in the stream of, a life. Aspirations are themselves in truth one part of actual life: to aspire within the context of one's actions, one's own personal history, is to live a life that synthesizes deed and aspiration, and, ideally, acknowledges what one has done with a full sense of cathartic closure and retrospective comprehension. This is the progress that Dencombe makes over his last days, progress occasioned by Doctor Hugh's devotion and progress inspired by literature: Doctor Hugh's sacrifice "worked together in [Dencombe's] mind and, producing a strange commotion, slowly altered and transfigured his despair" (p. 257). This transformation brings Dencombe to a final sense of buoyancy rather than "cold submersion," and it "shed an intenser light." He realizes that the very idea of a second chance, insofar as this idea removes us psychologically from lived experience, insofar as it bifurcates one's life—all of one's actual experience as mere preparation to be dismissed on the one side, and the idea of the real, genuine life to follow in an idealized future in the other—all of that is in truth the very content of what we saw described earlier as the abysmal illusion. Dencombe, in his final exchange with Doctor Hugh, expresses his newfound state of consciousness succinctly: "A second chance—*that's* the delusion. There never was to be but one. We work in the dark—we do what we can—we give what we have" (p. 258). Doctor Hugh has just said "You're a great success!" and Dencombe, taking this in, in his final moments, sees that it is only the delusion alienating himself from his work, from what he has in fact done, that would prevent him from knowing this deeply significant truth. His autobiographical words and their traction, and so his consciousness, his life in its last moments, have changed.

Much of the moral meaning of this tale (meaning, here once again, of a kind not reducible to the atomistic definitions of the words in which it is expressed) thus concerns the place we should give to aspirations and indeed the very real danger of this imaginative aspect of life. Aspirations should be construed as one significant part of one's real life and not as an idealized future, expressed as a separate, or indeed in the extreme case here as a hermetically sealed, compartment of consciousness. To this implicit moral significance Doctor Hugh adds that if Dencombe has in fact suffered despair and doubt about his creative work, then this is only another part, another element, of having "done it," and not of having merely prepared to do it. Dencombe, integrating the bifurcated aspects of his life into a whole identity where before there was only a fragmented, composite self, says, "We've done something or other." Doctor Hugh, now producing the line exemplifying the very greatest degree of compressed meaning (a meaning that we are only able to see against the background of all that has come before), says, "Something or other is everything. It's the feasible, it's *you!*" Dencombe *is* his work, his real life *is* manifest in that body of work (recall the discussion of Royce and Mead in Chapter 1), and this integration of self, this last-minute triumph

146   LIVING IN WORDS

over self-alienation, long sustained by the domination over the actual by the imaginary, eradicates the existential crisis. The meanings of the words "everything," "feasible," and particularly—and most significantly—"it's *you!*" in that very last exchange would be very difficult—I believe impossible—to articulate without giving the entire context of the utterance and without giving a full and convincing portrayal of the states of consciousness of these speakers—and particularly of in this case the *hearer* of the words, Dencombe. The same is true, of course, of the insistent words of Doctor Hugh, in defense of his claim, "But it's true." And the necessity of larger context for the discernment of the precise meaning of a particular utterance is rendered clearer still if the meaningfulness and plausibility of profoundly misleading words—words insistently articulating the separation of the ideal from the actual, the real from the aspiration, the first from the (imagined) second chance—have for Dencombe been exhausted. He is now free, if only in his final moments, of these self-alienating word-borne illusions and self-deceptions.[16] Acknowledging the veracity of Doctor Hugh's words and his own last great insight, his last and most important piece of self-knowledge, he utters the words: "It's true." Showing the meaning—*this* meaning—of this seemingly simple, and misleadingly brief phrase is, of course, precisely what James has here done. And it possesses a meaning that is, in *this* context, unambiguous—but that disambiguation is not the result of stripping away the context or the occasion or what the ideal-language picture regarded as "muddiness" in the interest of invariant word meaning. Just, indeed, the reverse. (And recall Virginia Woolf's remark discussed above in Chapter 2 concerning how little we actually understand of an event—and events are of course described in words—without first knowing in some detail about the person to whom the event happened.) These two words are deeply revelatory of who Dencombe is now, and of who he sees himself as being now. In the same way that the realm of the aesthetic in human life is much larger than the realm of art (the placement of artifacts on a mantle is not art), the realm of self-revelatory speech is very much larger than the realm of what we would ordinarily classify as autobiographical language.

It would certainly be possible, although it is not my purpose at present, to situate the position on self-integration, the position in moral philosophy that James is advancing through telling the tale of Dencombe, on a continuum of such positions in the history of ethical theory. Plato's position, along with any moral idealism following it that was developed under the influence of Platonism, would occupy one polar extreme; a position such as that adumbrated by Nietzsche in *Twilight of the Idols* would mark the other extreme.[17] Plato would tell us to devote

---

[16] For a compact depiction of the ultimate unworkability of the kind of second chance Dencombe desires, thus further articulating its illusory nature, see Lydia Davis, *Almost No Memory* (New York: Farrar, 1997), pp. 131–2.

[17] I offer a discussion of the significance for aesthetics of *Twilight of the Idols*, trans. R. J. Hollingdale (London: Penguin, 1968) in "Apollo's Revenge," *Historical reflections/Reflexions Historiques* 21, 1995:

ourselves wholly to the ideal, disregarding the projects, the experiences, and the vicissitudes of embodied life, looking only to higher things, abstract truths above the "divided line" (p. 204). Nietzsche would tell us, famously, that the very idea—the Platonic idea—of the real world above and beyond appearance has been only "lyingly added" (36). Aristotle falls between these extremes: within his fully developed view in the *Nicomachean Ethics* we find a position of moderation: idealism and aspiration certainly have their place, but what we do, and what we have done, is undeniably central, and not only to ethical evaluation—although that is hardly a small matter—but to who we are.[18] What we say is, of course, part of what we do (words as deeds), and the meanings of those uttered words are every bit as layered and complex in life as they are in literature. The affinity between the position put forward in literary form by James's and Aristotle's position is clear, as is the affinity to existentialist themes; in addition, the demonstration of the significance of context for meaning is, as I have suggested here and more fully elsewhere, closer to central themes in Wittgenstein's philosophy than we might at first have been willing to find plausible.

But before moving ahead, I want to pause to consider for a moment and from a higher altitude the relation between literature and philosophy that is emerging throughout these reflections.

Read with questions of meaning, verbal content, self-expression, relational perception and understanding, and autobiographical thought and language, the fiction of Henry James (along with Kundera, Murdoch, Woolf, Rousseau, and the authors coming up in the rest of this study) gives us good reason to move toward a position—indeed perhaps to effect what Wittgenstein called a change in our way of seeing (in this case brought in as a change of disciplinary consciousness)—in which we see that much of literature is and has been one manifestation of philosophy, if at one remove. Literature is not merely preparation for philosophy nor a body of work to be superseded once the imperatives of philosophy are extracted and then abstracted—against what is required for the real, traction-finding determination and clarification of meaning; the gems themselves are already in literature. And again, in the context of the present study, we see that a good deal of the clarification of meaning by close contextual analysis concerns self-revelatory, or broadly autobiographical, language. Thus Henry James (like the other authors) is perhaps himself something of a Doctor Hugh to the larger field of philosophy, bringing it in the direction of acknowledgment and integration of its

---

437–49. For a discussion of the significance for aesthetics of Plato's position (in *The Republic*), see Iris Murdoch, *The Fire and the Sun: Why Plato Banished the Artists* (Oxford: Oxford University Press, 1977).

[18] See Aristotle, *Nicomachean Ethics*, in *The Complete Works of Aristotle*, Vol. 2, ed. Jonathan Barnes (Princeton: Princeton University Press, 1984), pp. 1729–867. For much fuller elaborations of the view I am alluding to here, see Amelie Oksenberg Rorty, ed., *Essays on Aristotle's Ethics* (Berkeley: University of California Press, 1980), and, for a particularly helpful and humane discussion, see Jonathan Lear, *Aristotle: The Desire to Understand* (Cambridge: Cambridge University Press, 1988).

148 LIVING IN WORDS

various manifestations, seeing that one of the self-defining things the philosophical impulse has done is to not be hermetically sealed within its professionally defined discipline. In this section we've see that James's work itself goes a long way toward exhausting the plausibility of the belief that, as a brute and categorically neat difference in kind, philosophical content is one kind of thing, literary content another. Thus philosophy may, like Dencombe, recognize that it is what it has done, regardless of the particular disciplinary location of its activity.[19] Or perhaps philosophy can be as much like April as it is like Dencombe, displaying an oscillating identity, sometimes identifying more strictly with its past and containing itself within that past's self-definition, sometimes looking forward, severing its ties to the past where those ties impose a limiting self-concept and inaugurating a new season. Like April, it displays a double-aspected or bifocal identity that in one mood seeks to preserve its integrity through exclusion and negative definition (i.e., defining itself in terms of what it is not) and in another mood seeks to expand its self-understanding through acknowledgment and inclusion of its more far-flung expressions or manifestations. But this thought takes us back again to the example of Dencombe: if philosophy, as an expression of its self-acknowledgment and self-integration, were to utter "It's true!," a full explication of this utterance would require, as we have learned from James, a very convincing, plausible, nuanced depiction of the speaker's state of consciousness, along with the larger context within which, or the webbed background (to which we will return in detail in Chapters 5 and 6) against which, that utterance is made. That, as anyone can see, would not only be another story from the main focus of this book, it would be a story we could not finish—precisely because (for those working at the crossroads of philosophy and literature) we would find ourselves inside its unfolding narrative now.

So with these thoughts concerning the larger relation between literature and philosophy as the more far-reaching relational frame of reference, and with the more focused topic of expressive, self-revelatory, and self-composing language at that frame's center, let us turn to the king who needed to learn how to listen, how to think about the words of others—and how to change himself by changing his relation to language.

---

[19] I am referring here to authors as diverse as Hegel, the early Wittgenstein, and Richard Rorty; for discussions of these and other authors on the subject of philosophy's last moments, see Kenneth Baynes, James Bohman, and Thomas A. McCarthy, eds., *After Philosophy: End or Transformation?* (Cambridge: MIT Press, 1987). But of course the matter may be more complex: perhaps one of the things philosophy has done that it should itself acknowledge is to have ended (in one of its long-practiced manifestations, anyway) itself. Thus its own expanded self-identity may be a result of seeing that it has effected its own end (under one description) or auto-transformation. For fascinating discussions of the parallel state of affairs in the arts (and from which philosophy's self-conception might well learn), see Arthur C. Danto's various articulations of the post-historical condition throughout his critical and philosophical writings; see particularly *The Transfiguration of the Commonplace* (Cambridge, MA: Harvard University Press, 1981) and *After the End of Art: Contemporary Art and the Pale of History* (Princeton: Princeton University Press, 1997).

4.3 Lear as a Tragedy of Errors: "He hath ever but slenderly known himself" (Shakespeare's *King Lear*)

To require love is the surest way not to get it. To not know that is itself tragic. What I will suggest here is that the profound lack of knowledge from which the king suffers, and because of which so many others suffer, is at a foundational level linguistic. He does not truly understand the words of others, and—more importantly for present considerations—he does not possess the words that would both enhance and deepen his awareness of others and (inseparably interwoven with this) his knowledge of himself. With these issues to the fore, the play reveals itself as an exacting study of the centrally significant contribution language makes to the composition of moral selfhood.

The theme of language misunderstood and the characterological deficiency that promotes such misunderstanding is prominent from the start:[20] the manipulative and insincere responses of both Goneril and Regan are judged by Lear to well answer his demands, while that of the truly honest, loving, and sincere Cordelia yield only a threat ("Nothing will come of nothing"). What we call mere words, or empty words, are flying; in this verbal context Cordelia's silence says far more than anyone else speaking. But Lear is deaf to this potentially life-saving silence, just as he is deaf to sincerity and humane depth in an utterance.[21] One might say: he is incapable of seeing that the form of a statement or remark can be delivered without its content. Or worse: for him, empty unto himself, the form is all there is.[22] Shakespeare has anticipated this moral theme in the very precondition of the opening of the play: Lear's purpose as he enters is to divide his kingdom between his daughters and sons-in-law in order to retain the authority, the respect, the high station, of a king (the "form"), while casting off the duties, responsibilities, and ongoing multiple engagements required of a true king (the "content") that taken together justify and genuinely substantiate—or earn—the authority, respect, and station. And they substantiate the meaning of the word "king." (This difference is marked by our word "titular.")

The contrasts between the sensibilities of characters with which Shakespeare surrounds, or relationally situates, Lear are invariably instructive. As we proceed

---

[20] Herder wrote, "the first scene already carries within it the seeds of his later fate"; one way to say what Herder sees in this scene is the range of implications Lear's words herein open. See Johann Gottfried Herder, *Shakespeare*, trans. and ed. Gregory Moore (Princeton: Princeton University Press, 2008); this line p. 34.

[21] The difference in play here is well examined in the writings of Rush Rhees; see his *Wittgenstein and the Possibility of Discourse*, 2nd ed., ed. D. Z. Phillips (Oxford: Blackwell, 2006). See especially ch. 13, "Philosophy, Life, and Language," pp. 243–56.

[22] Sarah Beckwith, in her incisive and insightful *Shakespeare and the Grammar of Forgiveness* (Ithaca: Cornell University Press, 2011), captures the linguistic condition of Lear's court perfectly: "At the beginning of *King Lear* a daughter finds that she has nothing to say. Words of truth and of love are alike impossible at Lear's court. The play will show relentlessly, remorselessly, what a culture comes to look like when the paths to truthful expression are lost," p. 89.

150 LIVING IN WORDS

I will consider a number of these, but one of the contrasts that is most revelatory of inner content or its absence is the response of France to the fact that Lear has just deprived Cordelia of the very substantial dowry that (had the silence not just occurred) she would have brought to her marriage. France sees true content beneath mere form, true substance, true character, and it is precisely in Cordelia's silence and her resolute and character-affirming stance concerning the truth in relation to her father that he, France, sees a life companion. Lear, shouting out abusive descriptions of the now-disowned Cordelia, expresses only his incomprehension that anyone would want a now-dowry-vacated wife. With a sole measure of outward gain, he cannot comprehend the words of France any more than he has understood Cordelia's genuine and truth-respecting reticence. And another contrast, to that of Kent, is revelatory in a different way: Shakespeare, ingeniously, places Kent in the position of disguising himself (as "Caius") so that he can continue to serve and assist Lear after Lear, in another explosive fit of anger, has banished him; what Shakespeare is showing is that he, Kent, finds a way to continue the truth—the reality of his devotion to his king—beneath the appearance of Caius, so that Lear receives the benefit of Kent's service but in a way Lear does not recognize. On the level of action, this is precisely like Lear's relation to Cordelia's words. But with these themes identified, we should look more closely both at the words as they work within the lives of the characters and as they work for Shakespeare as philosopher behind and beneath those characters' words. (With the reflections concerning the relation between literature and philosophy closing the previous section in mind, one might say: in this sense, the philosophy is itself "content" beneath the "form" of the play, and without an attunement to it we as readers ourselves become "Lears" to the "Cordelia" of the play. But that consideration, like the previous remarks, stands at a "meta" level from the issue I wish to explore here.)

From the very inception the theme of the knowledge of another is in play, and it is as quickly answered in terms of inward content that makes such knowledge worthy of the effort of its gaining. Kent, on meeting Edmund, opens the space for further human understanding ("I must love you and sue to know you better," meaning that he hereby resolves to work his way into a fuller comprehension of Edmund as a person), and this is met by Edmund's "Sir, I shall study deserving," or that he will further strive to improve himself thus to warrant Kent's imaginative effort. With Shakespeare already sharply delineating the content of character, this entire genre of exchange is lost to Lear's walled-in moral vocabulary. And it is in this first scene of the first act that Cordelia, initiating the knowledge (hers) to ignorance (his) relation to her father, says (to herself—i.e., to an inward recipient of these words capable of comprehending them), "What shall Cordelia speak?" She answers with what can be heard as an active verb as description of her psychological reality: "Love." To which she adds, having just audited the exaggerated and hollow speeches of her sisters, "and be silent." But then, given Cordelia's

THREE TRAGEDIES OF THE UNEXAMINED LIFE   151

sensitivity to language, one can well imagine that she here also knows that "love" can also be heard as a noun, so that the action she prescribes to herself is not to love but, indeed, to speak love. In this case, what Cordelia sees within the implications of her fleeting private reflections is that being silent is itself the act of speaking love. Lear, as we shall shortly see, repeatedly fails to "hear," to comprehend, silence, to understand Cordelia's silence as itself a chosen verbal action, and thus to see what stands so meaningfully before him, i.e., a "speaking" of love, which is the actual present content of the "silent sentence" he uncomprehendingly believes to be absent and that he demands to (literally, expressly) hear.

Were there a question concerning whether the investigation being undertaken here by Shakespeare centrally concerns language, he definitively answers it by moving directly to Cordelia expressing her own suspicion of manipulative rhetoric, where she measures words against far greater true love: "I am sure my love's more ponderous than my tongue." She is devoted to showing rather than saying. And Kent, finding Lear's intemperance aimed at him, warns the king about the grave dangers of a king succumbing to rhetorical manipulation ("When power to flattery bows..."), and exemplifying what he is describing (by saying what he is saying forcefully and directly), says that honor, or truthfulness, or sincerity, are wedded to plain speech: "To plainness honor's bound." To be whom and what he is, both within himself and for his king, Kent here must speak a certain way. "When majesty falls to folly," the duty then falls to him to set the king and the king's circumstances aright by speaking aright. And seeing so clearly what Lear does not, he begins his performance of this duty by saying, dangerously, "See better, Lear." Ocular metaphors everywhere, this means: "Hear better, Lear."

With a cultivated moral imagination, and the correlated ability to hear, such an admonition would occasion reflection—perhaps deep and sustained reflection—in a person. In Lear, it occasions rage, threats, and Kent's banishment. Lear's first (catastrophe-generating) error was to not hear Cordelia's silence; now his second is to fail to hear, to contemplate, and to take seriously by acting upon, Kent's call. On (apparently, but not really) departing to his banishment, Kent, seeing significance in Lear's words beyond his (Kent's) personal case, says to Lear that in speaking the words of banishment Lear also banishes freedom itself; he says to Regan and Goneril that he hopes their "large speeches" may find deeds that genuinely exemplify them. And to Cordelia he remarks that she has thought well, spoken well and honestly, and done so (and in this context uniquely) in a way that truthfully and thus precisely aligns sincere thought with earnest words ("may gods take under their shelter she who justly think'st and hast most rightly said"). She is here the standard against which the words of others are measured. That is to say: (a) Lear's words are out of control, running now far beyond what he realizes or comprehends (in a way that recklessly severs intended utterance from that utterance's range of implications); (b) the sisters' words, their speeches, are out of proportion to anything remotely like what they will actually do; and

152 LIVING IN WORDS

(c) Cordelia, in her words and in her silence, stands alone. That solitary ground, as the honorable Kent sees, is powerfully held with only a few real words fighting a great swell of prismatic verbiage. As a gauge of the extent to which these sets of words (apart from Cordelia) are running amok, one might consider the extent to which we commonly expect speakers to have and maintain a grasp of the implications, or the entailments, of what they say: it would show either a blindness to or a disregard of meaning as conveyed in language for a speaker to not realize, in expressly making an assertion, that a range of "owned" implications extend from what is expressly said. Ordinarily, intention, utterance, and implication are understood as intricately intertwined, so that a speaker is expected to accept unstated implications, or reformulations that variously highlight one aspect or another of what was expressly said, as, as we say, "what they meant." Similarly, we expect speakers to draw boundaries on those entailment extensions and implications as they arise, rejecting misleading or "unowned" entailment expressions. Lear's words forcefully fly around the room with no grasp of this or of the practical fallout of his utterances (e.g., Cordelia leaving, or the new distribution of power, really a relational seismic event, between himself, Goneril, and Regan).

What Shakespeare next has France say is instructive, functioning as what Wittgenstein called a "reminder": France expresses his sense of disorientation at the words he is hearing from Lear. What he, like us, expects is that a person's words will exemplify a morally constitutive coherence across time.[23] And a close reading of France's words to the king reveals that for him such coherence is not only the measure of, but in a real sense the content of, character.[24] What France says here is subtle: he can only make sense of Lear's dramatic reversal of feeling for Cordelia (from his "most dearest" to her being disowned in a single linguistic test of the sisters) if she has been seen to "commit a thing so monstrous to dismantle so many folds of favor." But now the subtlety, said of Cordelia but aimed at Lear: His faith in the character of Cordelia is so unwavering, so unquestioningly strong, that he says only a miracle could plant in his mind the belief that she had actually done any such thing ("which to believe of her must be a faith that reason without miracle could never plant in me"). It is also in this exchange that Burgundy is placed in sharp contrast to France, thus casting France's virtue suddenly in higher relief—thus showing by contrast his fittingness for Cordelia: Burgundy says to Lear that if he receives the initially discussed dowry he will marry Cordelia, where

---

[23] This of course connects directly to Chapter 1, Section 1.3 above; there the issue concerned the circumstantial content of a person's words as used at a precise moment in a given exchange but where that usage is inflected by that person's prior experiential backlog; here that issue is expanded, bringing into view the way in which a person's long-form moral coherence is sustained within those words.

[24] I pursue this link between language and consistency in character further in "Othello's Paradox: The Place of Character in Literary Experience," in Garry L. Hagberg, ed., *Fictional Characters, Real Problems: The Search for Ethical Content in Literature* (Oxford: Oxford University Press, 2016), pp. 59–82.

THREE TRAGEDIES OF THE UNEXAMINED LIFE   153

France is saying that "love's not love" when it is mingled with practical concerns.[25] Shakespeare, showing that France comprehends the consistency of Cordelia's verbal actions (of course including the choice of silence) and thus knows deeply who and what she is by truly fathoming her words and non-words, compresses the point into what in this context is nothing short of a perfect sentence: "She is herself a dowry." The remark instantaneously places Burgundy in a low moral station while (here again) surpassing the comprehension of the impatient Lear. Separating one kind of value from another and seeing the polarized oppositions between them, France, in saying to Cordelia that she is now (characterologically and morally) richer upon being suddenly made (materially) poor, declares that his love for her has blossomed even more now that she is despised. And on saying goodbye to her sisters, Cordelia says that she now knows what they are—where this knowledge is the fruit of her having measured the content, the manipulative function, of their words. Cordelia, now tearful, like France, sees into persons because she sees into their utterances. It is shortly after this that Regan says of her father, with a dismissive, pragmatic harshness, that his worsening condition is in part a function of his age, but adds a second, not unintelligent observation: "Yet he hath ever but slenderly known himself." That is, even to her it is evident that Lear is a person who, as we colloquially say, speaks before he thinks, or more precisely, is a person from whom utterances and declarations and pronounce-ments and judgments erupt without there being a sense of inner composure, inner reserve, and a rich reflective life behind them. That missing composure and reserve (the Fool says to him, "Speak less than you know"), the conspicuously absent measured, thoughtful, confidence-inspiring sensitivity, would be the nat-ural correlate of a heightened sensitivity to language. Lear is a man who tragically does not listen to others and, because he does not listen to them, does not know how to reflectively listen to himself. Slenderly, indeed.

When Kent appears to Lear in disguise, upon being asked by Lear who he is, Kent replies that he is what he seems (a trustworthy servant of the king). It is, again, Kent adopting a disguise in order precisely to be what he actually is, and it is at this point that this circumstance is intertwined with the Fool telling Lear that he

---

[25] There is an obvious resonance here with Sonnet 116 ("love is not love Which alters when it alteration finds"). France's remark, like the sonnet, could be reasonably taken as a claim concerning who does and does not understand the meaning of the word "love." Note however that Helen Vendler, in exactingly drawing out the layered and nuanced meaning of the sonnet, regards it not as an autonomous statement or definition of love, but rather as a reply, and indeed stern repudiation, of an imagined interlocutor who has just previous to the first line of the sonnet used some of the words in the sonnet that indicate what she perfectly calls a "sordid algebraic diction of proportional alteration." We will see Lear employ precisely such "sordid algebraic" calculations below, thus in a sense needing the very dialogical refutation of a quantified debasement of the concept of love that she sees the sonnet as. It is also remarkable how much more subtlety of the sonnet comes to the surface when seen as dialogically engaged language rather than as independently asserted propositional content. See Helen Vendler, *The Art of Shakespeare's Sonnets* (Cambridge, MA: Harvard University Press, 1997), pp. 487–93 (this passage p. 492).

154 LIVING IN WORDS

(Lear) is in truth the real fool. (Lear, having given away his inherited royal position, strikes the Fool as unbelievably foolish.) And on being challenged by Lear about this, the Fool says to Lear that "Fool" is in fact the only genuine title Lear has left. This is supposed to be a joke, but like the disguised appearance carrying within it the reality of Kent, the Fool's words are, as we say, a little too true. Kent then notes precisely the twin meanings of the Fool's words: "This is not altogether fool, my lord"—that is, pay heed that this is not entirely a joke. And at the close of the exchange, the Fool expresses a wish for a teacher who can teach him to lie ("Prithee, nuncle [he repeatedly calls Lear "uncle"], keep a schoolmaster that can teach thy fool to lie. I would fain learn to lie"). Shakespeare is showing: truth in actual language is not reducible to nor containable within explicitly asserted propositional content. Like Kent in disguise to deliver his true self to his king, the Fool, in speaking a fool's nonsense, speaks the truth. Kent is a truthful false actor; the Fool is a truthful liar. And knowing himself, the Fool describes himself to the king as needing to learn to lie. That is, the Fool, in presenting what he says as jokes, is lying; they are factual descriptions of Lear's condition and situation, and so he finds himself always speaking the truth (thus in this sense needing to learn to lie). And his awareness not only of this layered truth-in-falsity relation but also that he serves at the pleasure of the king, and that he can be permanently cast out in a single phrase and so walks a very fine line, displays a capacity for self-reflection or self-knowledge that far outstrips Lear in every exchange. To compress the point: he knows that his very title is a lie. It is as if Lear, by instructive contrast with Cordelia, with Kent, and now with the Fool, is living in a narrow linguistic world in which assertions such as "snow is white" or "the cat is on the mat" are about as complex as things get. The unquestioned presumption of linguistic simplicity, in intricate contexts of human complexity, is a tragic error.

But I should also note: although I am casting the problem from which Lear suffers—and because of which so many others in his world suffer, in terms of a blunt focus on only the most literal propositional content, his fuller set of problems actually fan out from this base. For example, Kent sees the content within the Fool's joke that Lear does not, which is not strictly speaking a matter of seeing beyond propositional content. It is rather that Kent recognizes (non-reductively to explicitly asserted singular content) that an utterance can be two types of speech-act at once (e.g., a joke and a warning); Lear sees, understands, and in a very limited way listens, only mono-dimensionally. Similarly, Lear's failures to hear, his inability to truly listen, his insensitivity to others' subtle and layered reasons and complex intentions, and his resultant anemic capacity for genuine and sympathetic communication all also reach beyond the fairly contained issue of seeing only explicit propositional content or overrating the role direct propositions play in meaning. So my characterization of the problem here is meant to be broad and inclusive of the web of linguistically generated problems one would encounter who started with a demand for simple declarative statements and believed them to be foundational to all meaning.

There is an exchange with Goneril that is in these terms interwoven with philosophical significance. In response to her having criticized Lear's knights, he calls her a liar for having spoken against his unexamined presuppositions, but then, importantly, speaks to *himself*, calling his name in frustration ("O Lear, Lear, Lear!"). What he says speaks volumes beyond his immediate intentions: striking his own head repeatedly, he exclaims, "Beat at this gate that let thy folly in and thy dear judgment out!" What he means, narrowly, is that his head has served as the perceptual portal through which the folly that supplanted his good sense gained entry. But what this shows is that, in separating himself from the contents of his own mind, he does not stand in an intimate and self-defining relation to his own speech, his own words.[26] He sees himself as separate from those, and is now sitting in judgment of that verbal part of himself that he disavows, that he does not see as his own in the right way—he sees his speech as his, but not *of* him. For him, foolishness was *let in*, and on arrival it established a ventriloquist-like relation to what he said. And because words are deeds, it established a puppeteer-like relation to what he did. Instantiating one variety of self-deception, he attempts to stand apart from his own language as a mechanism for preserving a false self-image. "Slenderly" is the right word, and Shakespeare is steadily disclosing its deeper meaning.

Act II begins with a remarkable further commentary on language: Shakespeare has Cornwall disrupt any lingering presumption that straight speech, the direct utterance, is somehow more immune to dissimulation than a more artful phrase. The oversimplified picture at work here is: if we reduce, or "translate," the more embellished, poetic, literary, or sensitive usages of language to what are regarded as their blunt directly assertive counterparts, we will reduce impurity and thereby maximize the prospects for truth. Cornwall identifies Kent as one who has been "praised for bluntness" and of whom it is thought that because of "an honest mind and plain, he must speak truth." But he as quickly adds: "These kind of knaves I know, which in this plainness harbor more craft and more corrupter ends..." This in turn is followed immediately by Kent performing a linguistic act that advances the theme concerning what France saw in Lear's words above

---

[26] There is another way of describing the ethical significance of the words in play here. In a conversation about Dostoevsky's *Notes from Underground*, Wittgenstein observed, as reported by O. K. Bouwsma, that "there might be a way of saying what is true truly and a way of saying what is true falsely." (The example at hand concerned the underground man asserting "I am a spiteful person" but doing so in a way that in a crafted fashion put on display a certain attitude toward his self-description and so, as Wittgenstein is here reported to have said, is "posing" while telling the truth.) See O. K. Bouwsma, *Wittgenstein: Conversations 1949–1951*, ed. J. L. Craft and Ronald E. Hustwit (Indianapolis: Hackett, 1986), pp. 69–71. Lear, while telling the truth here, is speaking to himself in the third person, addressing himself by his surname, and thus in a "posing" sense is taking responsibility only at a distance. It is the truth, said in a false way, with a distanced relation to one's own words.

156 LIVING IN WORDS

concerning Cordelia: Kent adopts an idiom completely foreign to him ("sir, in good faith, or in sincere verity, under th' allowance of your great aspect, whose influence, like the wreath of radiant fire on flickering Phoebus' front"). He gets precisely that far when Cornwall interrupts to pointedly ask him what on earth he is talking about and why he is speaking like this ("What mean'st by this?"). Kent's answer is: "To go out of my dialect, which you discommend so much." Shakespeare—with profound insight into the self-compositional power of a person's language—is thus intertwining his exposure of the oversimplifying myth of a tighter connection between simplicity and truth with the theme of recognizing a person in, and by, their words. Kent, in these words, is to Cornwall fleetingly in disguise; against Lear's self-deceptive linguistic disavowal, language is in fact inseparable from identity.

Nor is language an arbitrary affair. Lear may have been, and may still think of himself, as an autocratic power; for him (or in his autocratic imagination) what he says, is. But he does not have this power over language, over meaning. In an exchange with Goneril leading to further emotional severance concluding in irreparable alienation, Goneril says, against his words, "All's not offense that indiscretion finds and dotage terms so." He can rename, redefine, as he likes— but words will not obey him. At this point in the play his losing his grip on this fact serves as a measure of his mental dissolution, but Shakespeare does much more within these passages. Lear's incomprehension of the concept "love" is, as I said at the outset, tragic. Shakespeare brings this to the surface here, with Lear—having already claimed, against everything that France sees, that Cordelia could not be of any value because she has no material value—now calculating the relative loves of Goneril and Regan by asserting that, since Goneril will leave him fifty knights and Regan only twenty-five, that Goneril thus loves him twice as much. This is an unwitting but still cruel mockery of human understanding. One could express this as: does he have *any* comprehension whatsoever of the meaning of the word "love" or its reach, its character, its depth?

It is near the opening of Act IV that Gloucester is employed to draw another telling contrast to Lear: recently blinded, for him inner vision is separate from, and not dependent upon, outward or actual vision. Announcing that he did not always see clearly when he still possessed sight, he thereby demarcates the imaginative space of insight. This is the essence of what is required to truly understand the words of others—and now it frames in a new way what Lear lacks. When Kent asks the Gentleman about Cordelia's reactions to the letters, he speaks beautifully of Cordelia maintaining an outward composure while still betraying inner delicate emotional experience that was growing to the point of overwhelming her: she was, on reading the letters in his presence, "a queen over her passions," with her subtle tears like "sunshine and rain at once." The composed and controlled smile was one thing; the tears another: "Those happy smilets that played on her ripe lip seemed not to know what guests were in her eyes, which parted thence as pearls

THREE TRAGEDIES OF THE UNEXAMINED LIFE   157

from diamonds dropped." And he sees, and then captures perfectly, the beauty in this quiet romantic sorrow as Cordelia's inner emotional crescendo gently manifests itself: "Sorrow would be a rarity most beloved if all could so become it," if all could make delicate sorrow such a rare thing of beauty. This is not to see a person; it is to see into a person. Gloucester describes this kind of human understanding and *in his words* opens conceptual space for it; the Gentleman exemplifies it and in his words articulates it; and Lear, in his arrogance and his impatience, has inwardly blinded himself to it. He sees—outwardly.

And, still another error, but even worse: We have seen that Lear hears in the same way, believing himself to be missing nothing. But let us pursue this: When Edgar presents himself to the blinded Gloucester as another person, Gloucester immediately perceives the difference in language as that difference would indicate a difference of person: he says, "Methinks thy voice is altered, and thou speak'st in better phrase and matter than thou didst." Edgar insists that only his garments have changed, but Gloucester "sees," through language he can hear, that something is wrong: "Methinks you're better spoken." The indissoluble relation between language and identity has surfaced a number of times throughout this study. One could put Shakespeare's philosophical point here perhaps in this way: language is a fingerprint. But as with a trained and cultivated musical ear, one has to have ears to comprehend its subtle content, to discern the identity-revealing minute parts. And much of that training in discernment, Shakespeare knows, will be painful experience: Edgar refers to himself as one "who by the art of known and feeling sorrows am pregnant to good pity." His sympathetic imagination is cultivated by sorrow; he has suffered into knowledge (he gently alludes to, without recounting, a difficult past), and that knowledge takes form as compassionate comprehension. Beyond Gloucester's perceiving a difference of person in Edgar's language (although that is something), it is Edgar's sensitive and able ear, conjoined to his equally sensitive and able tongue, that together serve as the conduits of his deep humanity. In him, suffering begets a form of moral beauty. Lear, by contrast, just suffers.

There is a point late in the play where Shakespeare provides a perfect analogy for the kind of meaning words can accrue and how they can present links to the past (as we first saw those relations explored in this study with Franz and Sabina, and Sabina and the former lover Tomas, in Chapter 1). Referring to ragged clothes as "weeds," Cordelia says, "Be better suited. These weeds are memories of those worser hours. I prithee, put them off." Like the garments in this context, a recalled phrase can be one that awakens either a small set, or a stream, or a flood, of memories and attendant images, of emotions remembered. The sensitive Cordelia sees such connections right and left; as if illustrating what Wittgenstein[27] was to

---

[27] Ludwig Wittgenstein, *Philosophical Investigations*, revised 4th ed., ed. P. M. S. Hacker and Joachim Schulte, trans. G. E. M. Anscombe, P. M. S. Hacker, and Joachim Schulte (Malden:

158   LIVING IN WORDS

observe at great philosophical depth, her life in words reaches far beyond what we think of as words themselves. She lives her life in words; Lear, by contrast imperious, impatient, one who talks over others and one who demands others to speak in voices he wants to hear, throughout his simplified thought, his blunt words, and his peremptory deeds, only repudiates that life. It is thus fitting to his moral psychology that at the end of the play he actually *wants* to retreat to prison with Cordelia—where he imagines they together will sing like birds in a cage, hear and discuss courtly gossip, and live in protection from the ups and downs of power and its unpredictable vicissitudes. And then he says: when she asks for his blessing, he will kneel down and ask her forgiveness. This is suddenly new: it is a glimmer of realization of who he is and what he has done. But—his final tragic error—this is too little, too late. Perhaps he senses that he could learn real language from Cordelia; perhaps he gains a first glimpse of how they could then actually talk to each other (he imagines that they will contemplate the mysteries of the universe together). But for him—and this is all too of the man—this seems possible only away from his life, only beyond the bounds of who he is, only in imprisoned retreat. What he does not see is that the retreat to prison would only be a literalization of the verbal prison in which he has lived all along.

In Stanley Cavell's classic essay "Must We Mean What We Say," he writes, "It sometimes happens that we know everything there is to know about a situation— what all of the words in question mean, what all the relevant facts are; and everything is in front of our eyes. And yet we feel we don't know something, don't understand something."[28] Lear never had a problem, narrowly speaking, of word meaning.[29] Yet he missed volumes. Confidently striding through the worlds of Kent, of Edgar, of the Fool (who repeatedly functions as Lear's personal Greek chorus with that chorus commenting both on the limits of his language and on his words themselves pulling him ever further into madness on the heath), and of Cordelia, his ear had no acuity. If in his plea to Cordelia to retreat with him he sensed something, it was, as Cavell puts it, that despite his being right there all the time, there was something he did not know, did not understand. Cavell here appeals to Socrates, who said that in such circumstances what we need is to be reminded of something. And Wittgenstein had written of assembling reminders

Wiley-Blackwell, 2009), see especially "Philosophy of Psychology: A Fragment" (formerly Part II), sec. xi, where the kinds of connections I am referring to here are examined at length in their connection with word meaning.

[28] Stanley Cavell, "Must We Mean What We Say?," in *Must We Mean What We Say? A Book of Essays* (Cambridge: Cambridge University Press, 1976), pp. 1–43; this passage p. 20.

[29] In this connection consider T. S. Eliot's remark (in the course of an essay on Yeats), "What is necessary is a beauty which shall not be in the line or this isolable passage, but woven into the dramatic texture itself; so that you can hardly say whether the lines give grandeur to the drama, or whether it is the drama which turns the words into poetry. (One of the most thrilling lines in *King Lear* is the simple: "*Never, never, never, never, never,*" but, apart from a knowledge of the context, how can you say that it is poetry, or even competent verse?)." *Selected Prose of T. S. Eliot*, ed. Frank Kermode (New York: Harcourt Brace Jovanovich Farrar, Straus and Giroux, 1975), p. 255.

THREE TRAGEDIES OF THE UNEXAMINED LIFE   159

for a particular philosophical purpose. Lear has not seen into what he knows, and he has not organized what he does know in the right, i.e., light-casting, sense-making way.[30] Were he able to look back over his exchanges with his daughters and with all those around him, were he able to see emergent patterns of his too-quick and invariably unconsidered responses, and were he able to cultivate within himself the ability to hear the nuances of the words of others by analogy to a trained musical ear and to see that how they say is as important as what they say, he could have lived in a world, waiting just beyond the reach of his comprehension, of enriched and humanized linguistic interaction. Tragically, he missed it.

Cavell writes, "When [a philosopher's] recommendations come too fast, with too little attention to the particular problem for which we have gone to him, we feel that instead of thoughtful advice we have been handed a form letter."[31] The fact that everyone knows the feeling of receiving a form letter in response to a heartfelt effort shows that we know the difference between the basic meaning of which Lear was aware and the kinds of meaning to which he was deafened, to which he was meaning-blind. This is just as we know the feeling of being given a stock phrase in response to an expression of suffering or a quiet call for help in a situation of emotional intricacy—precisely Lear's insufficient responses to Cordelia.[32] The kind of attention required is special, and, as Cavell continues the above passage, "Attention to the details of cases as they arise may not provide a quick path to an all-embracing system; but at least it promises genuine instead of spurious clarity." The all-embracing system for Lear is: He is king; he has three daughters; he will divide his kingdom among them; they must compete in statements of love. (That he is king is just about the full content of his

---

[30] Helen Vendler neatly articulates the kind of self-reflective process I am referring to here (and in doing so shows the connection between understanding a literary work and understanding a life); she writes of a poet at work, "A poet's compositional thinking becomes increasingly complicated when the experiences and imaginative discoveries of past decades have to be folded into the work of the present. In writing A Vision, Yeats reflected on how the salient events in one's life might retrospectively be given intellectual order, imagining an afterlife in which one would construct different schemes of arrangement of those events. One might relive one's life purely chronologically, reviewing it in the form of images unscrolling themselves in their original sequence. Or one might scroll those images backwards, finally understanding the earlier events (as one could not at the time) as foretastes and causes of later ones. Or one might order the significant events and images of one's life in a hierarchy, with the most emotionally decisive ones at the top, and so on down the ladder. In writing his late retrospective poetry, Yeats plays in comparable ways with the ordering of images; and once he has found and settled on a plan of arrangement for his significant images, the poem 'clicks' into place." In her Poets Thinking: Pope, Whitman, Dickinson, Yeats (Cambridge, MA: Harvard University Press, 2004), p. 92. This is the kind of imaginative process that coalesces into an encompassing understanding of a text, of a person, and of a person's words as they operate within their larger frame. Cordelia's, Kent's, Edgar's, and the Fool's (in his witty and clever self-references) exude this sense of connectedness and intertwining self-awareness; with the exception of the glimmer at the end, Lear's, loudly and harshly, do not.

[31] Cavell, "Must We Mean," p. 41.

[32] Shakespeare, in giving the final words of the play to Edgar, underscores the importance of the difference between genuine and formulaic speech. Looking back over what has transpired, and with a deceased king and daughter before him, he speaks of the respect language must show, and the depth it must find, to fit the circumstances it recounts. Edgar says, "The weight of this sad time we must obey. Speak what we feel, not what we ought to say."

160   LIVING IN WORDS

self-definition; hence "slenderly" once again.) His system leaves him bereft of real understanding and bereft of genuine clarity.

And so in closing this section, we return to the larger issues concerning the relation between literature and philosophy with which we closed the previous section. Philosophy as system building can (it need not, but it can) to varying degrees and in varying ways make Lears of us, and in our impatience we deafen our ears to precisely the kind of nuance (often shown in literature more than in philosophy) that the tradition that Ludwig Wittgenstein, John Wisdom, J. L. Austin, Rush Rhees, D. Z. Phillips, Stanley Cavell, Martha Nussbaum, Ted Cohen, Cora Diamond, Richard Eldridge, and now numerous others have developed. In an examination of the intertwined issues of word meaning and of what thinking is, Wittgenstein wrote: "These are, of course, not empirical problems; but they are solved through an insight into the workings of our language, and that in such a way that these workings are recognized—*despite* an urge to misunderstand them. The problems are solved, not by coming up with new discoveries, but by assembling what we have long been familiar with. Philosophy is a struggle against the bewitchment of our understanding by the resources of our language."[33] The want of insight into the workings of our language; the sustained urge to misunderstand; the failure to assemble what lies before us; the costly bewitchment of understanding: these phrases capture the condition of Lear.

Yet one should probably not embrace any generic claim concerning the connection between any philosophical methodology and Lear's condition: rather, one could learn from Lear to preserve an Austinian or closely attentive ear and the philosophical space for the work of such an ear, or to remain vigilant about the potential significance for philosophical understanding of seemingly small linguistic detail. This is easily said and difficult to accomplish. Be that as it may, from this vantage point too, it emerges that literature is a form of art that can deliver an otherwise unavailable amount of illuminating content of the kind for which Wittgenstein is calling in the above passage. Questions of meaning, of interpersonal understanding, of nuanced intention, of sophisticated interpretation, of implication and entailment, and of how words are deeds, are issues that are explored with microscopic acuity in literature. And so it can be in the too quick, or philosophically impatient, approach to such content, such literary explorations, that we risk becoming in small ways Lears. Here one can indeed consider the very idea of an example: if we see a literary text as reducible to an illustration of a briefly propositionally encapsulated philosophical thesis, we fail to attend to it for its more intricate significance and fail to discern the rich contribution this form of art can make to philosophy (e.g., where the propositional thesis would be, "There can be meaningful silences," and the illustrative example would be, "Cordelia"). But

---

[33] Wittgenstein, *Philosophical Investigations*, revised 4th ed., sec. 109.

like Shakespeare showing ever more deeply the meaning of "slenderly" as it functions within this play, we can grasp more deeply the meaning of "meaningful silence" by looking more closely, more exactingly, more acutely. This does not itself argue against methodological generality, but it does argue for particularity and for the interpretive patience that can alter or inflect the general claims at which we ultimately arrive and the words in which those claims are stated.

Cavell writes, "Euthyphro does not need to learn any new facts, yet he needs to learn something: you can say either that in the *Euthyphro* Socrates was finding out what 'piety' means or finding out what piety is."[34] Lear needed to become the person who could hear his daughter: he could have found out what her words mean as the finding out of who and what she actually is. And he would thus have been in a position to deserve love, and not merely to demand its thin simulacrum. Shakespeare's *King Lear* is, of course, a play in language, in words. But so much more deeply: it is a tragedy about language.

[34] Cavell, "Must We Mean," p. 21.

5
Moments of Self-Definition
Forging a Self in Language

When we enter an imaginary fictional world, the referents of the "we" are not the stable entities our intuitions concerning selfhood may lead us to believe. Those intuitions are in part supported by experiential considerations, but also—of central importance to this chapter—in part by linguistic ones. Experientially, we of course do not emerge from a fictional world changed beyond recognition: we know that it is we who underwent the literary experience. Linguistically, we believe that the reflexive referent of the first-person pronoun has not, by virtue of that literary engagement, changed in any wholesale sense from one entity to another. It is then all too easy to adopt, pre- or semi-reflectively, the strong presumption of identity fixity across time—including the time spent in that other, imaginary fictional world. Here I want to suggest that this overarching presumption blinds us to a more nuanced, remarkable, and once one sees it for all its power, in fact rather unexpected, truth about this variety of aesthetic experience. To support this suggestion concerning the decisive power displayed by the kind of literary experience I have in mind I will return, in the first section of this chapter, to the concepts of fixity and flux as we saw them in Chapters 1 and 2, but here as they apply to human selfhood in connection with belief and the way in which beliefs (and the language in which we express those beliefs, as we will see in connection with some views of Donald Davidson and Richard Rorty) serve to do no less than to make us who we are. In the second section, under the heading "The Textually Cultivated "I": Making up One's Mind," I will describe the three-level literary experience (introduced shortly in sketch form in this first section) that, as seen in examples from Goethe, Borges, Iris Murdoch, and Virgil, occasions the acts of self-reflection that allow us to articulate ourselves but in a way where the articulation itself becomes self-constitutive, i.e., determinative of who we are at that moment and then binding upon who we are in the future. And in the third section of this chapter, I will look, in connection with a view advanced by Arthur Danto, at the metaphorical structure of the relation between self and text that allows us, in a distinctive sense we will describe, to interact with literary texts in a self-constitutive way, or, in short, to make the texts our own.

Living in Words: Literature, Autobiographical Language, and the Composition of Selfhood. Garry L. Hagberg, Oxford University Press. © Garry L. Hagberg 2023. DOI: 10.1093/oso/9780198841210.003.0005

5.1 Possible Selves and Webs of Belief

In *Four Quartets*,[1] T. S. Eliot captures in finely chiseled form the opposition in play here between (1) the idea of fixity-of-self across time in a way impervious to the vicissitudes of experience, and (2) the idea of experience leaving its mark in such a way—indeed in a way both indelible and cumulative—that the experience becomes a part of the person who has it. On this latter view, experience then becomes, however small, one constituent part, one distinguishing and defining element, of the referent of the first-person pronoun. Eliot writes:

> Fare forward, travellers! not escaping from the past
> Into different lives, or into any future;
> You are not the same people who left that station
> Or who will arrive at any terminus,
> While the narrowing rails slide together behind you.

To not escape from the past into a different life is to preserve the fixity of the referent of the first-person pronoun. To not escape into any future is to not leave the content of one's present, one's identity, behind. Those words convey a sense of the permanence of selfhood, and they rely for their plausibility on the unspoken intuitions that support it. But then Eliot as quickly paints the opposing picture of personhood: in not being the same people who left the station, they are persons reshaped by the experience delivered to the self within that journey. And Eliot's line is delivered as a proclamation, as a strong rebuttal to the entrenched—and as we shall see blinding—presumption of fixity: "You are not the same people..." constitutes a polemical assertion designed to challenge the implicit assumption that they *of course* are the same people, to challenge the very self-referential belief he just articulated in the previous lines. But as a still stronger rebuttal, Eliot's next line aggressively asserts (against his imaginary interlocutors who presume fixity-across-experience) the more subtle point that they, as presently referred to, will not arrive at any terminus precisely because they, as a matter of ontological impossibility, cannot arrive there. Those who do, and can, arrive will of necessity—that is, by virtue of this easily concealed feature of personhood as it can be understood with heightened sensitivity to the self-formative power of experience—be different. To encapsulate the matter: this contrasting picture, focused upon and respectful of the power experience possesses to effect real change in the self that undergoes the experience, sees experience as constitutive. Its previous, opposing picture sees experience as a set of mere accretions, layered upon an underlying, but ultimately unchanged, person.

---

[1] T. S. Eliot, *Four Quartets* (San Diego: Harcourt Brace Jovanovich, 1988), p. 140.

164   LIVING IN WORDS

But then Eliot is never too quick to accept as given, or to give the last word to, a polemical duality. He has indeed captured these two opposing pictures of fixity and flexibility, but in his next line he intimates a way out of this dichotomy (as we shall see, a false dichotomy) of self-understanding. He writes:

> And on the deck of the drumming liner
> Watching the furrow that widens behind you,
> You shall not think "the past is finished"
> Or "the future is before us."

Here, in opposition to tracks that converge ultimately to a point (and indeed to one that vanishes), the liner carves a furrow in the sea that widens as it disperses. These are now the competing images for the relation between the self and its past—the first with an ever-diminishing record of its presence, the second with ever-broadening ripples of the implications of its actions. But it is, as he instructs through his admonishment ("You shall not..."), possible to think neither that the past is closed[2] and now diminished to invisibility and thus no longer a part of us, nor that the future lies before us as we, unchanged, move into it. Those words intimate a kind of freedom from a philosophical dichotomy that one does not simply announce, assert, or declare; instead, one earns such freedom of thought (in this case, as we shall see in this section rather important self-constitutive thought) by working through the intellectual impulses that lead us into, keep us within, and then, if momentarily free of them, all too easily pull us back into the presumptions and intuitions buttressing either side. We will return to this below, but first, we need to ask: How do the beliefs we hold operate in connection with self-fixity or self-fluidity?

I mentioned just above that some of the intuitions supporting the notion of the fixity of selfhood are linguistic: most briefly stated, in order for "I" to mean the same thing across time and differing circumstances, its referent, to ensure constancy of meaning, must, we all too easily think, remain the same. But there are

---

[2] I discuss the competing pictures of the closed versus the open past (and the sense in which the past can intelligibly be thought to be open) in *Describing Ourselves: Wittgenstein and Autobiographical Consciousness* (Oxford: Clarendon, 2008), passim, but here again Chapter 6, Section 6.3, "Iris Murdoch, the 'Unfrozen Past', and Seeing in a New Light," pp. 202–22, is particularly relevant to the present discussion. (This chapter in particular extends and works from discussions in that previous book, so in the following footnotes I will specify the relevant passages in that book for this present discussion.) The subject of the attempt to escape the past wholly, followed by the discovery that this is impossible within the confines of self-identity, has been a frequent literary theme. Lydia Davis explores this within the fictional setting of a short-term affair and its complex (and instructively inescapable) aftermath in her novel *The End of the Story* (New York: Farrar, Straus, Giroux, 1995); Julian Barnes examines the gradual mental erosion of a person increasingly obsessed with another's past in the setting of an historian discovering unsettling facts about his new lover (and his increasingly ruinous search for clues about that past in their present) in his novel *Before She Met Me* (London: Jonathan Cape, 1982). The titles themselves are somewhat telling.

SELF-DEFINITION: FORGING A SELF IN LANGUAGE   165

further, and more subtle, linguistic intuitions that would blind us to literature's self-constitutive power. It is all too easy to think, as Donald Davidson[3] has observed, that the relation of thought to talk is one of complete dependency, with some philosophers taking it as obvious that thought is primary and psychologically prior, with speech being wholly dependent for its content on the thought that is separate from and prior to it.[4] (This picture is only encouraged by phrases such as "the articulation of thought" or "the expression of thought," where these are construed on dualistic terms.) And a polemically opposed group of philosophers have come to regard such priority as a myth now shattered, arguing that thought is in fact only possible once speech is in place.[5] Be all that as it may, what is of special importance for the present discussion is to bring into brighter light the deeply embedded influence exerted by the thought-dependency thesis specifically on our thinking about the nature of the self *as it is described in language*: we think (here once again all too easily) that just as the content of language is dependent upon the prelinguistic thought that precedes it, so the self precedes, and is ontologically autonomous from, both (1) any third-person language used to describe it and (2) any first-person language used to express it.

The truth about this relation between thought and speech—I should say these relations—is I believe irreducibly complex,[6] and instructively so. And that complexity is something that is shown throughout whole stretches of literature in the finest detail. Davidson himself argues for a language-dependency position, and

---

[3] Donald Davidson, "Thought and Talk," in *Inquiries into Truth and Interpretation* (Oxford: Clarendon, 1984), pp. 155–70. For a particularly helpful discussion of Davidson in connection with the issues that follow, see Samuel C. Wheeler III, "Language and Literature," in *Donald Davidson*, ed. Kirk Ludwig (Cambridge: Cambridge University Press, 2003), pp. 183–206.

[4] I have examined the deep and powerful misleading force this linguistic picture exerts on our thinking about artistic meaning in *Art as Language: Wittgenstein, Meaning, and Aesthetic Theory* (Ithaca: Cornell University Press, 1995); in "Implication in Interpretation: Wittgenstein, Artistic Content, and 'The Field of a Word'," in *Mind, Language, and Action: Proceedings of the 36th International Wittgenstein Symposium*, ed. Daniele Moyal-Sharrock, Volker Munz, and Annalisa Coliva (Berlin: De Gruyter, 2015), pp. 45–63; in "In Language, beyond Words: Literary Interpretation and the Verbal Imagination," in *Interpretation and Meaning in Philosophy and Religion*, ed. Dirk-Martin Grube (Leiden: Brill, 2016), pp. 74–95; and in "Word and Object: Museums and the Matter of Meaning," in *Philosophy*, Supplementary Volume: *Philosophy and Museums* (Cambridge: Cambridge University Press, 2016), pp. 261–93.

[5] This presumption became entrenched as a given fact of the human condition, and thus as a kind of methodological axiom, in the structuralist and semiotic traditions, and appears in differing manifestations in the writings of Saussure, Barthes, Lacan, and many others. And Sartre's autobiography, after all, is titled *The Words*, trans. Bernard Frechtman (New York: George Braziller, 1964). Sartre provides a useful illustration of the distinction I will discuss in what follows in this chapter between a superficial acquaintance with a familiar string of words and a deeper and fuller understanding of their content as used by a particular person in a particular context for a particular purpose or intertwined set of purposes. Sartre writes, "I reread the last pages of *Madame Bovary* twenty times and ended by knowing whole paragraphs by heart without understanding any more about the poor widower's behavior."

[6] I discuss what I call here this irreducible complexity in *Describing Ourselves*, ch. 3, "The Self Speaking," pp. 76–118; ch. 6, "The Uniqueness of Person-Perception," pp. 185–222; and the third section of ch. 7, "On Philosophy as Therapy: Wittgenstein, Cavell, and Autobiographical Writing," pp. 240–57.

166 LIVING IN WORDS

although I believe it can be shown that this position cannot accommodate all cases (specifically cases in which we exactingly describe instances of thinking before speaking and some sensation-based cases of visual or musical thinking) and is thus reductive in precisely the sense Davidson himself finds objectionable, there are a number of points Davidson makes along the course of his argument that cast valuable light on present considerations. As one foundational starting point for his larger discussion, Davidson emphasizes the centrality of belief to many subcategories of thought (he mentions desire, knowledge, fear, and interest as only a few of these), giving the example of a person being glad that, or noticing that, or remembering that, or knowing that, a gun is loaded. In each case, he claims, this person "must believe that the gun is loaded" (p. 157). He writes:

> Even to wonder whether the gun is loaded, or to speculate on the possibility that the gun is loaded, requires the belief, for example, that a gun is a weapon, that it is a more or less enduring physical object, and so on. There are good reasons for not insisting on any particular list of beliefs that are needed if a creature is to wonder whether a gun is loaded. Nevertheless, it is necessary that there be endless interlocked beliefs. The system of such beliefs identifies a thought by locating it in a logical and epistemic space. (p. 157)

Although I think there are indeed some problems with this overarching way of stating the preconditions of belief that run along Austinian and Wittgensteinian lines (do we believe this gun is an enduring physical object because the last one turned out to be a hologram?), at present what I want to pursue is the significance for selfhood of the notion of a system of interlocking beliefs making a thought *possible*. And what is significant for the special kind of self-defining reading that it is the task of this chapter to identify and describe is the point concerning the open status of belief with regard to the thought made possible by the background nets of beliefs, nets that provide what Davidson called the logical and epistemic space within which the thought has its place, within which that thought is made possible and brought to life. Davidson puts it this way:

> Having a thought requires that there be a background of beliefs, but having a particular thought does not depend on the state of belief with respect to that very thought. (p. 157)

Seen one way, literature gives us a web of beliefs (to use W. V. O. Quine's phrase[7]) within which the thoughts of the characters living in that imaginary world are made possible. So in a sense—the more simple one—the world depicted in a

---

[7] See W. V. O. Quine, *The Web of Belief* (New York: Random House, 1970).

literary text is a world within which we, as readers, witness fictional characters thinking thoughts rendered possible by the webs of belief, explicitly (Smith is glad the gun is loaded) or implicitly (Smith acts upon the unspoken belief that the gun is an enduring physical object) present, in that world. And in another sense—the more complex one—we as readers witness characters entertaining thoughts to which their belief is not yet (described by the author as) extended, but where these entertained possible beliefs are themselves rendered possible by the belief web that locates them, gives them a home and a life, in logical-epistemic space. The simpler sense has been in place, one might say, from Homer (indeed from the first imaginary narrative). The second sense is also (but not ineliminably) woven throughout the history of literature; in recent times, Milan Kundera's and Iris Murdoch's novels, as we have seen in preceding chapters, are densely populated with such thought-entertaining characters (and this may be one of the indeterminate cluster of reasons they are classified as philosophical novels).

Now, Davidson's fundamental point (in the article being discussed presently, but this is also foundational to his larger philosophical project) is that to be able to so much as have thoughts, we must already be, as he puts it, "an interpreter of the speech of another" (p. 157). By "interpretation" he does not at this stage mean anything frightfully complex: his example is that of interpreting a person's raising his arm as a manifestation of (1) his desire to attract the attention of his friend, and (2) his belief that raising his arm will do so. (Here again, one might well say on Austinian-Wittgensteinian grounds that such a person is not raising his arm, i.e., he is not volunteering for something, but rather waving to his friend; but that critique of this line of thinking, however important, is not germane to what I am presently trying to use Davidson to bring out.) What is here called an interpretation is thus really what Davidson identifies as a "redescrib[ing] of certain events in a revealing way" (p. 151).

A redescribing of certain events in a revealing way. That, I will go on to suggest, is not the worst way of capturing the special kind of self-reflective activity in which a reader (again, of the certain kind under investigation here) engages. The literary novel is a complex and extensive web of indeterminate reach that provides the logico-epistemic space within which thoughts, on the part of a character, become possible. And it is the space within which that character can be depicted as entertaining thoughts, thoughts themselves made possible by other strands in that background web of beliefs (roughly, what Wittgenstein, along with the notion of the necessary "stage-setting" for a word to be a word that we encountered above, called "the scaffolding" of thought).

Literature, seen in the light of this set of Quineian-Davidsonian ideas, can then be seen as mimetic in a somewhat special way: the reader, at the simplest level, sees a narrative world depicted, where the complex web of explicit and implicit beliefs within that world makes thought (and in Davidson's sense, interpretation of speech and action) possible. And then at one higher or second mimetic level the

168   LIVING IN WORDS

reader of imaginative literature sees belief-neutral thought—often of a self-reflective kind, i.e., where the character, inside his or her imaginative logico-epistemic space, reflects on his or her actions, desires, motives, fears, aspirations, romantic ambitions, and so forth (we will see a case of this fairly fully in Iris Murdoch's *The Sea, The Sea* below). Within the novel, the granting of assent to the entertained belief by the character transforms it from an entertained belief to what I want now to call, in terms of the make-up of that character, a self-constitutive belief. The reader looks, as a spectator-outsider, into the mimetic world within which that process occurs, learns about it, and in a sense rehearses it (to which I will return below) in the act of reading. The reader indeed gets to know the character by witnessing the character's acquisition of beliefs, by witnessing the character's thoughts, and this itself is a mimetic reflection of the way we get to know people in life: people are defined in considerable part by their thought, and more specifically by the quality, character, moral content, degree of refinement, humane sensitivity, precision, and care shown in that thought.

At this second level, the reader, looking closely into that imaginative world, also sees the complexity of what one might call the negotiations involved in converting an entertained thought into a belief, where that belief then becomes both character-constitutive and part of the web background for other now-possible thoughts. The reader sees, in an extended narrative depiction, the process, with all its subtle variations, of taking on a thought as one we would defend, or one we hold to, or one we are convinced of, or one we feel sure about, or one we are sure about, and so forth. And these processes are, like their end results, i.e., the beliefs we take on, subject to moral evaluation by the first-person holder of the belief, and by second- and third-person others. Belief-holders can be proud, ashamed, or anything in between not only of their beliefs, but also of how they came to hold them, and others can and certainly do evaluate these processes of belief acquisition as well: that a holocaust denier[8] holds the belief he does is morally indicative of who and what he is, and how he came to that belief (it was consistent with or followed from his other intertwined beliefs; it was the result of his having been brutally tortured and brainwashed; it was subsequent to severe head trauma after which his epistemic responsibility was diminished, etc.) is similarly morally relevant in determining his character and condition. Again, the reader sees, in the highly variegated ways literature shows, the hardening of a possible view into a settled one. And in seeing this, the reader sees the forming, the strengthening, and the solidification of the morally constitutive epistemic content of a character.

Davidson emphasizes the easily forgotten truth, mentioned a few times in the preceding chapters, that "uttering words is an action," and that, understood as

---

[8] For a morally insightful discussion of a real case of such denial and its self-defining power, see Raimond Gaita, *A Common Humanity: Thinking about Love and Truth and Justice* (London: Routledge, 2000), pp. 157ff.

SELF-DEFINITION: FORGING A SELF IN LANGUAGE 169

such, a (linguistic) action "must draw for its teleological explanation on beliefs and desires" (p. 161). The term "teleological" might here be taken as a kind of shorthand for the open-ended process of situating what a person says, as action, into the larger frame of reference, the web, that makes that action intelligible. One benefit of seeing an utterance as an action is that we would not find it intuitively plausible for an action to have something called a meaning independent from the circumstances within that action was performed. Many do, however, find a parallel notion of pre-contextual word meaning or sentence meaning intuitively plausible, and the explicit categorization of speech as action helps to diminish the force of this misleading intuition. And it is precisely such linguistic actions, as they occur in the expanded contexts that make them possible for the actor and intelligible for the hearer (what Davidson calls, in his restricted sense, the "interpreter"), that are mimetically depicted in literature. Where revealing redescriptions of those linguistic actions are put forward and considered by the characters who utter them and their fictional interlocutors, we see the kind of interpretation that Davidson is discussing, indeed the processes that allow us to so much as make sense of ourselves and others—in action, or within what Wittgenstein called the stream of life. We see the processes within which characters have their own Davidsonian interpretations of themselves ("to explain why someone said something we need to know, among other things, his own interpretation of what he said, that is, what he believes his words mean in the circumstances under which he speaks," p. 161), sometimes maintaining these self-interpretations, and sometimes, through the process of revealing redescription, coming to a changed self-understanding. This process of self-understanding (and as we shall see more fully throughout this chapter, of self-constitution)—of central importance to the task of this chapter—very often takes the form of arriving at a changed understanding of what was meant by our words.[9] And this is often negotiated in terms of a speaker's beliefs concerning, as Davidson says, "how others will interpret his words" (p. 161). That, as we saw above, was Rousseau's concern.

It is at this juncture, this stage of the three-level aesthetic experience I am presently sketching, that we move to the third level. As we have seen, as readers we (1) see the extended and indeterminately bounded contexts within which beliefs, actions, and expressions are possible, and we (2) see characters performing actions (often of a linguistic kind) whose meaning we grasp as a function of having grasped the larger context and where their actions evince the beliefs they either hold or entertain. But beyond this, we (3) can *identify* with the character in his or her context of action and web of beliefs in such a way that we:

---

[9] I offer a discussion of how such retrospective meaning determinations are made, and how such changes are possible, in *Describing Ourselves*, ch. 5, sec. 1, "Meaning in Retrospect," pp. 154–84, especially pp. 154–62.

170 LIVING IN WORDS

(a) learn what it is, what it *means*, to perform expressive actions that evince belief in this highly particular way;

(b) learn what it is like to *be* the kind of person who holds these narrated beliefs and acts upon them—and, importantly, a person who interacts with others in certain ways and not others on the basis of those beliefs; and

(c) see the narrated fictional content as a rather grand metaphor for our own real or possible life circumstances.

We can thus imagine in a full way—i.e., at the imaginative depth necessary to truly fathom, truly comprehend both the possibility and the meaning of significant human actions—the circumstances as they take shape in external physical situations, in patterns and habits of human interaction, and in dispositions of character that would together lead us to be, indeed together *make* us to be, one kind of person or another. In these layered ways—ways considerably more complex than any oversimplified picture of lesson-learning literary didacticism could accommodate—much of moral significance is taking place within the imaginative world of aesthetic experience. And with the foregoing sketch (at this stage still only a sketch because not yet shown in detailed examples) of these three levels of the reader's experience behind us, we can begin to see how such aesthetic engagement can be of a kind that expands our imaginative reach, our understanding of others' webs of belief and the perhaps idiosyncratic ways in which a person's beliefs are interconnected, and—most importantly, I want to suggest—our understanding of what it means to hold those beliefs and the circumstances that make those beliefs and the actions that express them possible. Moreover, such aesthetic experience can be of a kind that is stronger still in terms of its self-constitutive power: it can elicit in the reader's consciousness an act of entertaining a belief (where this involves all that has been described at the first and second levels) that is, through the identification of the literary context as a metaphor for our own lives,[10] then taken on (through the process of epistemic acquisition to be shown more fully in the following sections) as one that we hold true. Such beliefs can be about the world, about others, or about ourselves—in all cases they are, because beliefs serve to define in part the content of personhood, self-constitutive, self-compositional. If about the world, (e.g., the history of the holocaust), they can determine the attitude (e.g., skeptical or immediately dismissive, or accepting and immediately supportive, among countless other attitudinal predispositions) with which we will approach many other intertwined possible beliefs. If about others, they can influence no less than the patterns, the character, the tone, and the

---

[10] Arthur Danto, in "Philosophy as/and/of Literature," in *The Philosophical Disenfranchisement of Art* (New York: Columbia University Press, 1986), pp. 135–61, has pointed out some promising directions on this point, directions to which I will return in Section 5.3 of this chapter below.

SELF-DEFINITION: FORGING A SELF IN LANGUAGE   171

content of our human interactions. And if about ourselves, such aesthetically occasioned beliefs can determine the extent to which we have earned self-understanding, the extent to which we possess self-knowledge, or in the negative case the extent to which we have become, as a matter of belief-hardened character, resistant to self-examination (King Lear above) or given over to patterned or chronic self-deception (Dencombe above).[11]

Richard Rorty has cast in high relief—perhaps, as I will suggest, in too high a relief—a feature of our identities that he calls "the contingency of selfhood."[12] (This constitutes one important articulation of the flux or malleability of selfhood that would facilitate the recognition of literature's formative power.) Rorty embarks on his examination of this defining feature of selfhood by reading a poem of Philip Larkin's where Larkin describes the content of self-knowledge (gained as the result of "walk[ing] the length of your mind") as inescapably idiosyncratic to the self-examiner. That body of gained self-knowledge—in Larkin's words "as clear as a lading list"—is what makes the difference between the I and what Rorty calls "all the other I's," and it is this exclusively self-known idiosyncratic content that we fear will be lost forever at death ("[s]ince it applied only to one man once, /And that man dying," as Larkin expressed it). Rorty interestingly sees the fear as the symptom of an achievement of self-knowledge— the strength of the fear of the loss of the impress on the self of the experiential content that makes each of us unique is just a measure of our knowledge of that content. But Rorty also sees in these lines a novel expression of a classic tension, a new flare-up of the ancient quarrel between the particularity of poetry and the desired universality of philosophy: Rorty describes this as "the tension between an effort to achieve self-creation by the recognition of contingency and an effort to achieve universality by the transcendence of contingency" (p.25).

As Rorty has discussed extensively in his *Philosophy and the Mirror of Nature*,[13] the deeply entrenched epistemology of universality—the discipline-hardened attitude which would discard the idiosyncratic, the particular, the contingent, as irrelevant "noise" from the outset—would lead us to value only that which, as experiencing selves, we have in common with all the other experiencing selves. Thus he writes:

They [the defenders of universality throughout philosophy's history] would thereby inform us what we really are, what we are compelled to be by powers

---

[11] I pursue one non-dualistically entrenched way of characterizing such cases of self-investigative resistance and self-deception in *Describing Ourselves*, ch. 3, sec. 3, "Real Introspection (and Kierkegaard's Seducer)," pp. 97–118.

[12] Richard Rorty, *Contingency, Irony, and Solidarity* (Cambridge: Cambridge University Press, 1989), ch. 2, "The Contingency of Selfhood," pp. 23–43.

[13] Richard Rorty, *Philosophy and the Mirror of Nature* (Princeton: Princeton University Press, 1979), passim.

172 LIVING IN WORDS

not ourselves. They would exhibit the stamp which had been impressed on *all* of us. This impress would not be blind, because it would not be a matter of chance, a mere contingency. It would be necessary, essential, telic, constitutive of what it is to be human. It would give us a goal, the only possible goal, namely, the full recognition of that very necessity, the self-consciousness of our essence.   (p. 26)

Rorty sets against this grand picture what he identifies as the view of Nietzsche, whom he credits with being the first to reject "the whole idea of 'knowing the truth'" (p. 27). If Nietzsche's "perspectivism amounted to the claim that the universe had no lading-list to be known" (p. 27), then, having "realized that Plato's 'true world' was just a fable, we would seek consolation, at the moment of death, not in having transcended the animal condition but in being that peculiar sort of dying animal who, by describing himself in his own terms, had created himself. More exactly, he would have created the only part of himself that mattered by constructing his own mind" (p. 27). Thus, on this view (one clearly polemically opposed to the presupposition of fixity), the content of self-knowledge will not be gained as the result of a process of discovery, but rather as the result of a process of creative self-narration. Here the self, as reflexively engaged author, "writes" itself—the story of its accumulated "impress" of experience, ordered into a self-definition with the strength of what Rorty, borrowing the term from Harold Bloom, calls a "strong poet," i.e., one who creates his own unique language of self-description out of that utterly contingent and experientially unique body of experience. And such a self (here following some of Nietzsche's thoughts on the matter) will not—because it metaphysically could not—be a mere token of a pre-established type, or "a copy or replica of something which has already been identified" (p. 28). The self, in this sense, is for Rorty in truth both ineliminably and inimitably contingent, as is the language, the narrative we assemble, to linguistically identify that self. This, again, would indeed all seem to go a long way toward describing the malleable self whose content is in part determined by the "impress" of literary content and the absorbed reader's reflections upon that content as sketched above.

The problem with this view, however—as I intimated—is that in placing itself *polemically* against the classically entrenched view, it dramatically overstates its case, ironically ascending to a universal claim concerning our identity that is designed to challenge the very possibility of making a universal claim concerning our identity. Rorty selectively assembles a mosaic from Nietzsche's writings, and then provides a summary that leaves out a number of other defining particularities of Nietzsche's work. Nietzsche does, in *The Twilight of the Idols*,[14] blast (Nietzsche calls his slim volume a piece of dynamite) away at what he there calls "The

---

[14] Friedrich Nietzsche, *Twilight of the Idols*, trans. R. J. Hollingdale (Harmondsworth: Penguin, 1990 [1889]).

SELF-DEFINITION: FORGING A SELF IN LANGUAGE   173

Problem of Socrates,"[15] giving a sharp-toned voice to some observations that Rorty elevates to a generalized position. But Nietzsche also emphasizes—of great importance to understanding precisely how Rorty goes wrong on the subject of selfhood, despite his having identified an important kernel of truth concerning what it is to be human—that along with the historically entrenched idea of the real world (that has for millennia been taken to be philosophy's grand task to describe) being removed as an epistemic ideal or endpoint, that the idea of the apparent world *goes out as well.*

This, for Nietzsche, is hardly throwing out the baby with the bath water—for him, there was no baby to begin with. But for Rorty, it would be to do so, precisely because of his having first taken on the polemicized, ancient-quarrel structure of the argument requiring position-formulation and counter-formulation. In fact, in a spirit perhaps closer to that of (at least) the later Wittgenstein, Nietzsche is undercutting the presuppositions of the debate, suggesting that to banish the idea of the real world—for us the objective universal facts of human selfhood—is *not at all* to thus lay the foundation for a universalizing anti-objectivist, all-is-contingency (or, like Heraclitus, all-is-flux) position. It is, rather, reminiscent of the lines of Eliot's work with which we began this chapter, to first break free of one constraining picture or conceptual model, but then also to come to see that this gives us the sense of liberation, of autonomy, to know how to resist that first constraining picture's polemically situated antithesis as well. In positioning Nietzsche as the *defender* of a grand view that stands in opposition to the classically entrenched epistemological presumption that Rorty has done so much to bring to light and to subject to scrutiny,[16] Rorty himself has failed to acknowledge, and to put to philosophical use, the very fine-grained particularities and contextually seated idiosyncrasies that, taken together, constitute Nietzsche's body of work. That body of work in this sense mimetically reflects the body of experience, the collective impress of life, that constitutes the content of self-knowledge, and it does so in highly particularized observations that—like human experience (understood in accordance with William James's relations-inclusive radical empiricism in Chapter 1, and not in accordance with Locke's atomistic picture of experience)—takes its meaning, its force, and its significance *within*, and not in any grander sense that serves a larger polemical purpose, above, the context of each utterance, each observation. Wittgenstein showed the profound importance of working through what one might call the etiologies of philosophically universalizing or overgeneralizing positions, tracking closely and

---

[15] *Twilight of the Idols*, "The Problem of Socrates," pp. 39–44. My following remarks concern also the section "How the 'Real World' at last Became a Myth," pp. 50–1.
[16] For helpful discussions of Rorty on the presuppositions of traditional epistemology, see Gary Gutting, "Rorty's Critique of Epistemology," in *Richard Rorty*, ed. Charles Guignon and David R. Hiley (Cambridge: Cambridge University Press, 2003), pp. 41–60, and Michael Williams, "Rorty on Knowledge and Truth," in the same collection, pp. 61–80.

174 LIVING IN WORDS

with exquisite care the pressures on thought, the intellectual attractions and snares that would lead us to turn away from what was misapprehended (often under the influence of entrenched epistemological presuppositions of precisely the kind Rorty has excavated) as the "noise" of particularities. But Wittgenstein, knowing where to stop, did so without then adopting an anti-objectivist position that itself amounted to an objective claim. It is all too easy, at just this juncture, to overstate the distinctive kind of fluidity, or, in a positive sense of the term, impressionability, of selfhood that I am suggesting is the raw material upon which formative literary experience acts.

Rorty, in what might fairly be called his polemical zeal (or at least a position-shaping exaggerated boldness), is perhaps too quick to equate the unique, the idiosyncratic, the highly particular, with contingency, and perhaps too quick to generically place those things, and other things in broad terms like them, into the category of "the contingent," which, also generically, is taken to oppose, indeed to preclude, the kind of stability that classical epistemology would, if true to its highest aspirations, correctly describe. As Austin and those in his tradition showed, shooting a donkey by mistake, by accident, inadvertently, by mishap, by misadventure, through confusion, through misidentification, and so forth, are, at the level of detailed particularity (and that is after all the level at which these words function), *very* different things: to generically group them all together as "unintentional action" and then to attempt to provide a general theory of that is, indeed, to obscure (rather than to reveal an imagined hidden essence of) the very specific action that drew our attention to the case in the first place.[17] And so picking up the thread of the discussions above concerning the larger relations between literature and philosophy, the making of these fine distinctions, and the describing of the detailed highly particularized contexts of human engagement within which we importantly distinguish the accident from the mistake, the inadvertent from the mishap, is one of the services philosophically significant literature performs. What Rorty's grand view (constructed out of an overgeneralized and selective reading of Nietzsche that is positioned in opposition to a preceding grand view) misses, through the too-quick identification of the unique, the idiosyncratic, the particular with the generically contingent, is that a kind of objectivity is possible, a kind of descriptive veracity is possible, not despite, but rather *because of*, a clear focus on the unique, the idiosyncratic, the particular. It will not—and this is what Rorty is absolutely right about (where this rightness is not merely a function of his powers as a "strong poet," i.e., it is not merely because he said it in particularly convincing or resonant rhetoric)—be an objectivity or

---

[17] For an exemplary awareness of the all-important subtleties of the descriptions of actions (and the significance of those very subtleties for the dismantling of overarching general questions concerning action description), see Frank B. Ebersole, "The Analysis of Human Actions," in his *Language and Perception: Essays in the Philosophy of Language* (Washington, D.C.: University Press of America, 1979), pp. 199–222.

SELF-DEFINITION: FORGING A SELF IN LANGUAGE   175

veracity born of verified correspondence between a *post factum* statement and prelinguistic state of affairs. But to claim that then the content of self-knowledge will be purely, inescapably, and wholly a matter of self-descriptive *creativity* is to go too far, to cast the valuable point beneath all of this in far too high relief, which in turn blinds us to other meaning-determining nuance. Indeed, to see the extreme claim Rorty is making as plausible, one might already be woven into a web—in this case caught in it—of belief that intertwines with (and makes possible and gives a home to) this too-bold claim, and one of these interwebbed beliefs may well be that language is, in its most fundamental nature, descriptive, rather than constitutive, of complex entities like human selves. That presumption would prevent us from seeing the nonpejorative "bootstrapping" character (as mentioned above) of self-definition where that definition advances incrementally by the accrued items of self-constitutive language. The stability of selfhood that Rorty's strong neo-Heraclitean thesis declares mythical may well be real enough *in a sense* after all, but we get into a position to see this only once we have freed ourselves of the blinders imposed by large-scale position-formulating polemics. Indeed, what we might then see would be suitably particularized to the individuals in question, and respectful of their idiosyncratic experience and its multiple and complex resonances within that life span (true to Larkin's observation, and true to what we saw in the case of Kundera's Sabina and Franz), which itself would be a lesson on a larger scale about self-understanding. But it would not take the form of a generic, philosophical theory that might be named as an "ism." Literature so often sets out to show such self-constitutive language in action with the fine contextual detail necessary to truly understand the words used in the transaction; philosophy so often sets out with presuppositions on both sides of the polemicized debate (and often where both sides share one heretofore unexamined presumption[18]) that, directly contrary to its clarificatory ambitions, in fact prevents a clear view of this most human process.

Rorty, in short, runs the risk of occluding the distinction between life and art in such a way that the content and structure of autobiographical understanding seems nothing more than a whimsical construction, rendered in a free-form manner independent of any epistemic constraints. And that would fail to acknowledge important—in some cases life-defining—distinctions we make between right and wrong, acceptable and unacceptable, illuminating or unilluminating, plausible and implausible, self-descriptions. But he believes—and this is another place where he takes one essentially significant feature of the way we make sense of our lives and then quickly ascends far above the lifegiving particularities that

---

[18] I am alluding here to the methodological insight that is known as "Ramsey's Maxim," as discussed in Chapter 1; that maxim, as we see, takes on special force here in connection with the removal of misleading pictures that would stand in the way of a clear view of the self-constitutive dimension of literary experience.

176   LIVING IN WORDS

motivated this entire line of thinking in the first place—that such distinctions need to be grouped together and (sounding rather like a post-modern Schiller) then replaced, wholesale, by a heightened sense of *play*:

> This playfulness [of metaphorical[19] self-construction] is the product of their shared ability to appreciate the power of redescribing, the power of language to make new and different things possible and important—an appreciation which becomes possible only when one's aim becomes an expanding repertoire of alternative descriptions rather than The One Right Description. Such a shift in aim is possible only to the extent that both the world and the self have been de-divinized. To say that both are de-divinized is to say that one no longer thinks of either as speaking to us, as having a language of its own, as a rival poet. Neither are quasi-persons, neither wants to be expressed or represented in a certain way.

But if it were *all* a matter of simply working to expand, without end or limit in sight, our repertoire of alternative descriptions as instruments for understanding ourselves, we would lose not only the distinctions we make between the right and the wrong, the plausible and the implausible, and so forth as mentioned above. We would lose a set of highly significant distinctions we make *about the descriptions themselves*, e.g., the apt, the fitting, the concise, the resonant, the revealing, the intriguing, the suggestive, the just, the fair, the inverses of all of these, and countless others that, again, an Austinian linguistic investigation (and the kind that literature, along the course of its narrative path, so often undertakes) would detail.

What Rorty perhaps needed to put together was not his Heraclitean view with Davidson's conception of metaphor (where metaphors do "not *express* something which previously existed," p. 36), but rather his sense of freedom from the picture of the One Right Description with the views of Davidson's that we considered above. Davidson, giving his most rudimentary definition of interpretation, said that it is "a redescribing of certain events in a revealing way." Those redescriptions are not cut loose from the moorings of our deeply embedded intuitions concerning rightness,[20] wrongness, the apt, the inapt, the fair, the unfair, and all the rest in the Austinian catalogue of distinctions that are used as descriptions of utterances. But we see those distinctions, and we use those descriptions of utterances, only

---

[19] For an insightful discussion of the powerful role metaphor plays in human understanding, see Ted Cohen, *Thinking of Others: On the Talent for Metaphor* (Princeton: Princeton University Press, 2008), and his essay, of particular relevance here, "At Play in the Fields of Metaphor," in *A Companion to the Philosophy of Literature*, ed. Garry L. Hagberg and Walter Jost (Oxford: Wiley-Blackwell, 2010), pp. 507–20.

[20] For a most acute discussion of the sense of rightness and its (too often underappreciated) role in our interpretative and creative practices, see Michael Krausz, *Rightness and Reasons: Interpretation in Cultural Practices* (Ithaca: Cornell University Press, 1993); this of course directly connects back to the issue of multiple interpretations in Chapter 2, Section 2.1 above.

within the expanded frame, the indefinitely limited web of beliefs, associations, connotations, expectations, intimations, and so forth that, as we saw above, both show us what the words used in an utterance mean and more fundamentally make those utterances so much as possible in the first place. The distinctions between the kinds of utterances we make, the descriptions we employ of those utterances, and the ultimate acceptance or rejection of them are not—here Rorty is right— measured in any simple one-to-one way against the One Right Description to gauge their veracity. But it does not follow from this that they are thereby put forward, like or as mere articles of play or whimsy, without constraints, without measures, without the standards and justifications of rationality. That these constraints and measures are not reducible to One does not make them any less real (quite the reverse), nor does the Rortyan shattering of the myth of the One Right Description preclude objectivity in such distinctions and descriptions, ushering in an epistemologically undifferentiated play of subjectivity. Such distinctions and descriptions, like distinctions and descriptions concerning selfhood and self-identity, are made possible within that expanded web, indeed *within language, within words.* Only a grand picture of language as being utterly separate from, and posterior to—rather than indissolubly wound together with, and indeed constitutive of—the world would make us falsely believe that, because such distinctions and descriptions take place in language, they are thus always relative, always adventitious, always secondary to what really matters.

They aren't. We can indeed entertain (in the foregoing literary-imaginative sense) possible selves: we can construct, by focusing on a coherent collection of described characteristics to the exclusion of others, what we might call imaginary identities[21] (as indeed we did in Chapter 1) within the larger mental act of absorbed literary reading, asking ourselves as we proceed as readers to what extent, and in what precise ways, we are similar and different from them. This process yields, for reasons we have begun to see as the preceding chapters have progressed along their way, self-knowledge. And in autobiographical reflection we can, having rehearsed this process in literary reading, construct similarly entertained versions of ourselves, in one case (with generosity-to-self to the fore) emphasizing and collecting together instances of kindness, in another case (with past-felt negative emotion at the fore) emphasizing and collecting together causes for regret and self-recrimination. And so with a thousand other cases of inward self-portrayal. Where we judge—in the particularized, intricately contextualized Austinian way—an entertained self-description positively, i.e., as having a sufficient verisimilitude but where this verisimilitude is not measured simply and mono-dimensionally against the (mythical) One Right Description, we take it on as a part of who and what we are. The portrayal description, far from merely

---

[21] This is essentially a more fully elaborated version of the process of developing one's relationally constituted selfhood (as initially expressed in American pragmatism) that we saw in Chapter 1 above.

178 LIVING IN WORDS

adventitious and hardly detached from what really matters, becomes the very substance of selfhood. And that selfhood displays aspects both of fluidity and of fixity that are ungeneralizeable, unsimplifiable. Literature, as we will see, in a special double-focused way both shows this within the imaginary world of the narrative and occasions it within the real world of the reader.

5.2 The Textually Cultivated "I": Making up One's Mind

Private or self-directed soliloquy, or silent thought to oneself, often exhibits a public, or public-like, dimension that its image of metaphysically enclosed solitude would belie. Such self-directed thinking obviously takes place in autobiographical reflection, but it also takes place within, and in an important sense alongside, as we have now begun to see, absorbed literary reading. Goethe captures this in a remarkable passage in his autobiographical writings; the passage casts light on Goethe, on his compositional process, on the similarity of such thought to epistolary (and hence relationally intertwined) exchange, on the tellingly *dialogical* character of inward reflection (as we encounter it in Augustine, in Kierkegaard, in Wittgenstein, in Stanley Cavell, and many others), and more generally on the public dimension of self-directed soliloquy that I am pursuing presently. Goethe, having referred to his "peculiar habit of recasting even soliloquy as dialogue" (p. 424),[22] writes (instructively, in the third person):

> Being accustomed to spend his time preferably in company, he transformed even solitary thinking into social conversation, and in the following way: namely, when he found himself alone, he would summon up in spirit some person of his acquaintance.
>
> He would ask this person to be seated, pace up and down by him, stand in front of him, and discuss whatever subject he had in mind. The person would occasionally answer him and indicate, with the customary gestures, his agreement or disagreement; and everyone has a particular way of doing this. Then the speaker would continue, and expand on whatever seemed to please his guest; or he would qualify what the latter disapproved of, and define it more clearly, and even finally be willing to abandon his thesis. The most curious aspect of this was that he never chose persons of his closer acquaintanceship, but those he saw only rarely, nay, often some who lived in far-off places and with whom he had merely a passing relationship. But usually they were persons more receptive than communicative in nature, open-minded and prepared to be calmly interested in matters within their ken, although sometimes he would also summon

---

[22] Johann Wolfgang von Goethe, in *From My Life: Poetry and Truth*, trans. Robert R. Heitner, ed. Thomas P. Saine and Jeffrey L. Sammons (Princeton: Princeton University Press, 1994), p. 424.

SELF-DEFINITION: FORGING A SELF IN LANGUAGE   179

contentious spirits to these dialectical exercises. Persons of both sexes, and of every age and condition, submitted to this and proved agreeable and charming, because the conversation was only about subjects they liked and understood. Yet many of them would have been greatly amazed had they been able to find out how often they were summoned to those imaginary conversations, since they would hardly have come to a real one.

It is quite clear that such thought-conversations are closely related to correspondence, except that the latter responds to an established familiarity, while the former creates a new, ever-changing familiarity for itself, with no reply.

This passage paints a portrait of a thinker engaged in the process of making up his mind by speculatively reflecting on possible beliefs. This involves both (1) recognizing what Rorty called the contingency of our views, our stances, and our positions as they take on greater specificity when compared to other possible positions, and (2) working through an expanding and deepening awareness of what it means to hold these possible beliefs. This also describes the character of autobiographical reflection, just as it describes the special kind of literary absorption of which I am pursuing a fuller account throughout this chapter. To identify some of this passage's elements:

(1) To so quickly turn "solitary thinking into social conversation" just is in a sense to recognize, with Wittgenstein (on the topic of privacy and private language[23]) that, to put the point strongly, there *is* no solitary thinking in the profoundly solitary (i.e., utterly non-dialogical) sense.[24]

(2) To have the imagined interlocutor answering and indicating with gestures just is to situate the initial remark being answered into an expanded web of (possible) belief, and to embody that belief (with gestures) in a manner that preserves a mindfulness of the fact that *persons* make remarks and hold,

---

[23] The topic of Wittgenstein on privacy and private language is one with a long and much-debated history; for a recent insightful and richly multifaceted discussion of not only the main terrain of the issue but also its far-reaching implications, see Stephen Mulhall, *Wittgenstein's Private Language* (Oxford: Oxford University Press, 2006). I offer a brief discussion of the impact the notion of private language can have on our thinking in aesthetics in *Art as Language*, ch. 6, "The Silence of Aesthetic Solipsism," pp. 118–35.

[24] In is in this connection revealing that even a figure we might think of as private to the point of being near-solipsistic, i.e., Werther (in Goethe, *The Sorrows of Young Werther*), as he describes his interior world in his letters, nevertheless and indeed necessarily describes that interior world publicly, or in what we might call "public" language. In fact, Goethe writes, "The letters of Werther . . . probably owe their manifold appeal to the fact that their various contents were first rehearsed in imaginary dialogues with several individuals, whereas in the composition itself they seem to be directed to only *one* friend and sympathizer" (Goethe, *From My Life*, p. 425). To put it one way, the kind of deep privacy that we understand Werther to exemplify actually depends for its intelligibility on Goethe's public, dialogical imagination, just as our understanding of the words Werther uses to express himself in his letters are words we understand as tools for use in a larger public or relationally intertwined dialogical forum.

180   LIVING IN WORDS

discuss, and debate views, positions, stances, and beliefs—they are not abstract incorporeal propositions, but are entertained and held by contextually situated people.

(3) Following on the last element, if we truly imagine a possible belief, we imagine an individual person holding that belief (which, again, is precisely what literature shows with the requisite detail), and our capacity to imagine our holding it (if that belief is deeply different or, in Goethe's phrase, "far-off" from views we do hold) is not only to imagine human difference, but to become able—and here we answer, in a differently articulated way, Rorty's call to recognize our contingency—to imagine ourselves as a different person (where, again, belief webs are in considerable part what differentiates persons, Rorty's I and all the other I's, as we conceive of them both in life and in literature).[25]

(4) When a speaker exhibits a capacity to "continue, and expand," or "qualify" or "define more clearly," that speaker thereby shows a facility and ease of movement within the interwoven and indeterminately bounded web of which we saw Davidson speak, and where a speaker is "willing to abandon his thesis," that speaker is shifting, however large, however small, a part of belief-constituted selfhood. Indeed, that person will, in this imaginary dialogical engagement, through the process of more clearly defining his or her thesis as a result of a very close scrutiny and patient comparing and contrasting of views, positions, stances, and beliefs taken or held, more clearly define herself or himself.

(5) The very capacity to change our mind is itself a precondition for the possibility of self-creation, and it is accomplished not prior to, but here again rather *in*, language. The dialogical structure of self-directed reflection in part shows that. Thus it is *within* such reflection that we entertain beliefs, and it is here that we decide to take them on or not, to become the person whose self is constituted by—whose mind is made up by—such movements and settlements of thought. (It is also important to see here that the holding of a given belief or position—in politics, say—is not uniform across all cases of persons who hold it; i.e., to have held a very different view initially, and then to have worked through intricate issues in order to arrive at the present one, is very different from having simply held

---

[25] Goethe, previously in this autobiographical writing (*From My Life*), describes the process through which he himself becomes increasingly able to imagine himself, and then become, in this sense, a different person. It comes through his first imagining, then contemplating, and then finally resolving, in a self-constitutive way, to oppose his father's plans for him: "Now I really began to regard it as legitimate self-defense to resolve on the adoption of my own way of life and study, against his will and sentiments. My father's obstinacy in unknowingly opposing my plans encouraged me in my impiety, and it did not hurt my conscience to listen to him for hours while he told and retold me about the course of life and study I would have to pursue at the university and in the world" (p. 185). This, in short, is a dialogical (in this case contra-paternal) process of self-redefinition via resolution.

SELF-DEFINITION: FORGING A SELF IN LANGUAGE   181

from the outset the present view unproblematically. This is a fact that is much easier for literature than for philosophy to capture, given the high-resolution focus literature can offer on what we might here call epistemo-logical psychology.) To the extent to which we are "open-minded and prepared to be calmly interested" in Goethe's sense, we are—to precisely the degree of intellectual openness that is shown—mindful in a serious way of circumstantial mind-making contingency.

(6) To be, as we revealingly say, *conversant* in a subject is to be able to imagine a multiplicity of perspectives ("persons of both sexes, and of every age and condition"), and this, I am suggesting, is to be able to imagine in a full sense the sentences, the words, the language, that articulate them. That self-defining capacity (and this is the point most central to this entire chapter) is not only shown in literature, but also (at the third level described above) *occasioned* by it. To learn to be conversant with a subject is at least in part to learn to imagine, and those acts of imagining rest upon—indeed they reside within—language.

(7) Lastly, while it is right to emphasize and draw out the dialogical-linguistic character of the process Goethe has captured in this passage, it is not by any means thereby wrong to keep in mind that it *is* still a kind of self-reflective soliloquy we are discussing; it is still, in a sense, a private activity of mind—in precisely the sense that absorbed literary engagement is a private experience (within the expanded frame of a public language[26]). It is, despite the public and dialogical character of reflection, still *self*-constitu-tive reading we are discussing.

There are many places throughout Goethe's autobiographical writings where the themes he captures in the above passages are given full and detailed examples: in writing of his early student years in Leipzig, he refers to "intolerable demands" (p. 192) that were intolerable precisely for the reason that they suppressed what he felt, at that stage of his development (or within the belief web of that self), naturally disposed to say. He was "prohibited from alluding to pithy Bible passages and from using naïve expressions out of the chronicles"; he had—important for our present concerns—to forget that he had read certain authors and to "dispense with everything [his] youthful enthusiasm had embraced." In short, he was being in a perhaps more than metaphorical sense "edited" and then "recast" into a different (linguistically constituted) person. While at the early stage of this self-transition he felt himself a lost soul ("I felt paralyzed in the core of my being") and he felt himself anything but conversant as described in his passage

---

[26] I offer a discussion of some ways in which our ability to so much as understand the words we use to describe privacy is invariably already situated within a public context in *Describing Ourselves*, ch. 1, sec. 3, "Real Privacy (and Hidden Content)," pp. 33–43.

182 LIVING IN WORDS

above ("so that I could scarcely talk about the most ordinary things"), we see along the lengthy course of this gradual and not always easy process a person, to put it most bluntly, *working out who he is*. He shapes his identity, his moral, aesthetic, and linguistic sensibility, just as a sculptor begins by carving overall contours and then refines, feature by feature, from there. And then as we as readers see this process, we also, alongside of our outward-directed reading of Goethe's self-defining narrative, work on, and work out ourselves—through the above-mentioned process of inward-directed identification, comparison, contrast, differentiation, and all the other elements of imaginary interlocutorship.

The short story "The Book of Sand" by Jorge Luis Borges[27] can function as a remarkably adept allegory of the kind of self-constitutive reading we are presently pursuing. In the story Borges describes a stranger who appears at his (or the protagonist's—although as Borges has repeatedly called attention to the autobiographical content of his writing this is an unclear distinction) door eager to sell a strange and eerie book. The unnamed protagonist opens the book "at random" (p. 118)—indeed just as we always hear details, episodes, or encounters of a person's experience *in medias res*, and never in any complete way from a pure beginning—only to find that the book's contents (1) never appear on the same page again, i.e., he closely scrutinizes an illustration, then closes the book, and on reopening it to that page finds utterly different content there (and never sees that same illustration again), and (2) he could never, despite repeated attempts, get to the first or last page (every effort invariably yielded still a few more pages between the pages he was on and the cover binding). The webs of interwoven belief, the webs that serve to make us who we are, as Davidson observed, are of indeterminate reach—whenever we reach what we might take as the end of an inferential link from the entertained belief in question, we find that we can follow numerous individual strands still further. And the contingent (using the word with the cautions expressed above concerning Rorty) nature of our own present selfhood and the relationally enmeshed character of that self's experience always

---

[27] Jorge Luis Borges, *The Book of Sand*, trans. Norman Thomas di Giovanni (New York: Dutton, 1977), pp. 117–22. In connection with present issues it is worth having a look at his early essay, "The Nothingness of Personality," in Jorge Luis Borges, *Selected Non-Fictions*, ed. Eliot Weinberger (New York: Viking, 1999), pp. 3–9. He begins a number of paragraphs, each developing a separate line of thought, with the sentence "There is no whole self." It is fitting to the theme of this chapter that the words Borges uses concerning the problems of selfhood can be much more fully understood by considering the biographical setting in which he wrote that essay; see Edwin Williamson, *Borges: A Life* (New York Viking, 2004), pp. 98ff. For an interesting contrast, one that agrees with the centrality to human life of the question of the possibility and nature of "whole selfhood" but that gives it a different answer, see Milan Kundera, *Identity*, trans. Linda Asher (New York: HarperCollins, 1998). See especially p. 45: "He reminded me of what I must have said when I was sixteen. When he did that, I understood the sole meaning of friendship as it's practiced today. Friendship is indispensable to man for the proper function of his memory. Remembering our past, carrying it with us always, may be the necessary requirement for maintaining, as they say, the wholeness of the self. To ensure that the self doesn't shrink, to see that it holds on to its volume."

reconfigure experience;[28] they always weave it into a pattern generating a set of present and subsequent echoes or reverberations distinctive to *that* pattern that not only significantly change, through these echoes and reverberations, its linked associations and connotations in its presentations to the self, but more importantly they change *it itself*—the content of experience is never the same, because the context (in the pragmatic sense of ever-evolving relations discussed in Chapter 1 and because describing, or capturing in words, the person to whom things happen is exceptionally intricate, as we saw Woolf say in Chapter 2), strictly speaking, is never the same.

And just so, the reader's experience is never, in this sense, the same—the mind that comes to the text (as William James insisted) is always altered upon return to it, so the associative webs, the sometimes explicitly articulated, sometimes only dimly sensed linkages to the past, differ time to time. Thus what we might call "the same diagram," the same content, is never exactly, or in a very fine-tuned sense, findable again, just as the self that turns to the text comes to it not without a beginning that much precedes it (in terms of the past associations and the reflections it awakens or occasions), nor does that self close its story at the end of the book—its resonance, its impact, its sense, continue beyond that textual closing.[29] (One might call it an apparent narrative closing of the kind we saw with Aristotle in Chapter 3 that is in truth by its nature incompatible with final or henceforth-unchangeable closure; we will return to the idea of, in a special sense, rewriting the past in Chapter 6.) Just as we can become haunted by the past, or by aspects or episodes of it (recall Sabina with her unending desire to recapture a moment with Tomas), Borges's protagonist becomes haunted by the book whose contents, like sand, always shift, are always elsewhere upon return. He contemplates burning it—just as one can try to repudiate or even obliterate the past—but he fears that (like fearing the continuing and indeed increasingly haunting influence upon the future of that past) "the burning of an infinite book might likewise prove infinite and suffocate the planet with smoke" (p. 122). In the end, the protagonist—for us an image of the resolute denial or repudiation of all self-reflection (and thus like Don Giovanni in Chapter 4), an image of attempting to close and flee from what is by its nature perennially open—abandons the wondrous but threatening book in the basement (the subconscious?) of a library, where in addition to books, maps (charting out and understanding a life in

---

[28] This reconfiguration of experience as its relational meshing changes is, to my mind, helpfully understood in connection with the non-atomistic conception of experience articulated in American pragmatism and the writings of William James on perception; this thus links directly back to the discussion in Chapter 1, which may now be seen in this light.

[29] Indeed see, in this connection, Borges's own words closing the afterword he wrote for the collection in which this story appears: "I hope that these hasty notes I have just dictated do not exhaust this book and that its dreams go on branching out in the hospitable imagination of those who now close it" (p. 125).

184 LIVING IN WORDS

cartographic terms?[30]) and periodicals (continually updating and reweaving the past into the present and future?[31]) were kept. It was surreptitiously deposited on one of the basement's musty shelves and abandoned there.

Now, to stand back a bit, why should a willingness to embrace a reflective life, rather than to turn away from it, be a virtue? Why should this allegory of a reader's experience seem to deserve the words "denial," "repudiation," and "flee from"? At least in part, Davidson and Rorty, when woven together, have already answered the question. To fully and seriously imagine what it is to believe things other than we presently believe is, as I am suggesting, a way of coming to know ourselves and our self-constitutive beliefs fully, with far greater exactitude and refinement than we would have had without these literary occasions for reflection. To be made, through literary engagement, mindful of what is contingent about ourselves is to be made broader and more capacious in our human understanding. To turn from that process is to turn away from growth, from openness, to the narrow, to the familiar, to the—indeed like the finite book we cannot truly find (Borges's wondrous book is also a metaphor for all books)—closed. Rorty himself, reviving pragmatism in his idiosyncratic way, wrote that our self-narratives, themselves always implicitly evocative of Nabokov's line concerning life as "an unfinished poem" (p. 42 Rorty), "cannot get completed because there is nothing to complete, there was only a web of relations to be rewoven, a web which time lengthens every day" (pp. 42–3). And it is literature that affords an opportunity to reflect upon, to extend, to reweave, and—in the belief-as-entertained to belief-as-held process of self-directed epistemic acquisition described above—to create those self-constitutive relations of psychological association and meaning-contributing connotation.[32] But it is time to sum up where we are within a rather extended discussion and then to move ahead.

I said above that the kind of literary absorption (indeed, the reader's life in words) of which I am pursuing a fuller understanding in this chapter functions on three levels, with the third, more psychologically complex level itself dividing into three.[33] With the themes we have covered in this chapter to this point in play, we are in a position to see this three-tiered experience with much greater clarity. First, and simplest, we had characters as agents whose range of possible actions is itself made possible by the explicit and implicit belief webs within which they reside. To

[30] Cartographic and architectural metaphors are used very frequently in our language-games of self-description; this of course connects directly to the issues examined in Chapter 3 above on the relations between Wittgenstein's thinker and the draftsman.

[31] This is precisely the sense of the openness of the past of which Iris Murdoch wrote; see note 2 above.

[32] We are initially inclined to think of such relations in too-simple terms as invariably and wholly either discovered or created; I discuss this misleading dichotomy in Describing Ourselves, ch. 5, sec. 2, "The Pain and the Piano," pp. 163–75.

[33] I offer this, it should be noted, as a rough schematic of one kind of aesthetic experience; I would welcome what could initially seem counterexamples that would in fact further reveal the complexity, and the intricacy, of these mind-text relations.

SELF-DEFINITION: FORGING A SELF IN LANGUAGE   185

put to work in this context a resonant line from Emily Dickinson, they dwell in possibility, where the reach of the possible coextends with the reach of that indeterminately bounded web. And, as in life (but as we will shortly see with a reflective-contemplative distance that life doesn't in its ordinary course allow) we comprehend (also as in life) their actions to the extent that we comprehend the particularities of the contexts within which they act. That understanding depends on our cultivating a real sense of the scope, the reach, of possibility, but—to avoid Rorty's overstatement of freedom—also a sense of the limits, the constraints. Edward Said[34] has drawn attention to precisely this kind of double-aspectual understanding of human action through reference to the philosopher often thought to have most strongly emphasized unrestrained volitional freedom. Said writes:

> Let us return to Sartre. At the very moment that he seems to be advocating the idea that man (no mention of woman) is free to choose his own destiny, he also says that the situation,—one of Sartre's favorite words—may prevent the full exercise of such freedom. And yet, Sartre adds, it is wrong to say that milieu and situation unilaterally determine the writer or intellectual: rather there is a constant movement back and forth between them.

The character-constitutive beliefs that we see represented in fiction function in precisely this way, where to genuinely and truly understand, to fathom, what it means to hold a belief involves understanding what interwoven, and sometimes epistemologically interlocking, beliefs can and cannot be held or entertained by that character at that time of his or her development in that context. (It is for this reason that we can find a character—just as we may in life—morally blameworthy for not having had a thought he or she should have had, or not having thought harder about the ramifications of a belief upon which he or she has acted; such moral evaluations of mental action and inaction are made possible just by the scope of what indeed is, for that character, possible.)

So the first level of this kind of self-constitutive reader's experience, is simply (or perhaps not so simply, as we shall see in a moment) to see a character acting, in word and deed, upon a belief that is for this moment, for this particular action, prominent (having emerged on this occasion from that extensively webbed background or from Wittgenstein's scaffolding). Examples of this in literature truly are too numerous to mention: we see them in psychologically refined descriptions in Homer, Greek tragedy, Virgil, Dante, Shakespeare, George Eliot, Tolstoy, Dostoevsky, Edith Wharton, Proust, Iris Murdoch, and obviously countless others. But then, given an awareness of the psychological astuteness of these

---

[34] Edward W. Said, *Representations of the Intellectual* (New York: Random House, 1994), p. 74.

186 LIVING IN WORDS

authors, one wants to add that this matter indeed is perhaps not so simple: to *understand* the strength of the suppressed and concealed reaction of the old woman recognizing by his scar Odysseus dressed as a beggar just before he reveals his identity is to know more than a little about (1) her past with Odysseus as a boy, (2) the power of her instantaneously awakened recollection of all of that by the scar, (3) her thoughts and feelings concerning the present state of Penelope, (4) her seeing the courage of the father suddenly manifest in the son Telemachus in what immediately follows upon that moment of memory-web-activating recognition, (5) her almost Proustian sense of time past (specifically, the sense of time and what was a possible future made real by Odysseus' presence, thought to be irretrievably lost in the past) being suddenly and dramatically regained as Odysseus slays Penelope's increasingly impatient suitors, and surely many other things (extending as webs reaching out from those themes). To know the true content of her reaction at the recognition scene is to know a very great deal about humane content that extends vastly beyond what any philosophical picture or simplifying template of localized and immediately given experiential content (essentially, the reductive picture of experience given to us by British empiricism)[35] could account for. Humane understanding—the kind of awareness cultivated within this kind of reader's absorption—is anything but atomistic or experientially isolable or narrowly determinately bounded. What we would, with respect for the term, be able to call an *understanding* of Medea's terrible acts,[36] or the filial piety shown to Orestes,[37] or Dante's description of the place and condition of Ugolino,[38] or Casaubon's inwardly vacuous and aesthetically posturing ability to say the right thing (actually if we understand the case not that, but rather to parrot what sound like the right words),[39] involve an extensive grasp of humane content far beyond what an anemic description, or what we might initially think of as the brute facts alone, would capture. (And any attempt to state the brute facts quickly generates the sense that one does not at all know where to stop tracing out the webs in describing the act in question—think of the psychological complexity of Medea's act.) Examples of what it takes for such understanding, layered and intricate in all

[35] I refer here, as I have in previous chapters, to the picture of sensory experience put forward in Locke's *Essay Concerning Human Understanding* and subsequent writings on perception in that tradition. One might briefly characterize that as a kind of perceptual "snapshot" model, where each of the five sensory modalities continually takes in its atomistically isolated blocks of experience. The distortions brought in by this picture become especially visible when brought up against the intricacies of our perceptions of persons.

[36] Euripides, *The Medea*, trans. Rex Warner, in *The Complete Greek Tragedies, Euripides I*, ed. David Grene and Richard Lattimore (Chicago: University of Chicago Press, 1955), pp. 55–108.

[37] Aeschylus, *Oresteia*, trans. Richard Lattimore, in *The Complete Greek Tragedies, Aeschylus I*, ed. David Grene and Richard Lattimore (Chicago: University of Chicago Press, 1955), pp. 33–171.

[38] Dante Alighieri, *The Divine Comedy*, trans. Charles S. Singleton (Princeton: Princeton University Press, 1970). Ugolino is placed in the ninth circle of hell in quite inventive morally retributive circumstances; *Inferno*, cantos XXXII and XXXIII, pp. 339–59.

[39] George Eliot, *Middlemarch* (New York: New American Library, 1964).

SELF-DEFINITION: FORGING A SELF IN LANGUAGE   187

their complexity, are—if taken with the patient case-by-case attention that true understanding requires—everywhere throughout the history of literature. That gradually acquired sense of complexity carries over to our self-descriptions and self-definitions as well. All of that is the first level.

At the second level, we had the literary depiction of entertained belief, where that entertained belief stands against the backdrop of a network of related and settled, accepted, or held beliefs—in short, the body of beliefs to which, we might say, the entertained belief aspires and by which it is being considered as a candidate. Examples here are naturally legion as well, but perhaps one may stand for the many.

In Iris Murdoch's *The Sea, The Sea*,[40] Charles Arrowby, retired and now reflecting back on his earlier life in the ever-engaging world of the theater in London (where he was actor, director, and playwright), later in the novel is "in a sick trance" of mourning and self-recrimination at the drowning death of his friend Hartley's son Titus. Arrowby in these pages reflects on: (1) whether or not people to whom he tells things believe him; (2) to what extent he is right to blame himself (for not sufficiently watching over Titus and for not sufficiently warning him of the power of the sea in the first place); (3) to what extent the view of stone cottages, willows, butterflies, box hedges, rambler roses, and so forth have been transfigured, by association to the tragic loss, from images giving great pleasure to "the very images of sorrow," and to what extent (in terms of which entertained beliefs concerning his responsibility and the correlated extent to which these beliefs, once taken on board and interwoven as part of himself, profoundly and forever change his relations to the others and what one might call his moral relation to himself) he will ever be able to see them in what we call the same way again; and (4) what it is to now see the world and its inhabitants "through a black veil of misery and remorse and indecision [where the indecision is indeed about which self-constitutive beliefs to hold and which to reject] and fear"—where the object of the fear is precisely the set of consequences of those entertained beliefs once they are hardened into a part of who and what he is, where he realizes that his emotions of self-assessment will follow from these beliefs once settled. Murdoch captures the emotive potency of Arrowby's reflections in an unforgettable description of deep sadness: she has him say "and there was a feeling as if I carried a small leaden coffin in the place of my heart." Arrowby also (5) reflects on the meaning of silences (recall Lear's loving daughter), the very concept of which (let alone the nuanced particularities of) the philosophy of language could well learn from literature. Arrowby says, "We spoke little as we walked and I could see Lizzie looking at me now and then and she was thinking to herself: it is a relief to him to walk with me thus in silence. My presence, my silence is healing him." Murdoch

---

[40] Iris Murdoch, *The Sea, The Sea* (Harmondsworth: Penguin, 1978), pp. 400–3.

188   LIVING IN WORDS

here has Arrowby inwardly articulating his silent interlocutor's thoughts on the meaning of their companioned silence, showing that in this case he sees perfectly well what she is thinking.[41] And then adding a further layer of entertained belief (showing that the phenomenology of self-constitutive belief acquisition does not proceed one item at a time), Murdoch gives us (6) Arrowby reflecting upon the justifiability of the preceding thought, the preceding interpretation of silence (here Arrowby has become a somewhat complex interpreter of another's thought in Davidson's sense above), by adding to the previous the parenthetic reflection "(This last belief was probably justified)," where the meta-reflection implied by the word "probably" indicates its status as a candidate belief. Arrowby reflects ("I went over and over these things in my mind") upon why he failed to warn Titus, provisionally settling (and thus showing within the fiction that we have in life a stage of intermediate or provisional settling on what and what not to believe where these beliefs are strongly self-determining vis-à-vis who and what we are, and who and what we may or may not then become) on the view that he turned away from prudence in order to preserve reciprocally his sense of Titus and—this is especially important to his estimation of self-blame—Titus's sense of him. (He wanted to show the boy that he was indeed, like the boy himself, "strong and fearless"; warning the boy about the dangers of that water would have "spoilt the charm of that moment." Or, if he knew that he was not in this sense strong and fearless, he wanted to preserve the false appearance of this to the boy—which would in this case be all the more morally blameworthy.) Arrowby considers, going over in his mind, the very sentences he might have uttered to voice that suppressed (and what would have been lifesaving) prudence: "It's not that easy to get out" or "I don't think I will swim here"; such sentences, like those of less psychologically mimetic complexity from the *Odyssey* or *Medea* above, have a meaning as they roll into and out of his mind that is not only inflected by (that is to put the point too weakly), but in truth given content by, the circumstances of their contemplation.[42] To understand (again, in the fuller sense of understanding that fully warrants the term "understanding") those words is to understand these circumstances and the psychologically dire condition of the person who entertains them. And like the first level, all of this as well carries over to inform and refine

---

[41] For a helpful discussion of our knowing another's thoughts (against the misleading picture of hermetic or unbridgeable mental enclosure), see Ray Monk, "Getting inside Heisenberg's Head," in *A Companion to the Philosophy of Literature*, ed. Garry L. Hagberg and Walter Jost (Oxford: Wiley-Blackwell, 2010), pp. 453–64. See also in this connection Frank Kermode's discussion of *Middlemarch* in his afterword to that volume, specifically seeing the novel as (as Eliot herself puts it) a project of discovering "how ideas lie in minds other than my own," p. 814.

[42] For helpful discussions of the determination of what is often called (although this is in fact an interestingly dangerous metaphor) propositional content by precisely this kind of context-embeddedness, see here again Charles Travis, *Occasion-Sensitivity: Selected Essays* (Oxford: Oxford University Press, 2008).

our processes of self-description and self-definition. All of that, then, is the second level.

The third level of the literary experience it is my purpose in this chapter to characterize is one to which we now return to after seeing it initially sketched above, but now here too with a good deal more of the web (in this case all of the foregoing discussion) surrounding the following sentences that will articulate this experience and bring it more sharply into view. I said above that when identifying with a literary character we must first—in order for that identification to be psychologically possible—comprehend the context of that character's action, the web of belief (of settled, entertained, and, as Murdoch has shown, half-settled kinds) that makes the real and possible action intelligible. To clarify that, in so identifying, within this autobiographically engaged mode of literary absorption, we:

(1) grasp what it is, and what it means, to perform the actions that evince the action-determining belief held by the character;
(2) grasp what it is like to be a character who chooses to act on such a belief in this particular way (*we* might choose very different actions, indirect or secondary actions, or inactions to express those beliefs according to the patterns of action that constitute our character); and
(3) see the situation of the character with whom we vicariously identify as a metaphor for our life circumstances real or possible (knowing what we would do if... is as important to self-knowledge as knowing what we did do when... or what we will do when...). And coming to see what we would do is often a function of resolving (in the very act of reflecting upon such possibilities or Rortyan contingencies that literature affords) what we would do; i.e., the reflection-via-vicarious-identification becomes, through settling a disposition to react in this or that way or according to this or that pattern of reactions, self-constitutive.

In most succinct form: reading in this way—given an imaginative scope that yields the kind of genuine understanding described above—in significant part determines the content of selfhood. But if articulating this distinctively reflexive mode of aesthetic experience in these compact terms is merely to say it, where in literature is it more fully shown?

At the close of the *Aeneid*,[43] in mortal hand-to-hand combat with his nemesis Turnus, murderer of his most beloved comrade and dear friend Pallas, Aeneas hurls a spear with a force that "like a black whirlwind bringing devastation... passed clear through/ The middle of Turnus' thigh" (p. 401). This blow "Brought the huge man to earth, his knees buckling." With a groan expressing a dire

---

[43] Virgil, *The Aeneid*, trans. Robert Fitzgerald (New York: Random House, 1983).

190   LIVING IN WORDS

expectation of the worst from his onlooking supporters echoing from all sides, there follows a perfectly turned literary portrayal of (1) a moment of reflection, (2) a near-settlement on a belief, (3) a profound re-minding occasioned by the sudden perception of a meaningful artifact, (4) a correspondingly sudden reversal to the contrary belief, (5) a deep conviction or resolution taken on in the name of another (and yet—or even all the more because of this—one that makes Aeneas who he is), and (6) an irreversible and irreversibly character-defining action that follows as the consequence-in-action of all the preceding reflection. But, tellingly, a precondition for understanding this sequence is to first gain an awareness of the content of the plea uttered by the fallen Turnus with Aeneas' sword at his chest, that (in terms of meaning determinants) again not only inflects, but substantively contributes to, the sequence's content. Turnus, on his back and wounded beyond continuing to fight, "held his right hand out to make his plea" (p. 402):

> Clearly I earned this, and I ask no quarter.
> Make the most of your good fortune here.
> If you can feel a father's grief—and you, too,
> Had such a father in Anchises—then
> Let me bespeak your mercy for old age
> In Daunus, and return me, or my body,
> Stripped, if you will, of life, to my own kin.
> You have defeated me. The Ausonians
> Have seen me in defeat, spreading my hands.
> Lavinia is your bride. But go no further
> Out of hatred.

Turnus does a great deal with these words: he acknowledges what he has done, what he deserves, and what it would be unjustifiable and dishonorable to ask. He appeals to an element of our common humanity—he entreats Aeneas to remember both any father's grief at the loss of a child and to remember his own father— in this case a thought, an act of remembrance, capable of awakening powerful sentiment. Turnus speaks of the doubled or extended consequence if Aeneas does kill him, and then, once he is deceased, refuses the honorable return of his body. His words make Aeneas mindful of the contingency of his victory on this occasion, reminding him that he could easily have been in Turnus' position here (Turnus' massive strength uncharacteristically failed him in his attempt to hurl a great stone at Aeneas in the preceding passage), that there was no necessity to this outcome. But he acknowledges his defeat, acknowledges the disgrace of having been publicly seen in this defeat, and acknowledges the humiliation of his having non-heroically gestured, while fallen, for mercy. And in exchange for this multiple and layered acknowledgment, the web of associations he has strung, powered by the emotive fuel of the reference to a father's, and *his* father's, suffering (i.e.,

SELF-DEFINITION: FORGING A SELF IN LANGUAGE   191

weaving together his acknowledgment with the set of self-constitutive beliefs Aeneas has about his own father), Turnus implores Aeneas to save him the post-mortem indignity of an unreturned corpse and to save his family the added suffering of a burial and mourning denied.

All of this (and, in the fullest sense, the entire book that precedes it) is what gives content to the unforgettable sequence of events we see next:

> Fierce under arms, Aeneas
> Looked to and fro, and towered, and stayed his hand
> Upon the sword hilt.

We see fierceness calmed by reflection: we see a hand stayed, and to look to and fro is both an external and internal description, at once literal and metaphorical. Aeneas, towering, looks about him as he pauses in indecision, the emotion of fierce battle now cooling; and one sees him looking to the past and its claims, and then to the future and its possibilities, and then for moderation, for reduced severity—Turnus' words have awakened the reality of that possibility, that future contingency. And it appears that Aeneas, still wavering in indecision but now leaning in favor of Turnus' plea, is settling on a kind of self, resolving to be the kind of self, sensitive to and positively disposed toward such pleas from the vanquished, however despicable their previous deeds:

> Moment by moment now
> What Turnus said began to bring him round
> From indecision.

But at this moment—a moment that shows Aeneas for who he is in his thought, and that resolves who he is in terms of his immediately subsequent action—Aeneas sees the belt of Pallas that Turnus is wearing as a morally grotesque token of that previous murderous victory:

> Then to his glance appeared
> The accurst swordbelt surmounting Turnus' shoulder,
> Shining with its familiar studs—the strap
> Young Pallas wore when Turnus wounded him
> And left him dead upon the field; now Turnus
> Bore that enemy token on his shoulder—
> Enemy still.

It is at precisely the instant of this perception (another recognition scene) that Aeneas, now turning swiftly back to the claims of the past and away from even partial conciliation, in a very real sense simultaneously discovers, and yet decides,

192   LIVING IN WORDS

who and what he is. Because the circumstances, in all their detailed and occasion-specific subtlety, give rise to an experience, a sudden perception, that strongly aligns episodes and human connections from his past and thus delivers a clear and forceful trajectory from the past through the present and into the future, Aeneas both (1) volitionally comes out of indecision into unwavering resolution, and in the act, in doing so, simultaneously also (2) reveals himself to himself, thus discovering, and then as quickly staying true to, who he is, the kind of person he is, the kind of character he has. (This is precisely the interaction between self and context that we saw intimated in Said's mention of Sartre's view above.) One can say this is in part volition—he decides. And yet that decision, the moral phenomenology of which is exquisitely captured here by Virgil, is determined by character—it is thus not wholly decided, but to an extent discovered, by a most pressing emergent circumstance. It is in fact instructive that the dichotomized language of decision versus discovery, of making up one's mind versus disclosing one's mind, does not sit comfortably in this self-defining field. (This is the dichotomy that I said, chapters back, will ultimately prove insufficient.) As a hardened dichotomy template it has repeatedly been forced upon, but does not naturally emerge from, this region of self-confrontational human experience. Virgil's words show this:

> For when the sight came home to him,
> Aeneas raged at the relic of his anguish
> Worn by this man as trophy. Blazing up
> And terrible in his anger, he called out:
>
> "You in your plunder, torn from one of mine,
> Shall I be robbed of you? This wound will come
> From Pallas: Pallas makes this offering
> And from your criminal blood exacts his due."

"The relic of his anguish, worn by this man as trophy." I believe that the words "this man" should be heard in the tone of a profoundly invidious comparison to Pallas and extreme derision (as though the word "this" points contemptuously): "*this* man." It would be folly to attempt to separate off into distinct categories these words' power from their meaning—and their power comes from all that has come before that shows us the person, Turnus, as described by Aeneas' words. And it is Aeneas, the person as holder of beliefs and as life-and-death-determining actor upon them, who utters them and who gives them their point, indeed gives these words their life. Understanding the "web" within which those words function and have their point and power as linguistic action is, I want to say, to understand the meaning. Here again, only a shallower conception of or thinner standard for the word "understanding" could I think dispute this.

Most of us know what it is to be suspended in a state of "crossroads" indecision, what it is to emerge resolute in a future-determining way from that state, what it is to have eyes fall on a relic of our anguish, what it is to evince strong belief in the form of irreversible action. But to know these things is not an all-or-nothing affair, not a matter of *simply* knowing or not knowing, like knowing or not knowing the name of a dog or the temperature outside presently. Humane knowledge is severely miscast in these brutish scientistic terms (scientistic, not scientific, because scientific terms do not, against a false image of directly corresponding brute-fact language or what used to be called observation sentences, function in any such simple way either), and to know what it is like[44] to hold a view (in a suitably particularized context) amounts to much more than knowing the minimal decontextualized content of that belief. (I want to suggest that the very idea of the determinate minimal content of context-independent belief is a philosophical myth, or at the most an extremely reductive term of art. It is literature that helps us advance to a stage of linguistic sensitivity from which we can, against some sometimes-prevalent methodological presuppositions in the philosophy of language, see that and keep it in focus and to the fore.)

The first two of the subdivided parts of the third layer of the reader's experience, then, are fairly evident in a reading of Virgil's lines: we (a) see what it *means* to perform those life-and-self-determining actions; and we (b) grasp to an extent what it would be *like* to perform them. But what then of (c) seeing the situation or complex circumstances of the character into whose life we imaginatively project as a metaphor for our own lives?

Concerning Turnus, the extent to which we identify (and thus possibly gain or confirm self-knowledge from this identification) with him is the extent to which we are able to see his multiple eleventh-hour acknowledgment as sincere: in his last words he at least summons the decency to unambiguously state in a clear-eyed way what he has done and what, by virtue of this late clarity (a phenomenon, if differently inflected, that we have seen in Henry James's Dencombe in Chapter 4), he recognizes (where the scope of this recognition is calibrated within the ethos of his world, to remind us of the Rortyan elements in play here) that he deserves. We as readers may take a lesson from that, resolving to be better, and more clear-eyed (and not at the eleventh hour), about acknowledging our misdeeds. And in seeing the appeal to fatherhood (to the extent we take this as sincere and not manipulative) we see a flash of humanity, and this glimpse may well solidify our resolve to look for the humanity in others we find to be cold, alien, detached, indifferent, or even in the extreme case devoid of a sense of humane presence.[45] So in this fairly

---

[44] I allude here to the anti-reductionist essay, noted above, of Thomas Nagel's, "What Is it Like to Be a Bat?," *Philosophical Review*, 83, 1974: 435–50.

[45] The close study of the morally grotesque absence of such a sense shows us, I believe, a good deal about what its presence amounts to; that was essentially the project of Chapter 4, Section 4.1 above on Leporello's question concerning who is dead, the Commendatore or Giovanni.

194 LIVING IN WORDS

straightforward way, once we are positioned to see it, literary-characterological reflection on Turnus doubles as a morally self-constitutive act for us. So we do see in this passage about Turnus, if briefly, the third subdivision of the third layer. The case of Aeneas, however, is more nuanced, and instructively so.

We know what it is to emerge from a conflict with the upper hand, and we know what it is to act impulsively, thoughtlessly, imperiously, unilaterally, single-mindedly, unreflectively, self-aggrandizingly, and so forth. First, in seeing Aeneas *towering*, we see—to articulate some strands of the web surrounding that positioning, that circumstance, or in Sartre's sense, situation—not yet the actuality, but the possibility, of all of these types of action. That recognition of possibility—of multiple routes into morally blameworthy acts from this pre-decision moment in time—can itself instill (or re-instill) in us as readers, or remind us of the value of, a laudable moral caution, where such re-minding leads us to greater awareness, and thus to better choices, at just such decision points of our own. Second, in seeing Aeneas looking to and fro, we as readers are made to recall—we are, while following that unfolding narrative, here as well reminded[46] of—the value of taking stock, of looking around us, of remembering to *actively* look to see just where we are, to try to be (in Henry James's famous phrase) a person on whom nothing is lost. Third, in witnessing in our reader's imagination the staying of the hand, we are again in this doubled way reminded of deliberation, reflectiveness, the value of taking a moment to let cool the immediately felt impulse to act precipitously, to keep our wits about us. Fourth, in seeing a person brought round from indecision by taking the human measure of an appeal to fatherhood and kinship, we are—within the self-directed part of our imaginative world that parallels the literary narrative—reminded of the need to cultivate and strengthen such forms of responsiveness (and reminded of the virtue of patience and listening[47] upon which such responsiveness depends) in ourselves. All of this is relatively straightforward. But it is in seeing, fifth, the close of the epic story of Aeneas that the reader's relation to the text gets more complicated.

After having made his speech for Pallas, and just after the above line "And from your criminal blood exacts his due," we have the final act of the narrative described:

> He sank his blade in fury in Turnus' chest.
> Then all the body slackened in death's chill,

---

[46] I mean "reminded" in a broadly Wittgensteinian sense here, that is, the reorienting experience of being reawakened to sets or networks of connotations that connect the case before us to other cases previously known but until now forgotten or overlooked, and that thus bring out features of the case before us that were, prior to this re-contextualization in memory, obscured.

[47] What this suggests—rightly, I believe—is that listening is a far more important matter than has been generally acknowledged in moral philosophy. I describe what I take to be an exemplary case of such listening within artistic creativity and how ensemble close-listening mimetically reflects moral engagement, in "Jazz Improvisation and Ethical Interaction: A Sketch of the Connections," in *Art and Ethical Criticism*, ed. Garry L. Hagberg (Oxford: Blackwell, 2008), pp. 259–85.

SELF-DEFINITION: FORGING A SELF IN LANGUAGE 195

And with a groan for that indignity
His spirit fled into the gloom below.

Does this exemplify reflection-borne compassion? Is it to assess and respond to Turnus' vanquished appeal and to respond to the flash of humanity we see shining through the brutal exterior? Is it to expand the mind so that it capaciously encompasses an awareness of his good fortune and the contingency of his victory? Is it to cool impassioned impulses that would motivate and, unchecked, lead to perhaps ultimately undesirable irreversible action?

The picture of moral psychology that Virgil's text paints is not in any clear sense any of these. But it is an act that in an important sense *includes* (given what we have seen in the foregoing passages) all of these: the final act of Aeneas is one of considerable moral complexity, and it reminds us of the fact that moral actions are often of a complex kind with a particularized intricacy that simplifying reductive (i.e., motive-unifying) utilitarian (consequence-identifying) or deontological (duty-identifying) moral systems fail to capture. The moral psychology of Aeneas does, as we see in the foregoing passages, include reflection upon those reductive elements: both consequence calculation and duty consideration are in play. But *then*, with that reflection behind him, he moves to a resolute self-definition that here again is both chosen and yet in another sense determined by who and what he is—where who and what he is, and who he is to himself, is then immediately reinforced by the action. Now articulated within the example of Aeneas, this "bootstrapping" process, when seen through our doubled literary experience, reminds us of the Aristotelian[48] character of moral action that, becoming engrained through repetition and through self-defining moments (as is, perfectly, Aeneas' final act here) of resolution, makes us who we are. Such occasions, as mimetically represented in Aeneas' act, are like (i.e., have the same structure as) the beliefs that we first entertain and then, after a process of epistemic acquisition of the kind described above, take on as part of us. Aeneas reflects, is aware, is responsive, and is fully alive to where he is, but then in seeing the relic of his anguish, he also sees beyond where he is, and so the sense of who he is as interwoven with his sense of who Pallas was, together make one course of action impossible, and the other course of action—for him, within the ethos of his world—necessary. And, in seeing that, we as readers are reminded—made mindful of the self-individuating fact—that there are for us limits: there are things we simply will not abide, and outrages we cannot forgive. To recklessly or whimsically or arbitrarily (in Rorty's overstated and overgeneralized sense above) dispense forgiveness would, in the sense that the case of Aeneas portrays with such precision, be to take the "we" out of play, or to diminish, to erode, or in an extreme case of a violation of self-integrity, to begin to eradicate the selves that we

---

[48] Aristotle, *Nicomachean Ethics*, in *The Complete Works of Aristotle*, ed. Jonathan Barnes (Princeton: Princeton University Press, 1984).

196 LIVING IN WORDS

are—selves of which we have an abiding sense (which as I am suggesting literary experience cultivates) and to which we have an ongoing responsibility to respect and preserve (for which, as I am suggesting, literary experience provides occasion).

But before closing this chapter, more still needs to be said, and now with greater specificity, about what I have repeatedly called the "doubling" of the reader's experience, the process by which we make the textual narrative a metaphor for our own lives (the third strand of the third layer of the reader's experience as described above), and the process of aesthetic-to-moral "bootstrapping," i.e., the self-compositional power of this variety of reading that is at the very least autobiographically informative, and at most, nothing less than self-creative.

5.3 Metaphorical Identification and Self-Individuation

Arthur Danto has described the relation between the reader and the literary text as metaphorical in structure, and this proves to be an extraordinarily illuminating way of articulating one part of the distinctive experience on the part of the reader that I am pursuing throughout this chapter.[49] Danto's position, stated in its most succinct form, is that literature "is about each reader who experiences it" (p. 154). He is quick to set aside the obviously false claim that, for example, the primary subject matter of *Paradise Lost* is the story of the life of the person who reads it. But it is about that reader in the way, as Danto presents it, that Hegel said the work of art "reveals its purpose as existing *for* the subject, for the spectator, and not on its own account. The spectator is, at it were, in it from the beginning, is counted in with it, and the work exists only for this point, i.e., for the individual apprehending it" (p. 135).[50] And for Danto, in a way that is uniquely particularized to the individual reader, the literary work nevertheless exhibits a kind of universality: "The universality of literary reference is only that it is about each individual that reads the text at the moment that individual reads it, and [here Danto's idea connects explicitly to present concerns] it contains an implied indexical: each work is about the 'I' that reads the text, identifying himself not with the implied

---

[49] Arthur C. Danto, "Philosophy and/as/of Literature," cited in note 10 above. See also his illuminating interview "Why We Need Fiction: An Interview with Arthur C. Danto," *The Henry James Review*, 18(3), Fall 1997: 213–16. Although this is not the place to pursue the matter, it is worth noting that there are informative parallels between the self-reflective and self-finding process Danto is describing in literature and the painting of a self-portrait. For an insightful discussion, see Jodi Cranston, *The Poetics of Portraiture in the Italian Renaissance* (Cambridge: Cambridge University Press, 2000); see especially p. 98: "A category of portraiture explicitly devoted to representing oneself, self-portraits claim to present the 'I,' the maker, through the circumstances of their making...The process and the product contribute toward presenting some aspect of the artist's self, that part beyond the physical, with the act of painting constituting and generating as much of the artist's self as the completed representation."

[50] Hegel, *Werke*, 15:28; translated as *Aesthetics: Lectures on Fine Art*, trans. T. M. Knox (Oxford: Oxford University Press, 1975), p. 806.

reader for whom the implied narrator writes, but with the actual subject of the text in such a way that each work becomes a metaphor for each reader: perhaps the same metaphor for each" (p. 155). Part of what makes metaphor an attractive concept to bring in to describe the reader-text parallel relation is precisely that it possesses (Danto does not put it exactly this way) the "doubled" structure described above—it is clearly literally false to say that the *Odyssey* is about reader A rather than about the trials and tribulations of Odysseus; it is clearly false to say that *The Sea, The Sea* is about reader B rather than about the later-life autobiographical reflections and reconsiderations of retired thespian Charles Arrowby; it is clearly false to say that the *Aeneid* is about reader C and not about the inward and outward travails and triumphs of Aeneas. Juliet is not the sun; and yet, in a sense far too important, and far too illuminating to allow any residue of positivism to crush, she is. And in *that* sense, Danto rightly insists, "for each reader I, I is the subject of the story. The work finds its subject only when read" (p. 155). Thus it is in a simple (too simple) sense clearly false to say these things about these texts and the readers A, B, and C, and yet, like the claim about Juliet, in another distinct sense—indeed a sense closely related to the literary cultivation of our sense of self—they are not at all clearly false. As they read of Odysseus, Arrowby, and Aeneas they—with a doubled consciousness, a bifocal concentration—read of themselves. This way of putting it would suggest (and Danto sees this danger and steers clear of it) that, as the lives, outward and inward, of the protagonists are mimetically depicted in the text, and we as readers clearly are not authorially empowered to change that text (i.e., we can't through an act of will, manifested as a kind of reader-as-writer psychokinesis, change the words on the page), then the doubled narrative of our lives, to the extent that the works are in this metaphorically structured way about us, will be fixed in their mimetic content as well. We would, in that case, look into the text and—bifocally doubled—simultaneously look into ourselves, therein seeing, like the fixed printed words of the text, the fixed representation of ourselves.[51] This, as Danto rightly insists, is too passive a way of picturing the reader's psychology here: the truth, as I also have been suggesting from various avenues of entry (T. S. Eliot, Davidson, Rorty, Goethe, Borges, Murdoch, and Virgil) into the topic throughout this chapter, is far more active—and far more interesting. The content of the reflection in a mirror is wholly fixed by the features of the real object or person that is reflected in it; this is strict mimesis. It is a mirror held up to a *pre-existent* reality. But the reflection we see in literature is—rather strikingly (and this was the point I called "rather unexpected" in the introduction to this chapter) once we stop to think of it—in

---

[51] The metaphorical picture of the self as a text, one that we look into and read prewritten content that is fixed prior to the act of reading, is one that has been presumed as unproblematically helpful by many. I suggest otherwise in "Wittgenstein's Voice: Reading, Self-Understanding, and the Genre of *Philosophical Investigations*," special issue of *Poetics Today* 28(3), Fall 2007: 499–526.

198　LIVING IN WORDS

part of our own making. Juliet is not the sun—and yet she is. We do not have authorial or psychokinetic powers over the text—and yet, if in a way we must quite cautiously describe, we do. Danto writes, "Because of this immediacy of identification, it is natural to think, as theorists from Hamlet upward have done, of literature as a kind of mirror" (p. 156). But he continues with what is most important for present concerns:

> not simply in the sense of rendering up an external reality, but as giving me to myself for each self peering into it, showing each of us something inaccessible without mirrors, namely that each has an external aspect and what that external aspect is. Each work of literature shows in this sense an aspect we would not know was ours without benefit of that mirror: each discovers—in the eighteenth-century meaning of the term—an unguessed dimension of the self. It is a mirror less in passively returning an image than in transforming the self-consciousness of the reader who in virtue of identifying with the image recognizes what he is. Literature is in this sense transfigurative, and in a way which cuts across the distinction between fiction and truth. There are metaphors for every life in Herodotus and Gibbon.　(p. 156)

Danto does not here go into just what precisely is that "something inaccessible without mirrors," or what precisely is "the aspect that one would not know is ours" without this kind of experience of literary absorption. (Although the blunt answer "We know it when we see it" would not, as anyone who has gained some self-knowledge through this kind of literary absorption probably implicitly knows, be an entirely bad one.[52]) I want to suggest that such otherwise-inaccessible (or at least otherwise difficult to obtain—Danto may have overstated the case) content of the indexical "I" is the kind of thing described throughout the preceding two sections of this chapter: it is, through vicarious identification, coming to see ourselves as one contingent self realized from a matrix of other, web-interrelated

---

[52] The experienced idiosyncratic content of the moment of self-recognition as the criterion for, or definition of, such experience need not be viciously circular in the way it may seem to a superficial glance; there is much discussion of the "ah-ha" experience in psychoanalysis that casts light on this phenomenon, and these experiences can, in some cases, assume the authority of a legitimation or confirmation. Yet they are by no means *intrinsically* verifying: the criteria for their credibility will emerge in the expanded contexts where the words in which such experiences are expressed have their life. This particular issue is examined in a literary setting in James Joyce, *A Portrait of the Artist as a Young Man* (New York: Viking, 1972). See, for example, the problem as it is illustrated on p. 153: "A restless feeling of guilt would always be present with him: he would confess and repent and be absolved, confess and repent again and be absolved again, fruitlessly. Perhaps that first hasty confession wrung from him by the fear of hell had not been good? Perhaps, concerned only for his imminent doom, he had not had sincere sorrow for his sin? But the surest sign that his confession had been good and that he had had sincere sorrow for his sin was, he knew, the amendment of his life.—I have amended my life, have I not? he asked himself." The answer to this last question will take form within the expanded context of his life and working out, and through, the ramifications of the self-directed belief, and not by consulting exclusively what we call the inner experience.

SELF-DEFINITION: FORGING A SELF IN LANGUAGE   199

possible selves, where we ever more finely chisel (and in this sense we are coauthors of the text) the portrayals of ourselves along with, or in subtle contrast to, the other side of our doubled concentration, the protagonist with whom we experience the immediate identification. We see here again that we gain knowledge not only of who and what we are in a passive sense (although the simpler side of the experience, where we recognize telling similarities to the protagonist, will work in this fairly simple way), but as a function of the active process, the self-compositional process of thinking through (as we saw in—or actually parallel to or bifocally with—the case of Aeneas' final choice above) the "what-we-would-do-when" questions that take as many particularized formulations as there are imaginary literary worlds. And again (going back to the Davidsonian element in play here), we understand the words that describe those scenarios just to the extent that we—in the fuller and deeper sense of the word "understand" employed above—understand the webs of belief, and the possible and actual action and interaction upon those beliefs, that give those words sense. An unguessed dimension of the self becomes through this process a known one, but in ways where, like Aeneas, we nevertheless volitionally make up our minds in a self-constitutive way that makes us who we are. It is indeed, as Danto describes it, a process that transforms the self-consciousness of the reader. A metaphor, as we have seen briefly, cuts with a fine epistemological disregard[53] across the distinction between truth and falsity, as does (as Danto also puts it) this kind of transfigurative literature. The occasion for this reflexive contemplation, the fiction, is (in a narrow or strict sense) false by definition. But the other half of the doubled experience, where we gain self-knowledge often by making constitutive self-resolutions, much like the claim about Juliet, is not.

But there is still another dimension, also deserving of fuller elucidation, concerning the image of ourselves that we create and then identify with (Danto's words were "who in virtue of identifying with the image recognizes what he is"). Much has been written about the problem of moral improvement through fiction.[54] The appeal to metaphor offers a fairly concise way (a way that does not run afoul of the many difficulties that beset conceptions of literary didacticism[55]) of schematically picturing this process (where the details of the literary case are then

---

[53] I perhaps should say why I think my allusion here to Kirk Varnedoe's *A Fine Disregard: What Makes Modern Art Modern* (New York: Abrams, 1990) is reasonably apt in this case. In both cases (i.e., in artistic creation and self-description—Varnedoe of course discusses the artistic side of the comparison implied by the allusion) the full awareness of the rules being broken in the act of breaking them opens the way into further creative work that would otherwise have remained beyond the bounds of the possible.

[54] For a helpful orientation, see Noel Carroll, "Art, Narrative, and Moral Understanding," in *Aesthetics and Ethics: Essays at the Intersection*, ed. Jerrold Levinson (Cambridge: Cambridge University Press, 1998), pp. 126–60.

[55] See, for a particularly discerning discussion, Joshua Landy, "A Nation of Madame Bovarys: On the Possibility and Desirability of Moral Improvement through Fiction," in Hagberg, ed., *Art and Ethical Criticism*, pp. 63–94.

200 LIVING IN WORDS

positioned into the schematic). If, as Danto suggests, we are active, self-transforming agents in making the portrayal (through something like the intricate comparative and then self-determining process I have described in the preceding sections of this chapter, where again a certain circumstantially limited flexibility of self, of possible and actual belief, and of possible and actual self-description come into play), then there is no reason why we would not be able, in being reminded of particular aspects of our selfhood and possible selfhood, to cast those aspects in higher relief in our self-picture. And this would accentuate the characteristics we, in our ideal (or closer-to-ideal) realizations of ourselves, want exemplified in us as persons. Like Aristotle, who in the course of his aesthetic thinking said that an artist can portray us better, as, or worse than we in fact are, so, as "coauthors" of the reflexive side of our doubled attention, we as readers could (parallel to the work of the literary authors considered in the previous sections) arrive at a finely chiseled (i.e., exactingly described) self-image. This, it is true, would in part reflect only what we want to become, not what we are (although such an image serving as an internal regulative ideal toward which we aspire is no small moral matter). And indeed, if the image we sculpt is far removed from the cold truth about the subject of the portrayal, i.e., us, then this process could, it would seem, become an instrument for self-deception. But then recall what we saw in the doubled reading of Aeneas' moral psychology above. To the extent that we take on, and resolve to hold, characteristics that are us at our best (e.g., most attentive, most sympathet-ically imaginative, most generous-minded, most kind, most mindful of the mater-ial or psychological constraints under which others we might too easily criticize have acted, most aware of subtlety in human affairs, most discerning of motives behind appearances, most sensitive to what can for a particular person mobilize insecurities, etc.) in precisely the way we saw entertained beliefs become held beliefs and thus become part of who and what we are, we can self-constitutively resolve to be that person (or to a fuller extent approximate that person). And thus, as Danto, if perhaps too schematically, expresses it, we can indeed transfigure ourselves through the experience of literature.[56] Or, to reemploy Davidson's phrase, we enact through this absorbed literary reading a layered auto-dialogical process where we grow into the ability—with all the serious linguistic understand-ing upon which this depends—to "redescribe certain events [in this case the events of our lives that are selected as episodes in a life-narrative] in a revealing way."

Still, the characterization of this process as a kind of inward dialogical *negoti-ation* can seem counterintuitive, and before concluding this chapter we should pause to reflect on the reasons for this. In initially coming to the subject of autobiographical reflection we may well expect the classically entrenched and

---

[56] See in this connection Iris Murdoch's journal entry: "Man is a creature who makes pictures of himself, and then comes to resemble the picture," quoted in Peter J. Conradi, *Iris Murdoch: A Life* (New York: W. W. Norton, 2001), p. 272.

SELF-DEFINITION: FORGING A SELF IN LANGUAGE   201

extremely simple dichotomy to keep in order, or in a sense undergird, all of the rest of the proceedings. We might expect that there are statements concerning how things are in the world external to my mind (these would on this simple scheme be classified objective descriptions) and those concerning how things are within my mind, independent of the world (these would, by contrast, be classified subjective descriptions). And in a manner corresponding to a simplified picture or model of the mind that is complicit with this oversimplifying dichotomy, we might intuitively believe that any question of the first world-describing type can always be judged *against* an external measure of veracity, i.e., how the world actually is. For such statements, we too easily think (and, given the richness and complexity of both outward and inward descriptive life, this in truth is an appalling oversimplification), skepticism is always, indeed inelibinably at home, because even our greatest degree of felt certitude ("Obviously the earth is flat"; "Obviously we will never travel to the moon") is and will remain open to falsification or correction. And a place, so we think, for skepticism is reserved even in cases of presently verified simple assertions ("I am now standing on a sandy beach gazing at the surf") by maneuvers such as Descartes's dream argument. It appears, given these too-simple reflections and the undergirding upon which they stand, that self-descriptive, or internally reflexive statements are invariably closed to skepticism; this is really nothing more than the classic picture of privileged access to our own mental contents applied to self-descriptive sentences. Our knowledge that Jones is gullible requires that we make a distinction between what is the case and what Jones believes (and the kind of thing he is habitually willing to believe); no such wedge can, we think too quickly on this model, be driven in the first-person case, because the contents therein described are immediately given to the self-describer. This is not the place to pursue this matter at considerable length, but it perhaps is the place to say that this picture, this conceptual model, illicitly presumes from the outset that the function of autobiographical language is essentially and invariably mimetic; i.e., it provides a representation after and apart from the inward facts of the first-person case. The power of Danto's point, following Hegel's, is to redirect us away from this embedded presumption, and in his remarks we can begin to see the active power of self-descriptive language in shaping, giving content to, again no less than constituting, the reality it allegedly describes. To express the point in a formula, one might say: Such language is in truth more self-defining than self-describing. Or (cautiously): more self-creative than self-reflective.

One of the evident great gifts of literature to humane self-understanding is that it can provide the exacting language within which questions concerning selfhood are asked, where the articulation of such questions generates in turn the language in which the self-constitutive answers are given. What this chapter has offered is one way of articulating the special place where beliefs about the self (understood through reference to Davidson, Rorty, and now Danto as well) comingle with that

202   LIVING IN WORDS

self and thus provide—forming a kind of virtuous circle, or functioning in a way that is virtuously a self-fulfilling prophecy—the referential content of the indexical that that self-descriptive belief is about. To take one final (misleadingly simple) case of this—autobiographical writing is full of far more extensive and intricate cases— asking a question voiced in tandem with the travails of a protagonist concerning our own courage and then, upon reflection, answering it positively through reflection upon a set of possible-contingency "What if...?" questions can itself, in subsequent cases where courage is called for, make us more courageous. Thus:

(1) The state of courageousness is not invariably there prior to this self-negotiating process;

(2) The language we use to discuss that courageousness is not invariably secondary to it, not invariably mimetic; and

(3) Our self-understanding concerning it will be made available in, and not (as we are inclined to think of it in accordance with the over-simple dichotomy between the objective and the subjective fields described above that shapes our preliminary intuitions against the active process of self-negotiation) prior to and separable from, language.

Now, it might be argued (if the embedded misleading presumptions concerning fundamental objectivity and subjectivity considered above are especially difficult to dislodge) that the distinctive self-creative reader's process that I have been pursuing throughout this chapter is, however matters may appear when all the foregoing considerations concerning self, belief, and self-determining resolution are brought together, not *genuinely* self-constitutive; resolutions of this self-reflective kind yielding reflexive belief are made—here is the argument—and broken all the time, and anyone with a sufficient grasp of the distinctively human side of human nature knows that. Thus the self-believer may take on any reflexive belief he or she likes; this will not (returning to the threat of self-deception mentioned above) be a reliable guide to the truth about the settled or abiding content of that person, nor will such a belief serve as a criterion for what it is or will be true to say of that person.

First, I would say that this fails to sufficiently acknowledge the considerable extent to which, as covered above, our belief constellations actually do make us who we are (e.g., the person who is proud to be the kind of person who would never believe in the holocaust). The person who makes this objection is simply not looking at a sufficiently broad and detailed range of cases. Beliefs about the self undeniably are (once we clear away the blinding over-simple categories and dislodge the simplified conceptual pictures that put them in place) in many cases constitutive of that self. But there is more to say to this anti-constitutive argument than this blunt—if factually forceful—head-on repudiation. It is possible that we resolve and re-resolve frequently, but never succeed in avoiding the

SELF-DEFINITION: FORGING A SELF IN LANGUAGE   203

revocation of the resolution, never get the chosen action or group of actions repeated, or performed in such a way that it hardens into an Aristotelian character trait. On this topic Richard Moran has made some particularly helpful remarks. Moran writes that this line of argument about this kind of self-reflector

> suggests that his reflection on his best reasons for belief or reasons for action still leaves it an open question what he will actually end up believing or doing. This is not a stable position one can occupy and continue to conceive of oneself as a practical and theoretical deliberator. One must see one's deliberation as the *expression and development* of one's belief and will, not as an activity one pursues in the *hope* that it will have some influence on one's eventual belief and will. Were it generally the case (for Sartre's gambler, say) [who upon considered reflection seriously resolves to stop going to the gaming tables] that the conclusion of his deliberation about what to think about something left it still open for him what he does in fact now think about it, it would be quite unclear what he takes himself to be *doing* in deliberating. It would be unclear what reason was left to *call* it deliberation if its conclusion did not count as his making up his mind; or as we sometimes say, if it didn't count as his coming to know his mind about the matter.[57]

Another way to put this galvanizing point would be say that, if the self-reflecting gambler proceeds as he does, then this is in fact not a case of considered and serious reflection leading to a self-constitutive resolution, not genuine deliberation *of the kind in question*. It is not such a case because that quite flatly is not, in their intertwining and indeterminate webs of significance, implication, and connotation, what the words "self-constitutive resolution" and words like them mean. And with this observation concerning how we use the words like "deliberation" and perhaps "resolution" in place, we can now put it very briefly: the skeptics can argue that a given case of belief-settling resolution may be disguised irresolution and so not truly self-constitutive, and one can reply that yes, there can be such cases—but those are then cases we might group together under the heading of *akrasia* or weakness of will, or, if differently described psychologically, indeed under the heading of self-deception. But they are, by virtue of the hardly small matter of the usage of our words, not the cases we are presently talking about. As one would thus expect, *they*—by contrast with the real cases they superficially resemble—are not instructive vis-à-vis our self-creative engagement with literature: they undermine nothing of relevance here. Questions concerning self-deception and the construction of a false self-image will arise in very specific, and very particular,

---

[57] Richard Moran, "Self-Knowledge: Discovery, Resolution, and Undoing," in *Privileged Access: Philosophical Accounts of Self-Knowledge*, ed. Brie Gertler (Aldershot: Ashgate, 2003), pp. 159–77, this passage p. 173.

204 LIVING IN WORDS

circumstances: a general skepticism concerning self-constitutive self-deception is not warranted, not at home here.

The picture of mental privacy, of the hermetically sealed Cartesian mind, suggests unmediated non-inferential access to our inner world—where that world would have its fixed stability and determinate content prior to our describing it. Thus it would, by virtue of this hermetic priority, have a metaphysically ensured immunity to the power of language. But the actual inner world, the one we inhabit as absorbed readers, is as we have seen in this chapter not at all like that. The reader's inner world does not conform to that metaphysical picture, and we should neither wittingly nor unwittingly force our understanding of personally engaged reading to conform to that false model (just as Ryle taught us not to unreflectively presume that the inner world must be modeled upon the outer[58]). Nor, I am suggesting, should our conception of autobiographical or self-descriptive language be modeled upon a too-easily adapted picture of world-to-language correspondence, or of invariably mimetic, ex post facto language. The interwoven and possibility-engendering webs of belief of the kind we discussed with Davidson, the kind of moderate, realistic, or non-overstated (i.e., limited by the Sartrean "situation") contingency of selfhood we discussed with Rorty, and the kind of self-transfiguring metaphorical relation between text and self we discussed with Danto, are anything but out of place in our articulation of the reader's role as a special kind of textually doubling coauthor of a self-image. In fact, what we might call our stance toward ourselves when engaged to this self-constitutive degree in literary experience is deeply reminiscent of Hegel's remark about our stance toward art more generally: we come to it and find, in a distinctive reflexive way that shows its dependence on the mind of the beholder, that we are and were already there.

T.S. Eliot painted the competing pictures of on the one hand the fixity of the referent of the first-person pronoun and on the other the Heraclitean fluidity of the "I." We, as Eliot's travelers in literary worlds, as imaginative readers, do not, as he said, really escape from the past into different lives, but nor are we exactly the same people who left the station. The truth of the matter, as we saw Eliot intimate, escapes this over-simple dichotomy—and his literary words now resonate with both greater volume and greater extension in their philosophical significance. Earlier in that poem, Eliot wrote, "You must go through the way in which you are not" (p. 29), a line now for us linked to Danto's remarks about the literal falsity of the instructive metaphor. And Eliot wrote, in a way now interwoven with the subtle comparative and belief-acquiring process of doubled attention through which we define ourselves, "And where you are is where you are not" (p. 29): we are not these protagonists, and yet we are. Our situations are not theirs—and

---

[58] Gilbert Ryle, *The Concept of Mind* (New York: Barnes and Noble, 1949).

yet, in a way I have tried to help articulate throughout this chapter, they are. But most importantly in connection with present purposes, Eliot wrote that words "reach into the silence" (p. 19)—for us, the transformational process through which a self's words reach into what, in the language-game of selfhood (one that is founded on spatial metaphors) we call its own interior. And they are words that do so with a self-constitutive power that immediately falsifies any conception of literature as mere diversion or escape; in truth, they give voice to what was, and may otherwise have remained, inarticulate, and they have the power to help create what we can too easily believe they merely describe. Of such words, Eliot wrote that they "will not stay in place,/ Will not stay still" (p. 19). For reasons we have seen, for the profoundly transfigurative service such words can perform when in motion or when in the serious aesthetic play of reflexive negotiation, we should not want them to. "I" is central among them.

6

The Sense of Self

The experience of self-compositional reading; the question, the philosophical problem, of word meaning and the deepened way that, in the light of literature, we answer it; the way that our words carry our identities—these are all, as I have suggested throughout this study, contributors to the sense of selfhood that we bring to the world of human experience that we describe, interrelate, and then integrate into a long-form autobiographical narrative. But what of self-compositional rereading? What does rereading tell us about word meaning, as that issue informs our understanding of the role language plays in selfhood? Does rereading offer a light-casting analogue or parallel to the inward process of revising not only our understanding of ourselves, but indeed, ourselves?, And first, in what contexts might we appeal to a concept of self-rewriting? These are the questions motivating the first two sections of this chapter; in the third section, we will in closing take a brief retrospective view of the six main steps of this study.

6.1 The Self Rewritten: The Case of Self-Forgiveness

Self-forgiveness is a complex phenomenon that, instructively, takes its identity relationally, and not merely episodically. That is to say, the phenomenon is not one that is hermetically contained within our own reflexive consciousness, but rather is one that by its nature extends out across the divide between ourselves and others, and one that extends beyond the bounds of the present, reaching back into the past and extending forward into the future across temporal bounds as well. It is, in short, not a phenomenon we can enact in a single moment and achieve in full as the result of one decisive inward act of momentary resolution. Like the making of a life-narrative, self-forgiveness develops as a process over time: its character, like narrative, is of a kind that prevents its reduction to a momentary episode. It is thus no surprise that the processes of self-forgiveness are ones that occur as part of, and as interwoven with, a life-narrative, and not merely as the isolated dots of a life's episodes that such a long-form narrative would connect. And as I will suggest in what follows, such processes of self-forgiveness become themselves self-constitutive, in such a way that the self being forgiven is indeed significantly changed by, and within, that very process of forgiveness. But before turning to that

---

Living in Words: Literature, Autobiographical Language, and the Composition of Selfhood. Garry L. Hagberg, Oxford University Press. © Garry L. Hagberg 2023. DOI: 10.1093/oso/9780198841210.003.0006

issue directly, I will begin this section with an example borrowed (although I will extend it far beyond his description of the case) from Stanley Cavell.[1]

Suppose we have been in close, intimate, and intricate conversations with a confidant about his marital aspirations for some time, and we know that his deepest and indeed profound affections are wholly engaged with a woman who is presently on the verge of deciding to enter into a conventional, socially predictable, and uninspired marriage with someone deemed, in the least adventurous sense, suitable. Our confidant, we know from our conversations, sees before him a chance to live his way into a possible future that would be fueled by genuine passion, profound love, and an exhilarating sense of expanded possibility—if only he can find the opportunity to speak to the woman in question in a way that is private, uninterrupted, and unburdened by the constant threat of the intervention of those who expect her to proceed with the conventional arrangements and thus embark upon, by contrast, a lifeless marriage. Our friend at this moment feels and believes (whether true or not) deeply—and we thoroughly know this of him (a fact in this case essential to creating the moral difficulty of self-forgiveness)—that, in short, this is his One Big Chance. He and we know that he would do anything to have those precious few hours alone with the companion of this possible future, to offer her, through his declaration and proposal, the clear and unambiguous opportunity to avoid making what he clearly sees as a mistake of life-ruining proportions. And so we tell him that we happen by chance to have learned that she will be on a train, traveling alone, that stops near us at 1:00 p.m. with a wait of an hour, at which point the train will depart for her destination where she will be greeted by the prospective husband and his family and its web of pressing expectations. Full of hope and imagining with increasingly detailed specificity his possible future, he departs with a mind full of potentially life-transforming phrases for the station. To our great surprise and alarm, he returns, utterly dejected, shortly later, informing us that the time we gave him was incorrect, and that the summer schedule (of which we were unaware, having presumed that the winter schedule would continue) changed the time to a 12:00 noon stop, and that, desperate, he hoped to speed by automobile to the next stop to board the train there, only to discover to his anguish that there was not a stop before the final destination. The woman thus arrives there, greets her husband-to-be and his family, quietly accepts the fact of uninspired conventionality, and with decreasing frequency she thinks back to what might have been; he becomes a solitary, heartbroken, existentialist. When, just after missing the train, he returns to us dejected, we hear of all this to our horror, and the first words we hear come out of our mouths are: "I am so, so sorry. This is unbelievably terrible. I'll never forgive myself. This should never have happened."

---

[1] Described in a paper Cavell delivered to a meeting of the North American Nietzsche Society at the American Philosophical Association, Philadelphia, December 2008.

208   LIVING IN WORDS

From this example I want to pursue three threads: the first thread, the meaning of the word "never" in the phrase "I'll never forgive myself"; the second thread, the meaning of the word "should" in "This should never have happened"; and most fundamentally the third thread, the act we herein say we will never perform, i.e., the act of self-directed forgiveness.

So the first thread: The word "never" here functions not as the irrevocable self-imposed moral proscription it appears to be, but rather as a measure of the difficulty of the act of self-forgiveness in this case, which itself is a measure of the harm we have done to our confidant by having acted to close the very door to the future he most profoundly wanted, in effect consigning the parties to disappointment or lifelong compromise. It is I think worth noting here that the particular details of the case are what give the word "never" here its occasion-specific force, and it is with this contextualized force that it serves to open the way, as a sort of implicit preamble, to the lengthy process of not just saying, but truly delivering, an apology (one that we sense we will need and want to make over time and that will be manifested in various ways involving words, deeds, emotional tone, gesture, physiognomic expressivity, patterns of sensitivity and attentiveness, and so forth). It is also instructive that what in a sense stands behind the word "never," a word that in this exchange is delivered as an understood exaggeration for dramatic (but not for that reason expressively insincere) strength cannot be reduced to either unwitting action or thoughtless action. (Incidentally, the word "never" does here function as an irrevocable proscription to *forgetting* the case.) It is not that we simply unwittingly told him the wrong train time—not exactly. Nor is it that we simply thoughtlessly told him the wrong time—not exactly. We certainly did not tell him the wrong time wittingly (that would in this case have been viciously cruel and involve a very different story), but for that reason alone the case is not (contrary to what could here be a moral misapplication of the law of excluded middle) one of unwitting moral action. It is also true that we did not give enough thought at the moment of telling him the train time—but it is not for that reason reducible to an act of simple thoughtlessness (as we may do in, say, casually or even cheerfully mentioning in a social group, with our suffering confidant present, the date and time of the woman's upcoming wedding to the suitable groom-to-be). What both misdirected attempts at moral-act reduction do is to try to reduce the case to a hermetically contained episode with a single determinate name, one that has action boundaries that are neat and not relationally inter-twined across persons and across time.[2] But in fact—well, in *particularized* fact—the word "never" in this context indicates not what an atomistic dictionary definition of the isolated word might specify, but rather a far more nuanced

---

[2] This builds on Chapter 2, Section 2.3 concerning the problem of the individuation of an action, and *Describing Ourselves*, ch. 7. One could say with some plausibility that Ian McEwan's *Atonement* (New York: Anchor, 2003) shows what I am suggesting here over much of the novel's span.

content, suggesting indeed that the apology that will be enacted will be one that takes place across time, that will reach far into the future, that will be quickly responsive and especially sensitive to our confidant's disappointment and pain, and that will remain mindful (hence the literal application the term actually has to forgetting rather than to self-forgiving as mentioned above) of the "unsealed" or ever-growing, ever-expanding consequences of this one extremely unfortunate act. And so: the more subtle function of the word "never" as we are examining it in this context itself serves to acknowledge the unbounded, non-hermetic nature of an act of self-forgiveness.

The second thread casts a different light on the language we use to initiate the outward apology that makes the inward act of self-forgiveness possible and that thus sets in motion word-borne self-change. The word "should" here is in fact of extreme interest, and we owe it to Charles Griswold's[3] illuminating study of forgiveness that we are now in a position to clearly see why this is so. Throughout his study Griswold makes clear that narrative, and the narrative structuring of events where that narrative weaves the kinds of relational interconnections I will be emphasizing here, is essential to forgiveness: indeed, I would say (to put the point perhaps more extremely than Griswold would endorse) that without such narrative structuring, the very idea of an act of forgiveness would be unintelligible. And he agrees that forgiveness, to be rightly understood, must be seen as a process ensuing over time, and not merely as an "end result" (p. 98). Griswold's foundational point, one that strikes me as surely right (and one, as we shall see, that is stable enough to build on), is that, because human life unfolds in time and across long-term phases or periods, that our self-narrations are thus of necessity ongoing and of an interweaving kind. The process indeed stands parallel to the process of contrapuntal composition in music.[4]

This is hardly the simple point that my over-brief way of putting it here might suggest: notions such as permanent closure and completeness in connection with any action description are called into question by this observation. So to make the point slightly less briefly: if action descriptions are not hermetically bounded (here the themes of Chapter 2, Section 2.3 return again, but now in the context of self-revision), why should we retain (that is, if we do, after Chapter 2, Sections 2.1 and 2.2) any genuine confidence in so much as the residue of an atomistic picture of actions themselves as hermetically bounded? That is, why should we distrust the language we actually use—language that is itself resistant to false or premature descriptive closure—in favor of a superimposed picture of prelinguistic physical or bodily actions? If actions themselves, as are their descriptions, relationally

---

[3] Charles Griswold, *Forgiveness: A Philosophical Exploration* (Cambridge: Cambridge University Press, 2007).

[4] I discuss the connection between what is commonly thought of as absolute music, specifically contrapuntal composition, and the structuring of sense-making life-narratives, in "Kivy's Mystery: On What the Formalist Can (or Could) Hear," *Journal of Aesthetics and Art Criticism*, 2021: 366–76.

210 LIVING IN WORDS

constituted (in the way we have discussed the matter in Chapters 1 as well as 2 above), in the interest of descriptive accuracy we ought in fact to extinguish, rather than preserve, the desire to see actions at bottom (i.e., the kinds of thing a conventional method of action analysis would lead us into) as intrinsically "neat." This thus connects once again to William James and the anti-Lockean conception of human experience, but we can now see here how the prejudice in favor of atomistic objects manifests itself in autobiographical form, precisely where physical events are thought of as real, the relations between them less so. And (as has already been intimated in the discussion of the circumstantially situated word "never" just above) I want to add to this fundamental ontological point that the meanings of the words we use to weave those narrative threads are themselves evolving and continually reweaving themselves in accordance with the evolving contexts of their usage.

Now, just how does the word "should" in the sentence, "This should never have happened" show this? Griswold I think emphasizes that life-narratives (within which, I will suggest, self-forgiveness takes place in a self-changing way) do not merely *describe* (at least not in any simplistic "language-directly-corresponding-to-fact" fashion), but indeed, *characterize* what is happening or what has happened (p. 99). And in doing so, it reshapes it or reimagines it.[5] To characterize something is, in a sense, to give it a face, to give it a set of recognizable features, to describe it in a way that brings it to life and gives it a place. The word "should" above, seen in this light, is one that characterizes the unfortunate life-changing act as one that has a face we wish we had never seen, that has features of highly undesirable consequences that we wish we had never recognized, that gives the act a life we wish it did not have, and—most importantly for present concerns—gives it a place in an unfolding narrative that it, indeed, should not have. The possible future that our confidant saw extending before him—the one that he deeply believed would bring him happiness—was a future of narrative continuity, with themes unfolding along lines that were, by virtue of his knowledge of the woman in question and the details of his imagined future with her, the fulfillment of his present (as woven through and emerging from the past) hopes and aspirations. Here, within this context and on this particular occasion of utterance (and every utterance is particular in this respect, a point we might still usefully take from the tradition of ordinary-language philosophy), the word "should" is thus a word that points to a narrative future that has run out of control, that has run off its tracks, that is utterly unlike any of the possible narrative futures we might have heartily and readily endorsed. (Remorse too would not be possible without such narrative

---

[5] But this respect for the power of language by no means endorses any extreme relativism: Griswold adds that we do "not thereby fabricate it out of thin air" (p. 99). I return to this below in connection with MacIntyre.

ruptures, but that is another matter.[6]) Those tracks in a very real sense are tracks of extrapolation not only from the past, but also from (as Griswold rightly emphasizes) our linguistic characterizations, as they have developed across the phases of an unfolding life, of that past. It is they, those words of characterization, that have the power of pointing directions, of drawing dotted lines into the future not yet filled in, of giving a life a sense of how and where it, indeed, as we say, *should* go. One might say that such tracks are really only fanciful literary tropes projected over life, but that is to give them too little power and too little seriousness—they are *already* embedded within the structure of life (and for this reason literature is mimetic in a way that is deeper than obvious resemblance—recall the Aristotelian considerations in Chapter 3 above). And indeed one way of understanding Griswold's remark about the reimagining that may take place in narrative evolution is to look closely at the distasteful and very unfortunate hard labor that our confidant must now undertake: he must reimagine his life in a way that now integrates the developmental trajectories that we all see, according to his earlier self-identifying narrative threads, should (as we compactly say) never have happened. But if we see clearly, given a detailed awareness of that life's hopes, aspirations, and unfolding teleology, that such a rupture in a life's projected narrative should never have happened and that we are the agents of precisely this having happened, what then do *we* do with that unwelcome article of self-awareness? And so we now turn to the main third thread, the issue of forgiving *oneself* for having done the long-arc harm to our confidant.

Griswold makes a particularly important point here: he observes that self-forgiveness is rightly frequently suspected of abuse (e.g., "preachers caught *in flagrante* and forgiving themselves with lightning speed," p. 122), and this description of the example captures precisely what is important: lightning speed is incompatible with the nature of a reflexive act of forgiveness. Against the multi-form possibilities of abuses (letting oneself off the hook far too easily, as we say), and especially because we are forgiving ourselves not in our own name—our usual sphere of "ownership" in cases of other-forgiveness—but rather in the name of the one who was injured, it is by the nature of the case incumbent upon us to employ precisely what we might think of as a transposed kind of literary imagination, thinking our way with genuine imaginative sympathy into the experience of the injured. And the measure of the success of this imaginative effort is the extent to which we become able to feel warranted resentment against the one who perpetrated the injury, i.e., ourselves. And in so transcending ourselves, we arrive at the doubled state in which we are able to look back on who we are and what we have done *as if* we are seeing another. This, I want to suggest, is instructively parallel in

---

[6] For a particularly insightful discussion that shows a deep awareness of the point concerning the particularized usage or moral terms, see Raimond Gaita, *Good and Evil: An Absolute Conception* (London: Routledge, 2004), pp. 43–63.

212 LIVING IN WORDS

an unobvious way to our experience of literary texts, where we vicariously enter into a life-narrative not our own but see it as if it were, but then transcend what would otherwise be the limits of our selfhood in the act of imaginative reading.

The meaning of our third thread, the phrase "to forgive ourselves," thus requires for its intelligibility both (1) an act of sympathetic imagination with the other, and (2) a transcendent relation to ourselves of a kind that I believe we rehearse in literary engagement. And it requires temporal considerations, as already suggested. But also: if (3) it is too quick, it is false. If (4) it does not pattern itself across time and action, it is insincere. If (5) it is out of sequence (another kind of temporal consideration), i.e., if we forgive ourselves before the injured party forgives us (Griswold makes this point, p. 124), we run the risk of adding disrespect to injury. And if (6) it does not reasonably follow upon the other's forgiveness, where we implicitly or explicitly pride ourselves on having superior moral standards considerably higher than the damaged party's, we only add smug self-aggrandizement to the harm we have already caused. And if (I would add this to the ground Griswold covers) we dramatize the suffering we undergo as a result of our own act, thus (7) putting ourselves in a position to try to claim that the blame we place upon ourselves makes the blame of any other (including the injured party) redundant and thus unnecessary, we only add self-centeredness and self-importance to a real injury we mask behind the false face of our own advertised guilt. It is easy to imagine words that show all of these failings of self-assessment: we utter to our injured confidant (1) a sentence beginning with the words "Well if I were you..." thus from the outset failing at thinking our way into *his* life, in effect displacing that entire life with the first-person pronoun. Or (2) we utter words indicating an inability to see ourselves from the outside[7] (as it were) or as a third party, producing phrases of the "Still, regardless of what you say, from my point of view..." kind. Or (3) we say (rather inhumanly in this circumstance—but then that makes the point), "Well, there's nothing that can be done, so it's really time to let that go." Or (4) a day or week later, we are saying "get over it: that was then, this is now," showing no heightened sensitivity or mindfulness of the consequences of our action as they extend into the future. Or (5) we say, "Well, I've forgiven myself, and you should too. We need to get beyond this" (interestingly and distinctively ugly, that phrase). Or (6) we say, "I don't care what you say about it, I shall never forgive myself. Only I can suffer at this depth, etc. etc." (a phrase that would be laughable were it not a lucid microcosm of interpersonally tragic folly). Or (7) we say, "I blame myself so much more than you will ever blame me, etc." (and so, by implication, you might as well go away and drop it). All of these are failures to engage seriously, and they tellingly fail to

---

[7] This is an interestingly dangerous spatial metaphor; one brief way to capture the danger here is to say that the asymmetry between the first- and third-person case is not equivalent to the metaphysical distinction between the inner and the outer.

THE SENSE OF SELF   213

vicariously enter into the narratively unfolding life of another in such a way that (here's the core of the point) we satisfy the circumstantial preconditions of true self-forgiveness. Indeed, phrases that constitute the moral inverses of all these would constitute the words within which self-forgiveness actually becomes possible. And they thus contribute (each in distinct ways calling for scrutiny of the kind we gave the word "never" above) to the meaning of the phrase central to our third thread.

But that third thread possesses still other aspects, aspects that importantly contribute to its meaning. It would be simple, attractive, conceptually neat, and deeply erroneous to posit a partitioned self in order to account for the very possibility of self-forgiveness. (Attempts to explain the possibility of self-deception have followed similar lines, and failed for the same reasons—they are far too simple to accommodate what Griswold rightly describes as the complex phenomenology in play here.) In the case of a partitioned mind, self-forgiveness would be other-forgiveness internalized. One part of us told our confidant the wrong train time, the other part of us forgives that first part. This modeling of self-forgiveness on other-forgiveness thus moves inside a single mind the interpersonal process that is enacted when our confidant forgives us for having caused the consequences that extend long into his future (or again, for having derailed his hoped-for Aristotelian narrative teleology). But the phenomenology is far more interesting than any such oversimplifying partition model would suggest, and here we turn to the self-constitutive or self-compositional dimension of self-forgiveness.

Griswold makes a helpful point at this juncture: "Self-forgiveness could not restore basic dignity; rather, it assumes a perspective from which the self already possesses it" (p. 126). If we see the implications of this, we see that the self-forgiver must possess in advance of the forgiveness some measure of the dignity that the act itself restores or at least buttresses. But that is not the implication of greatest or deepest interest: in fact, the self *that has first satisfied the preconditions described above and that fails in none of the ways described above* takes on, as a character trait, what it itself grants (this is not unlike the circumstance depicted in Escher's famous drawing of the hand drawing the hand). This circular process might well be described as "bootstrapping," but it is important to remember from preceding chapters that, in this self-compositional case (again, as opposed to other areas in philosophy where the term is clearly negatively valued) this term can well and rightly be used in a non-pejorative sense. The self grants the dignity and sense of moral equanimity that it comes to increasingly recognize in itself, which makes that self ever more capable of granting it. And (as Griswold also mentions) this recursive process eventually restores what he calls the sense of wholeness (p. 126)—which also incidentally weighs against the too-convenient model of a partitioned self. Thus, in the sense mentioned above where we simultaneously identify with a character in fiction but also stand apart from that narratively entwined persona, so the self-forgiver engages with himself or herself in this

214 LIVING IN WORDS

doubled way. Doubled, but not partitioned: it is one identity seeing bifocally, not two persons gazing from a distance upon each other.

Now, let us change the case above: suppose it is we who have done the damage to ourselves. Let's say (to extend an example of Griswold's and bring it together with Cavell's case) that we are now the person trying to catch the train, and we know the correct schedule. But because of chronic drug abuse we sleep through it and miss the all-important stop. Same result, same loss, different agent. This self-harming example generating the need for self-forgiveness better captures the (non-viciously) circular or bootstrapping aspect of this complex phenomenology. In response to such cases of self-injury and the accompanying need for self-forgiveness, Griswold writes,

> One must reframe one's view of oneself and see oneself in a new light; make a commitment to change one's ways; confront honestly and fully the injury one has done to oneself; have compassion for oneself, and refrain from objectifying oneself as though one were a 'moral monster'; develop a narrative that explains how one came to do wrong, what emendatory steps one will take, and that expresses how one 're-frames' one's view of oneself. As in the interpersonal case, a narrative of oneself as injured and accusing will also be called for. Crucially, one must take responsibility for oneself. The target of forgiveness remains the agent, not the deed.

A large part of what it takes to come to see ourselves in a new light[8] is to act upon ourselves within the self-reconstructing doubled phenomenology I am attempting to bring out. And again, that action (self-forgiveness) at one time both gives and takes: it gives compassion, understanding, insight, self-knowledge, and it takes instruction, improvement, and the kind of resolution that changes the person who makes it. In the preceding case and as we have seen above, my understanding my confidant *as a person* invariably involves my grasping the extrapolations of his layered and contextually nuanced event and action descriptions that, woven together, form a life-narrative, where those extrapolations constitute projections into his future. Simply put, I have a good sense of what does and does not fit, a good sense of what has been helpfully discussed as rightness in this regard (as we

---

[8] I explore one way of describing such change in *Describing Ourselves*, pp. 202–22. Wittgenstein's remarks on aspect perception, as one might expect, can prove especially useful in the context of self-understanding. But the discussion of relationally constituted events, actions, and descriptions can also prove useful in elucidating what "new light" or "new aspect" might here mean: a new set of intertwining relational connections and linkages that (here again anti-atomistically) make the action—as remembered from the past and described in the present—what it is. It is in this context that we can see that the over-hardened distinction between finding a connection and making a connection is not in truth a polar matter, not an either/or proposition with verified observation sentences on the one side and an interpretive free-for-all on the other. A wide range of cases connects the two poles, one increment at a time.

THE SENSE OF SELF   215

saw in Chapter 2, Section 2.2),[9] and I know the difference, down to fairly intricate matters, between what would constitute fulfillment and what would constitute narrative rupture in that life. Precisely the same is true of my knowledge of myself; indeed, I want to suggest that such knowledge of rightness and fittingness with regard to a self's coherence and cogency (at the level of the finest and most exacting detail) is one essential part of the content of self-knowledge. Or to put it another way, this is a way of articulating the content that self-knowledge is *of*.

To make a commitment to change one's ways is to resolve to be different than one has been, and the point I want to add to Griswold's list of conditions in his preceding passage is that, given the moral bootstrapping phenomenon under discussion here, one is made more able to make and keep such resolutions as one continues to make them; it is the moral equivalent (and reminiscent of points Aristotle[10] makes) of building muscle—the more one lifts, the more one is able to lift. To confront the injury honestly and fully is to avoid the kinds of rhetorical redecoration of the situation that I described above (and to describe oneself as a moral monster is merely to abdicate responsible control and volitional power through a dramatizing redescription); to develop the narrative I am suggesting is ineliminable is to use, in exacting and acute ways, the words and phrases under examination presently. And to take responsibility for ourselves is both shown and, as I am suggesting here, enacted, in the words of self-description we employ (in the ways we saw illustrated in Chapters 1 and 5). Griswold's last point in the passage above is vitally important to gaining a full understanding of the complex phenomenology of self-forgiveness, and it is a point that consequential ethical methodologies seem designed to miss: the target of the forgiveness is the *agent*. To say, "If only I hadn't done *that*" is to give our attention and focus to the external action in the physical world that constitutes the intrusion to the extrapolated and projected narrative as we envision it extending into the future. The first-person pronoun in the sentence escapes (and thus we escape) scrutiny, and the sentence either leads us to presume, or shows that we already presume, that we as persons are stable and fixed entities before, during, and after the ill-fitting misdeed. If by contrast we say, "If only *I* hadn't done that," we get a different orientation—one that fits with everything about the content of self-knowledge and self-reconstitution that I am suggesting here. (Emphases are not always morally inert.) The recognition that it is the self's action, and that this particular action fell short of the expectations that self holds of itself, opens the space within which resolution takes place, the space within which moral aspiration is possible.

---

[9] For a particularly lucid and precise discussion of this matter see Michael Krausz, *Rightness and Reasons: Interpretation in Cultural Practices* (Ithaca: Cornell University Press, 1993) and *Limits of Rightness* (Lanham: Rowman and Littlefield, 2000); the most important elements of Krausz's investigation were discussed in Chapter 2, Sections 2.1 and 2.2 above.

[10] Aristotle, *Nicomachean Ethics* (New York: Bobbs Merrill,1962), esp. Book 2, sec. 1, pp. 32–5 and Book 7, secs. 1–10, pp. 174–201.

216 LIVING IN WORDS

Now, let us change the example one last time, this time with an eye to moral luck. We tell our confidant the wrong time, he arrives just before 1:00 p.m., but the train happens to be late and so he catches the train with minutes to spare, sits with the woman in question, delivers his life-changing words, prevents her from opting half-heartedly for conventionality, and lives his way with her into the intellectually and emotionally electrified future he envisioned. For the strict consequentialist, all is well, and that's the end of the story. For us, the matter is more interesting. Suppose the next time we see him, radiating happiness, he says to us, "Can you believe how lucky I was that she was on the train, and that you knew of it, etc." Here, we might say, "Yes, that was extraordinarily fortunate." But then that constitutes a slight sin of omission, does it not? What perhaps you should say is, "You don't know just how lucky we both were!" and then tell him the full story. To not do so is to leave him ignorant of a fact that seems morally relevant in three ways: (1) it reveals how *extremely* fortunate he was, which will inflect and in its way augment, however subtly, his appreciation of the situation he now enjoys; (2) it reveals how fortunate *we* were (thus escaping all the myriad negative consequences of the case as initially described above); and—here the interesting complication emerges—(3) it reveals what we might well have done to him, in the other possible world in which the train was on time (as, let's say, it usually is—this is morally relevant in that it helps to measure the extent of the danger in which we put him). To not let him know this is a form of concealment, and it would pretend that consequences are in fact all that matter in moral life. (Although this would take us rather far from the present focus, here in fact we see one way in which the subscription to one moral theory or another can *itself* be subject to moral evaluation: one might not want to be the kind of person who might yield to the temptation to too quickly embrace the oversimplifying consequentialism that would eradicate these subtleties and the nuanced layers of moral responsibility along with them.) To let him know is in part to further celebrate ("And see how close to the edge of massive romantic loss you actually were!"), but it is also to let him know that we did not actually know the correct time but spoke, *under these extremely important and irreplaceable circumstances,* as though we did. This is itself something for which we will need a lesser and slighter form of forgiveness from him (although the need for this lesser forgiveness is a comparative luxury, given the contrast of the other contingency in which he misses the train—but it is certainly not for that reason nothing). And then we will also need a similarly lesser and slighter form of forgiveness from ourselves. It will still be, in that relationship, despite the happiness engendered by the success, something to get over. And the way, the process, of getting over and through this particular kind of act of self-forgiveness, although described well in Griswold's passage above, here occurs with a difference: we take responsibility for what *might* have been, given what we in fact actually did. And so again, our engagement with that counterfactual thought or scenario is deeply akin to our engagement with literary texts. We learn from

THE SENSE OF SELF   217

reflecting on it, and—beyond that—we reshape, or subtly restructure, who and what we are (through even the most subtle and intricate forms of bootstrapping resolution), just as we do in the self-defining moments of imaginative literary absorption. We, in a sense, rewrite ourselves.

So what then of tying our three threads in this section together? The first thread concerned the fairly narrowly contained issue of the meaning of the word "never" as one example of the care we need to give to our scrutiny of, and consequent understanding of, the words out of which we make the narratives of our relationally intertwined moral engagements. The second thread concerned the perhaps more intricate meaning of the word "should" as it functions within a pronouncement that a given event should never have happened (when seen against the backdrop of the projected moral teleology of a self we intimately know). And the third, considerably more involved still, concerned the complex phenomenology of the act of self-forgiveness, which I characterized in terms of doubled reflexive action and non-pejorative bootstrapping, with a comparison to a kind of self-constitutive literary engagement.

The way these three threads interweave with each other might be seen in reconsidering some remarks of Alasdair MacIntyre's on narrative.[11] Citing Dr. Johnson's notes on his travels in France (e.g., "There we waited on the ladies—Morville's.—Spain. Country towns all beggars. At Dijon he could not find the way to Orleans.—Cross roads of France very bad. Five soldiers.—Women.—Soldiers escaped." . . .), MacIntyre writes, "What this suggests is what I take to be true, namely that the characterization of actions allegedly prior to any narrative form being imposed upon them will always turn out to be the presentation of what are plainly the disjointed parts of some possible narrative." This is precisely the kind of characterization of which Griswold wrote and that led to my suggestion of the need for, and value of, the close scrutiny of the words we use to so characterize. But to take in generalized isolation what MacIntyre has said here can deeply mislead: what MacIntyre has said can suggest, utterly falsely (and this is a point to which Griswold is by the way fully aware and finely sensitive), that the dots of Johnsonian isolated fact are compatible with the superimposition of many different narratives to connect them, where *any organizing pattern is as good as any other*. This form of radical relativism with regard to self-narrative formation is unacceptable for its severe mischaracterization of, or complete failure to acknowledge, the constraints that come into play under conditions of autobiographical self-scrutiny. To see this in better focus we need to see how our three threads come together. MacIntyre continues: "We can also approach the question in another way. What I have called a history is an enacted dramatic narrative in which the characters are also the authors." To say that the characters are authored by

---

[11] Alasdair MacIntyre, *After Virtue* (Notre Dame: University of Notre Dame Press, 1984), all passages quoted p. 215.

218   LIVING IN WORDS

themselves is a memorably strong way of capturing the point I have been making concerning the self-constitutive aspect of acts of self-forgiveness: the phenomenology is indeed, in precisely this respect of doubled action, complex, i.e., where the characters *are* the authors. (That is one way of saying what "bootstrapping" here means.) But MacIntyre next adds what is most important for present concerns: "The characters of course never start literally *ab initio*; they plunge *in medias res*, the beginnings of their story already made for them by what and who has gone before."

The words "of course" function here because we are talking about nothing less than human beings, and they are the sorts of entities that are by their nature enmeshed in self-compositional (but not whimsically relative or subjectively fanciful) narrative—and as discussed above, the extent to which we understand them as persons, and know what is and is not fitting or right for them in terms of their moral teleology, is the extent to which we actually know that narrative. To know what went before, as MacIntyre puts it, is to know the content and direction of that life-narrative, and it is that, *and only that*, which allows the finely detailed sense of what fits and why. And to see what in this sense came before for ourselves is what it means to gain the retrospective self-knowledge (which itself permits extrapolation and projection into the future) that will allow us to know what is and is not fitting, what does and does not exemplify the sense of rightness for us as the persons we are (where we often see that measured against the person we want to be). The narratives we in one sense create are, in light of our knowledge of what went before, narratives we find to be possible, and we make those narratives out of words to which we owe a good deal of attention. The engagingly complex act of self-forgiveness presents us with a microcosm within which we can see both the self-constitutive power of words and the self-restructuring power of the agents using them. It is in those words that, as our own authors, we create the characters that we then discover ourselves to be.

But as I said in the introduction to this chapter, following the discussion of rewriting the self, we would consider the idea of rereading and what light that might cast on self-composition and self-understanding.

6.2 Wittgenstein, Rereading, and Self-Understanding

Why would we ever read anything again? There is the obvious answer: to remind ourselves of what we may have forgotten. But that is nowhere near the most interesting reason. David Hume, in his classic essay "Of the Standard of Taste,"[12] writes that "At twenty, Ovid may be the favorite author; Horace at forty; and

---

[12] David Hume, "Of the Standard of Taste" (1757), reprinted in Alex Neill and Aaron Ridley, eds., *The Philosophy of Art: Readings Ancient and Modern* (New York: McGraw-Hill, 1995), pp. 255–68.

THE SENSE OF SELF   219

perhaps Tacitus at fifty."[13] Reading Ovid, Horace, Tacitus—and any other literary author—will not be the same at twenty, forty, and fifty. Yet the words are obviously the same. So if we subtract the word meanings that remain the same across these temporally and experientially disparate readings, what is the remainder? What makes them different? And what of the presupposition buried within the formulation of this question: that is, should we assume that there *is* such a thing as word meaning that remains invariant beneath the differences?

There are, despite everything I have said throughout this study starting from Chapter 1, Section 1.3, countless cases throughout the practical affairs of life that seem to leave word meaning intact and untouched by context, by the experiential backlog in play, by the resonances chiming throughout that backlog, by the ever-more-cultivated sensibility of the reader in question. A detective, on finding the perpetrator's name inscribed on a carpet in blood by the victim, does not go back to reread repeatedly to see if it now names another name or if it says the same as before. The master of ceremonies in an awards ceremony does not continually reread the name of the winner on the card just opened from the sealed envelope, and so forth. And beyond names (which, as I'll return to below, initially at least appear to stack the deck in favor of an anti-Heraclitean fixity of meaning), we do not reread instruction manuals or furniture-assembly pamphlets to gain insight into the vicissitudes of our souls. But Hume knew that literary meaning is not like those cases; as we saw T. S. Eliot say in Chapter 5, "words will not sit still."[14]

The *words*—meaning here the printed letters—of Ovid's *Metamorphosis* do not change. If their senses were fixed unambiguously, by extension there would be determinate fixity of the entire work, and its interpretation would be a matter of correctly matching, to the point of completion, the exacting description of that meaning content with the words that together comprise the work. Yet at twenty (or younger), one may be fascinated by the wondrously inventive transformations of one entity into another. But at thirty, or forty, one may know that to see a person, or oneself, change from one kind of person into another, or to see a person or oneself reveal an ethical reality previously hidden beneath a very different appearance, can be something other than entertainingly fascinating. Similarly, at fifty, seeing, through literature-induced reflection, that oneself has changed through a gradual transmutation into a person one at twenty (i.e., on first reading) one did not want to be,[15] is also far from frivolous imaginative diversion. For such

---

[13] "Of the Standard of Taste," p. 266.

[14] T. S. Eliot, *Four Quartets* (New York: Harcourt, Brace, Jovanovich, 1988 [orig. 1943]), in Burnt Norton, sec. V: "Words strain,/ Crack and sometimes break, under the burden,/ Under the tension, slip, slide, perish,/ Decay with imprecision, will not stay in place,/ Will not stay still."

[15] This phenomenon, as one might expect, is of considerable moral-philosophical interest. See Rush Rhees, "The Tree of Nebuchadnezzar," *The Human World*, no. 4, 1971: 25; and Frank Cioffi, "Explanation, Self-Clarification, and Solace," in *Wittgenstein on Freud and Frazer* (Cambridge: Cambridge University Press, 1998), pp. 128–54, esp. pp. 144–7.

220 LIVING IN WORDS

individuals, the content of the very concept of metamorphosis has changed; the significance of the fiction is no longer hermetically contained within that fictional world. Speaker's intention, narrowly defined, didn't change it; experience did.

Hume is speaking primarily about aesthetic preference, but his observation brings the just-mentioned point concerning one of the functions of rereading into sharper focus: character changes, or the erosion of ideals, or the abandoning of aspirations, often take place incrementally over an extended duration. Similarly, on the positive side, the achievement of those aspirations, the holding true to those ideals, the deepening and improving of character, the sharpening of discernment, also often take place across broad expanses of time. Revisiting a literary text that we knew well at an earlier time but that we have not seen for many years can serve to demarcate an earlier point of selfhood—a stabilized moment of time in the progressive Heraclitean flux—against which we can measure the degree of change, for good, for ill, or for both in distinct respects. Rereading, in this particular sense, becomes an instrument of self-knowledge; this experience also gives content to what we call the sense of self. That is to say: One can see what it was we used to see in Ivan Karamazov, what we did not see in Dmitri, what we perhaps naively saw in Alyosha, all of which informs what we now see in ourselves. The wisdom of Tacitus, the recognition of the depth of his understanding of the ways of the world, informs us at one remove[16] about what we ourselves inwardly possess as an experientially earned capacity to recognize and to fathom such wisdom when we see it placed before us. But to put the question here again in subtractive terms: if we read Tacitus or Dostoevsky at twenty, unproblematically know the meanings of all the words in both books, and subtract that earlier reading from our reading at fifty, what is, and what precisely accounts for, the remainder?

Recall what Wittgenstein wrote about the misleading image—a compelling one that can be difficult to dislodge—of the fixity of meaning in *Philosophical Investigations* 426:

> A picture is conjured up which seems to fix the sense unambiguously. The actual use, compared with that traced out by the picture, seems like something muddied. Here again, what is going on is the same as in set theory: the form of expression seems to have been tailored for a god, who knows what we cannot know; he sees all of those infinite series, and he sees into the consciousness of human beings. For us, however, these forms of expression are like vestments, which we may put on, but cannot do much with, since we lack the effective power that would give them a point and purpose.

---

[16] This, now in this context, is another exemplification of the process described in Chapter 1, Sections 1.1 and 1.2 above as it is nested within the relational conception of selfhood.

THE SENSE OF SELF   221

> In the actual use of these expressions we, as it were, make detours, go by the side roads. We see the straight highway before us, but of course cannot use it, because it is permanently closed.[17]

Now, the picture, Wittgenstein here suggests, offers the false but compelling image of the hermetic fixity of the words that make up *The Brothers Karamazov*; a god's view—here also then setting in place, on this model, a conception of the ideal critic—would be a full and exacting encompassing knowledge of the determinate meaning of each word, and hence each sentence, as contained within the frame of the work. And so, against this picture, our actual usages of such words and sentences seem muddied. But that comparison, Wittgenstein is implying (and perhaps should have said here more directly), is itself a false one: the seeming muddiness is only a secondary illusion born of the prior illusion of the dreamed-of fixity. We, down here on the ground of actual usage like Franz and Sabina in Chapter 1 and like Charles Arrowby in Chapter 5, rely on the contextually seated nuances that together give our words and sentences point, power, and purpose. And as we have seen, closely examining the *using* of words, the *using* of sentences, shows us precisely their point, power, and purpose that, in truth, clarify rather than muddy. In *Philosophical Investigations* 432, Wittgenstein writes: "Every sign *by itself* seems dead. *What* gives it life?—In use, it *lives*. Is it there that it has living breath within it?—Or is the *use* its breath?"

"Or is the *use* its breath?" Well, indeed; and by now in this study this is a familiar point. But how do we get this to help us with our problem concerning rereading, with the interpretive deepening, with the fifty-minus-twenty remainder?

Let us step back for a moment: Literary language is, after all, one kind of use of our language. But it is dangerously easy to picture literary language as a kind of subdivision of the larger Venn diagram, where all uses within that set are in essence of the kind seen in the card identifying the winner; a name read by the master of ceremonies. It may, we might think, be much more complex, but—says the picture—it will, by virtue of being language, by virtue of being within the Venn diagram where inclusion is determined by the presence of that essence, invariably be built upon that foundation. And in this (supposed essence-revealing) case the meaning is wholly fixed by the writer, and wholly and exhaustively received by the reader (in this case the MC). If all language were in essence like that, then this would be nothing less than the straight highway before us, and all linguistic inquiry could proceed on that foundation. But again: it is literary language that shows us more forcefully than anywhere else that this dreamed-of highway is

---

[17] Ludwig Wittgenstein, *Philosophical Investigations*, revised 4th edition by P. M. S. Hacker and Joachim Schulte, trans. G. E. M. Anscombe, P. M. S. Hacker, and Joachim Schulte (Malden: Wiley-Blackwell, 2009), Sec. 426.

222 LIVING IN WORDS

permanently closed. The reason Wittgenstein reread (as repeatedly reported to his friends)[18] *The Brothers Karamazov* many times over many years, is that he was endlessly exploring the sideroads, the adventurous detours. And with the ground covered to this point in this study, I want to suggest that what he found there was not predictable from his earlier travels, not merely a set of small extensions from what he had already seen in that book. Something larger, and something more revealing for present considerations, was taking place in his rereading.

It would be strange—actually to the point of unimaginability—to suggest that persons should be entities with a demarcated fixity of experiential content, so that the understanding of a person could be final, complete, and exhaustive in the way we too easily picture the (ideal) understanding of a word. No sentient being could be like that—indeed the very act of suggesting such stasis would invoke sudden and radical change in the way the suggester is perceived (if it could be taken seriously, which I think we instructively doubt). Stanley Cavell has drawn special attention, in his discussion of Wittgenstein on seeing-as, to the way in which our relations to our words stand as allegories of our relations to others. Others, and our relations to them, are—often of wondrous complexity—in constant flux; we encounter them, like their and our words, within (and never prior to or separate from) what Wittgenstein called the stream of life. Cavell writes of the duck-rabbit figure that "the beauty of the thing lies, first, in the fact that the figure is so patently all in front of your eyes,"[19] and this, I want to suggest, is directly parallel to the fact that all of the words of Ovid, of Horace, of Tacitus, and of Dostoevsky are before our eyes at twenty, forty, and fifty. But Cavell calls attention to a facet of this perceptual-interpretive phenomenon that is most salient for present consider-ations: "you can see, as patently as you can see the figure itself, that the flip from one reading to another is due solely to you, the change is in you."[20] It would be easy—as indeed it has been for many theorists of interpretation—to say that this shows that the difference between the reading at twenty and the rereading at fifty is wholly in us, wholly a subjective matter of what we bring to an inert text. But here ordinary language—as it so often is on close inspection—is subtle: we speak of what we now, later in life, see *in* Tacitus, see *in* Dostoevsky—and not of what we layer over it. This drop of grammar[21] is not, I think, insignificant.

Cavell calls attention to the intrinsic complexity of the phenomenon in ques-tion here: aspect seeing invites into play "an unexpected range of concepts" that "can be given application and in which one is brought to sense the complexity

---

[18] See Rush Rhees, ed., *Recollections of Wittgenstein* (Oxford: Oxford University Press, 1984), pp. xvi, 4, 44, 72, 85–7, 102, 107–8.

[19] Stanley Cavell, *The Claim of Reason: Wittgenstein, Skepticism, Morality, and Tragedy* (Oxford: Oxford University Press, 1979, reprint 1999), p. 354. See also Cavell's "The Touch of Words," in *Seeing Wittgenstein Anew*, ed. William Day and Victor J. Krebs (Cambridge: Cambridge University Press, 2010), pp. 81–98, esp. p. 85.

[20] Cavell, *The Claim of Reason*, p. 354.

[21] See Wittgenstein, *Philosophical Investigations*, Pt. II, Sec. xi, p. 233, no. 315.

THE SENSE OF SELF 223

of their crossing—e.g. imagination, interpretation, experience, impression, expression, seeing, knowing, mere knowing, meaning, figurative meaning."[22] It is, I believe, precisely this complexity that one has to preserve in order to gain clarity about the perceptual-interpretive process here that will help answer our question concerning the content of the rereading "remainder."

It has been attractive to many to attempt to reduce this kind of perception-interpretation to only one of the concepts on Cavell's list (and thus to analyze down, here again, to an alleged essence). Some argue that imagination is basic or foundational here, so for us the personal or idiosyncratic imaginative content on the part of the rereader would fully account for the remainder—which is then regarded as not really in or of the text. On this view, we really saw all there was to see at twenty (and here one will use phrases such as "strictly speaking"). Some will focus on the interpretation, where this is informed by the cognitive stock of the rereader (e.g., the Marxist will see class struggle, the Freudian will see psycho-dynamics, the semiotician will see signs in interactive play, etc.), so we use the text as a set of illustrations of front-loaded stock, where the change of stock accounts for the change in rereading. Some will make expression central, so that the expressive content believed to have been "sent" by, for example, Dostoevsky becomes the criterion for correct criticism, so a change in the act of rereading is thought to be a function of a change in our beliefs concerning intended expressive content. Some will focus on the gap between plain or direct meaning (which we got at twenty because we knew the meanings of the words) and figurative or indirect meaning, where the change in rereading is accounted for in terms of seeing events described in the text as metaphors, drawn from narrated particulars within the text, for universal life events beyond the literal reach of those particular narratives. And we could say similar things for the other concepts on Cavell's list: experience, impression, seeing, knowing, and mere knowing. But again, what one needs for conceptual clarity—as Wittgenstein shows in his extensive remarks on aspect seeing—is to preserve the complexity and to allow the interaction of these concepts to take place as they may in particular cases. To reduce them all to one template of generic aspect perception is only to dream of the straight highway. But the closed highway, and Wittgenstein's open sideroads and detours, concerned linguistic meaning, not visual perception. So what, more precisely, is the connection between them?

Cavell continues, now discussing the phenomenon of aspect blindness, saying:

> He [Wittgenstein] immediately introduces his term "noticing an aspect"...I point to two late junctures in the progress of this notion of an "aspect": "The aspect presents a physiognomy which then passes away" (p. 210); and "The

---

[22] Cavell, *The Claim of Reason*, pp. 354–5.

224 LIVING IN WORDS

importance of this concept [of aspect blindness] lies in the connection between the concepts of 'seeing an aspect' and 'experiencing the meaning of a word'" (p. 214).[23]

It will become important for us below to note here: the analogy that both Wittgenstein and Cavell are identifying as centrally important—between aspect perception and the experience of word meaning—carries with it the corollary analogy between not being able to see an aspect and not being able to fathom the fuller significance of a word or sentence. But Cavell continues:

> Putting together the ideas that noticing an aspect is being struck by a physiognomy; that words present familiar physiognomies; that they can be thought of as pictures of their meaning; that words have a life and can be dead for us; that "experiencing a word" is meant to call attention to our relation to our words; that our relation to pictures is in some respects like our relation to what they are pictures of; I would like to say that the topic of our attachment to our words is allegorical of our attachments to ourselves and to other persons.[24]

Our relation to our words is no more simple, nor any more reducible to any one explanatory template, than is aspect perception; the relation of the person who knows the name of the winner, types it on a card, seals it, and then hands it to the MC is not the essence upon which later complexity is layered. He knows the name of the winner, that his name stands for, goes proxy for, refers to that person, and that the MC will, on reading the card, recognize the name and the person to whom that name refers. But as will be evident, acting on, living by, so impoverished a model of word meaning would ridiculously, or tragically, leave us utterly bereft of any human interaction or human understanding. The model, applied to literary meaning, would do equal damage. Thus Cavell, I think, might have gone further: It is true that our (irreducibly complex) attachment to our words is allegorical of our attachments to ourselves and to other persons, but it is not only that: the words to which we are attached are, in very many cases, the vehicles or the very means of, indeed the content of, our attachments to others. The connection is at once allegorical and more than allegorical.

But then Cavell does in a sense see this, if he does not quite say it. He writes:

> My words are my expressions of my life; I respond to the words of others as their expressions, i.e. respond not merely to what their words mean but equally to their meaning of them...[25]

---

[23] Cavell, *The Claim of Reason*, p. 355.　　[24] Cavell, *The Claim of Reason*, p. 355.
[25] Cavell, *The Claim of Reason*, p. 355.

THE SENSE OF SELF   225

One might say here—indeed I for one want to say here—that to understand a human being does not mean to know, in any reduced or minimally basic way, the meanings of their words; Franz and Sabina knew, or at least sensed, that in Chapter 1. The phrase "If you see what I mean" is very rarely, if ever, reducible to, or restated as, "If you know the meanings of the words I am using." Similarly, getting one to see the point—the point, purpose, or power—of what one is saying very rarely comes down to a narrow matter of *definition*. Cavell points to the kind of thing that is required by saying "to imagine an expression (experience the meaning of a word) is to imagine it as giving expression to a soul." He adds "(The examples used in ordinary language philosophy are in this sense imagined)"; I want to add that the literary words we reread, the literary characters with whom we engage and to whom we extend, work out, rehearse, and prepare our human understanding, are precisely in this sense imagined. And the words in them—like the words of persons—solicit our engagement[26] because they, in their way, give expression to a soul. But then how close is the connection, how tight is the link, between the two sides of Cavell's allegory? Cavell writes:

> The idea of the allegory of words is that human expressions, the human figure, to be grasped, must be *read*. To know another mind is to interpret a physiognomy, and the message of this region of the *Investigations* is that this is not a matter of "mere knowing." I have to read the physiognomy, and see the creature according to my reading, and treat it according to my seeing. The human body is the best picture of the human soul—not, I feel like adding, primarily because it represents the soul but because it expresses it. The body is the field of expression of the soul. The body is of the soul; it is the soul's . . . [27]

The physiognomy, the figure that is expressive of the soul, *must be read to be grasped*. "Mere knowing is weak, anemic, insufficient to the task": fathoming another human soul will never be reduced to this—just as the complexly inter-twined perceptual-interpretive acts of aspect seeing will never be reduced to a single essence-capturing template. These Cavellian reflections—reading a person, attending to difference, fathoming a soul (often in, with, and through words)—taken together, can remind us of the true complexity of the form of attention required to genuinely understand another's words, sentences, and expressions *as actually used*—in short, their linguistic life. And, rather than "merely knowing" anything, we continually reread, by sideroads and adventurous detours, persons, aspects, and (literary) words.

---

[26] For an extraordinarily helpful discussion of such solicitation of our engagement, our human interest, see Ted Cohen, *Thinking of Others: On the Talent for Metaphor* (Princeton: Princeton University Press, 2008), ch. 4: "Real Feelings, Unreal People," pp. 29–51.
[27] Cavell, *The Claim of Reason*, p. 356.

226 LIVING IN WORDS

One might think it strange, or perhaps naïve in a particularly academic or unworldly way, that Wittgenstein thought seriously of moving to, and settling in, Russia.[28] And it has been said that the deep impression that Dostoevsky's insights made on him in large part motivated this desire, this dream. But if the words we and others use are constitutive of, definitive of, life in the way Cavell has articulated, and if the insights voiced in the language of a great Russian author come from imagined (in Cavell's Wittgensteinian sense) Russian character, then the dream begins to seem less naïve and perhaps more richly aware of the linguistic constituents of the world that the person initially perceiving only naïve daydreaming realizes. (Indeed, one could say that if there is a naïve element in play here, it will be shifted more onto that person, once the depth of these linguistic issues is glimpsed).

There is more ground to dig before we bring all of this fully to the surface, but given the conception of words (with Cavell's remarks in mind) taking shape here in this final chapter concerning the sense of selfhood more broadly and the issue of rereading particularly, it is also becoming clearer why Wittgenstein said to his friend Maurice Drury, "When I was a village schoolmaster in Austria after the war I read *The Brothers Karamazov* over and over again. I read it out loud to the village priest. You know there really have been people like the elder Zosima who could see into people's hearts and direct them."[29] Reading out loud is physiognomic. And there are indeed real people whose deepest characteristics, their uncanny abilities in human understanding, are represented by (because they can see like, and speak with a power like) Zosima. We, and they, understand better and more richly through the comparison of life to literature and literature to life. Of Wittgenstein's insistence that all his considerable financial holdings be given, irrevocably, to his siblings, his sister said:

> Anyone who knows Dostoevsky's *The Brothers Karamazov* will remember the point when it is said that the thrifty and careful Ivan could well find himself in a precarious situation one day but that his brother Alesha [formally Alexey, informally also called Alyosha], who has no idea about money and possesses none, would certainly never starve, since everyone would be glad to share what they had with him and he would accept it without any reservations. I knew all this for certain, and did everything to fulfill Ludwig's wishes down to the last detail.[30]

---

[28] See Norman Malcolm's "Introduction" to Rhees, ed., *Recollections of Wittgenstein*, p. xviii, and in the same volume, Fania Pascal's "A Personal Memoir," pp. 44–5.

[29] Quoted in Rhees, ed., *Recollections of Wittgenstein*, in M. O'C. Drury's "Some Notes on Conversations with Wittgenstein," p. 86.

[30] Rhees, ed., *Recollections of Wittgenstein*, in John King's "Recollections of Wittgenstein," p. 72.

The constitutive, or self-compositional, words that Wittgenstein found in literature were not restricted to, nor contained within, that imaginary realm.

When Wittgenstein's friend John King mentioned that he had read *The Brothers Karamazov* some years earlier, Wittgenstein immediately "questioned [King] searchingly about this,"[31] exploring what King did and did not see in the book (King launched a close rereading of it not long after this exchange). And later in that conversation with King, while discussing a performance of *King Lear* that they had each seen at separate times, "Wittgenstein said that he had been astonished that so young a man could play an old man's part to such perfection. He thought he [the young actor] playing the elderly Lear had made only one mistake. In answer to Cordelia's 'Nothing,' Lear replies, 'Nothing will come of nothing.' [We saw one way of describing Lear's problem—a problem of his relation to his words—in Chapter 4.] Wittgenstein spoke these words as he thought they should be spoken, in hollow tones and clutching his diaphragm, as they came from the very heart of his being."[32] To question searchingly, to intimate what more there is to see, to see that words voiced with a certain physiognomy is to better and more fully express the state of a soul—these are forms of human understanding that are manifest in, and conducted through, our words. And they are depths of meaning that are not fathomable from any simple concept or template of atomistically contained word meaning. It is not, and could not be, a matter of what Cavell calls in this context "mere knowledge."

We might ask, or be asked, the question: "What do you see in the exchange with the Grand Inquisitor?" Wittgenstein writes, "'Seeing as...' is not a part of perception. And therefore it is like seeing, and again not like seeing."[33] The words "Like seeing" suggest that it is not just imaginative projection, not just a subjectivist, arbitrary, or viewer-idiosyncratic superimposition (of the kind discussed in Chapter 2 concerning the sense of rightness). Yet the contrast, "not like seeing," suggests that aspect perception, the seeing of X as Y, or in the light of Y, or in the connotative web of Y, is not going to be confirmed or disconfirmed in the way that the presence of an ambiguous line drawing before us (recall Cavell's "we see all of it, so the change is in us") will or can be, or in the way that the simple referent of a name (as in the MC's envelope) will definitively give that name's meaning. This, as Wittgenstein untangles the matter, is a false dichotomy—we don't have to choose.

But we don't have to choose between what, *precisely*? We easily think that at least the simple cases of word meaning are just that: simple, uniform, straightforward, where both sides of this perception/projection dichotomy are clearly

---

[31] Rhees, ed., *Recollections of Wittgenstein*, in John King's "Recollections of Wittgenstein," p. 72.
[32] Rhees, ed., *Recollections of Wittgenstein*, in John King's "Recollections of Wittgenstein," p. 73.
[33] Wittgenstein, *Philosophical Investigations*, Pt. II, Sec. xi, p. 207.

228   LIVING IN WORDS

demarcated. But do we even really have simplicity and uniformity in linguistic usage and meaning in what we regard as simple cases? Wittgenstein writes:

> I look at an animal; someone asks me: "What do you see?" I answer: "A rabbit."—
> I see a landscape; suddenly a rabbit runs past. I exclaim: "A rabbit!"
>   Both things, both the report and the exclamation, are expressions of perception and of visual experience. But the exclamation is so in a different sense from the report: it is forced from us.—It stands to the experience somewhat as a cry to pain.[34]

Here one wants (if impelled by the picture of the straight highway) to say: Well, say what you will, but in both cases the words are exactly the same, so the simple, straightforward meaning is—must be—the same, period. But that misses considerably more of the human element in this seemingly most simple case than it captures—the report (one has to extend the example somewhat to make full sense of this as a *report*, e.g., is this some kind of eye exam, or a question to a child learning language, or...?; but let us proceed with Wittgenstein's term) is a different kind of utterance than that of the exclamation. And the difference in kind is made not by the words spoken (although they are, importantly, spoken, enunciated, differently—recall Wittgenstein's Lear above), because *they* are (on the level of machine-like word identification) the same. The difference is made by the difference in our relations to our words, by the differences to which Cavell was

---

[34] Wittgenstein, *Philosophical Investigations*, Pt. II, Sec. xi, p. 207. It would require a separate paper to discuss this fully, but Wittgenstein's example here, brief as it is, seems to weigh against the plausibility of any minimal semantics, where what are identified as the same propositions are so identified because of sameness of wording. (Then the debate concerning contextualist semantics begins from there, arguing that propositional content is in part constituted by relational, external, or contextual features that differentiate content within sameness of wording.) The radical point contained in this example—one easy to miss with an image of "the straight highway" in mind—is that we should look to the most minute distinctions of usage within context, so that the telling differences are brought out in such high relief that we keep in the forefront of our minds a sense of how *we*, in Cavell's sense, actually use language (to a degree where we arrive at a question concerning what we so much as meant by the phrase "the same proposition," and indeed whether what we have in play here is a *proposition*.) Or to put it another way: to say (insensitive to meaning-determining nuance and to who is speaking) that a given combination of words will make up the same proposition does not leave us with sufficient means to distinguish between a person speaking and a parrot "speaking." (As Cavell reminds us, we respond to the words persons say and that it is *they* who are saying it equally.) Or still another way: minimal propositional content alone would fail to distinguish between what persons do in exchanging ideas and what computers do in (what we may misleadingly call) "exchanging" content in the form of words, i.e., they can transmit data back and forth; they do not exchange ideas. Wittgenstein's example, seemingly most simple ("a rabbit"), starts from the ground of embodied linguistic practice, not from embedded preconceptions concerning simplifying models; one could argue that one's model is, and another's is not, able to accommodate Wittgenstein's subtle difference here. But the point is whether one needs to, or ever would, arrive at any such model with a vast array of such details (the side roads, the detours) in clear view. That is what makes the position deeply radical, it is what makes it an alternative to theory formulation, and it is what makes it so easy to miss (i.e., to see it as an isolated case-based observation that is prefatory to theory formulation) in the context of the contemporary debate.

THE SENSE OF SELF   229

pointing, the differences that, I am suggesting, make them what they are. Who is speaking, in what state of being and state of mind, to whom, for what purpose, to what point, and with what power? Sensitivity to these kinds of questions is the sensitivity we bring with greater experience and greater cultivation to the words of others, to our own words, and to the words of others as we hear them with imagined physiognomies in literary texts. Words as apparently simple as "A rabbit" are not, on closer inspection, the same or invariant across contextual change, so the model at one end of our polarized dichotomy, the model or picture of simply putting into words a brute simple perception, is already oversimplified.

And what if (as Wittgenstein next discusses) we look for some time directly at a face across a room and then suddenly see that it is the face of a friend whom we have not seen for many years—we now "see" the younger face within, or beneath, the older present face that we see, and we suddenly cry out "Jones!" (This is much like the experience of hearing a melody and recognizing its coherence as a melody but not recognizing it as a variation on an earlier theme, and then suddenly recognizing it as, hearing it as, one.) This is both, in Wittgenstein's previous terms, report and exclamation—so even this dichotomy is over-simple, even it will not stay still.[35] Recall Cavell's list of concepts that can come into play in such cases; the question here becomes which elements of this complexity we want to bring out in higher relief, for what presently emergent purposes. If just the ocular, we speak of just what we see. If the recognition of Jones's face within the older to-that-point unrecognized face, we will speak of sudden recognition. If we wish to emphasize the special way Jones raises one eyebrow as the trigger of our sudden recognition, we will emphasize facial expression. If we emphasize what Jones meant to us at an earlier point in life, the rush of thoughts and emotions triggered by seeing the younger Jones "behind" this face now, we will speak of imaginative memory. And so forth. The irreducible complexity, the variance in emphasis given our present interests, given who is speaking, given what we know of the character and past experience of the person speaking, how what we are seeing and hearing resonates with our own character and past experience; all of this contributes to the "unexpected range of concepts." Wittgenstein, in the middle of his examination of aspect seeing, stopped to stand back and observe: "Here there is an enormous number of interrelated phenomena and possible concepts."[36] What we may initially have taken to be the simple, straightforward perceptual side of the dichotomy itself dissolves into ever more subtle complexity. This is why such cases are usually the more absorbing the more one looks (the more one rereads).

And what of the other side, the other polemical extreme of the perception/projection dichotomy as it can structure our thought on this issue? It does exactly the same. The reader of Dante's *Divine Comedy* who has a detailed knowledge of

---

[35] See Wittgenstein, *Philosophical Investigations*, Pt. II, Sec. xi, p. 208, remark 145.
[36] Wittgenstein, *Philosophical Investigations*, Pt. II, Sec. xi, p. 209, remark 155.

230 LIVING IN WORDS

Virgil's *Aeneid* and Homer's *Iliad* and *Odyssey* sees connections, influences, precedents, thematic developments, allusions, references, intertwined variations, and subtle similarities and differences in modes of speech and expression that the reader coming to the work "cold," as we say, cannot. Similarly, the expert in Florentine politics sees a network of connections, references, allusions, score settlings, and so forth that the "cold" reader does not see at all. And both the literary and political readers will see lines of influence stemming from Dante's work that are there but that Dante of course could not have seen. Literary imagination and historical-political imagination are contributing here, but in ways that we would describe as enabling the readers to see what is in the work. Or actually: what is in the words. We are able to make ever finer, ever more subtle distinctions between those readings that are enlivened and deepened by literary and historical/political imagination and those readings that are prismatically distorted by preconception—but these, like the other pole, will without exception be context-specific; no formula or generalized interpretive manifesto will help us here, precisely because any such generalized manifesto will fail to capture the meaning-determinative nuances that make the words what they are. And if the imaginative enrichment of the reread text comes from lived experience rather than literary or political scholarship, we may speak more of what we see in the text, but we still make fine distinctions that show which of many possible concepts of reading are in play or are brought out in higher relief. To put it paradoxically: on this score, all generalizations are false.

Wittgenstein provides a telling example that can itself be seen in the light of the present discussion. He writes:

> Hold the drawing of a face upside down and you can't recognize the expression of the face. Perhaps you can see that it is smiling, but not exactly what *kind* of smile it is. You cannot imitate the smile or describe its character more exactly.
>
> And yet the picture which you have turned round may be a most exact representation of a person's face.[37]

Upside down, we can see that the face is smiling. But we cannot imitate it or describe its character. Words themselves, Cavell said, exhibit a physiognomy, and we have to look closely at them, and—as we might now say—right side up (i.e., not as mere illustration of a preconception concerning brute perception or over-imaginative projection), to see what *kind* of "smile" they have. Like a facial expression, they will have it in that moment, from that speaker, to that hearer, for that purpose, as that response, provocation, invitation, etc., and with that power.

---

[37] Wittgenstein, *Philosophical Investigations*, Pt. II, Sec. xi, p. 208, remark 150.

THE SENSE OF SELF 231

Is then anything in language simple? To go back for a moment to our starting point, what about, after all, a simple name? Does it, can it, operate beneath, or outside of, the complexity of which Cavell and Wittgenstein speak, complexity that, the closer we look, seems linguistically omnipresent? Consider, in the light of all of the foregoing (should the phrase "in light of all the foregoing," as we say, go without saying for all linguistic usage?), this passage from *The Brothers Karamazov*; it is Alyosha knocking on a door, entering, and saying his name (how much simpler, we might ask, could things be?):

"Who's there?" shouted a man in a loud and angry voice.

Alyosha opened the door and crossed the threshold. He found himself in a regular peasant's room. It was large and cluttered with belongings of all sorts. There were several people in it. On the left was a large Russian stove. From the stove to a window was a string with rags hanging on it. There was a bed against the wall on each side, right and left, covered with knitted quilts. On the one to the left was a pyramid of four print-covered pillows, each smaller than the one beneath. On the other bed there was only one very small pillow. The opposite corner of the room was screened off by a curtain or sheet hung on a string. Behind this curtain could be seen bedding made up on a bench and a chair. A rough square table of plain wood stood in front of the middle window. The three windows, each of four tiny greenish mildewy panes were shut, so that the room was not very light and rather stuffy. On the table was a frying pan with the remains of some fried eggs, a half-eaten piece of bread, and a small bottle with a few drops of vodka.

A woman of refined appearance, wearing a cotton dress, was sitting on a chair by the bed on the left. Her face was thin and yellow and her sunken cheeks betrayed at the first glance that she was ill. But what struck Alyosha most was the expression in the poor woman's eyes—a look of surprised inquiry and yet of haughty pride. While he was talking to her husband, her big brown eyes moved from one speaker to the other with the same proud and questioning expression. Beside her at the window stood a young girl, rather plain, with scanty reddish hair, poorly but very neatly dressed. She looked disdainfully at Alyosha as he came in. Beside the other bed sat another female figure. She was a very sad sight, a young girl of about twenty, but hunchback and crippled "with withered legs," as Alyosha was told afterwards. Her crutches stood in the corner. The strikingly beautiful and gentle eyes of this poor girl looked with mild serenity at Alyosha. A man of forty-five was sitting at the table, finishing the fried eggs. He was small and weakly built. He had reddish hair and a scanty light-colored beard, very much like a wisp of tow (this comparison and the phrase "a wisp of tow" flashed at once into Alyosha's mind). It was obviously this man who had shouted to him when he knocked on the door. Seeing Alyosha, the man got up from the bench on which he was sitting, and wiping his mouth with a ragged napkin, came up to him.

232 LIVING IN WORDS

"It's a monk come to beg for the monastery. A nice place to come to!" the girl standing in the left corner said aloud. The man looked toward her and answered in an excited and breaking voice, "No, Varvara, you are wrong. Allow me to ask," he turned again to Alyosha, "what has brought you to—our retreat?"

Alyosha looked at him There was something angular, flurried and irritable about him. Though he had obviously just been drinking, he was not drunk. There was extraordinary impudence in his expression, and yet, strange to say, at the same time there was fear. He looked like a man who had long been kept in subjection and had submitted to it, and now had suddenly turned and was trying to assert himself. Or, better still, like a man who wants to hit you but is horribly afraid you will hit him. In his words and in the intonation of his shrill voice there was a sort of crazy humor, at times spiteful and at times cringing, and continually shifting from one tone to another. The question about "our retreat" he had asked as it were quivering all over, rolling his eyes, and coming up so close to Alyosha that Alyosha instinctively drew back a step. He was dressed in a very shabby dark cotton coat, patched and spotted. He wore checked trousers of a light color, long out of fashion, and of very thin material. They were so wrinkled and so short that he looked as though he had grown out of them like a boy.

"I am Alexey Karamazov," Alyosha began.[38]

"I am Alexey Karamazov." What do we see in this name?

One could say that the meaning of the name, technically, is nothing but the existent particular that is its referent (in this case a living human being). That would be the dreamed-of straight highway. But the question of meaning that is relevant to the question of rereading is: What does it mean to *us*? What does the name mean to the real users of it? What will it mean when we hear it? Well, we might say: A person who begins by seeing the size of a room and people in it, who then sees the placement of things—appliances, beds, chairs, etc. in it, but as he does he takes in still more informative details—the distribution of pillows, the quality of the fabric and its meaning for who these people are. He sees the texture of the table, the uncleaned windows, the quality of light, the atmosphere, and traces of some recent activities (eating and drinking) within the room. Then: he sees the aspect of a refined appearance over the look of sunken-cheeked illness, but with the expressive power of the eyes coming out for him in highest relief. And he sees the oscillating attention in these eyes, with their physiognomy of a proud, haughty, and questioning look. He sees the dignity of neat dress extracted from poor materials, he sees disdain in a glance, he sees striking beauty and gentleness radiating from the eyes of the physically unfortunate girl; he sees, and quantifies,

---

[38] Fyodor Dostoyevsky, *The Brothers Karamazov*, trans. Constance Garnett, ed. Manuel Komroff (New York: Signet, 1957), pp. 184–5.

THE SENSE OF SELF   233

serenity. He is aware of phrases flashing into his own mind (phrase-born suddenly dawning aspects), and he is aware of the interaction of these phrases with his perception. He sees himself misperceived; he sees angularity of character; he sees the unexpected and unusual admixture of impudence and fear in the same bearing and countenance, unpredictably together in the same expression at the same time. He saw the look of recently emerging assertiveness; in a flash he saw this description as one improved by, revised by, the look of one who wants to hit you but is constrained by fear. He knows what it is to see a divided person before him; he knows when he sees a person barely overpowering his own impulses. He hears the meaning-determining power of intonation; he hears shifting tones that sound deranged; he reads persons and the words of persons. He sees how words spoken were said (as if quivering); he sees his own instinctive, immediate, and embodied back-stepping, self-protective physical reactions and draws reflective conclusions from them. All of this inflects the content of his name for us as readers—we see a whole world of sensibility in that name when he pronounces it; it is, in Cavell's sense, *his* name as *he* is speaking it. And of course, at a "meta" level, we see what we see in observing that distinctive sensibility (one reminiscent of Henry James's phrase, "a person on whom nothing is lost"), and we see in his act of knocking on a door and stepping into a room what it is to be awake to, alive to, a rich environment in which rapid-fire perceptions and reflections interact, intertwine, and bring the words we use to life.

Is all of that in the name? Yes. Is it content we can miss, in whole or in part? Yes. Is it the kind of thing we see more fully, and more deeply, on rereading and from a position of more cultivated literary sensitivity and more life experience? Yes. And is it the kind of thing that can refine our descriptions, refine our perceptions (recall Alyosha's quick redescription where the recast formulation occasions the dawning of a new aspect over the surface, as it were, of the previous one), and cast light, through words, on our own experience? Certainly.

"I am Alexey Karamazov"? We have here only one relatively brief passage prefacing his uttering of his name, and yet no one would describe what we have here as a simple ostensive referent, simple meaning content. But the truth of the matter is far more complex still: by the end of the book we have hundreds of such character-revealing, mind-revealing, sensibility-revealing passages, and all of that—far too complex in content to reiterate in one descriptive list, far too complex to imaginatively encompass at one moment—is in his name. (With Cavell's remarks in mind: not in *the* name Alexey, but in *his* name Alexey—like the real names that we use of *persons*.) It is content that is assembled across, distributed across, repeated readings. It did not take Wittgenstein long to realize that an atomistic conception of word meaning, a picture of unitary, precise, bounded, and invariant linguistic content—however initially attractive is the image of the straight highway—was destined to miss, in terms of what language actually is, far more than it captured, and destined to obscure (despite its false

234 LIVING IN WORDS

initial promise) far more than it clarifies. Given the frequency and emphatic delivery to friends across his life of his recommendation to read and reread *The Brothers Karamazov*, and given the fit between what Dostoevsky's texts show and the philosophical issues he addresses, it is perhaps not overly fanciful to suggest that the close and absorbed reading and rereading of the literary works he found most compelling was itself part of his philosophical work. It certainly showed him the sideroads and their unpredictable interweavings.

But let us come back then directly to the problem of characterizing the difference between the reading at twenty and the reading at fifty. Frank Cioffi[39] has called attention to the criticism Wittgensteinian philosophical work has received from some quarters for its criticism of, or even denigration of, empirical explanation. This is an easy matter to misunderstand, and getting clear on it—as Cioffi's work significantly helps us achieve—helps to describe in fairly brief scope the difference between the two readings (and thus the reason for, and the value of, rereading). Wittgenstein's hostility to the very idea of empirical or cause-and-effect explanation in aesthetics[40] is particularly well known, and goes to the heart of the matter here. Cioffi writes:

> In the course of his apparent derogation of empirical knowledge, Wittgenstein employs two sets of contrasts. One, most generically stated, is between explaining something in the way an event is explained and attaining to a more explicit understanding of what makes it that particular something.[41]

This distinction, then, is between:

(1) explaining something on the model of cause-and-effect event explanations (the airplane crashed because it ran out of fuel; the fire started from a frayed extension cord under a carpet; the airplane has lift because the shape of the wing creates lower pressure above the wing than below it, etc.); and
(2) working one's way into a more fully explicit, more fully articulated comprehension of the features, characteristics, connotations, aspects, relational interconnections, and so forth that make the thing or experience what *it* is.

This latter form of comprehension is not reducible to, nor does it conform to, generic explanatory templates (unlike the preceding cause-and-effect examples).

---

[39] Frank Cioffi, "Explanation, Self-Clarification, and Solace," in *Wittgenstein on Freud and Frazer*, pp. 128–9.

[40] See Wittgenstein, *Lectures on Aesthetics, Psychology, and Religious Belief*, ed. Cyril Barrett (Oxford: Blackwell, 1966); Garry L. Hagberg, "Wittgenstein's Aesthetics," *Stanford Encyclopedia of Philosophy* (Palo Alto: Stanford University, 2007); Roger Scruton, "A Bit of Help from Wittgenstein," *British Journal of Aesthetics*, 51(3), 2011: 309–19.

[41] Frank Cioffi, "Explanation, Self-Clarification, and Solace," in *Wittgenstein on Freud and Frazer*, p. 128.

THE SENSE OF SELF   235

Contrast what is needed to explain the physics and optics of pigment saturation with what is needed to ever more exactingly and deeply capture in words what makes an expanse of focused time spent with a set of Rembrandt self-portraits so absorbing. To put the matter in the briefest scope: the latter is the kind of reflection rereading occasions. Cioffi continues:

> Less generically, it is between explaining an event and coming to understand what the feelings and thoughts are which give it depth.[42]

This kind of understanding will come—usually piecemeal and as the result of absorbed reflection—in linguistic form, where the words we use in connection with (or as we saw above in Wittgenstein's remarks, in multi-concept interwoven interaction with) our experience are, in Cavell's sense, *our* words; in Wittgenstein's sense, they are complex, invariably contextually inflected ones. It is, as Wittgenstein insists, here and only here that they come to life, and it is here, as Cavell suggests, that they *can* have life. To use these words as if they are uniform instruments with prespecified determinate content and preconceived uses is—here is the reason for Wittgenstein's impatience with the empirical model—to use the proverbial jackhammer to attempt to repair a Swiss watch or (to use Wittgenstein's image) to attempt to repair a spider web with one's fingers. If our words were much simpler than they are, and if our usages of them were circumscribed causes aiming at predetermined effects, the only difference between the reading at fifty would be that many more irrelevant associations or connotations are brought by the reader's mind to project over, and thus only obscure, the evident and plain meaning on the page of which the twenty-year-old would then have the clearer, less obstructed view. But that is only philosophical mythology, one of the misdirections given by the atomistic picture and its lingering conceptual residue. The reason we know that the range of legitimate interpretation of *The Brothers Karamazov* is not demarcated by the collection of dictionary definitions of all the words contained within it is that we know that real words—live words, our words—do not work like that.[43] It is a happy fact that they do not sit still.

As we have seen throughout this section of this chapter, one way to describe the endlessly complex and inventive ways our words, our sentences, open on to each other is to speak of sideroads and detours. But another way to speak of the ranges of meanings a rereader can explore when our words are at work—in life and in literature (biographers and autobiographers are, in the sense developed in this

---

[42] Frank Cioffi, "Explanation, Self-Clarification, and Solace," in *Wittgenstein on Freud and Frazer*, p. 128.

[43] It is perhaps here worth noting: No one ever thought of this as a reasonable way of proceeding to demarcate the bounds of legitimate criticism, but if the atomistic picture were true, and if we speaking humans actually spoke in accordance with this picture (in which case it is not clear we could recognize ourselves as humans), everyone would find this suggestion readily plausible.

236 LIVING IN WORDS

section of this chapter, rereaders of life)—is to speak of the field of a word. Wittgenstein writes:

> A *great deal* can be said about a subtle aesthetic difference—that is important.— The first remark may, of course, be: "*This* word fits, *that* doesn't"—or something of the kind. But then all of the widespread ramifications effected by each of the words can still be discussed. That first judgment is *not* the end of the matter, for it is the *field* of a word that is decisive.[44]

The fact that a great deal can be said, Wittgenstein insists, is important. It shows, against the atomistic picture, how words open up, expand, reach out, connect. That is what we explore in finding articulations of experiential content in life, and it is what we do in finding articulations of significance, of a range of implications, of meaning-determining connections, of symbolically powerful relations in literature. Alyosha saw that the second formulation fit better than the first; it awakened a new aspect that proved more exacting, more fitting, more right (as we saw it in Chapter 2), more narratively organizing (as we saw it in Chapter 3), to the circumstance. "The widespread ramifications effected by each of the words"— that is to articulate the significance of the articulation itself, of the verbal formulation. And it is the field the rereader explores, always by sideroads where (linguistic) life is lived, where there are tales (with emergent Aristotelian structures) to tell.

We began this section with Hume and the subtractive problem: what is the content of the difference in readings that we all know is there, but that we may find difficult to describe (beyond simply saying that we now see more in it, which only restates the question)? There is a picture, we saw, of fixed meaning lurking in the conceptual subterrain, and that picture would suggest that all of the difference must come from projections over the primary textual content by the rereader. But once excavated and examined, here again, now in this context, that picture of determinate fixity of word meaning did not survive scrutiny. This led to our look into aspect seeing, what it is to see one thing in the light of another, the way this works with words as well as with visual perception, and the need to preserve, rather than reduce, for the sake of clarity and accuracy, the complexity and multiplicity of the concepts that can come into play here to describe what we are seeing, or what we are seeing-as, or what we are seeing-in. Experiencing the meaning of a word was then seen to be a considerably more interesting and variegated nest of phenomena than the naming model, or the atomistic model, could predict, and this brought us to the allegorical (and more than allegorical) relation between our attachments and connections to our words and our

---

[44] Wittgenstein, *Philosophical Investigations*, Pt. II, Sec. xi, p. 230, remark 297.

THE SENSE OF SELF   237

attachments to ourselves and others. The question of understanding the words of others, of ourselves—our own and owned words—thus becomes as humanly interesting and intricate a matter as the question of deeply or thoroughly understanding a person. The contrast here is: Do we want to see a word as standing in a naming relation to a physical referent, or, in Cavell's phrase, as expressing a soul? Human beings, or the complexities of human character, are themselves both in a sense read and reread; both words and persons exhibit physiognomies. Wittgenstein's Lear showed this in microcosm.

So what we actually mean by what on first glance we take to be the simplest words turns out, within the contexts that give them life, to be not so simple.[45] Nor is seeing the younger face we knew suddenly emerge from the face we did not immediately recognize—on the level of brute sensation, nothing has changed; yet on the level of human recognition, everything has. And it is important to keep in mind that in this case as discussed, the recognition is *correct*: it is not merely a whimsical projection, and yet it is thought-dependent. This stood directly parallel to the rereading of Dante in the light of Virgil. Similarly, what we cannot see in a drawing of a face held upside down is parallel to what we cannot see in a bare name: "Alyosha" before witnessing his sensibility in action, and "Alyosha" after— on the level of meaning and comprehension, nothing, and yet everything, has changed. Reformulations of descriptive phrases cast new light, awaken new aspects, and reveal, or forge, new connections—this is the substance of rereading in life and in literature, aiming at progress toward greater, deeper, more precise understanding that is distributed across time, across Wittgenstein's repeated rereadings. This is a kind of knowledge, an ever-growing recognition of meaning, that is not the summative result of accumulated empirical causal explanations. And so to encapsulate the point of this section of this chapter: it is the kind of knowledge that gives content to our sense of selfhood, the sense of internally contained but externally intertwined personal sensibility.

So my initial question, framed in subtractive terms and asking for a characterization of the remainder, may have been based on a too-simple—and still fairly common, despite the work of Wittgenstein, Austin, Wisdom, Cavell, McDowell, and others in this tradition—conception of word meaning. The thought was, if the words themselves remained constant across rereadings, wherein lay the difference? But words, rightly understood, are vastly more sophisticated, vastly more complex, and very much more ours than that starting simplistic template

---

[45] A close reading of Wittgenstein, *Philosophical Investigations*, Sec. 257 provides an inoculation (against precisely this oversimplification) that is as powerful as it is succinct; the concept of naming an object, or naming a sensation, is *already within* language and thus cannot be understood as an act of christening prior to language that can then explain how, in essence, language functions. (*Explanans, explanandum.*) The notion of a "language-game" (as designed to therapeutically loosen the grip of the picture of simple ostensive naming as the essence or foundation of language) proves especially helpful here.

238 LIVING IN WORDS

could so much as intimate, much less accommodate. The simple, invariant, or trans-contextual meanings were never really there to begin with. Indeed, with our relations to our words—and all that this entails, as we have surveyed the matter here—in clearer view, I should perhaps now ask how one could think that there could ever be a rereading *without* a very considerable difference. So what then, is Wittgenstein—what are we—pursuing in rereading? Nothing less than the comprehension of a form of life—the life of our words—that constitutes the irreducible content of humane understanding. But this sentence—like Alyosha Karamazov saying his name—can only be understood in light of everything that has preceded it.

6.3 Coda: Self-Compositional Reading, Seeing Connections, and the Self as a Work-in-Progress

We began with reasons to see the self in relational terms—as the center of a constellation of interconnections of an ever-evolving and internally dynamic kind. And in the course of considering that, we have seen something of the nature of human selfhood hidden within aesthetic experience, understood one way. Following that, we considered some of the reasons for suggesting that the understanding—that is, the serious and deep understanding—of a person's words is often coequal with understanding that person. Intimacy, insight, and empathy all depend on this. We then uncovered some of the complexities (where a grasp of complexity rather than a reduction to simplified generalities is viewed as the result, the reward, the progress, of a philosophical investigation) of self-interpretation, and some analogies between self-interpretation and the interpretation of works of art. And in connection with this, we considered some of the issues concerning the individuation of an action in relation to self-description and in relation to biographical and autobiographical writing. These considerations then led into what we termed the "architecture" of selfhood and self-understanding and the way in which the arrival at a settled self-defining narrative structure can be a cathartic achievement. That architecture, as we saw, is very often a matter of perceiving relations between life events, between words, between deeds, and between all of these in an intertwined way, where literature can serve as a powerful prompt text. But then it turned out that this was not exclusively a matter of perceiving (pre-existing) relations or connection, but in many cases it is also a matter of making those relations, those connections as well. Those relations and connections, as we saw, can realign the past, thus engendering what George Herbert Mead pithily termed "the unpredictable past."[46] And all along the way we

---

[46] George Herbert Mead, in *Pragmatism and Classical American Philosophy*, ed. John Stuhr, 2nd ed. (New York: Oxford University Press, 1999), p. 544. In these pages Mead also wrote: "The accepted past lies in a present and is subject itself, to possible reconstruction"; "We are constantly reconstructing the

THE SENSE OF SELF 239

have considered literary cases, literary characters, who put flesh on the bones of these philosophical ideas, characters who teach us something we otherwise would have missed or for which we would not have found a voice, or who show us, as cautionary tales, what insufficient reflection, insufficient narrative self-understanding or awareness, can cause within the constellations of our relations.

However, if *composition*, rather than construction or constitution, is our governing model for what transpires in the reader's inner world, then how precisely does this creative act unfold? How should we describe its process? Those questions led us to an examination of the relation between webs or networks of belief and the formation of selfhood, and the special way in which we can inside the imaginative world of literature "try on" sets of beliefs in order to expand the reach of our understanding and to see, beyond the reach of our present identities, "possible selves."

But then we are after all one actual person, and not another possible one, and so we looked into the making of textually cultivated selves and the imaginative and yet self-compositional act of making up our minds, of resolute self-individuation, within literary experience. And although the process of self-individuation has been a theme running through this entire study, in the final sections we looked into how words pragmatically work as self-compositional instruments, how they can constitute the substance of self-understanding, how rereading, properly understood, provides a model for word-borne self-reflection as a continuously developing self-compositional process. And these reflections led to an opening allowing us to see how an inward process very like self "rewriting" becomes possible, and the special role that metaphor can play in self-individuation.

The phrase "continuously developing," however, suggests that there is no terminus of self-composition, no endpoint marked by a finally settled self-understanding, no permanent boundary to what is the self. And given all of the foregoing, this suggestion seems correct: self-compositional reading has no end; the seeing of connections, and the making of them, never ends; and selves, in this sense, are like works of art and literature, offering ever-new constitutive relations, ever-new meaning-generating juxtapositions. Selves are thus not only like art, but also, indeed, like language itself. And hence the inexhaustibility of a work of art becomes a mimetic representation of the human self as an ever-dynamic work-in-progress. (Given the enlivening aspect of this observation, it should be cause for celebration, not consternation.) Composers of course do finish symphonies, string quartets, piano sonatas, jazz pieces, sound installations, and

---

world from our own standpoint. And that reconstruction holds just as really with the so-called 'irrevocable' past as with reference to a future"; and "The histories that we have transcribed would have been impossible to the pens of our fathers as the world we live in would have been inaccessible to their eyes and to their minds." Mead's claims here stretch across generations, across multiple lifespans. But I am suggesting that the process he describes can occur within a life, biographically or autobiographically understood.

240 LIVING IN WORDS

countless further categories of musical works. But that "finishing" is actually the point where life begins for the work and not where it ends. In that second sense, they are never finished and are not the kinds of entities that could be. Like us.

But before closing, there is one final issue to briefly consider. It is sometimes thought that the structures of self-understanding as we might draw them from literature are in an ontological sense unreal, fanciful, or merely imaginary. But in fact (the fact here being our actual linguistic practices, our language), if we look back (in Chapter 5) to the discussion concerning the trying on of webs of belief, we can see how we make distinctions between imaginary and real selves, between fanciful and justified interpretations of a literary character, or (to return to Chapter 2) between projected and perceived interpretations, where the sense of rightness plays an important role. But those are distinctions we draw in particular circumstances and not in a generic or overarching sense.

In truth, these self-interpreting, self-authoring, sense-making structures are no more ontologically fanciful than are patterns as we perceive them within a set of dots on a page. Because it is true that the page exists as brute physical matter, and because the dots exist as patterns of physical ink on a physical page, one can easily think that the pattern perceived in the arrangement of those physical entities is not real, and one then demarcates what is factual or not accordingly. Once brought to the light of day, this is a fairly simple fallacy of a misappropriated and overgeneralized concept: a distinction we would actually make here between the real and the not-real in pattern perception would be made in order to distinguish an illusory or falsely apparent pattern (as in visual illusions) from the real pattern that is present. And so we would cling to the philosophical claim that the pattern is not real only if we first have assented, either explicitly or on the level of presuppositional intuition, to a somewhat crude extensionalism, a doctrine claiming that only things extended in space and measureable in terms of weight, length, width, and so forth are real, everything else being imaginary. This strange view—really a manifestation of the most grand and over-general categorization of the world into mind and matter—would suggest that paperweights are real, while love, mathematics, higher aspirations, perceived resemblances between faces, the way we see character in aesthetic sensibility, and the melancholy in a melody are not. (The melody is like the pattern; the melody can reach, or soar, or dip, or fly, or intertwine only if we perceive the *melody*, and not only the independent and isolated physically sounded notes out of which it is composed. It is not *really* only notes. Analogously, Picasso's *Portrait of Kahnweiler* is not in truth *only* brushstrokes, and what is there does not reduce—without massive and senseless loss—to them.) The kind of self-understanding and reflexive restructuring, the kind of active literary engagement, the way of seeing language, the way of describing the acquisition and powers of autobiographical language, the parallel modes of artistic and self-interpretation, and the sensibility we create and enact within aesthetic experience, and indeed a full-bodied recognition of the importance of aesthetic experience, are all free of the shuttering effects of this doctrine. (The interestingly hopeless Don Giovanni, as we saw in Chapter 4, is probably not, and King Lear's blunt fact-shouting conception of language accords well with it.) In truth, such patterns, such self-compositional structures, such autobiographical connections, such relations, are as real as the language in which they are recorded and in which they take form. And they take form and solidify, or bend, or alter, or extend into the future or reach into the past, over and across the time of a life.

Reflective reading of the kind I have examined neither merely imposes from the outside a narrative form on experiential chaos, nor unearths fully formed pre-existent structures buried within that experience. The process is a more subtle negotiation that does not conform to easy generic categories. Connection making, connection seeing, and connection finding are all interrelated elements of the insight we gain into a life as lived: such insight does not often come passively, and it is of a kind that does not reduce to simple causal explanation or the kind of thing that empirical experimentation could capture. The content of self-understanding, and of other-understanding, is of a different kind, but it is not for this reason any less ontologically respectable. The examining of life, at least as discussed here, is not conducted in a laboratory. Or: the laboratory is literature and other genres and technologies (e.g., theater, film, television, etc.) of narrative art informed by philosophy.

We started with the American pragmatists, and in closing we might return to them. I have suggested that a distinctive kind of reading yields a widely experi-enced yet little articulated and examined self-compositional process that is in turn described in self-referential writing or autobiographical description, where that self-description then solidifies in the character, intellectual tone, and sensibility of the reader/writer, thus becoming the newly revised or augmented self that approaches the next text (hence my non-pejorative use of the term "bootstrap-ping"). C. S. Peirce wrote:

> A person is not absolutely an individual. His thoughts are what he is "saying to himself," that is, is saying to that other self that is just coming into life in the flow of time.[47]

This captures much of the human situation in two sentences. But it was still another American thinker, Ralph Waldo Emerson, who asked the profound question at the heart of humanistic inquiry: "Where do we find ourselves?" The answer may be: in words.

---

[47] *The Collected Papers of Charles Sanders Peirce*, ed. Charles Hartshorne and Paul Weiss (Cambridge, MA: Harvard University Press, 1931–6), Vol. 5, p. 421.

Bibliography

Aeschylus, *Oresteia*, trans. Richard Lattimore, in David Grene and Richard Lattimore, eds., *The Complete Greek Tragedies, Aeschylus I* (Chicago: University of Chicago Press, 1955), pp. 33–171.

Dante Alighieri, *The Divine Comedy*, trans. Charles S. Singleton (Princeton: Princeton University Press, 1970).

G. E. M. Anscombe, "Wittgenstein: Whose Philosopher?," in A. Phillips Griffiths, ed., *Wittgenstein Centenary Essays* (Cambridge: Cambridge University Press, 1991), pp. 1–10.

Aristotle, *Nicomachean Ethics*, trans. Martin Ostwald (Indianapolis: Bobbs-Merrill, 1962).

Aristotle, *Nicomachean Ethics*, in Jonathan Barnes, ed., *The Complete Works of Aristotle*, Vol. 2 (Princeton: Princeton University Press, 1984), pp. 1729–867.

Aristotle, *Poetics*, trans. Stephen Halliwell (London: Duckworth, 1987).

Marcus Aurelius, *Meditations*, trans. Robin Hard (Oxford: Oxford University Press, 2011).

Renford Bambrough, "Aristotle on Justice: A Paradigm of Philosophy," in Renford Bambrough, ed., *New Essays on Plato and Aristotle* (London: Routledge & Kegan Paul, 1965), pp. 159–74.

Renford Bambrough, "How to Read Wittgenstein," in Godfrey Vesey, ed., *Understanding Wittgenstein* (Ithaca: Cornell University Press, 1974), pp. 117–32.

Kenneth Baynes, James Bohman, and Thomas A. McCarthy, eds., *After Philosophy: End or Transformation?* (Cambridge: MIT Press, 1987).

Sarah Beckwith, *Shakespeare and the Grammar of Forgiveness* (Ithaca: Cornell University Press, 2011).

R. P. Blackmur, ed., *The Art of the Novel* (New York: Charles Scribner's Sons, 1962).

Jorge Luis Borges, *The Book of Sand*, trans. Norman Thomas di Giovanni (New York: Dutton, 1977).

Jorge Luis Borges, *Selected Non-Fictions*, ed. Eliot Weinberger (New York: Viking, 1999).

Jacques Bouveresse, *Wittgenstein Reads Freud*, trans. Carol Cosman (Princeton: Princeton University Press, 1995).

O. K. Bouwsma, *Wittgenstein: Conversations 1949–1951*, ed. J. L. Craft and Ronald E. Hustwit (Indianapolis: Hackett, 1986).

Daniel Brudney, "Styles of Self-Absorption," in Garry L. Hagberg and Walter Jost, eds., *The Blackwell Companion to the Philosophy of Literature* (Malden: Wiley-Blackwell, 2010), pp. 300–27.

Herman Capellen and Ernie Lapore, *Insensitive Semantics* (Malden: Wiley-Blackwell, 2005).

Noel Carroll, "Art, Narrative, and Moral Understanding," in Jerrold Levinson, ed., *Aesthetics and Ethics: Essays at the Intersection* (Cambridge: Cambridge University Press, 1998), pp. 126–60.

Quassim Cassam, ed., *Self-Knowledge* (Oxford: Oxford University Press, 1994).

Stanley Cavell, "Must We Mean What We Say?," in his *Must We Mean What We Say? A Book of Essays* (Cambridge: Cambridge University Press, 1976), pp. 1–43.

244 BIBLIOGRAPHY

Stanley Cavell, *The Claim of Reason: Wittgenstein, Skepticism, Morality, and Tragedy* (Oxford: Oxford University Press, 1979).

Stanley Cavell, *In Quest of the Ordinary: Lines of Skepticism and Romanticism* (Chicago: University of Chicago Press, 1988).

Stanley Cavell, *This New yet Unapproachable America: Lectures after Emerson after Wittgenstein* (Chicago: University of Chicago Press, 1989).

Stanley Cavell, "The *Investigations'* Everyday Aesthetics of Itself," in Stephen Mulhall, ed., *The Cavell Reader* (Oxford: Blackwell, 1996), pp. 376–89.

Stanley Cavell, *Little Did I Know: Excerpts from Memory* (Stanford: Stanford University Press, 2010).

Stanley Cavell, "The Touch of Words," in William Day and Victor J. Krebs, eds., *Seeing Wittgenstein Anew* (Cambridge: Cambridge University Press, 2010), pp. 81–98.

Frank Cioffi, "Wittgenstein's Freud," in Peter Winch, ed., *Studies in the Philosophy of Wittgenstein* (London: Routledge and Kegan Paul, 1969), pp. 184–210.

Frank Cioffi, "Explanation, Self-Clarification, and Solace," in his *Wittgenstein on Freud and Frazer* (Cambridge: Cambridge University Press, 1998), pp. 128–54.

Frank Cioffi, "Wittgenstein and the Fire-Festivals," in his *Wittgenstein on Freud and Frazer* (Cambridge: Cambridge University Press, 1998), pp. 80–106.

Ted Cohen, *Thinking of Others: On the Talent for Metaphor* (Princeton: Princeton University Press, 2008).

Ted Cohen, "At Play in the Fields of Metaphor," in Garry L. Hagberg and Walter Jost, eds., *A Companion to the Philosophy of Literature* (Oxford: Wiley-Blackwell, 2010), pp. 507–20.

Peter J. Conradi, *Iris Murdoch: A Life* (New York: W. W. Norton, 2001).

Jodi Cranston, *The Poetics of Portraiture in the Italian Renaissance* (Cambridge: Cambridge University Press, 2000).

Arthur Danto, *The Transfiguration of the Commonplace* (Cambridge, MA: Harvard University Press, 1981).

Arthur Danto, "Philosophy as/and/of Literature," in *The Philosophical Disenfranchisement of Art* (New York: Columbia University Press, 1986), pp. 135–61.

Arthur Danto, *After the End of Art: Contemporary Art and the Pale of History* (Princeton: Princeton University Press, 1997).

Arthur Danto, "Why We Need Fiction: An Interview with Arthur C. Danto," *The Henry James Review* 18(3), Fall 1997: 213–16.

Donald Davidson, "Actions, Reasons, and Causes," in *Essays on Actions and Events* (Oxford: Clarendon Press, 1980), pp. 3–19.

Donald Davidson, "Mental Events," in *Essays on Actions and Events* (Oxford: Clarendon Press, 1980), pp. 207–27.

Donald Davidson, "Psychology as Philosophy," in *Essays on Actions and Events* (Oxford: Clarendon Press, 1980), pp. 229–44.

Donald Davidson, "On the Very Idea of a Conceptual Scheme," in *Inquiries into Truth and Interpretation* (Oxford: Clarendon Press, 1984), pp. 183–98.

Donald Davidson, "Thought and Talk," in *Inquiries into Truth and Interpretation* (Oxford: Clarendon, 1984), pp. 155–70.

Donald Davidson, "A Nice Derangement of Epitaphs," in E. Lepore, ed., *Truth and Interpretation: Perspectives on the Philosophy of Donald Davidson* (Oxford: Basil Blackwell, 1986), pp. 433–46.

Donald Davidson, "Knowing One's Own Mind," *Proceedings and Addresses of the American Philosophical Association*, 60, 1987: 441–58, reprinted in *Self-Knowledge*, ed. Quassim Cassam (Oxford: Oxford University Press, 1994), pp. 43–64.

Donald Davidson, "Problems in the Explanation of Action," in P. Petit, R. Sylvan, and J. Norman, eds., *Metaphysics and Morality: Essays in Honour of J. J. C. Smart* (Oxford: Basil Blackwell, 1987), pp. 35–49.

Lydia Davis, *Almost No Memory* (New York: Farrar, 1997).

William Day and Victor J. Krebs, *Seeing Wittgenstein Anew* (Cambridge: Cambridge University Press, 2010).

Edward J. Dent, *Mozart's Operas*, 2nd ed. (Oxford: Oxford University Press, 1947).

Keith DeRose, "Contextualism: An Explanation and Defense," in J. Greco and E. Sosa, eds., *The Blackwell Guide to Epistemology* (Malden: Blackwell, 1999).

Descartes, Rene, *Meditations*, ed. John Cottingham (Cambridge: Cambridge University Press, 1996).

Cora Diamond, "Henry James, Moral Philosophers, Moralism," in Garry L. Hagberg and Walter Jost, eds., *The Blackwell Companion to the Philosophy of Literature* (Malden: Wiley-Blackwell, 2010), pp. 268–84.

Don Giovanni, trans. Ellen H. Bleiler (New York: Dover, 1964).

Fyodor Dostoyevsky, *The Brothers Karamazov*, trans. Constance Garnett, ed. Manuel Komroff (New York: Signet, 1957), pp. 184–5.

M. O'C. Drury, "Some Notes on Conversations with Wittgenstein," in Rush Rhees, ed., *Recollections of Wittgenstein* (Oxford: Oxford University Press, 1984), pp. 76–96.

Frank B. Ebersole, *Things We Know: Fourteen Essays on Problems of Knowledge* (Eugene: University of Oregon Books, 1967).

Frank B. Ebersole, "The Analysis of Human Actions," in his *Language and Perception: Essays in the Philosophy of Language* (Washington, D.C.: University Press of America, 1979), pp. 199–222.

George Eliot, *Middlemarch* (New York: New American Library, 1964).

T. S. Eliot, *Four Quartets* (San Diego: Harcourt Brace Jovanovich, 1988).

Euripides, *The Medea*, trans. Rex Warner, in David Grene and Richard Lattimore, eds., *The Complete Greek Tragedies, Euripides I* (Chicago: University of Chicago Press, 1955), pp. 55–108.

Simon Evnine, *Donald Davidson* (Stanford: Stanford University Press, 1991).

K. T. Fann, ed., "Assessments of the Man and the Philosopher," in *Ludwig Wittgenstein: The Man and His Philosophy* (New York: Dell, 1967).

Raimond Gaita, *A Common Humanity: Thinking about Love and Truth and Justice* (London: Routledge, 2000).

Raimond Gaita, *Good and Evil: An Absolute Conception* (London: Routledge, 2004).

Judith Genova, in *Wittgenstein: A Way of Seeing* (London: Routledge, 1995).

Hans-Johann Glock, *A Wittgenstein Dictionary* (Oxford: Blackwell, 1996).

Johann Wolfgang von Goethe, *From My Life: Poetry and Truth*, trans. Robert R. Heitner, ed. Thomas P. Saine and Jeffrey L. Sammons (Princeton: Princeton University Press, 1994).

Goethe, *Wilhelm Meister's Apprenticeship*, ed. and trans. Eric A. Blackall in cooperation with Victor Lange (Princeton: Princeton University Press, 1995).

Warren Goldfarb, "I Want You to Bring Me a Slab: Remarks on the Opening Sections of the 'Philosophical Investigations,'" *Synthese* 56, 1983: 265–82.

Nelson Goodman, *Ways of Worldmaking* (Indianapolis: Hackett, 1978).

Mitchell Green, *Self-Expression* (Oxford: Oxford University Press, 2007).

Charles Griswold, *Forgiveness: A Philosophical Exploration* (Cambridge: Cambridge University Press, 2007).

Gary Gutting, "Rorty's Critique of Epistemology," in Charles Guignon and David R. Hiley, ed., *Richard Rorty* (Cambridge: Cambridge University Press, 2003), pp. 41–60.

246 BIBLIOGRAPHY

P. M. S. Hacker, *Wittgenstein's Place in Twentieth-Century Analytic Philosophy* (Oxford: Blackwell, 1996), p. 100.

P. M. S. Hacker, "Is There Anything It Is Like to Be a Bat?," *Philosophy* 77, 2002: 157–74.

Garry L. Hagberg, *Meaning and Interpretation: Wittgenstein, Henry James, and Literary Knowledge* (Ithaca: Cornell University Press, 1994).

Garry L. Hagberg, "Apollo's Revenge," *Historical Reflections/Reflexions Historiques*, 21, 1995: 437–49.

Garry L. Hagberg, *Art as Language: Wittgenstein, Meaning and Aesthetic Theory* (Ithaca: Cornell University Press, 1995).

Garry L. Hagberg, "Wittgenstein's Aesthetics," *Stanford Encyclopedia of Philosophy* (Palo Alto: Stanford University, 2007).

Garry L. Hagberg, "Wittgenstein's Voice: Reading, Self-Understanding, and the Genre of *Philosophical Investigations*," *Poetics Today* 28(3), Fall 2007: 499–526.

Garry L. Hagberg, *Describing Ourselves: Wittgenstein and Autobiographical Consciousness* (Oxford: Clarendon Press, 2008).

Garry L. Hagberg, "Jazz Improvisation and Ethical Interaction: A Sketch of the Connections," in Garry L. Hagberg, ed., *Art and Ethical Criticism* (Oxford: Blackwell, 2008), pp. 259–85.

Garry L. Hagberg, "Implication in Interpretation: Wittgenstein, Artistic Content, and 'The Field of a Word'," in Daniele Moyal-Sharrock, Volker Munz, and Annalisa Coliva, eds., *Mind, Language, and Action: Proceedings of the 36th International Wittgenstein Symposium* (Berlin: De Gruyter, 2015), pp. 45–63.

Garry L. Hagberg, "Wittgenstein, Verbal Creativity, and the Expansion of Artistic Style," in S. Greve and J. Macha, eds., *Wittgenstein and the Creativity of Language* (London: Palgrave, 2015), pp. 141–76.

Garry L. Hagberg, "Word and Object: Museums and the Matter of Meaning," in *Philosophy*, Supplementary Volume: *Philosophy and Museums* (Cambridge: Cambridge University Press, 2016), pp. 261–93.

Garry L. Hagberg, "In Language, beyond Words: Literary Interpretation and the Verbal Imagination," in Dirk-Martin Grube, ed., *Interpretation and Meaning in Philosophy and Religion* (Leiden: Brill, 2016), pp. 74–95.

Garry L. Hagberg, "Othello's Paradox: The Place of Character in Literary Experience," in Garry L. Hagberg, ed., *Fictional Characters, Real Problems: The Search for Ethical Content in Literature* (New York: Oxford University Press, 2016), pp. 59–82.

Garry L. Hagberg, "Playing as One: Ensemble Improvisation, Collective Intention, and Group Attention," in George Lewis and Ben Piekut, eds., *Oxford Handbook of Critical Improvisation Studies* (New York: Oxford University Press, 2016), pp. 481–99.

Garry L. Hagberg, "The Ensemble as Plural Subject: Jazz Improvisation, Collective Intention, and Group Agency," in Eric Clarke and Mark Doffman, eds., *Creativity, Improvisation, and Collaboration: Perspectives on the Performance of Contemporary Music* (Oxford: Oxford University Press, 2017), pp. 300–13.

Garry L. Hagberg, "In the Ruins of Self-Knowledge: Oedipus Unmade," in Paul Woodruff, ed., *The Oedipus Plays of Sophocles: Philosophical Perspectives* (Oxford: Oxford University Press, 2018), pp. 65–98.

Garry L. Hagberg, "A Portrait of Consciousness: Joyce's *Ulysses* as Philosophical Psychology," in Philip Kitcher, ed., *James Joyce's Ulysses: Philosophical Perspectives* (Oxford: Oxford University Press, 2020), pp. 63–99.

Garry L. Hagberg, "Kivy's Mystery: On What the Formalist Can (or Could) Hear," *Journal of Aesthetics and Art Criticism*, 2021: 366–76.

BIBLIOGRAPHY 247

Garry L. Hagberg, "The Mind in Time: Proust, Involuntary Memory, and the Adventure in Perception," in Anna Elsner and Tom Stern, eds., *Proust*, Routledge Philosophical Minds (2022).

Jane Heal, "Wittgenstein on Dialogue," in T. J. Smiley, ed., *Philosophical Dialogues: Plato, Hume, Wittgenstein*, Proceedings of the British Academy 85 (Oxford: Oxford University Press, 1995), pp. 63–83.

Georg Hegel, *Werke*, 15:28; translated as *Aesthetics: Lectures on Fine Art*, trans. T. M. Knox (Oxford: Oxford University Press, 1975), p. 806.

Johann Gottfried Herder, *Shakespeare*, trans. and ed. Gregory Moore (Princeton: Princeton University Press, 2008).

David Hume, "Of the Standard of Taste" (1757), reprinted in Alex Neill and Aaron Ridley, eds., *The Philosophy of Art: Readings Ancient and Modern* (New York: McGraw-Hill, 1995), pp. 255–68.

Henry James, Preface to *Roderick Hudson*, in *The Novels and Tales of Henry James*, Vol. 1 (New York: Scribner's, 1907).

Henry James, "The Middle Years," in Frank Kermode, ed., *The Figure in the Carpet and Other Stories* (London: Penguin: 1986), pp. 235–58.

William James, "The Stream of Thought," in Frederick Burkhardt, ed., *The Works of William James: The Principles of Psychology*, 3 vols. (Cambridge, MA: Harvard University Press, 1981 [orig. pub. 1890]).

William James, *The Works of William James: The Principles of Psychology*, 3 vols., ed. Frederick Burkhardt (Cambridge, MA: Harvard University Press, 1981 [orig. pub. 1890]).

William James, *The Works of William James: Essays in Radical Empiricism*, ed. Frederick Burkhardt (Cambridge, MA: Harvard University Press, 1976 [orig. pub. 1904]).

William James, *The Works of William James: Pragmatism*, ed. Frederick Burkhardt (Cambridge, MA: Harvard University Press, 1975 [orig. pub. 1907]).

Eileen John, "Literature and the Idea of Morality," in Garry L. Hagberg and Walter Jost, eds., *The Blackwell Companion to the Philosophy of Literature* (Malden: Wiley-Blackwell, 2010), pp. 285–99.

James Joyce, *A Portrait of the Artist as a Young Man* (New York: Viking, 1972).

Joseph Kerman, *Opera as Drama* (New York: Vintage, 1952).

Frank Kermode, *The Sense of an Ending* (Oxford: Oxford University Press, 1967).

Frank Kermode, ed., *Selected Prose of T. S. Eliot* (New York: Harcourt Brace Jovanovich Farrar, Straus and Giroux, 1975).

Frank Kermode, "Memory," in his *Pieces of My Mind* (New York: Farrar, Straus, Giroux, 2003), pp. 289–306.

John King, "Recollections of Wittgenstein," in Rush Rhees, ed., *Recollections of Wittgenstein* (Oxford: Oxford University Press, 1984), pp. 68–75.

Michael Krausz, *Rightness and Reasons: Interpretation in Cultural Practice* (Ithaca: Cornell University Press, 1993).

Michael Krausz, *Limits of Rightness* (Lanham: Rowman and Littlefield, 2000).

Michael Krausz, *Interpretation and Transformation: Explorations in Art and the Self* (Leiden: Brill, 2007).

Milan Kundera, *The Unbearable Lightness of Being* (New York: Harper Perennial, 1987).

Milan Kundera, *Slowness* (New York: Harper Perennial, 1997).

Milan Kundera, *Identity* (New York: Harper Perennial, 1998).

Joshua Landy, "A Nation of Madame Bovarys: On the Possibility and Desirability of Moral Improvement through Fiction," in Garry L. Hagberg, ed., *Art and Ethical Criticism* (Oxford: Blackwell, 2008), pp. 63–94.

248 BIBLIOGRAPHY

Jonathan Lear, "Katharsis," *Phronesis* 33(3), 1988: 297–326.

Jonathan Lear, "Transcendental Anthropology," in his *Open Minded: Working out the Logic of the Soul* (Cambridge, MA: Harvard University Press, 1998), pp. 247–81.

Alasdair MacIntyre, *After Virtue* (Notre Dame: University of Notre Dame Press, 1984).

Norman Malcolm, "Introduction," in Rush Rhees, ed., *Recollections of Wittgenstein* (Oxford: Oxford University Press, 1984), p. xviii.

Norman Malcolm, "Language Game (2)," in his *Wittgensteinian Themes: Essays 1978–1989* (Ithaca: Cornell University Press, 1995), pp. 172–81.

James McConkey, *The Anatomy of Memory* (New York: Oxford University Press, 1996).

Brian McGuinness, "Freud and Wittgenstein," in *Wittgenstein and His Times*, ed. Brian McGuinness (Oxford: Basil Blackwell, 1982), pp. 27–43.

Jonathan Miller, ed., *Don Giovanni: Myths of Seduction and Betrayal* (New York: Shocken, 1990).

Ray Monk, "Getting inside Heisenberg's Head," in Garry L. Hagberg and Walter Jost, eds., *A Companion to the Philosophy of Literature* (Oxford: Wiley-Blackwell, 2010), pp. 453–64.

Richard Moran, "Self-Knowledge: Discovery, Resolution, and Undoing," in Brie Gertler, ed., *Privileged Access: Philosophical Accounts of Self-Knowledge* (Aldershot: Ashgate, 2003), pp. 159–77.

Stephen Mulhall, *Wittgenstein's Private Language* (Oxford: Oxford University Press, 2006).

Iris Murdoch, *The Fire and the Sun: Why Plato Banished the Artists* (Oxford: Oxford University Press, 1977).

Iris Murdoch, *The Sea, The Sea* (Harmondsworth: Penguin, 1978).

Vladimir Nabokov, *Speak, Memory* (New York: Vintage, 1989).

Thomas Nagel, "What Is It Like to Be a Bat?," *The Philosophical Review*, 83(4), 1974: 435–50.

Alexander Nehamas, *Nietzsche: Life as Literature* (Cambridge, MA: Harvard University Press, 1985).

Friedrich Nietzsche, *Twilight of the Idols*, trans. R. J. Hollingdale (Harmondsworth: Penguin, 1968).

Martha C. Nussbaum, "Perceptive Equilibrium: Literary Theory and Ethical Theory," in Garry L. Hagberg and Walter Jost, eds., *The Blackwell Companion to the Philosophy of Literature* (Malden: Wiley-Blackwell, 2010), pp. 241–67.

Eric T. Olson, *The Human Animal: Personal Identity without Psychology* (New York: Oxford University Press, 1997).

Fania Pascal, "Wittgenstein: A Personal Memoir," in Rush Rhees, ed., *Recollections of Wittgenstein* (Oxford: Oxford University Press, 1984), pp. 12–49.

C. S. Peirce, *The Collected Papers of Charles Sanders Peirce*, ed. Charles Hartshorne and Paul Weiss (Cambridge, MA: Harvard University Press, 1931–6).

Adam Phillips, "The Telling of Selves: Notes on Psychoanalysis and Autobiography," in his *On Flirtation: Psychoanalytical Essays on the Uncommitted Life* (Cambridge, MA: Harvard University Press, 1994), pp. 65–75.

George Pitcher, "About the Same," in Alice Ambrose and Morris Lazarowitz, eds., *Ludwig Wittgenstein: Philosophy and Language* (London: Allen and Unwin, 1972), pp. 120–39.

Hilary Putnam, "Meaning and Reference," in A. P. Martinich and David Sosa, eds., *Analytic Philosophy* (Oxford: Blackwell, 2001), pp. 90–6.

W. V. O. Quine, "Two Dogmas of Empiricism," reprinted in his *From a Logical Point of View* (Cambridge, MA: Harvard University Press, 1953), pp. 20–46.

W. V. O. Quine, *The Web of Belief* (New York: Random House, 1970).

BIBLIOGRAPHY   249

Rupert Read, Phil Hutchinson, and Wes Sharrock, *There Is No Such Thing as a Social Science: In Defence of Peter Winch* (London: Routledge, 2008).

Rush Rhees, "Wittgenstein's Builders," in his *Discussions of Wittgenstein* (London: Routledge and Kegan Paul, 1970), pp. 71–84.

Rush Rhees, "The Tree of Nebuchadnezzar," *The Human World*, 4, 1971: 23–26.

Rush Rhees, ed., *Recollections of Wittgenstein* (Oxford: Oxford University Press, 1984).

Rush Rhees, *Wittgenstein and the Possibility of Discourse*, 2nd ed., ed. D. Z. Phillips (Oxford: Blackwell, 2006).

Richard Rorty, *Philosophy and the Mirror of Nature* (Princeton: Princeton University Press, 1979).

Richard Rorty, *Contingency, Irony, and Solidarity* (Cambridge: Cambridge University Press, 1989), Chapter 2, "The Contingency of Selfhood," pp. 23–43.

Jean-Jacques Rousseau, *The Confessions*, trans. J. M. Cohen (Harmondsworth: Penguin, 1953).

Jean-Jacques Rousseau, *Reveries of the Solitary Walker*, trans. Russell Goulbourne (Oxford: Oxford University Press, 2011).

Gilbert Ryle, *The Concept of Mind* (London: Routledge, 2009 [orig. pub. 1949]).

Edward W. Said, *Representations of the Intellectual* (New York: Random House, 1994).

Jean-Paul Sartre, *The Words*, trans. Bernard Frechtman (New York: George Braziller, 1964).

Joachim Schulte, *Experience and Expression: Wittgenstein's Philosophy of Psychology* (Oxford: Oxford University Press, 1993).

Roger Scruton, "A Bit of Help from Wittgenstein," *British Journal of Aesthetics*, 51(3), 2011: 309–19.

William Shakespeare, *Othello, the Moor of Venice*, in W. G. Clarke and W. A. Wright, eds., *The Plays and Sonnets of William Shakespeare*, Vol. 2 (Chicago: University of Chicago Press, 1952).

John J. Stuhr, ed., *Pragmatism and Classical American Philosophy: Essential Readings and Interpretive Essays*, 2nd ed. (New York: Oxford University Press, 2000).

Ronald Suter, *Interpreting Wittgenstein: A Cloud of Philosophy, a Drop of Grammar* (Philadelphia: Temple University Press, 1989).

Bela Szabados, *In Light of Chaos* (Saskatoon: Thistledown Press, 1990).

Leo Tolstoy, *What Is Art?*, trans. Aylmer Maude (Oxford: Oxford University Press, 1898).

Charles Travis, *Occasion Sensitivity: Selected Essays* (Oxford: Oxford University Press, 2008).

Kirk Varnedoe, *A Fine Disregard: What Makes Modern Art Modern* (New York: Abrams, 1990).

Helen Vendler, *The Art of Shakespeare's Sonnets* (Cambridge, MA: Harvard University Press, 1997).

Helen Vendler, *Poets Thinking: Pope, Whitman, Dickinson, Yeats* (Cambridge, MA: Harvard University Press, 2004).

Virgil, *The Aeneid*, trans. Robert Fitzgerald (New York: Random House, 1983).

Kendall Walton, "Categories of Art," *The Philosophical Review*, 79(3), July 1970: 334–67.

Samuel C. Wheeler III, "Language and Literature," in Kirk Ludwig, ed., *Donald Davidson* (Cambridge: Cambridge University Press, 2003), pp. 183–206.

Bernard Williams, "Don Juan as an Idea," in Julian Rushton, ed., *Don Giovanni* (Cambridge: Cambridge University Press, 1981), pp. 81–91.

Michael Williams, "Rorty on Knowledge and Truth," in Charles Guignon and David R. Hiley, eds., *Richard Rorty* (Cambridge: Cambridge University Press, 2003), pp. 61–80.

Edwin Williamson, *Borges: A Life* (New York: Viking, 2004).

250 BIBLIOGRAPHY

Peter Winch, *The Idea of a Social Science* (London: Routledge, 1958).

John Wisdom, *Philosophy and Psycho-Analysis* (Oxford: Basil Blackwell, 1953).

Ludwig Wittgenstein, *The Blue and Brown Books* (Oxford: Basil Blackwell, 1958).

Ludwig Wittgenstein, *Lectures and Conversations on Aesthetics, Psychology, and Religious Belief*, ed. Cyril Barrett (Oxford: Basil Blackwell, 1966).

Ludwig Wittgenstein, *Philosophical Remarks*, trans. Raymond Hargreaves and Roger White (New York: Harper and Row, 1975).

Ludwig Wittgenstein, *Culture and Value*, ed. G. H. von Wright and Heikki Nyman, trans. Peter Winch (Oxford: Basil Blackwell, 1980).

Ludwig Wittgenstein, *Philosophical Investigations*, revised 4th ed., ed. P. M. S. Hacker and Joachim Schulte, trans. G. E. M. Anscombe, P. M. S. Hacker, and Joachim Schulte (Malden: Wiley-Blackwell, 2009).

Richard Wollheim, "The Art Lesson," in his *On Art and the Mind* (Cambridge, MA: Harvard University Press, 1974), pp. 130–51.

Richard Wollheim, *The Thread of Life* (Cambridge, MA: Harvard University Press, 1984).

Richard Wollheim, "Art, Interpretation, and Perception," in his *The Mind and Its Depths* (Cambridge, MA: Harvard University Press, 1993), pp. 132–43.

Virginia Woolf, "A Sketch of the Past," in her *Moments of Being*, 2nd ed., ed. Jeanne Schulkind (San Diego: Harcourt, 1985), pp. 61–160.

G. H. von Wright, ed., *A Portrait of Wittgenstein as a Young Man, from the Diary of David Hume Pinsent 1912–1914* (Oxford: Basil Blackwell, 1990).

Index

Note: Footnote numbers are indicated by 'n.' following the page numbers.

For the benefit of digital users, indexed terms that span two pages (e.g., 52–53) may, on occasion, appear on only one of those pages.

Aeneid/Aeneas (Virgil) 102–3, 196–8, 229–30
  act of resolution 189–96
  Aeneas' final act 189–96
  moral psychology 195–6, 199–200
  recognition 191–4
  self-constitutive beliefs 190–2
  self-definition 191–2, 195–6, 198–9
Aeschylus: *Oresteia* 185–7
aesthetic experience 240–1
  American pragmatism 19
  beliefs 170–1
  music 7
  relational aesthetic experience 7–8
  self-constitutive power of 19, 170–1
  selfhood and 238–9
  self-investigative work within 25n.45
  see also art
aesthetics
  aesthetic life 36–7
  empirical explanation 234
  interpretive pluralism 52
  see also art; aesthetic experience
American pragmatism 241
  aesthetic (literary) experience
    self-formation 19
  Cartesian model of selfhood: critique of 3–8, 11, 16–17
  consciousness as relational 5–8, 17
  literary experience and relational conception of selfhood 7, 13–14, 17–19
  relational conception of experience 5–11, 13, 17–18, 98–9, 183n.28, 209–10
  relational conception of selfhood 3–13, 15–17, 19–20, 47–8
  see also James, William; Mead, George Herbert; Peirce, C. S.; Royce, Josiah
Amis, Martin 35n.60
architecture
  architecture as gesture 90–2
  architecture of selfhood 86, 95–6, 99–100, 238–9
  draughtsman/autobiographer comparison 96–9

language/architecture comparison 92–3
  thinker/draughtsman comparison 86–100
  Wittgenstein's work on modernist house for his sister, Vienna 89, 95, 100
Aristotle 100–7
  action, representation of 101–2, 104–6, 110
  categorical exactitude 60–1
  catharsis 102, 104–6
  episodic structure as the weakest structure 131–2
  ethical theory 146–7
  habits 121
  love 128–9
  mimesis 101–2, 105–6, 116–17
  Nicomachean Ethics 33n.58, 116–17, 128–9, 146–7, 199–200, 215
  odiousness of a bad man falling 132–3
  plot: beginning, middle, end 102–3
  plot: defining elements 101–6
  plot structure 104–7, 110, 114, 116–17
  Poetics 100, 108, 110, 116–17, 132–3
  recognition 106–7, 122–3
  tragedy 102, 104–7
  unity of the plot 101–2, 104, 106
art
  artistic boundary indeterminacy 54, 57–8, 72–3, 85
  mimesis 140–1
  work of art as existing for the spectator 196–8
  work of art as mimetic representation of the human self 239–40
  see also architecture; aesthetic experience; aesthetics; literature; music/musical comparisons
Austin, J. L. 92–3, 160–1, 166–7, 174–8, 237–8
autobiographical language 240–1
  catharsis 111
  mimesis 200–1, 204
  psychophysical law and 78
  self-constitutive power of 56
  self-revelatory language 145–8
  see also autobiographical writing; language

252 INDEX

autobiographical understanding
  autobiographical/biographical understanding
    comparison 41
  autobiographical content (inward) 41–5
  autobiographical reflection 21, 91n.9, 123–4,
    142, 177–9, 200–1
  holism 75–8
  relational conception of words 33–4
  relational-linguistic nature of 21
  self-composition 48
  self-directed thinking 178
  self-knowledge 42–4, 48
  self-understanding 41
  sense of closure 47
  understanding a life on the model of literary
    understanding 48
  word meaning 48
  see also autobiographical understanding:
    structures; literary characters and
    autobiographical understanding;
    self-understanding
autobiographical understanding: structures 85
  architecture of selfhood 86, 95–6, 99–100,
    238–9
  Aristotelian frameworks 100–7, 110,
    114, 116
  catharsis/narrative catharsis 107–17, 238–9
  draughtsman/autobiographer
    comparison 96–9
  life-narrative simplification 89–90, 111–12
  life-structuring 111, 116–17
  memory 111–14
  mimetic narratives 108
  plot structure 104–12, 116–17
  self-representation 111
  Wittgenstein: thinker/draughtsman
    comparison 86–100
  see also Aristotle; Wittgenstein, Ludwig
autobiographical writing
  autobiographical truth/veracity 46–7, 74–5,
    79–84, 100, 105–6, 114–16, 141
  challenges 83–5, 100–1
  childhood events 83–4
  constructivist view 55–6
  "finished" autobiography 116–17, 141, 209–10
  language-games of the self 98–9
  propositional attitudes and person's
    behavior 73
  as reading off internal content and reporting it
    externally 24
  realist view: autobiography as *ex post facto*
    descriptions 55–6
  scheme/content dichotomy 80–1
  self-deception 107–8, 116

  self-doubt 80–1
  working on oneself 95–100
  see also autobiographical language

Bambrough, Renford 60n.4
behaviorism/behavioristic reduction 51, 73–4
  Don Giovanni 121–7, 132, 134
beliefs 162–78, 239–40
  aesthetic experience 170–1
  context-independent belief 193
  Davidson, Donald 75–6, 78, 168–9, 204
  Davidson, Donald: beliefs and thought 165–8
  entertained belief 167–8, 182–3, 187–9, 199–200
  holism 75–8
  isolated behaviors and 75–6
  literary characters: webs of beliefs 166–70,
    184–7, 189
  reader 167–71
  self-constitutive three-tiered reader's
    experience 184–205
  self-directed belief 198n.52
  settled belief 187–90
  understanding of persons's beliefs and
    understanding of them as persons 37n.62,
    187–9
  see also making up one's mind; self-
    constitutive belief
biography/biographical writing
  autobiographical/biographical understanding
    comparison 41
  biographers' understanding of their
    subjects 38, 40–1
  catharsis 105–6
  challenges 85
  holism 75–6
  scheme/content dichotomy 80–1
  truth 79–80
  see also Conradi, Peter J.: *Iris Murdoch: A Life*
bootstrapping 195–6
  bootstrapping of selfhood 69–70
  non-pejorative bootstrapping 174–5, 217, 241
  self-forgiveness 213–15, 217–18
Borges, Jorge Luis
  "Book of Sand, The" 182–4
  "Nothingness of Personality, The" 182n.27
  self-constitutive reading 182–3
Brothers Karamozov, The (by Dostoevsky) 52, 235
  Alyosha Karamozov 220, 226, 231–4, 236–8
  Dmitri Karamazov 220
  fixity of meaning 221
  Ivan Karamazov 220, 226
  Wittgenstein and 226–7
  Wittgenstein's rereading of 221–2, 226, 233–4
  see also Dostoevsky, Fyodor

INDEX 253

Campbell, James 15–16
Camus, Albert 13–14
Cavell, Stanley 40, 160, 206–7, 214, 227, 228n.34, 237–8
  aspect blindness 223–4
  aspect seeing (Cavell's list) 222–3, 229, 236–7
  Claim of Reason, The 126n.5, 222–5
  learning the meaning of a word/scene of instruction 34
  Little Did I Know 33n.58, 42n.67
  "Must We Mean What We Say" 158–61
  names 232–4
  reading a person 225
  "our relations to our words" 222, 224, 235–7
  physiognomy and words 223–5, 230
  rereading 222, 225
  Wittgenstein on seeing-as 222–4
Chekhov, Anton: "Gusev" 84–5
Christo: *Wrapped Reichstag* 54–5, 57, 69–70, 82–3
  boundary indeterminacy 54, 57–8
  unfolding self-constitution 69–70
Cioffi, Frank 234–5
Coetzee, John Maxwell 13–14
Cohen, Ted 160
comparison
  comparison and relational description 21–2
  literary experience and making comparisons 12–14, 18, 20
  self-understanding through literary characters comparisons 22
  word-borne comparisons 21
connective analysis 88–9, 97–8
Conradi, Peter J.: *Iris Murdoch: A Life* 38–41
  impersonation 38–9
  Murdoch and Bayley's word meaning 39–40
  word meaning 39–40, 48
consequentialism 216–17
constructive realism
  Krausz, Michael 54–8, 69
  self-interpretation 69, 71–2
constructivism 56
  autobiography: constructivist view 55–6
  cultural object/entity 57
  interpretation 53, 57–8, 63–4
  multiplism and 53, 68–9
  radical constructivism 56, 66–7, 69–70
  self-interpretation 66, 68, 70–2
contextualism 27n.48

Dante 93–5, 185–7, 237
  Divine Comedy, The 185–7, 229–30
Danto, Arthur 204–5
  reader/text relation: metaphorical structure of 196–200, 204–5

self/text relation: metaphorical structure of 162, 200–1
Da Ponte, Lorenzo: *Don Giovanni* 118, 120–6
  see also *Don Giovanni*
Davidson, Donald 75–85, 196–8
  beliefs 75–6, 78, 168–9, 204
  beliefs and thought 165–8
  boundedness of human experience 75–8, 81–2, 85
  empiricism, critique of 76–7
  explanatory singularism 75–6
  holism 75–9
  interpretation 167–9, 176–7, 199–200
  metaphors 176–7
  mind as a theatre 75
  "Psychology as Philosophy" 78
  psychophysical law 78–9, 81–2
  scheme/content dichotomy 80–2
  "Thought and Talk" 166–7
  thought/speech relation 164–7
Debussy, Claude 114–15
Descartes, René
  Cartesian model of selfhood 3–5, 19–21, 24, 50, 204
  Cartesian model of selfhood: critique of 3–8, 11, 16–17, 50
  Cartesian model of selfhood and self-understanding 50–1
  neat inner/outer dichotomy 50–1
  universal doubt 4–5
Diamond, Cora 160
Dickinson, Emily 13–14, 184–5
Don Giovanni (by Mozart and da Ponte) 118–34
  behaviorism 121–7, 132, 134
  Commendatore's death 119–21, 132
  Commendatore's statue 129–33
  concealment/dissimulation 118–19, 127–8, 130, 134
  deception 128–9
  Giovanni's death 130–2
  Giovanni's episodic sensory diversion 121–2, 130–1, 134
  Giovanni's inner vacuity 117, 119–20, 124–31, 133–4
  Giovanni's mask as redundant 134
  humane acknowledgment as precondition of self-acknowledgment 120–3, 126–7
  Leporello/Giovanni comparison 119–20, 123, 126–9
  Leporello's question 119–20, 125, 134
  love 128–9
  masked ball 127–8, 134
  most powerful line in the opera 133
  music/musical comparisons 125–6, 130–1, 133

254 INDEX

Don Giovanni (by Mozart and da Ponte) (*cont.*)
  opening scene 118–19, 128–9, 132
  opera's episodic design 123, 131–2
  person-perception as precondition of
    self-perception 124–7, 130, 132, 134
  precondition of selfhood/inner human
    content 121, 130–1, 133
  self in *absentia* 117–34
  self-ignorance 131–2
  self-reflection 122, 130–2
  tragedy 121, 130–3
Dostoevsky, Fyodor 13–14, 74–5, 79,
  185–7, 222
  Notes from Underground 155n.26
  Wittgenstein and 221–2, 226–7, 233–4
  see also *Brothers Karamozov, The*
doubt
  Descartes: universal doubt 4–5
  false doubt 81
  as relationally embedded 4–5, 16–17
  self-doubt 80–1

Eldridge, Richard 160
Eliot, T. S. 158n.29, 196–8, 204–5
  Four Quartets 163–4, 173–4, 204–5, 219
Emerson, Ralph Waldo 241
empiricism
  atomistic conception of experience 76–7,
    98–9, 186n.35
  British empiricism 7–8, 185–7, 209–10
  critique of 7–8, 75–7, 234–5
  James, William: radical empiricism 5, 10,
    17–18, 173–4
  Locke, John 5–6, 186n.35, 209–10
Escher, M. C. 89–90, 98–9, 213–14
essentialism 1
Euripides: *The Medea* 185–9
experience
  boundedness of human experience 75–8,
    81–2, 85
  context-sensitive and sensibility-sensitive
    experience 82–3
  empiricism: atomistic conception of
    experience 76–7, 98–9, 186n.35
  holism 75–9, 84–5
  interpenetration of experience 82–4
  relational conception of 5–11, 13, 17–18,
    77–8, 98–9, 183n.28, 209–10
  repetition of experience as impossible 6–7,
    82–3, 83n.33, 182–4
  "resonances" between experiences 84–5
  self-constitutive power of experience 163
  see also literary experience
extensionalism 240–1

Freud, Sigmund 74–5, 108–10

Genova, Judith 90–2
George Eliot (Mary Ann Evans) 17–18, 79,
  185–7
  Middlemarch 185–7
Goethe, Johann Wolfgang von 196–8
  From My Life: Poetry and Truth 178–80,
    179n.24
  self-directed soliloquy 178–9
  Sorrows of Young Werther, The 179n.24
Goodman, Nelson 54–5
Griswold, Charles 209–14, 217–18

Hegel, Georg 196–8, 200–1, 204
Heraclitus 1–2, 6–7, 13–14, 16–17, 31, 173–4
holism
  autobiographical understanding 75–8
  beliefs 75–8
  Davidson, Donald 75–9
  experience 75–9, 84–5
Homer 93–5, 166–7, 185–7
  Iliad 229–30
  Odyssey 105–6, 187–9, 196–8, 229–30
Horace 13–14, 218–19, 222
Hume, David 236–7
  critique of 7–8
  "Of the Standard of Taste" 218–19
  preferring Ovid at twenty, Horace at forty, and
    Tacitus at fifty 13–14, 218–20
  scheme/content dichotomy 80–1

interpretation
  "Community of Interpretation" 13
  constructivism 53, 57–8, 63–4
  cultural object/entity 52–3, 57, 62–3, 66
  interpretive practices 54–9, 64, 71–2
  literature 13
  multiple interpretations and singular
    selves 52–9
  multiplism/interpretive pluralism 52–3, 68–9
  radical constructivism 56, 66–7, 69–70
  realism 53, 57–8, 63–4
  Royce, Josiah 11–13
  singularism 52–3, 68–9, 72
  singularism vs multiplism debate 53–4, 62–3,
    66, 68–9
  Wollheim, Richard 99n.25
  see also interpretive rightness; Krausz, Michael;
    self-interpretation
interpretive rightness 53, 59–73, 240
  Aristotle: categorical exactitude 60–1
  de-psychologizing of 65–6
  interpretive understanding 62–4

Krausz, Michael 53–4, 62–4, 66–7
  limits of rightness 53–4
  self-interpretation 53, 67–72
  Wittgenstein, Ludwig 59–66
  see also interpretation; Krausz, Michael;
    self-interpretation

James, Henry 10, 17–18, 79
  "relations end nowhere" 8–9, 116–17, 140–1
  see also "Middle Years, The"
James, William 5–11, 26
  British empiricism, critique of 7–8, 209–10
  consciousness as relational 5–8, 17
  Essays in Radical Empiricism 10
  literary experience and relational construction
    of selfhood 7, 17
  naming 8–10, 17–18
  radical empiricism 5, 10, 17–18, 173–4
  relational aesthetic experience 7–8
  relational conception of experience 5–11,
    17–18, 98–9, 183n.28, 209–10
  relational conception of language 8–10, 17
  relational conception of selfhood 5–7, 10–11,
    15–17, 19–20
  relational perception 6, 10–11, 26, 31, 43–4
  repetition of experience as impossible 6–7,
    83n.33, 183–4
  rhythm of language 9–10
  sensibility 6
  "Stream of Thought, The" 5
  "What Pragmatism Means" 10
  "World of Pure Experience, A" 10
  see also American pragmatism
Joyce, James 198n.52

Kant, Immanuel 54–5, 80–1
Kermode, Frank
  on Nabokov's *Speak, Memory* 47–8
  on Rousseau's *Confessions* 47
  on Wordsworth's *Prelude* 48–9
King, John 227
King Lear (by William Shakespeare) 117,
    149–61, 227
  Cordelia and King Lear 149–53, 156–61
  deafness to words/silence 149–59
  Fool and King Lear 152–5, 158–9
  knowledge of others 150–1
  language, comments on 149, 153–61,
    159n.32
  language and identity 155–8
  language and self-composition 149, 155–6
  love 149–53, 156, 159–61
  metaphors 151
  music/musical comparisons 157–9

performance seen by Wittgenstein 227
  self-deception 155–6
  self-knowledge, lack of 149, 152–4, 159–60
  self-reflection 153–4, 159n.30, 170–1
  tragedy 149, 152–3, 156–9, 161
  word meaning 153–6, 158–61
  see also Shakespeare, William
Krausz, Michael 53–9, 64
  artistic boundary indeterminacy 54, 57–8,
    72–3, 85
  Christo: *Wrapped Reichstag* 54–5, 57–8
  constructive realism 54–8, 69
  interpretive rightness 53–4, 62–4, 66–7
  limits of rightness 53–4
  Limits of Rightness 52, 59
  multiplism 52
  radical constructivism 56, 66–7, 69–70
  *Rightness and Reasons: Interpretation in
    Cultural Practice* 52n.1
  selfhood: boundary indeterminacy 72–3, 85
  self-interpretation 52, 54, 66–72
  singularism vs multiplism debate 53–4, 62–3,
    66, 68–9
  therapeutic project 66–7
  Wittgenstein, Ludwig and 54–6, 58–9, 61–3,
    67, 72–3
  see also interpretation
Kundera, Milan
  Identity 23n.43, 182n.27
  Slowness 23n.43
  see also "Words Misunderstood"

language
  ideal language 134–6, 145–6
  King Lear 149, 153–61, 159n.32
  King Lear: language and self-composition 149,
    155–6
  language/architecture comparison 92–3
  language/character intrinsic
    connection 150–1
  language/philosophy relation 160–1
  moral philosophy and philosophy of language
    in literary form 142–3
  relational conception of language 8–10,
    17, 24
  relation between language, identity, and self-
    understanding 118
  self-constitutive power of 163, 200–2
  self-defining power of 200–1
  selfhood and 164–5
  thought/speech relation 164–6
  see also autobiographical language
Larkin, Philip 171
Lear, Jonathan 110–11, 113–14

256 INDEX

literary characters
  catharsis and 105–6
  character-constitutive beliefs 185
  readers's identification with 18, 193–4,
    196–205, 213–14
  relationally and self-comparatively engaging
    with 13–14, 18
  self-interpretations of 168–9
  self-knowledge and 193–4
  self-reflection 22, 193–4
  webs of beliefs 166–70, 184–7, 189
  webs of beliefs and reader 167–71
literary characters and autobiographical
    understanding 19–49
  comparison and relational description 21–2
  literary character: understanding another
    character 22, 38
  reader: understanding a literary character 22, 38
  relational conception of words 26
  self-understanding through literary characters
    comparisons 22
  see also autobiographical understanding;
    "Words Misunderstood"
literary engagement 240–1
  literary absorption 17–18, 23, 179, 181, 184–5,
    189, 198–9, 204, 216–17
  as private experience 181
  self-constitutive power of 6, 18, 164–5,
    174–5, 184
  self-forgiveness and 212–13
  self-negotiated identities 18
  see also literary experience
literary experience 16, 162
  making comparisons 12–14, 18, 20
  relational conception of selfhood and 7,
    13–14, 17–19, 21
  self-knowledge and 23
  self-negotiations 13–14, 202
  see also experience; literary engagement
literature
  concept of 1–3, 16, 18–19
  family-resemblance features of 12, 16
  interpretation 13
  as laboratory 241
  literature/commercial fiction
    distinction 18–19
  literature/philosophy relation 147–50, 160–1,
    171, 174–5, 187–9
  mimesis 167–9
  philosophical value of 78–9
  relational aesthetic experience 7
  relational construction of selfhood and 7, 16–17
  self-constitutive power of 164–5, 171, 174–5,
    177–8, 185–7, 204–5

self-defining capacity of 181
universality of literary reference 196–8
see also literary characters; literary
  engagement; literary experience
Locke, John
  empiricism 5–6, 186n.35, 209–10
  *Essay Concerning Human
    Understanding* 186n.35
  scheme/content dichotomy 80–1
  Sensation/Reflection distinction 121–2
  theory of language 7–8
Lodge, David 13–14

McConkey, James 84–5
MacIntyre, Alasdair 217–18
Machiavelli, Niccolò 11–12
making up one's mind 178–96
  belief/web of belief 179–80, 182–3
  capacity to change our mind as precondition
    for self-creation 180–1
  "crossroads" indecision 193
  decision vs discovery/making up one's mind vs
    disclosing one's mind 191–2
  dialogical character of inward reflection 178,
    180–1
  Goethe's autobiographical writings 178–82
  privacy 179, 179n.24, 181
  Rorty's "contingency of selfhood" 179–80,
    182–3
  self-constitutive beliefs 180–1, 184
  self-directed soliloquy 178–9, 181
  see also beliefs; self-constitutive belief
Marcus Aurelius: *Meditations* 37n.62
Margalit, Avashai 123–4
Mead, George Herbert 14–16, 19–20
  "accepted past" 14, 238n.46
  "emergent, the " 15
  realignments of the past in memory 14–15,
    18, 238–9
  "sociality" 15–16
  see also American pragmatism
meaning see word meaning
memory
  autobiographical understanding:
    structures 111–14
  creative dimension of 113–14
  emotional memory 113
  Mead: realignments of the past in
    memory 14–15, 18, 238–9
  memory-dependent forms of writing 113–14
  memory recognition 111–13
  Nabokov, Vladimir 84–5
  verbal memory 113
  Wittgenstein, Ludwig 111–14

INDEX 257

metaphors
Davidson, Donald 176–7
King Lear 151
metaphorical identification and self-individuation 196–205, 239
metaphorical picture of the self as text 196–8
Rorty, Richard 176–7
self-description 184n.30
self-interpretation and metaphorical truth 70
"Middle Years, The" (by Henry James) 134–49
aspirations 138, 144–6
autobiographical veracity 141
context and meaning 135–7, 142–3, 145–7
displacement 136–8
heartfelt utterance 135–6, 143–6
language-games 141
late-stage high-resolution 117, 138–9, 142–4
literature and philosophy 147–8
Middle Years, The 137–40, 142–4
mimesis and creativity 140–1
moral philosophy 137–8, 142–3, 146–7
narrative closure 141
opening words 136–7
second chance at selfhood 136–9, 143–6
self-acknowledgment 139–46
self-alienation 138–9, 141–2, 144–6
self-deception 117, 145–6, 170–1
self-image borne by false self-descriptions 141, 144–6
self-integration 145–7
see also James, Henry
Milton, John: *Paradise Lost* 196–8
mimesis
Aristotle 101–2, 105–6, 116–17
art 140–1, 239–40
autobiographical language 200–1, 204
literature 167–9
"Middle Years, The" 140–1
mimetic narratives 108
tragedy 108
moral philosophy
listening 194n.47
"Middle Years, The" 137–8, 142–3, 146–7
philosophy of language in literary form and 142–3
moral psychology 99n.25, 157–8, 195–6, 199–200
Moran, Richard 202–3
Mozart, Wolfgang Amadeus 93–5, 97–8
see also *Don Giovanni*
multiplism 52
constructivism 53, 68–9
singularism vs multiplism debate 53–4, 62–3, 66, 68–9

Murdoch, Iris 185–7
comparison and relational description 21–2
diaries by 21–2, 97–8
impersonation 38–9
Nuns and Soldiers 35n.60
Sea, The Sea, The 167–8, 187–9, 196–8
second novel, work on 42–4
self-constitutive belief 167–8, 187–9
self-investigative writings 23
self-presentation 38–9
settling of belief 187–9
music/musical comparisons 29n.53, 78, 93–5, 96n.22, 102–3, 114–15, 209, 239–40
aesthetic experience 7
Don Giovanni 125–6, 130–1, 133
King Lear 157–9
"Words Misunderstood" 31, 33, 35–6, 40, 48

Nabokov, Vladimir: *Speak, Memory* 47–8, 84–5, 184
Nagel, Thomas 193n.44
name/naming
Alyosha (*The Brothers Karamozov*) 231–4, 237–8
Cavell, Stanley 232–4
James, William 8–10, 17–18
meaning of 232–3, 236–7
Wittgenstein, Ludwig 237n.45
Necker Cube 64, 66–7
Nietzsche, Friedrich 1–2, 7–8, 16
"antecendentia of action" 73–4
"Problem of Socrates, The" 172–3
Rorty, Richard and 172–5
truth/real world 172–4
Twilight of the Idols 146–7, 172–3
Nussbaum, Martha 160

Ovid 13–14, 218–20, 222
Metamorphosis 219–20

Peirce, C. S. 241
Cartesian model of selfhood: critique of 3–5, 7–8, 16–17
"How to Make Our Ideas Clear" 4
"Issues of Pragmaticism" 4–5
relational conception of selfhood 4–7, 10–11, 16–17
"Some Consequences of Four Incapacities" 3–5
see also American pragmatism
Phillips, Adam 108–10
Phillips, D. Z. 160
philosophical myth 79–80, 193, 235

258 INDEX

philosophy of language 54–5, 90–2, 136–7, 142–3, 187–9
Picasso 35, 93–5, 97–8
Portrait of Kahnweiler 240–1
Pinsent, David 29n.53
Plato
  Euthyphro 161
  moral idealism 146–7
  Socrates 121–2, 158–9, 161
  truth 172
Platonism 146–7
  literature, concept of 1–2, 13–14, 16, 18–19
Pontalis, J.-B. 108–10
propositional attitudes 73, 75–80, 83–4
Proust, Marcel 185–7
psychoanalysis 87, 108–10, 136n.10, 198n.52
psychology
  Davidson: psychophysical law 78–9, 81–2
  epistemological psychology 180–1
  moral psychology 99n.25, 157–8, 195–6, 199–200
  philosophical psychology 79

Quine, W. V. O. 75–6, 166–8

"Ramsey's Maxim" 2, 5, 56, 175n.18
reader
  beliefs 167–71
  identification with literary characters 18, 193–4, 196–205, 213–14
  imaginary identities 177–8
  making resolutions 23
  metaphorical identification and self-individuation 196–205
  reader/text relation: metaphorical structure of 196–200, 204–5
  self-constitutive three-tiered reader's experience 184–205
  self-reflection 167
  understanding a literary character 22, 38
reading
  double reading 196–200, 204–5, 213–14
  literary and historical/political imagination and 229–30
  reading out loud 226
  reflective reading 241
  self-compositional reading 238–41
  self-constitutive reading 182–3
  self-definitional reading 23
  self-directed thinking 178
  "we are what we read" 18
  see also rereading
realism
  autobiography as *ex post facto* descriptions 55–6

cultural object/entity 57
interpretation 53, 57–8, 63–4
  self-interpretation 66, 68, 70–2
  singularism and 53, 68–9
recognition
  Aeneid/Aeneas 191–4
  Aristotle 106–7, 122–3
  image-recognition 112–13
  memory recognition 111–13
  Wittgenstein, Ludwig 111–12
relational conception of selfhood 238–9
  American pragmatism 3–13, 15–17, 19–20, 47–8
  consciousness as relational 5–8, 17
  experience, relational conception of 5–11, 13, 17–18, 98–9, 183n.28, 209–10
  language, relational conception of 8–10, 17
  literary experience and 7, 13–14, 17–19, 21
  relational aesthetic experience 7–8
  relational perception 6, 10–11, 24, 26, 31
  self-forgiveness 206–7
  self-interpretation 13
  words, relational conception of 20, 24, 26
  see also selfhood
relativism
  radical relativism: self-narrative formation 217–18
  scheme/content dichotomy 80–2
rereading 206, 218–39
  aspect-perception/"seeing-as" 222–4, 227, 229, 236–7
  autobiographers and biographers as rereaders of life 235–6
  Cavell, Stanley 222, 225
  functions of 219–20
  Hume: preferring Ovid at twenty, Horace at forty, and Tacitus at fifty 13–14, 218–20
  name, meaning of 232–3
  perceptual-interpretive phenomenon 222–3, 229
  purpose of 220
  "remainder" 222–3
  selfhood and 220, 237
  self-knowledge 220
  Wittgenstein and *The Brothers Karamazov* 221–2
  word meaning 219, 235–8
  see also reading
revisionism 14, 97–8
Rhees, Rush 87–8, 160
Rorty, Richard 196–8
  "contingency of selfhood" 171–80, 182–3, 204
  freedom 176–7, 184–5
  life as "an unfinished poem" 184
  metaphors 176–7

Nietzsche, Friedrich and 172–5
One Right Description 176–7
Philosophy and the Mirror of Nature 171–2
self-description 175–8
self-knowledge 171–2, 174–5
Rousseau, Jean-Jacques
autobiographical writing 44
Confessions 44–7, 168–9
lying/concealing 44–7
Reveries of the Solitary Walker 44
self-investigative writings 23
sense of the words 45–6
Royce, Josiah 15–16, 43–4
Cartesian model of selfhood: critique
of 11
"Community of Interpretation" 13
interpretation 11–13
relational conception of selfhood 11–13,
19–20
self/not-self contrast 11–12, 18
see also American pragmatism
Ryle, Gilbert 6
dualism, critique of 73–4, 204

Said, Edward 184–5, 191–2
Sartre, Jean-Paul 13–14, 165n.5, 194
volitional freedom 185, 191–2
Words, The 165n.5
scheme/content dichotomy 80–2
Schopenhauer, Arthur 112–13
self-composition 13, 123–4
endpoint 239–40
King Lear: language and self-composition 149,
155–6
literary experience and 23
self-compositional narrative 217–18, 239
self-compositional reading 238–41
self-constitution
aesthetic experience, self-constitutive power
of 19, 170–1
autobiographical language, self-constitutive
power of 56
"contingency of selfhood" 171
experience, self-constitutive power of 163
language, self-constitutive power of 163,
200–2
literary engagement, self-constitutive power
of 6, 18, 164–5, 174–5, 184
literature, self-constitutive power of 164–5,
171, 174–5, 177–8, 185–7, 204–5
self-constitutive reading 182–3
self-constitutive self-deception 203–4
self-constitutive three-tiered reader's
experience 184–205

self-forgiveness as self-constitutive
process 206–7, 213–18
words, self-constitutive power of 24,
37n.62, 218
self-constitutive belief 168–71, 201–3
Aeneid/Aeneas 190–2
belief-settling resolution 203–4
making up one's mind 180–1, 184
process of settling self-constitutive belief 187–9
Sea, The Sea, The 167–8, 187–9
self-constitutive resolution 203–4
self-descriptive belief 201–2
see also beliefs
self-deception 65–6, 199–200, 203–4, 213
autobiographical writing 107–8, 116
King Lear 155–6
"Middle Years, The" 117, 145–6, 170–1
self-constitutive self-deception 203–4
word meaning 35
self-definition
Aeneid/Aeneas 191–2, 195–6, 198–9
language, self-defining power of 200–1
literary characters: self-reflective moment of
self-definition 193–4
literature, self-defining capacity of 181
self-definitional reading 23
self-description 73–85, 241
challenges of 83–5
descriptive accuracy 81–2, 111
individuation of action 73–85, 238–9
metaphors 184n.30
"Middle Years, The": self-image borne by false
self-descriptions 141, 144–6
objective/subjective descriptions
dichotomy 200–2
problems of constitutive self-
description 175–6
Rorty, Richard 175–8
self-descriptive belief 201–2
self-descriptive projects of analysis 108–10
truth 79–80
visual language of 99–100
self-forgiveness 206–18
apology 208–9
bootstrapping 213–15, 217–18
"if only I hadn't done that" 215
"I'll never forgive myself" 207–9, 217
literary engagement and 212–13
moral-act reduction 208–9
moral luck 216–17
non-hermetic nature of 208–9
as process 208–9, 213
reflexive act of forgiveness 211–12
relational conception of selfhood 206–7

260 INDEX

self-forgiveness (*cont.*)
 remorse 210–11
 self-change 209–11, 215
 as self-constitutive process 206–7, 213–18
 self-directed forgiveness 208, 211–17
 self-injury and 214
 self-rewriting 216–17
 "this should never have happened" 207–13, 217
selfhood 206
 architecture of selfhood 86, 95–6, 99–100, 238–9
 boundary indeterminacy of 72–3, 85, 239–40
 Cartesian/dualistic model of selfhood 3–5, 19–21, 24, 50–1, 74–5, 204
 "contingency of selfhood" 171–80, 182–3, 198–9, 204
 Don Giovanni: self in *absentia* 117–34
 fixity of selfhood: linguistic intuitions 163–5
 fixity vs flux 15, 53, 68, 162–5, 177–8, 204–5
 individual as non-dividable singular self 72
 language and 164–5
 metaphorical picture of the self as text 196–8
 "Middle Years, The": second chance at selfhood 136–9, 143–6
 multiple interpretations and singular selves 52–9
 rereading and 220, 237
 self as work-in-progress 238–41
 sense of self 123–6, 128, 196–8, 206, 220, 226, 237
 text/self relation: metaphorical structure of 162, 200–1
 Wittgenstein: working on oneself 95–100
 words and 27, 241
 see also relational conception of selfhood
self-identity 69–70, 148n.19, 164n.2, 176–7
 literary absorption and 23
 relational self-identity 15
self-individuation 239
 metaphorical identification and self-individuation 196–205, 239
self-interpretation 50–1, 59, 62–3, 69–70, 98–9, 238–41
 constructive realism 69, 71–2
 constructivism 66, 68, 70–2
 foundationalist model of 70–2
 interpretive rightness 53, 67–72
 Krausz, Michael 52, 54, 66–72
 literary characters: self-interpretations of 168–9
 metaphorical truth 70
 realism 66, 68, 70–2
 relational conception of selfhood 13
 see also interpretation; interpretive rightness

self-knowledge
 autobiographical understanding 42–4, 48
 King Lear: lack of self-knowledge 149, 152–4, 159–60
 Larkin, Philip 171
 literary characters and 193–4
 literary experience and 23
 rereading 220
 Rorty, Richard 171–2, 174–5
self-reflection 70–1, 121, 135, 162, 239
 autobiographical reflection 21, 91n.9, 123–4, 142, 177–9, 200–1
 denial of 183–4
 dialogical character of inward reflection 178, 180–1
 Don Giovanni 122, 130–2
 King Lear 153–4, 159n.30, 170–1
 literary character and 22, 193–4
 reader 167
 self-directed soliloquy 178–9, 181
self-transformation 204
 literary experience and 204–5
 moral improvement through fiction 199–200
 self-forgiveness 209–11, 215
self-understanding
 autobiographical understanding 41
 Cartesian model of selfhood and 50–1
 inner/outer dichotomy 50–1
 mental state as criterion 59–60
 preconception of understanding 50–1
 relations between language, identity, and self-understanding 118
 self-understanding through literary characters comparisons 22
 as state or process 50–1
 structures of 240–1
 visual language of 99–100
 Wittgenstein, Ludwig 50–1
 see also autobiographical understanding; autobiographical understanding: structures
sensibility 26, 34, 88, 219, 241
 aesthetic sensibility 48, 240–1
 Brothers Karamozov, The 232–4, 237–8
 context-sensitive and sensibility-sensitive experience 82–3
 Don Giovanni 119–20, 123
 James, William 6, 17
 literary sensibility 11–12, 17
Shakespeare, William 185–7
 language/character intrinsic connection 150–1
 as philosopher 149–50
 Sonnet 116 153n.25
 see also *King Lear*

singularism
  explanatory singularism 75–6
  interpretation 52–3, 68–9, 72
  singularism vs multiplism debate 53–4, 62–3, 66, 68–9
skepticism 10–11, 99–100, 107–8, 200–1
  moral attributes 128–9
  motive-skepticism 116–17
  scheme/content dichotomy 80–2
Socrates 121–2, 158–9, 161
Sophocles: *Oedipus Tyrannus* 102–3, 133, 185–9
Szabados, Bela: *In Light of Chaos* 92n.14

Tacitus 13–14, 218–20, 222
Tolstoy, Leo 105n.41, 185–7
tragedy
  Aristotle 102, 104–7
  catharsis 102, 104
  Greek tragedy 185–7
  as mimetic art 108
  see also *Don Giovanni*; *King Lear*; "Middle Years, The"

Varnedoe, Kirk 199n.53
Vendler, Helen 153n.25, 159n.30
Virgil 93–5, 162, 185–7, 196–8, 237
  see also *Aeneid*/Aeneas

Wharton, Edith 185–7
Williams, Bernard 134
Wisdom, John 87, 108–10, 160, 237–8
Wittgenstein, Ludwig 7–8
  "assembling reminders for a particular purpose" 41–2
  autobiographical truth 100, 105–6
  behaviorism 74–5
  Cartesian model of selfhood: critique of 50, 81–2
  criticism of 234
  Dostoevsky and 221–2, 226–7, 233–4
  dualism 74–5
  Einstellung/Eine Einstellung zur Seele 118, 124–7, 130–4
  empiricism, critique of 234–5
  family-resemblance metaphor 2, 16
  "field of a word, the" 20, 40, 45, 235–6
  Freud, Sigmund and 108–10
  happy/unhappy man 144n.15
  inexpressible, the mysterious 93–5, 99–100
  interpretive rightness 59–66
  Krausz, Michael and 54–6, 58–9, 61–3, 67, 72–3
  language-games 28n.50, 32, 61, 63, 74–5, 81–2, 84–5, 89–90, 95, 237n.45
  language and philosophy 160–1

manifestation of understanding 61–2
memory 111–14
naming 237n.45
perspicuity 86–7, 89–92
perspicuous overview/view 86–7, 89–92, 97–100, 116
perspicuous relations 86–100
philosophical therapy 86–90, 95–6, 98–100, 110–11
privacy and private language 179
recognition 111–12
"reminder" 152–3, 158–9, 194n.46, 237–8
report and exclamation 228–9
rereading 221–2, 226, 233–4, 237–8
same propositions and sameness of wording 228n.34
saying/showing meaning 142–3
"scaffolding" 128–9, 134, 167, 185–7
seeing-as 222–4, 227, 229, 236–7
self-understanding 50–1
straight highway/"dream of the straight highway" 134–5, 221, 223, 228–9, 232–4
stream of life 17, 31–2, 168–9, 222
thinker/draughtsman comparison 86–100
understanding as state/process 61, 63, 65–6
universalizing or overgeneralizing positions 173–4
way of seeing 89, 95–6, 99–100, 111, 147–8
winner as "the one who gets there last" 99–100, 116–17, 143n.14
word meaning 23n.42, 31–2, 59, 160, 233–4, 237–8
word meaning: learning of 34
working on oneself 95–100
work on modernist house for his sister, Vienna 89, 95, 100
Wittgenstein, Ludwig: works by
  Blue Book, The 28n.50
  Culture and Value 86, 90–7, 99–100, 107
  Lectures and Conversations 111, 114–16
  Philosophical Investigations 28n.50, 59–66, 89–92, 111–14, 134–5, 220–1, 227, 229–30, 237n.45
  Philosophical Remarks 90–2, 92n.14
  Tractatus 90–5, 143n.12, 144n.15
Wollheim, Richard
  cognitive stock 25n.45, 71
  interpretation 99n.25
  Thread of Life, The 85n.40, 99n.25
Woolf, Virginia: "A Sketch of the Past" 82–4, 145–6
  interpenetration of experience 82–4
  self-description: challenges of 83–5

262 INDEX

word meaning
  aspect perception and experience of word
    meaning 224
  atomistic conception of 233–4, 236–7
  autobiographical understanding 48
  compressed meaning 145–6
  Conradi, Peter J. 39–40, 48
  context and 135–7, 142–3, 145–8, 219, 221,
    228–30, 235, 237–8
  fixity of meaning 26, 134–5, 220–2, 236–7
  King Lear 153–6, 158–61
  learning of 33–4
  "Middle Years, The" 135–7, 142–3, 145–7
  name, meaning of 231–3, 236–7
  rereading 219, 235–8
  self-deception 35
  sense of words 45–6
  simple cases of 227–9, 231, 237–8
  Wittgenstein, Ludwig 23n.42, 31–2, 34, 59,
    160, 233–4, 237–8
  Wittgenstein: "field of a word" 20, 40, 45,
    235–6
  Wittgenstein: saying/showing meaning
    142–3
  "Words Misunderstood" 25–7, 31–7, 48
  see also words
words
  Cavell: "our relations to our words" 222, 224,
    235–7
  Cavell: physiognomy and words 223–5, 230
  intention, utterance, and implication as
    intricately intertwined 151–2
  our relations to our words 228–9, 236–8

  our relations to our words stand as allegories
    of our relations to others 222
  persons as vehicles of words and words as
    vehicles of personhood 27
  physiognomy and 223–5, 230, 236–7
  relational conception of words 20, 24, 26
  self-constitutive power of words 24,
    37n.62, 218
  selfhood and 27, 241
  Wittgenstein: same propositions and sameness
    of wording 228n.34
  "Words Misunderstood": relational
    conception of words 24–6, 28–9, 32–6
  see also word meaning
"Words Misunderstood" (by Milan
    Kundera) 23–37, 42–3
  bowler hat 28–33, 40, 46
  language-games 32, 37
  learning the meaning of a word 33–4
  linguistic incomprehension 27–8, 32
  music/musical comparisons 31, 33, 35–6, 40
  relational conception of words 24–6, 28–9,
    32–6
  relational perception 26, 28–31, 43–4
  romantic restoration 28–9
  "Short Dictionary of Misunderstood Words,
    A" 33–4, 36–7
  Unbearable Lightness of Being, The 23
  "understanding a person" 37
  word meaning 25–7, 31–2, 35–7, 48
  see also Kundera, Milan

Yeats, W. B.: *Vision, A* 159n.30